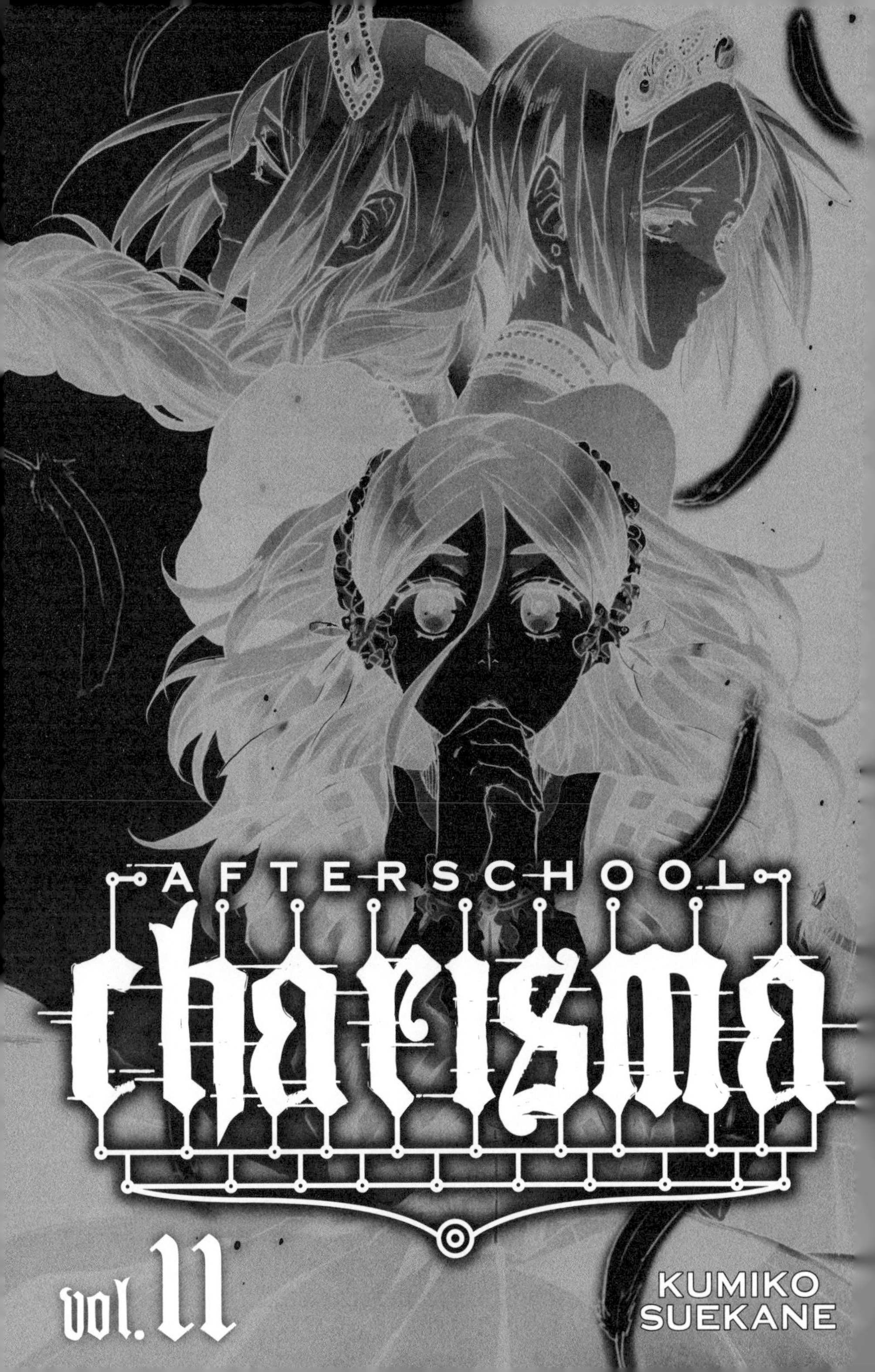
AFTERSCHOOL
charisma
vol. 11
KUMIKO
SUEKANE

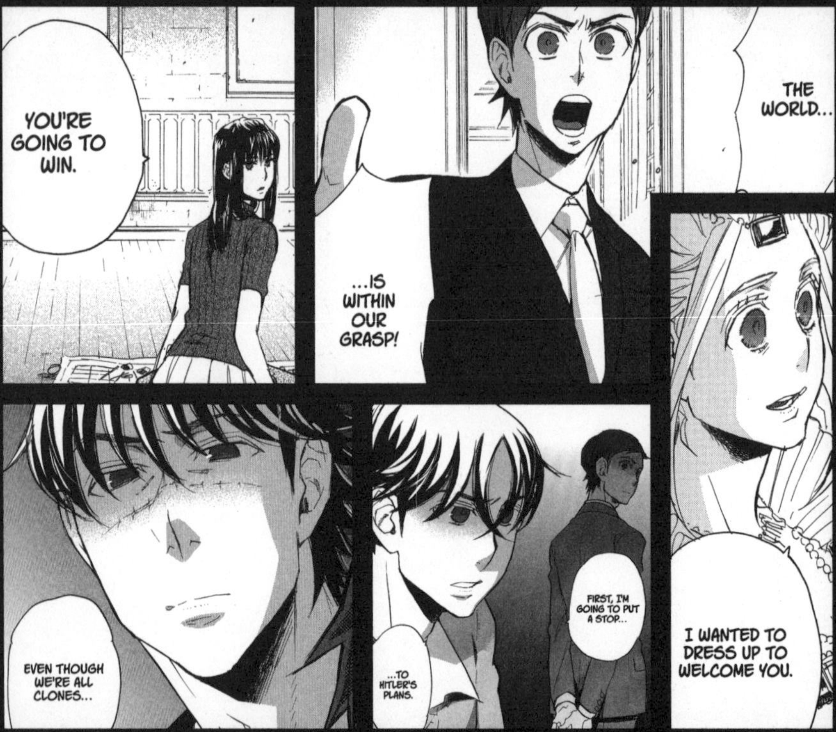
THE WORLD...
...IS WITHIN OUR GRASP!
YOU'RE GOING TO WIN.
I WANTED TO DRESS UP TO WELCOME YOU.
FIRST, I'M GOING TO PUT A STOP...
...TO HITLER'S PLANS.
EVEN THOUGH WE'RE ALL CLONES...

## story

THE YEAR IS 2XXX, AND AT ST. KLEIO ACADEMY, A SCHOOL FOR THE CLONES OF FAMOUS HISTORICAL FIGURES, SHIRO KAMIYA IS THE ONLY NON-CLONE. A GROUP OF TERRORISTS CONSISTING OF ST. KLEIO ALUMNI—AN OLDER GENERATION OF CLONES—ATTACK THE ACADEMY, KILLING JOAN AND VARIOUS OTHER STUDENTS. FOR SOME REASON, MANY OF THE TERRORISTS ALSO TAKE THEIR OWN LIVES IN THE PROCESS. THE ONLY TERRORIST CAPTURED IS A YOUNG MAN CALLED KAI, WHO BEARS A STRIKING RESEMBLANCE TO SHIRO. KAI FLEES THE ACADEMY, TAKING ELIZABETH AND HITLER WITH HIM.

HITLER BEGINS PUBLICLY DENOUNCING ST. KLEIO TO THE PRESS, GARNERING A GREAT DEAL OF PUBLIC SUPPORT AND SYMPATHY. MEANWHILE, SHIRO TRIES TO RUN AWAY FROM THE TREMENDOUS PRESSURES OF HIS ROLE BUT IS APPREHENDED WHEN MARIE CURIE BETRAYS HIM.

KUROE REVEALS TO SHIRO THAT SHIRO AND HIS FATHER, KAMIYA, ARE BOTH CLONES OF DOCTOR X, THE FOUNDER OF THE ACADEMY; THAT ROCKSWELL WAS ALSO AT THE ACADEMY AS A BOY; AND THAT KAMIYA KILLED X BUT THE ACADEMY COVERED UP THE INCIDENT.

NOW SHIRO KNOWS THE TRUTH, BUT HE STILL DECIDES TO FIGHT BACK AGAINST HITLER TO DEFEND THE CLONES' FUTURE. TO THAT END, HE LEAVES ST. KLEIO WITH A TEAM OF FRIENDS, INCLUDING NIGHTINGALE, IKKYU AND FREUD. THEY BEGIN THEIR DEFENSE BY PRESENTING NAPOLEON TO THE PUBLIC, TO COMPETE AGAINST HITLER...

# character

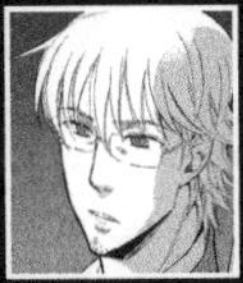

**Dr. Kamiya**
"Father" to Shiro and professor at St. Kleio

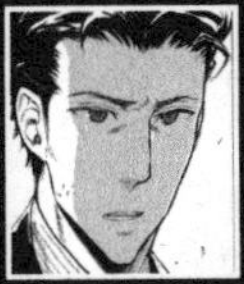

**Kuroe**
Professor at St. Kleio

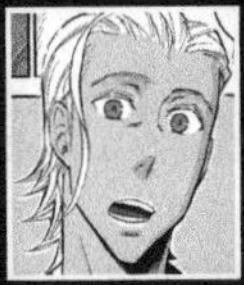

**Rockswell**
Director of St. Kleio

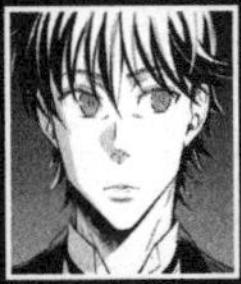

**Kai**
Graduate of St. Kleio

## students of st. kleio academy

(Clones of Historical Figures)

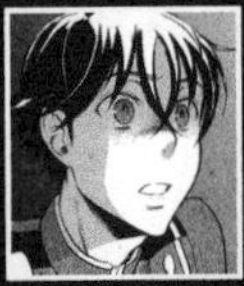

**Shiro Kamiya**
Clone of St. Kleio's founder

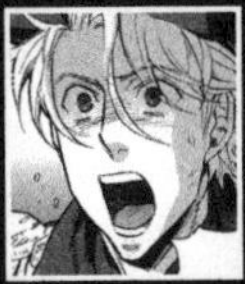

**Napoleon Bonaparte**

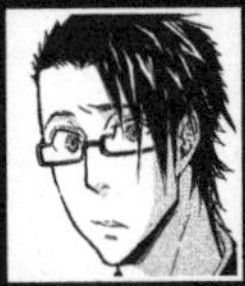

**Ikkyu Sojun**

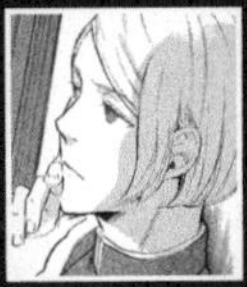

**Sigmund Freud**

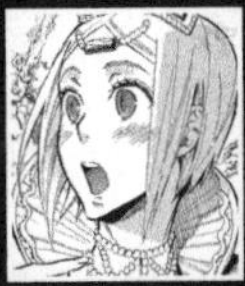

**Elizabeth I**

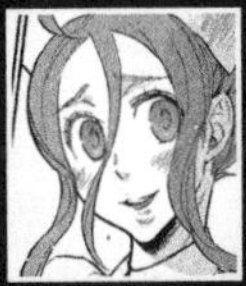

**Florence Nightingale**

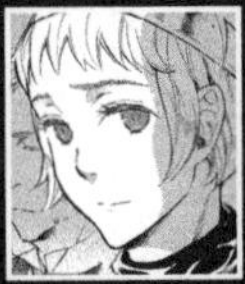

**Joan of Arc**
*burned at the stake

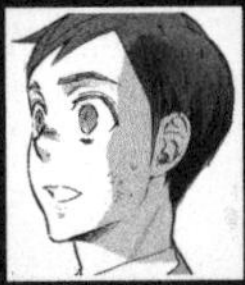

**Adolf Hitler**

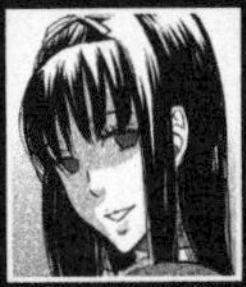

**Himiko**

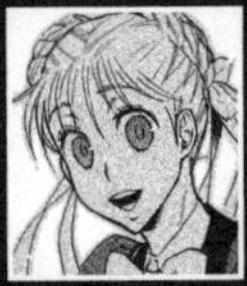

**Marie Curie**
(Madame Curie)

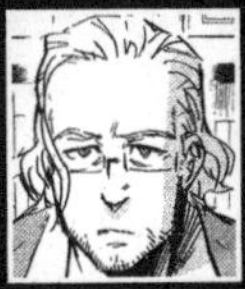

**Leonardo Da Vinci**
Former Director of St. Kleio

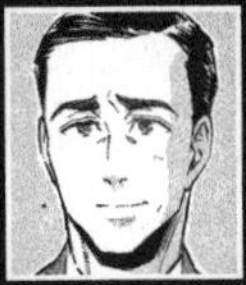

**Robert Green**
Politician

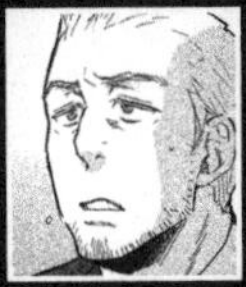

**Benjamin**
Journalist

St·KLEIO
11

afterschool
charisma

c o n t e n t s

CHAPTER sixty-one

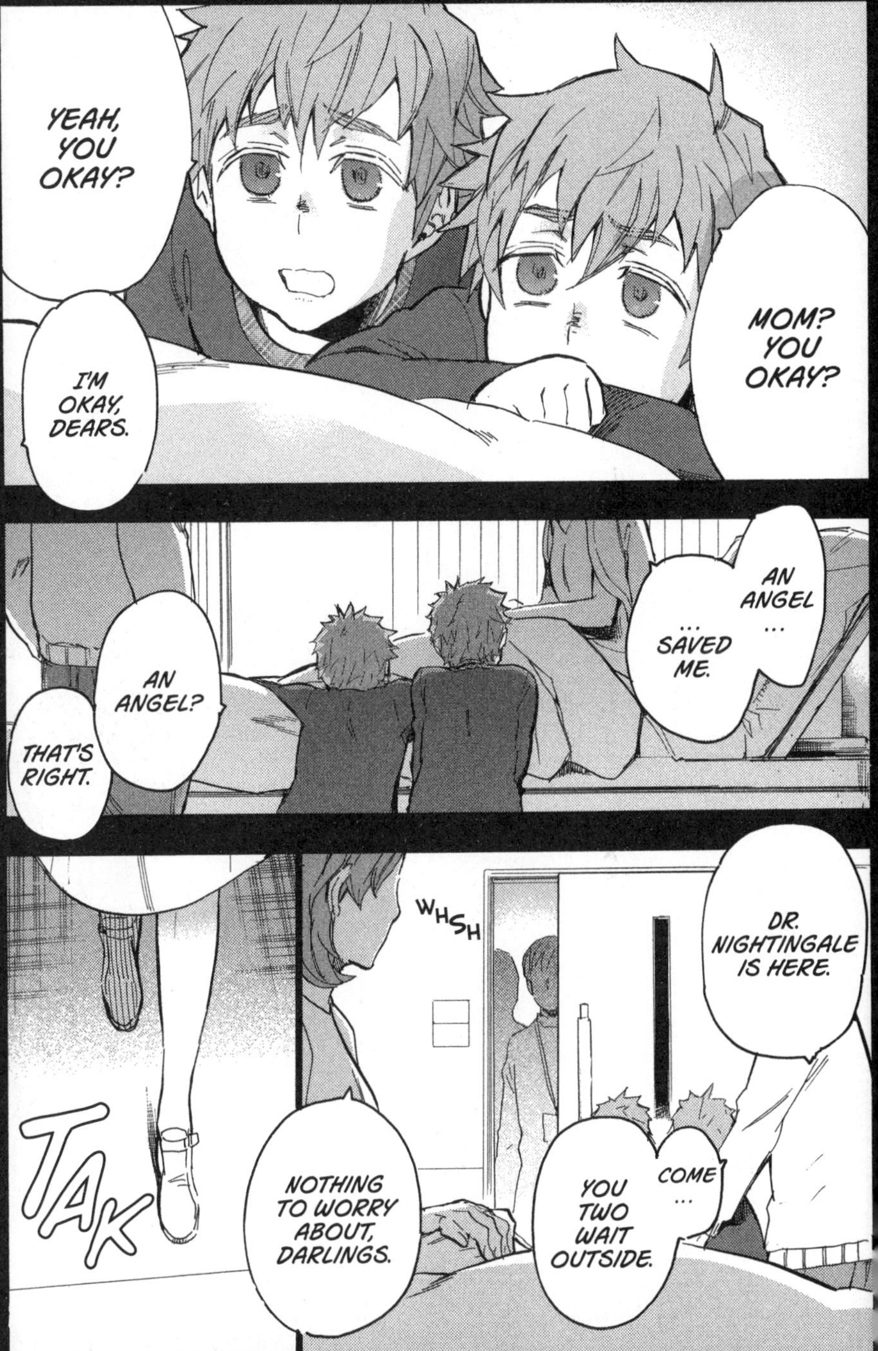
MOM? YOU OKAY?
YEAH, YOU OKAY?
I'M OKAY, DEARS.
AN ANGEL ... SAVED ME.
AN ANGEL?
THAT'S RIGHT.
DR. NIGHTINGALE IS HERE.
WHSH
COME ...
YOU TWO WAIT OUTSIDE.
NOTHING TO WORRY ABOUT, DARLINGS.
TAK

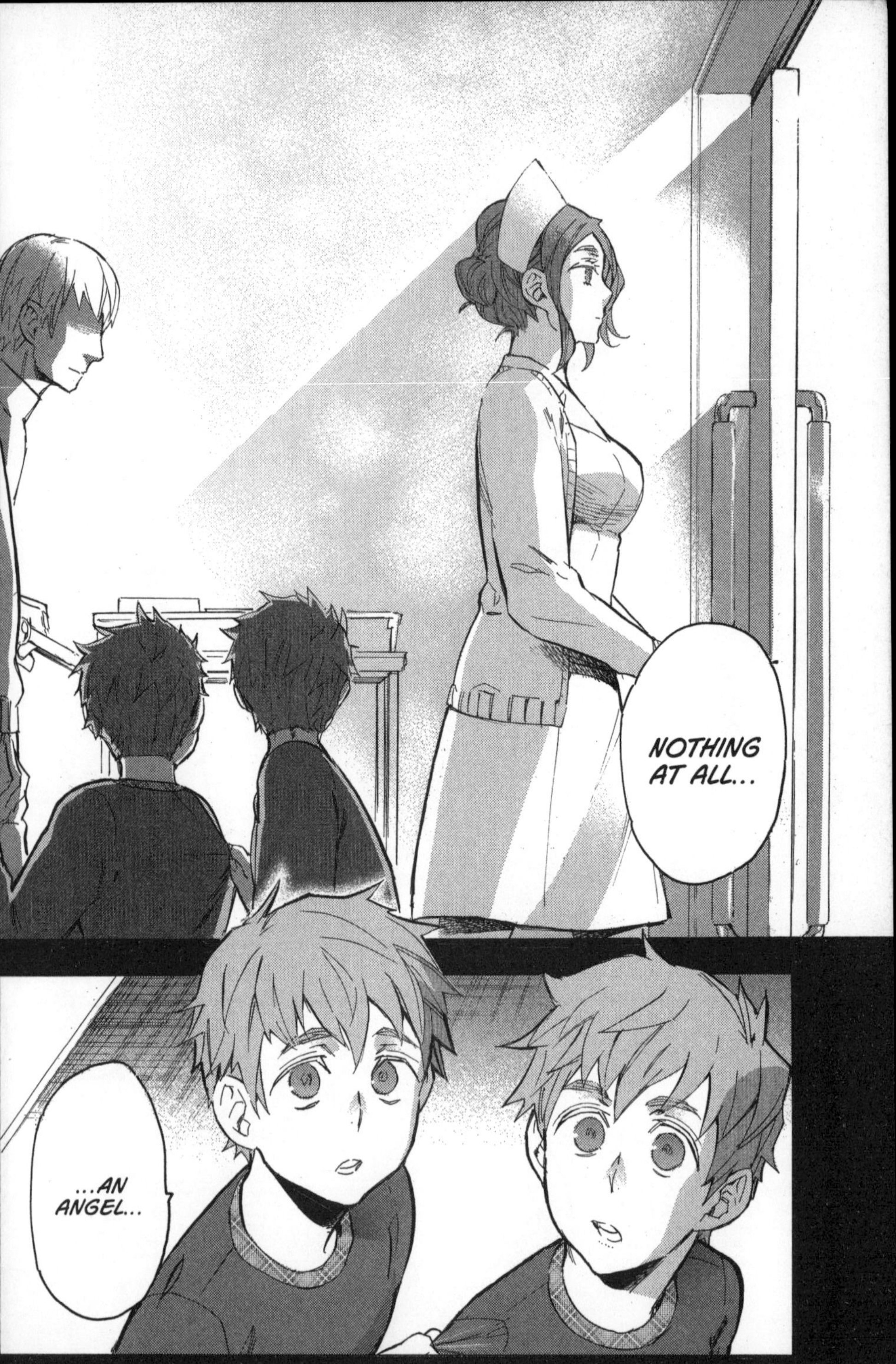
NOTHING AT ALL...
...AN ANGEL...

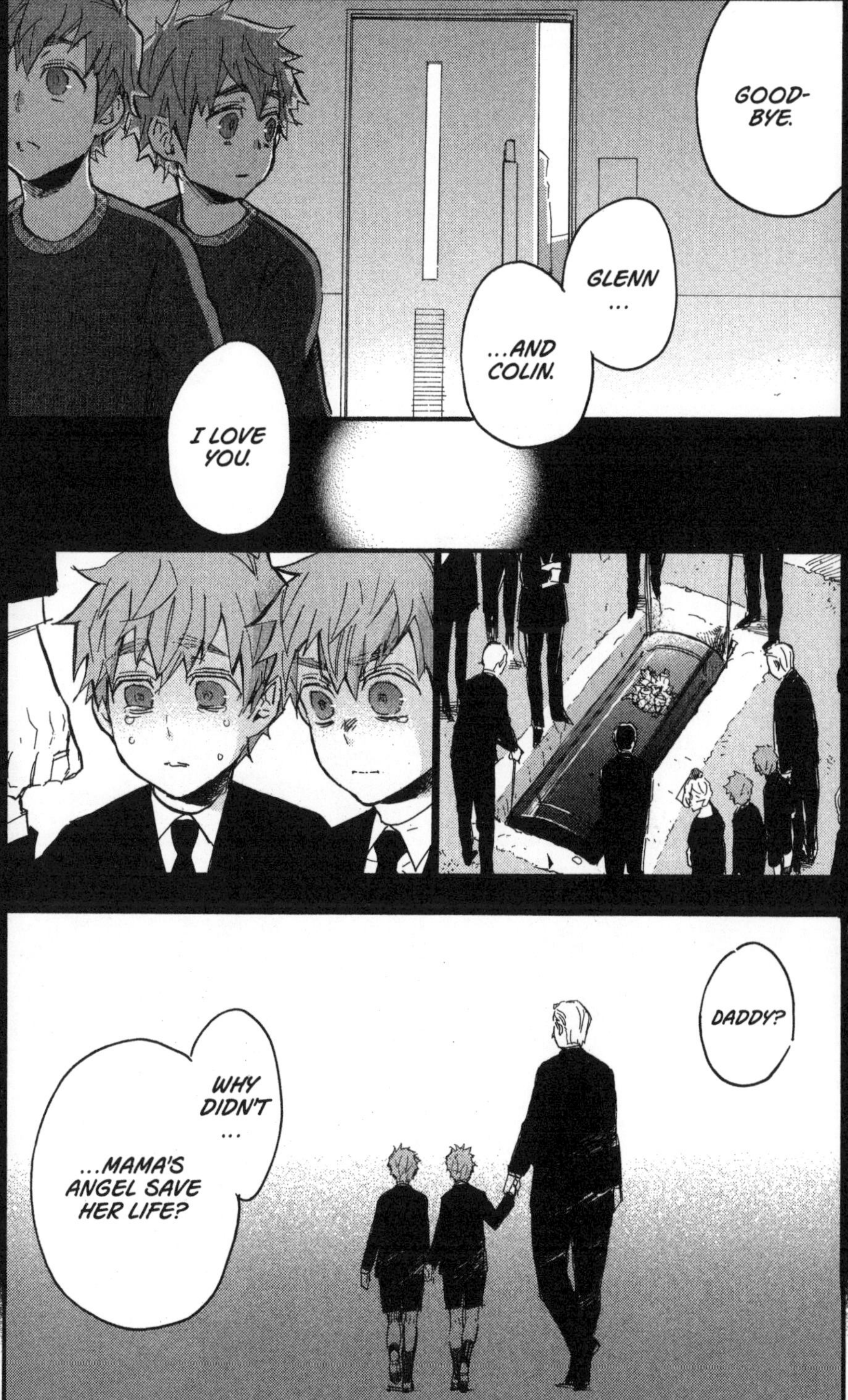
GOOD-BYE.
GLENN ...
...AND COLIN.
I LOVE YOU.
DADDY?
WHY DIDN'T ...
...MAMA'S ANGEL SAVE HER LIFE?

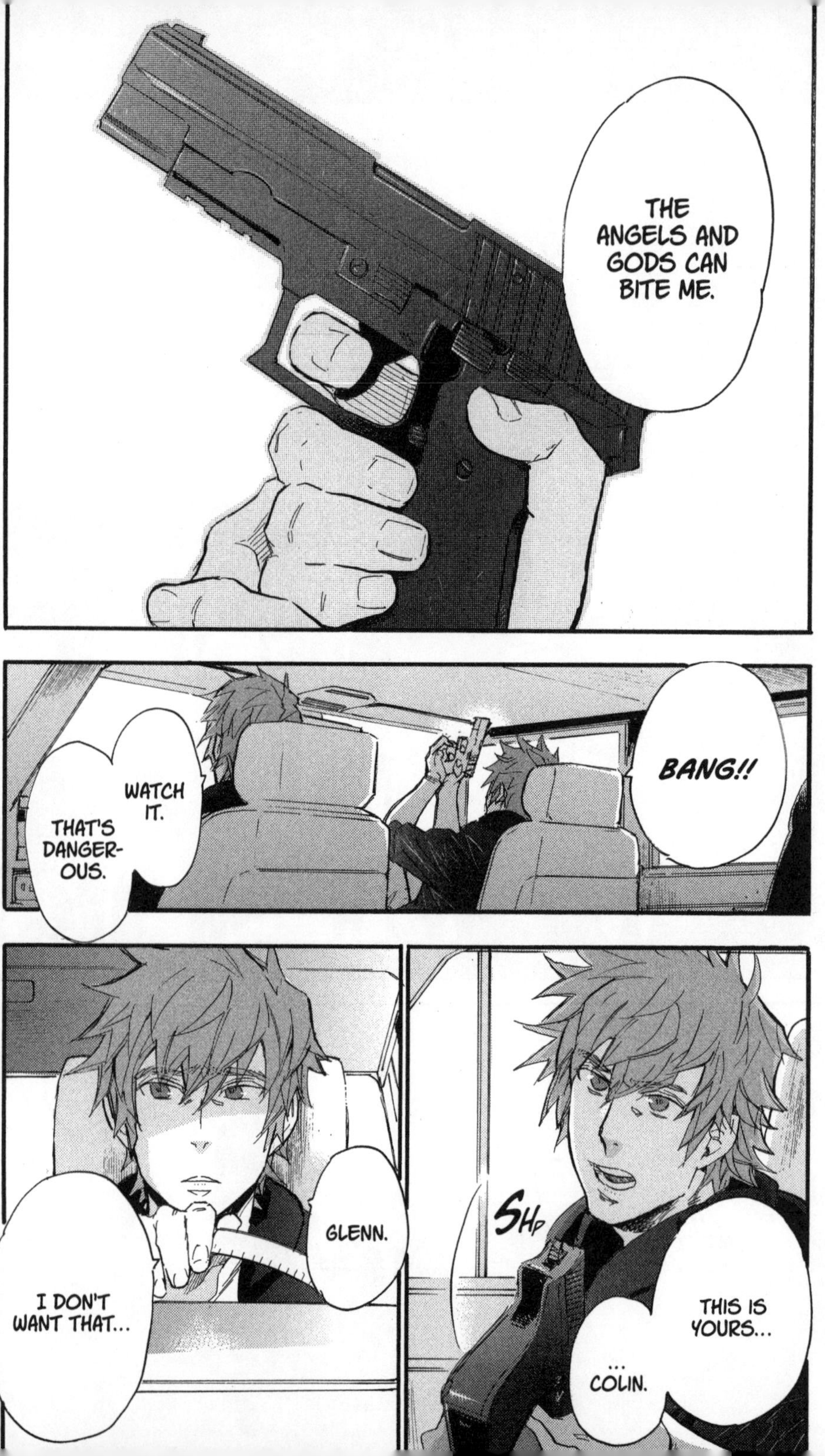
THE ANGELS AND GODS CAN BITE ME.
BANG!!
WATCH IT.
THAT'S DANGER-OUS.
SHP
THIS IS YOURS...
... COLIN.
GLENN.
I DON'T WANT THAT...

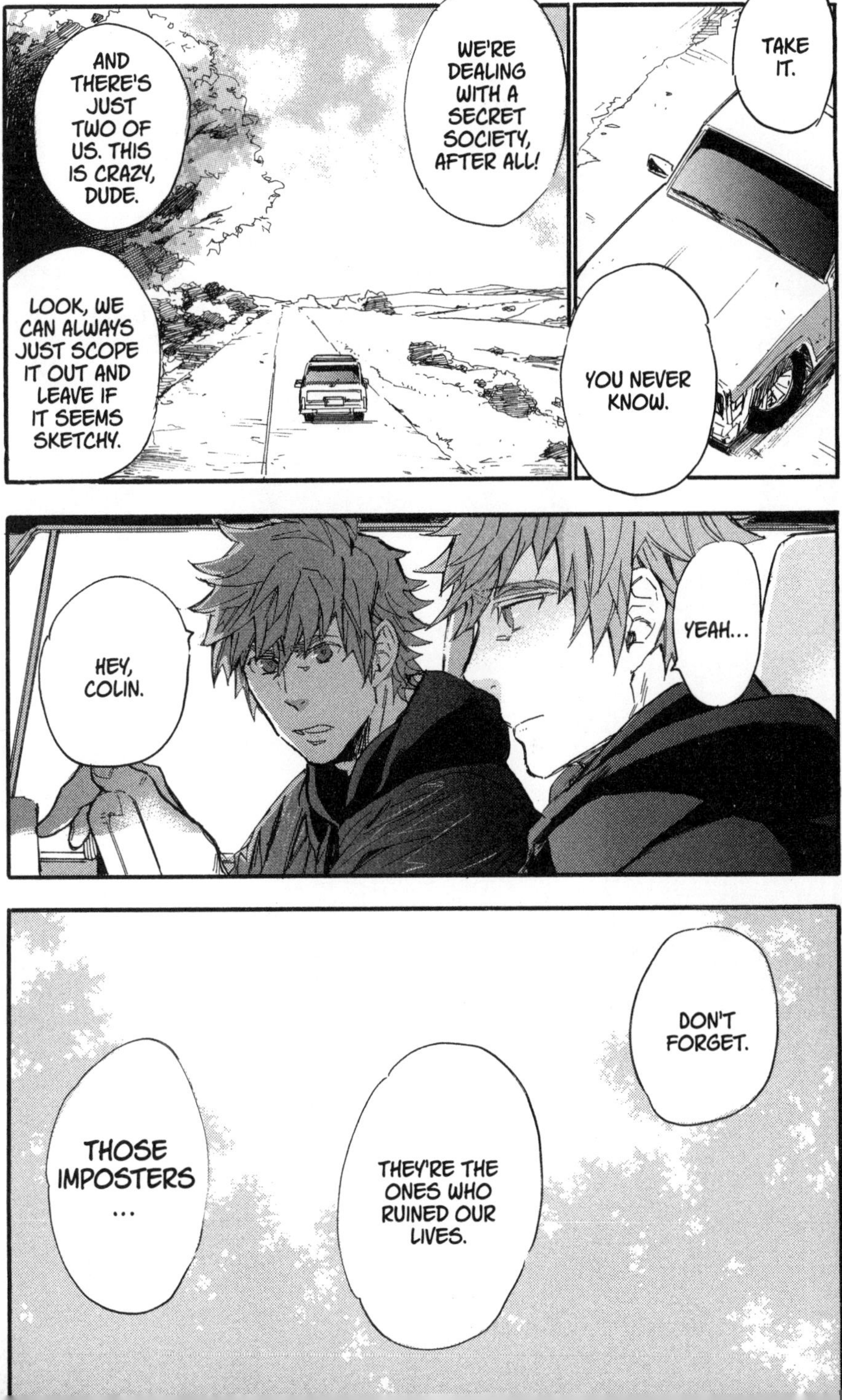
TAKE IT.
YOU NEVER KNOW.
WE'RE DEALING WITH A SECRET SOCIETY, AFTER ALL!
AND THERE'S JUST TWO OF US. THIS IS CRAZY, DUDE.
LOOK, WE CAN ALWAYS JUST SCOPE IT OUT AND LEAVE IF IT SEEMS SKETCHY.
YEAH...
HEY, COLIN.
DON'T FORGET.
THEY'RE THE ONES WHO RUINED OUR LIVES.
THOSE IMPOSTERS ...

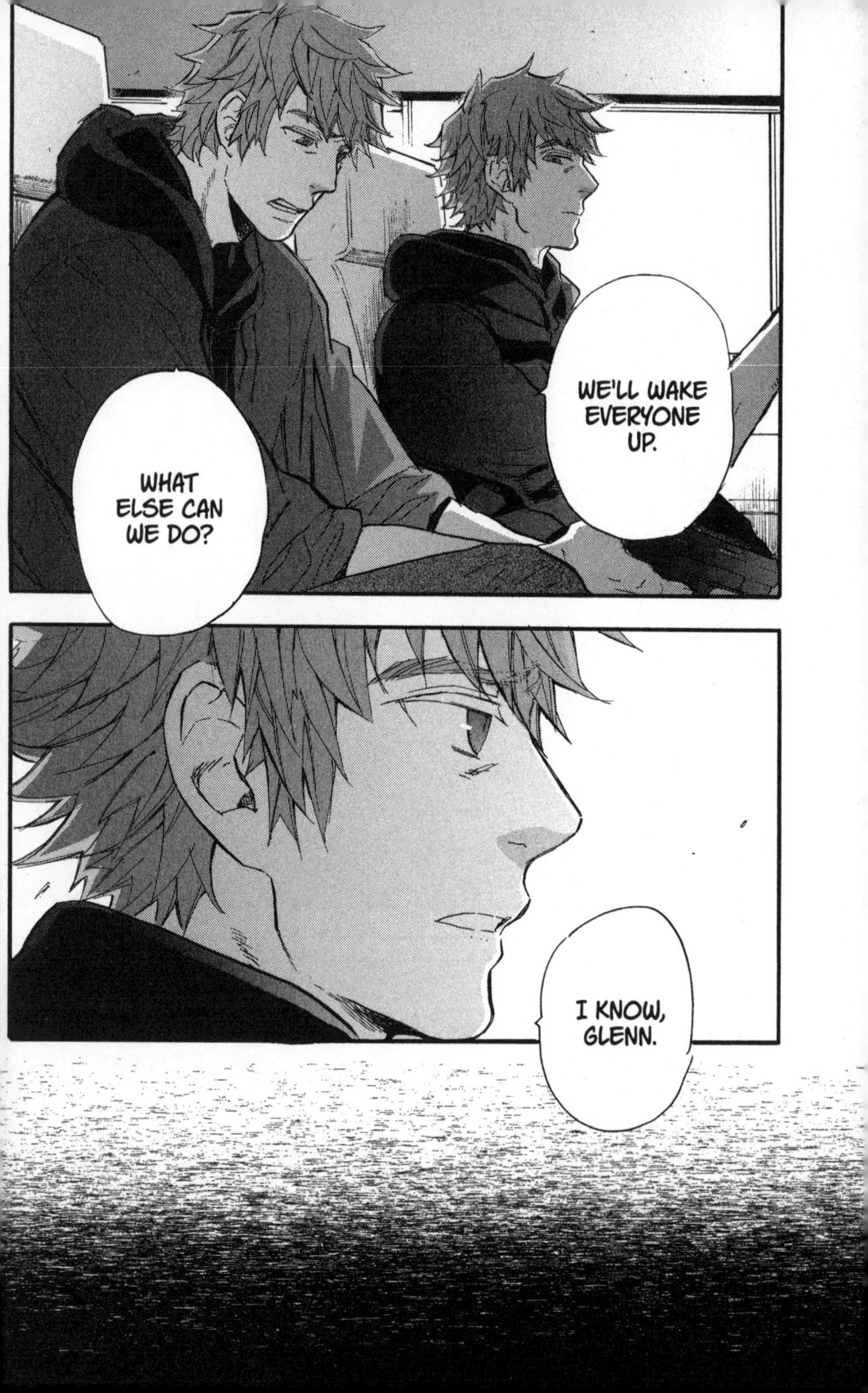
WE'LL WAKE EVERYONE UP.
WHAT ELSE CAN WE DO?
I KNOW, GLENN.

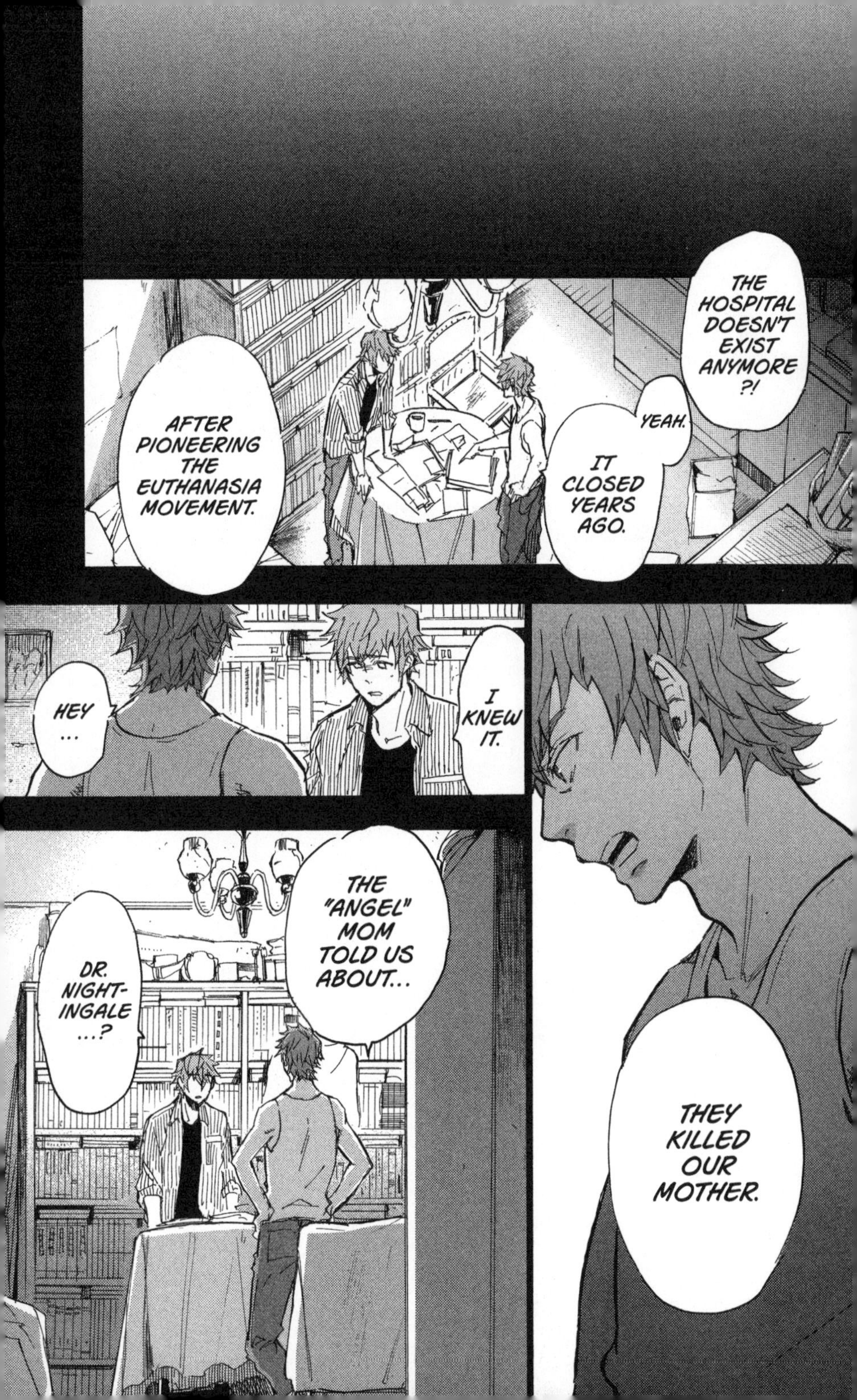
THE HOSPITAL DOESN'T EXIST ANYMORE ?!
YEAH.
IT CLOSED YEARS AGO.
AFTER PIONEERING THE EUTHANASIA MOVEMENT.
THEY KILLED OUR MOTHER.
I KNEW IT.
HEY ...
THE "ANGEL" MOM TOLD US ABOUT...
DR. NIGHT-INGALE ...?

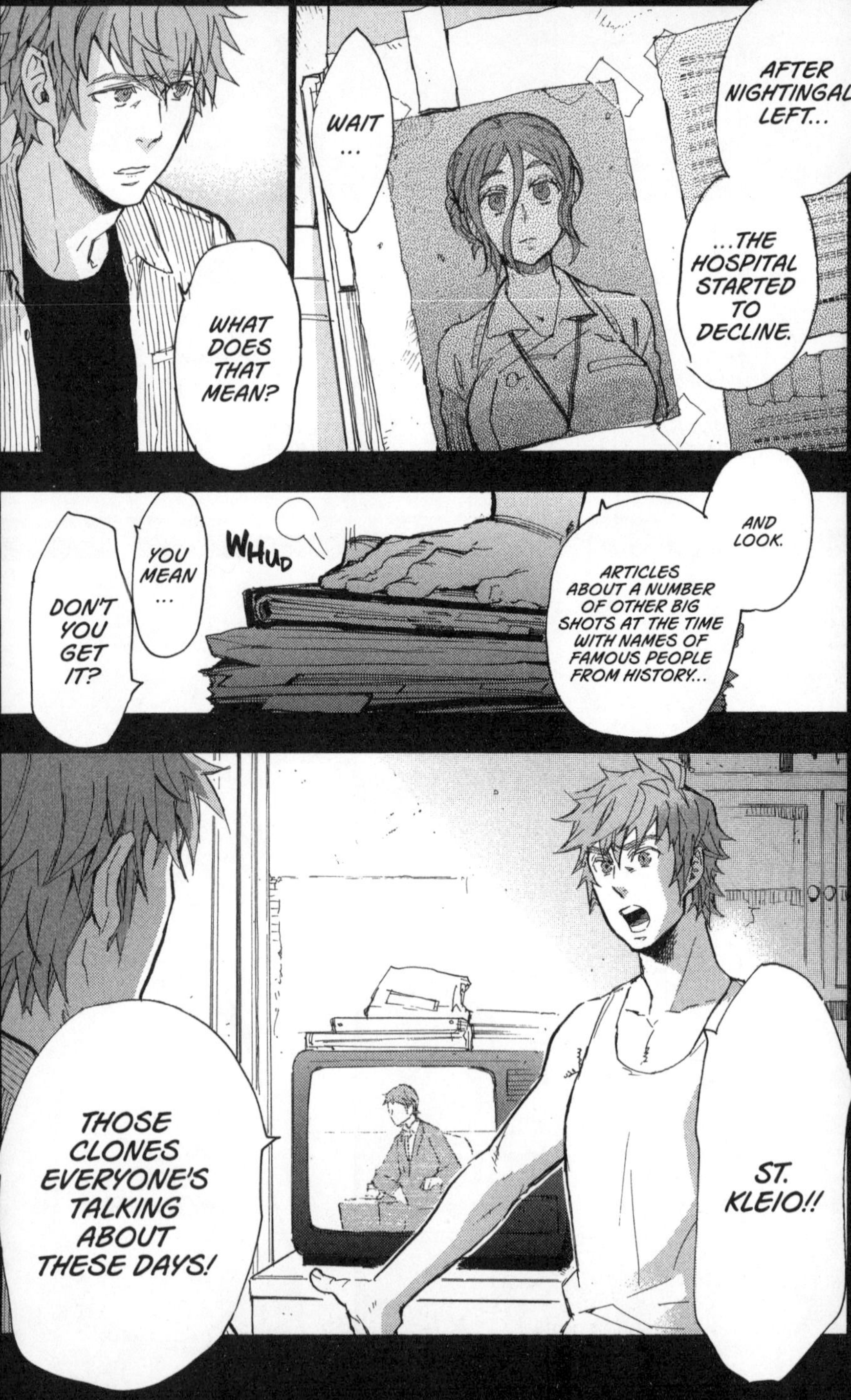
AFTER NIGHTINGALE LEFT...
...THE HOSPITAL STARTED TO DECLINE.
WAIT ...
WHAT DOES THAT MEAN?
AND LOOK.
ARTICLES ABOUT A NUMBER OF OTHER BIG SHOTS AT THE TIME WITH NAMES OF FAMOUS PEOPLE FROM HISTORY...
WHUD
YOU MEAN ...
DON'T YOU GET IT?
ST. KLEIO!!
THOSE CLONES EVERYONE'S TALKING ABOUT THESE DAYS!

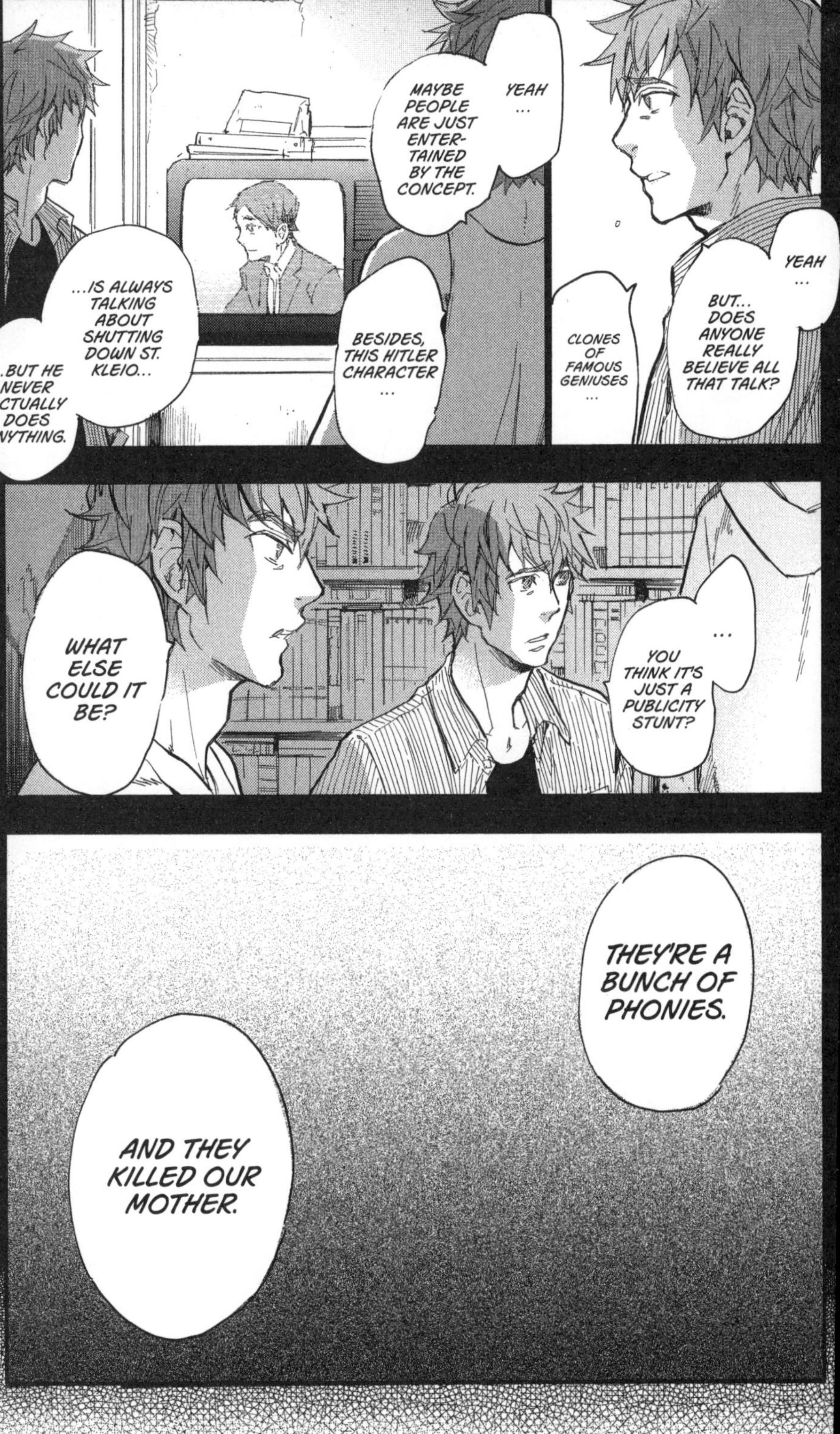
YEAH...
BUT... DOES ANYONE REALLY BELIEVE ALL THAT TALK?
CLONES OF FAMOUS GENIUSES...
YEAH...
MAYBE PEOPLE ARE JUST ENTERTAINED BY THE CONCEPT.
BESIDES, THIS HITLER CHARACTER...
...IS ALWAYS TALKING ABOUT SHUTTING DOWN ST. KLEIO...
...BUT HE NEVER ACTUALLY DOES ANYTHING.
...
YOU THINK IT'S JUST A PUBLICITY STUNT?
WHAT ELSE COULD IT BE?
THEY'RE A BUNCH OF PHONIES.
AND THEY KILLED OUR MOTHER.

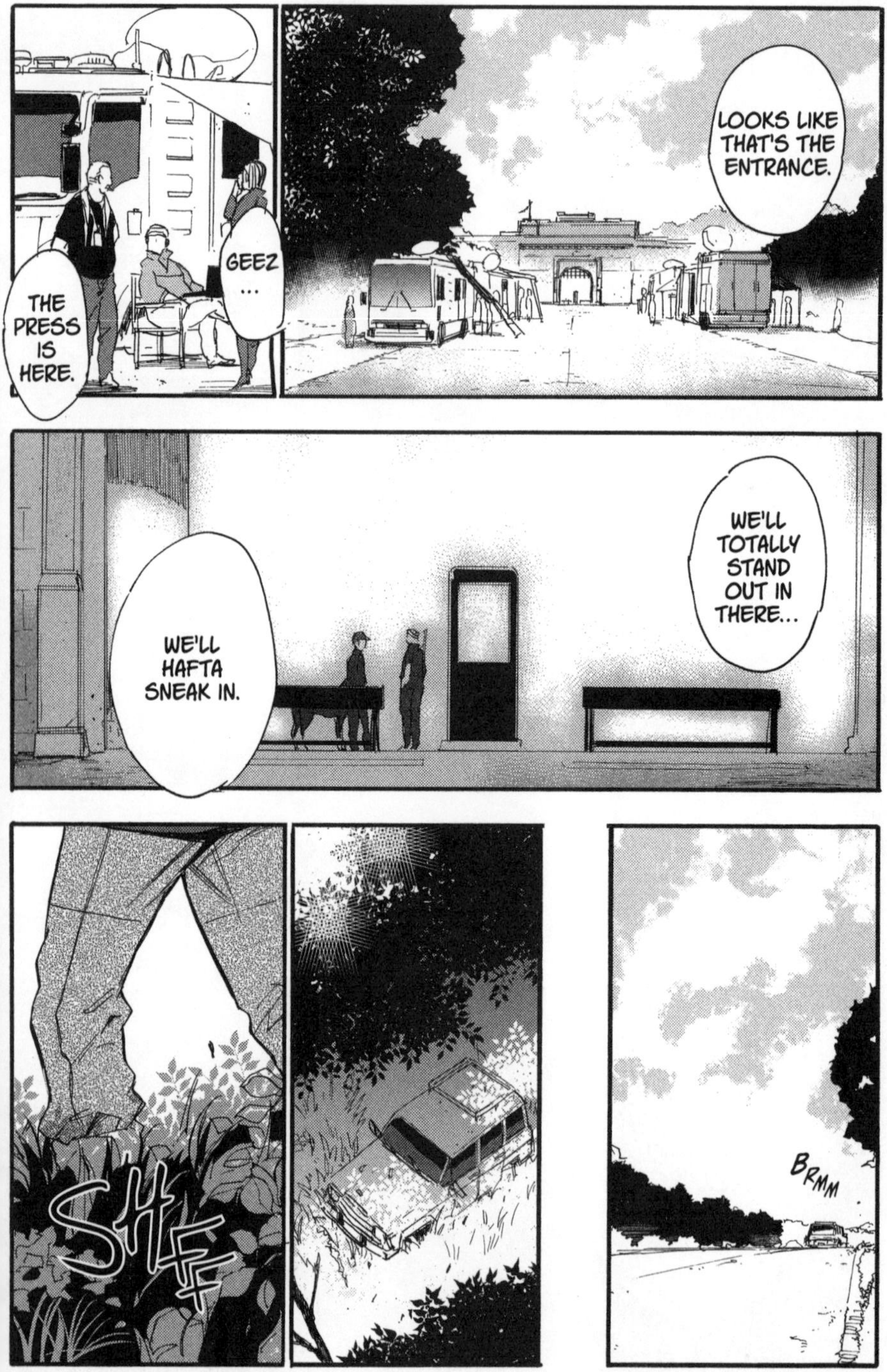
LOOKS LIKE THAT'S THE ENTRANCE.
GEEZ ...
THE PRESS IS HERE.
WE'LL TOTALLY STAND OUT IN THERE...
WE'LL HAFTA SNEAK IN.
BRMM
SHFF

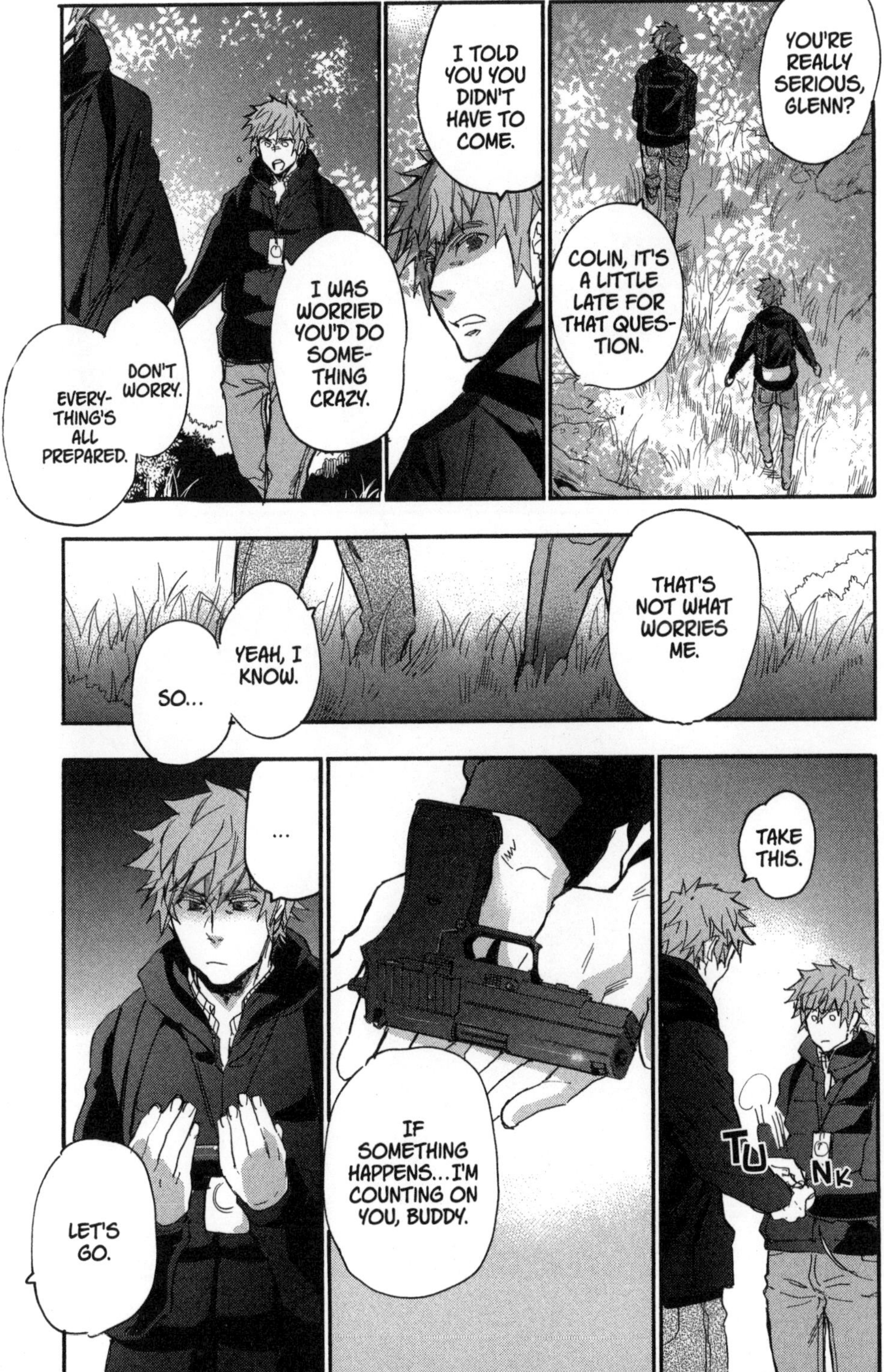
YOU'RE REALLY SERIOUS, GLENN?
COLIN, IT'S A LITTLE LATE FOR THAT QUESTION.
I TOLD YOU YOU DIDN'T HAVE TO COME.
I WAS WORRIED YOU'D DO SOME-THING CRAZY.
DON'T WORRY.
EVERY-THING'S ALL PREPARED.
THAT'S NOT WHAT WORRIES ME.
YEAH, I KNOW.
SO...
TAKE THIS.
TUNK
IF SOMETHING HAPPENS...I'M COUNTING ON YOU, BUDDY.
...
LET'S GO.

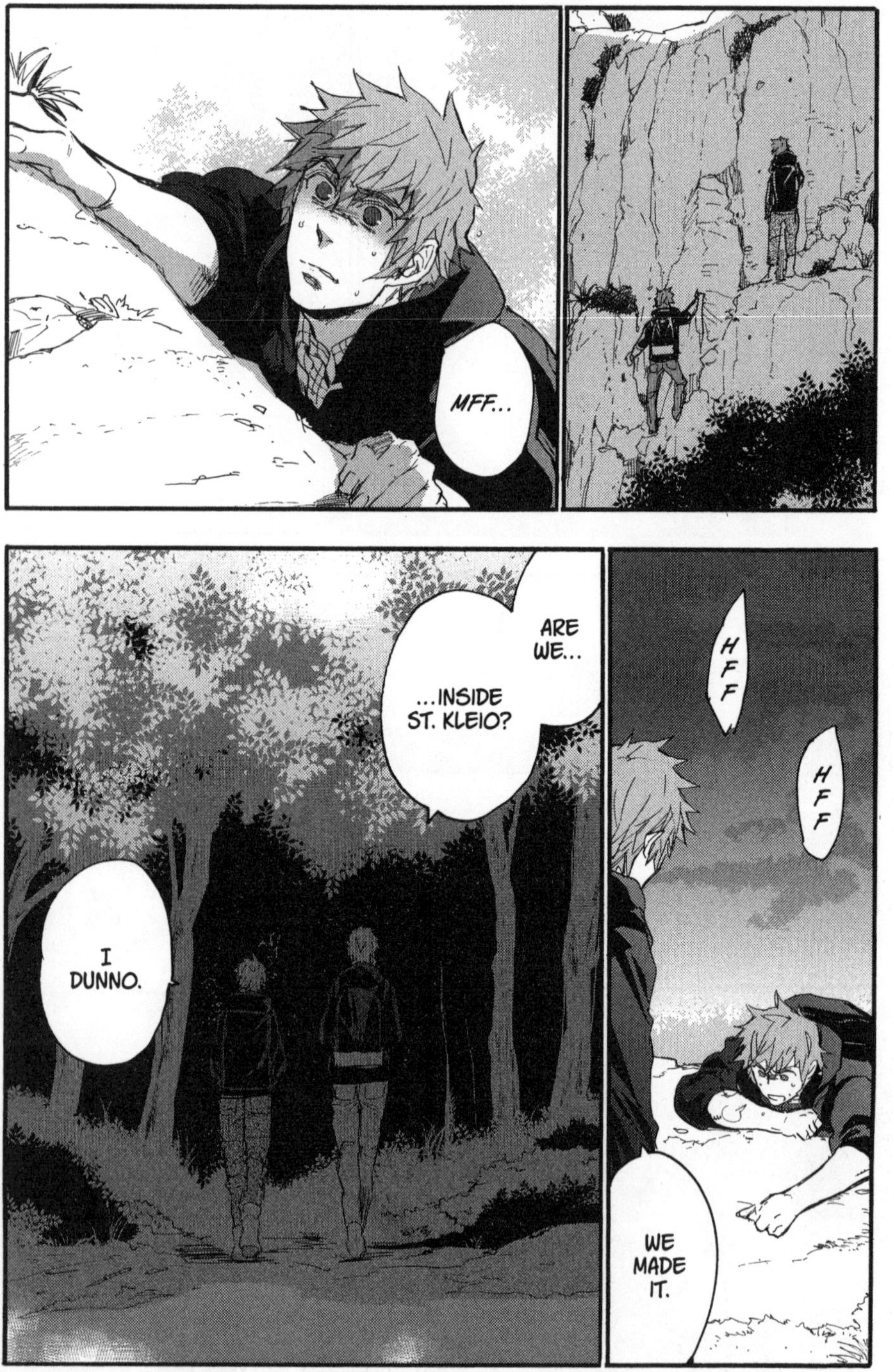
MFF...
HFF
HFF
WE MADE IT.
ARE WE...
...INSIDE ST. KLEIO?
I DUNNO.

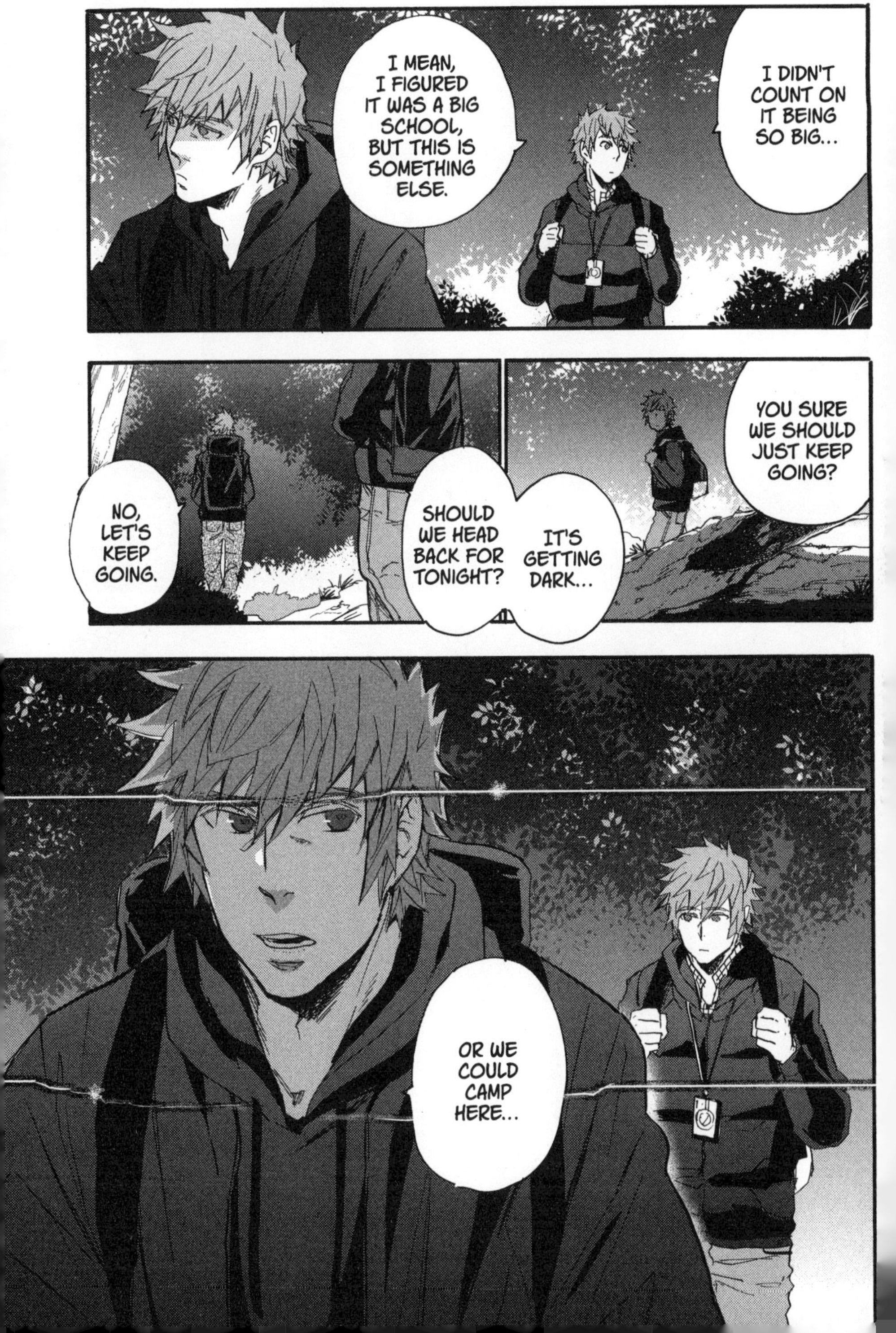
I DIDN'T COUNT ON IT BEING SO BIG...
I MEAN, I FIGURED IT WAS A BIG SCHOOL, BUT THIS IS SOMETHING ELSE.
YOU SURE WE SHOULD JUST KEEP GOING?
IT'S GETTING DARK...
SHOULD WE HEAD BACK FOR TONIGHT?
NO, LET'S KEEP GOING.
OR WE COULD CAMP HERE...

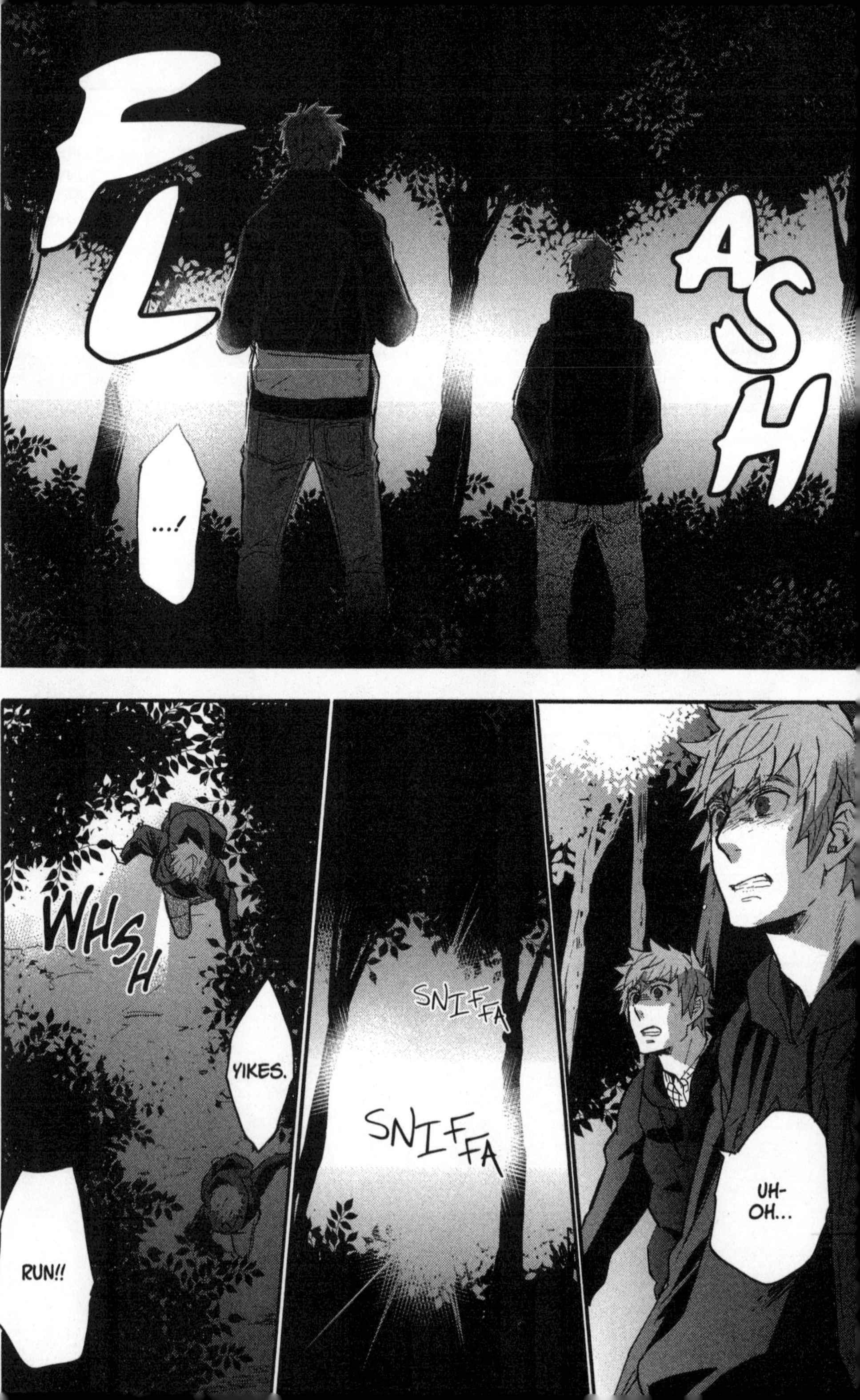
FLASH
...!
UH-OH...
SNIFFA
SNIFFA
YIKES.
WHSH
RUN!!

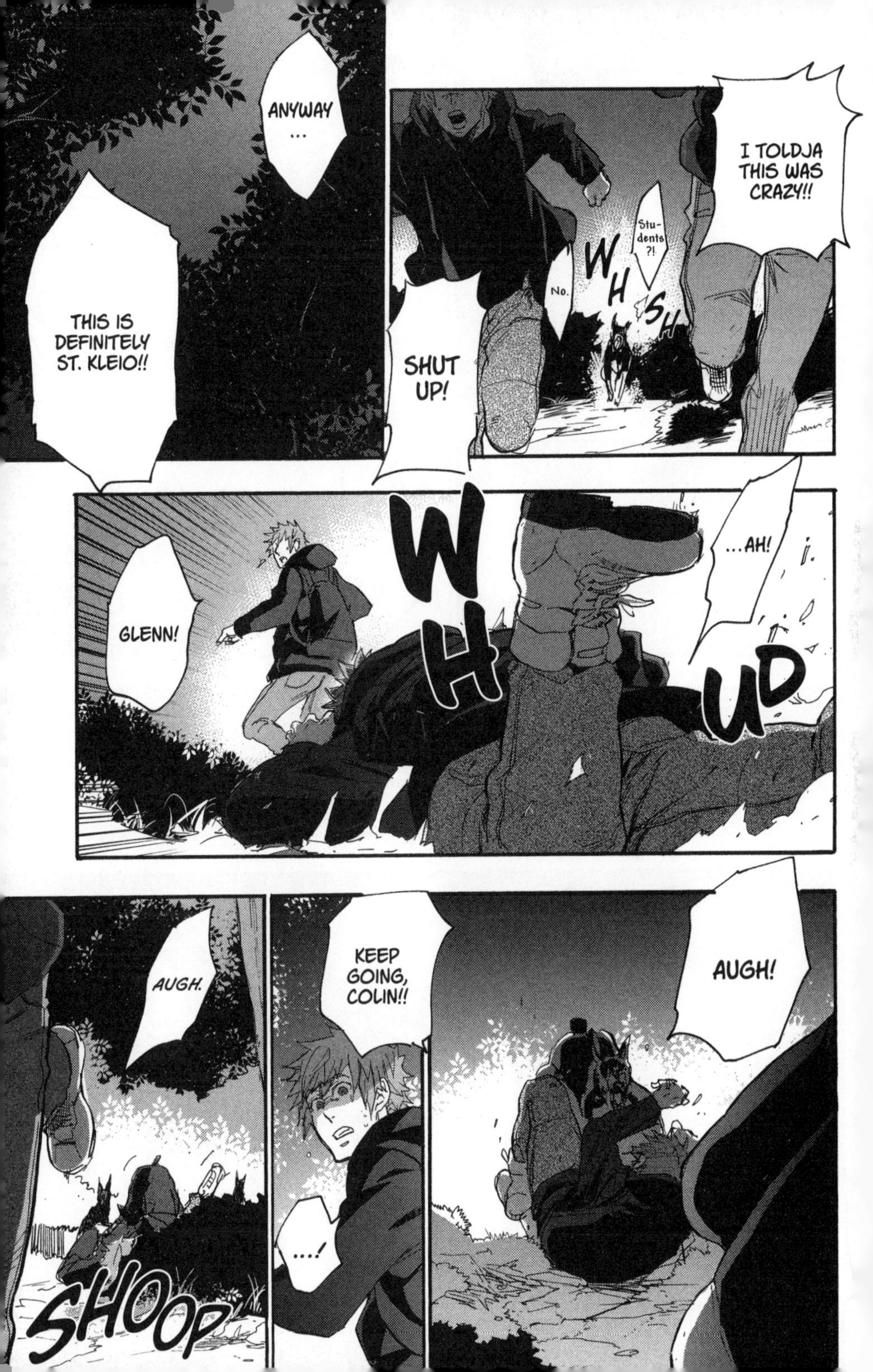
I TOLDJA THIS WAS CRAZY!!
Students?!
WHSH
No.
SHUT UP!
ANYWAY ...
THIS IS DEFINITELY ST. KLEIO!!
...AH!
WHUD
GLENN!
AUGH!
KEEP GOING, COLIN!!
...!
AUGH.
SHOOP

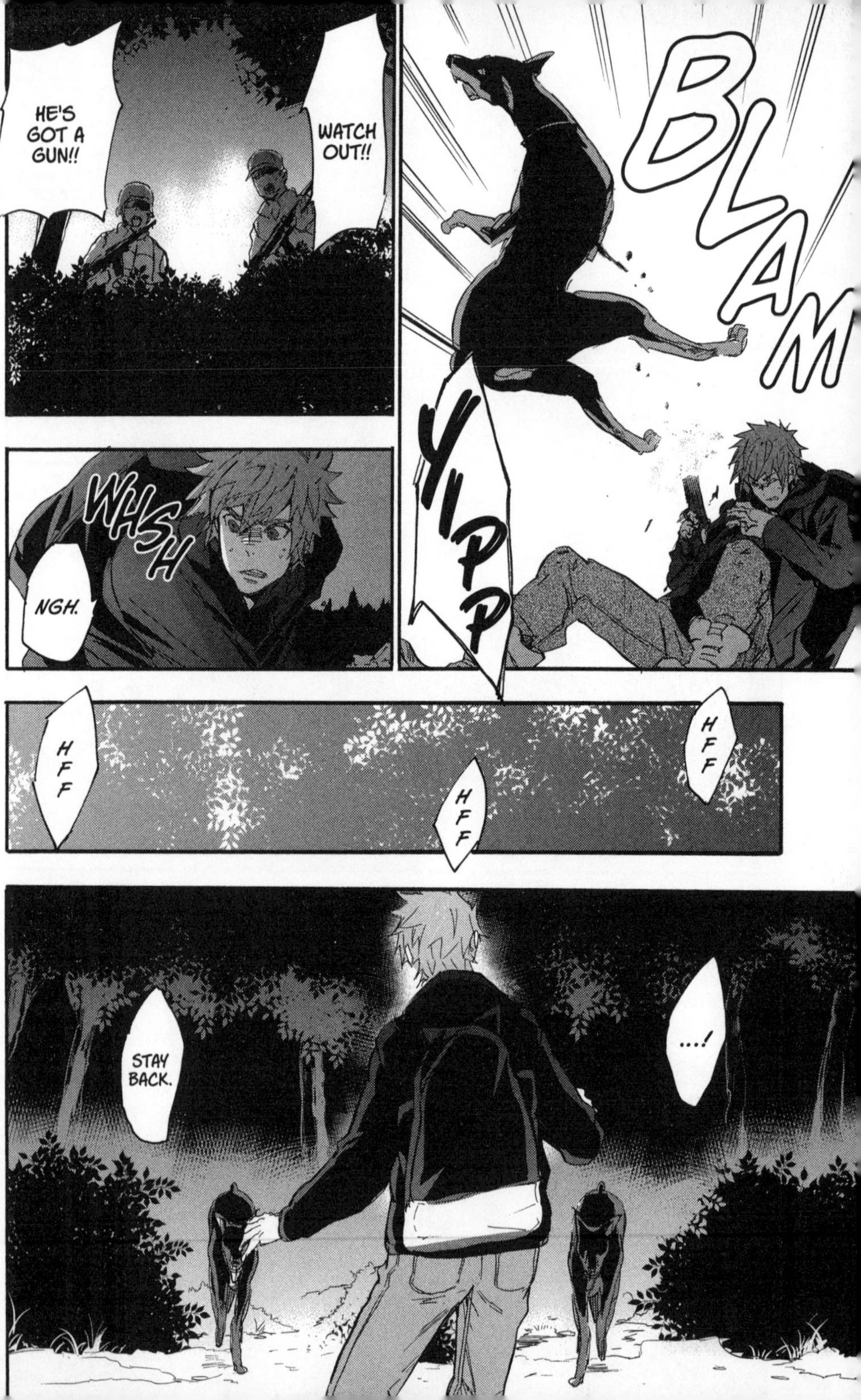
BLAM
YIPP
WATCH OUT!!
HE'S GOT A GUN!!
WHSH
NGH.
HFF
HFF
HFF
...!
STAY BACK.

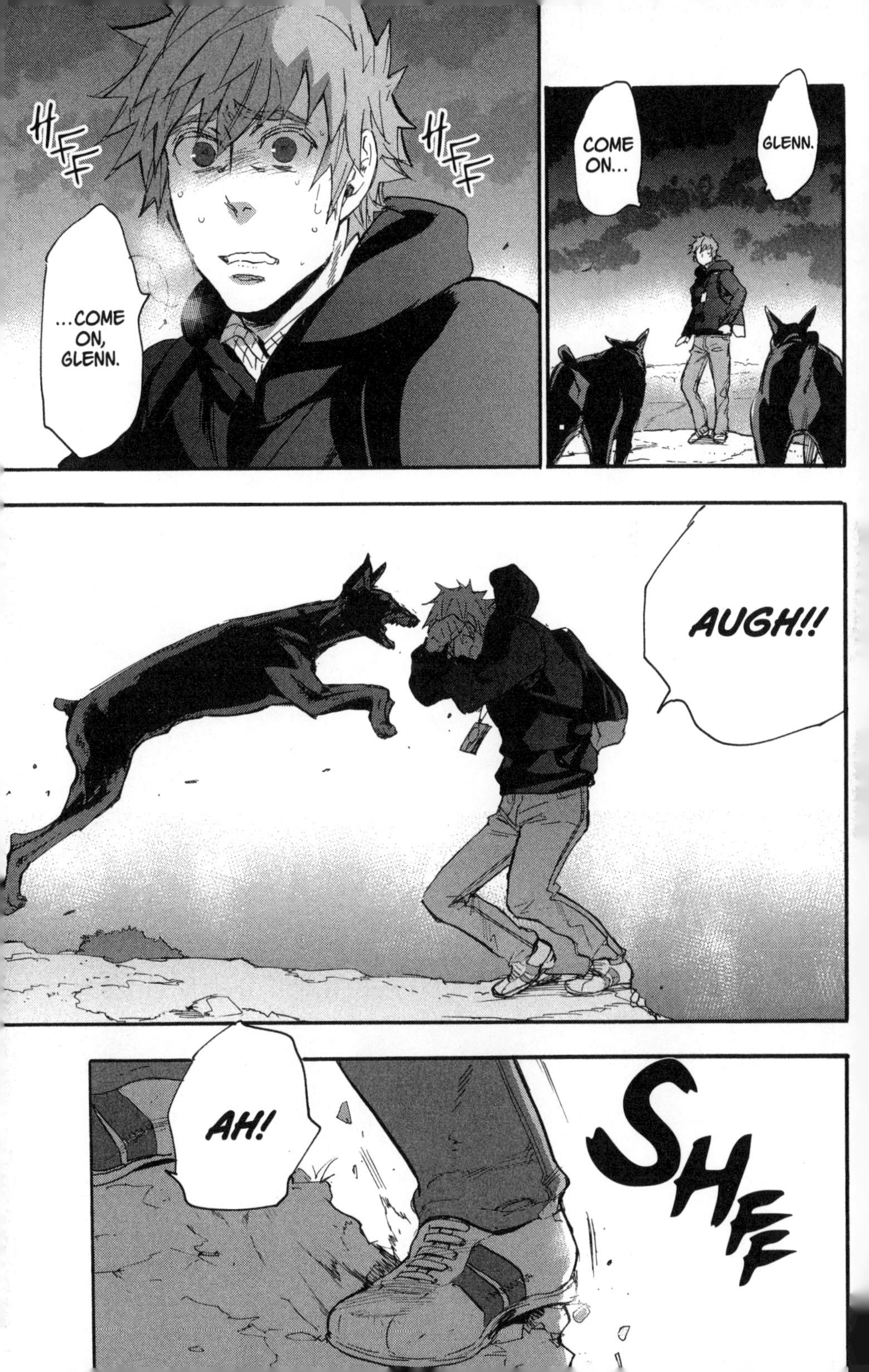
GLENN.
COME ON...
HFF
HFF
...COME ON, GLENN.
AUGH!!
SHFF
AH!

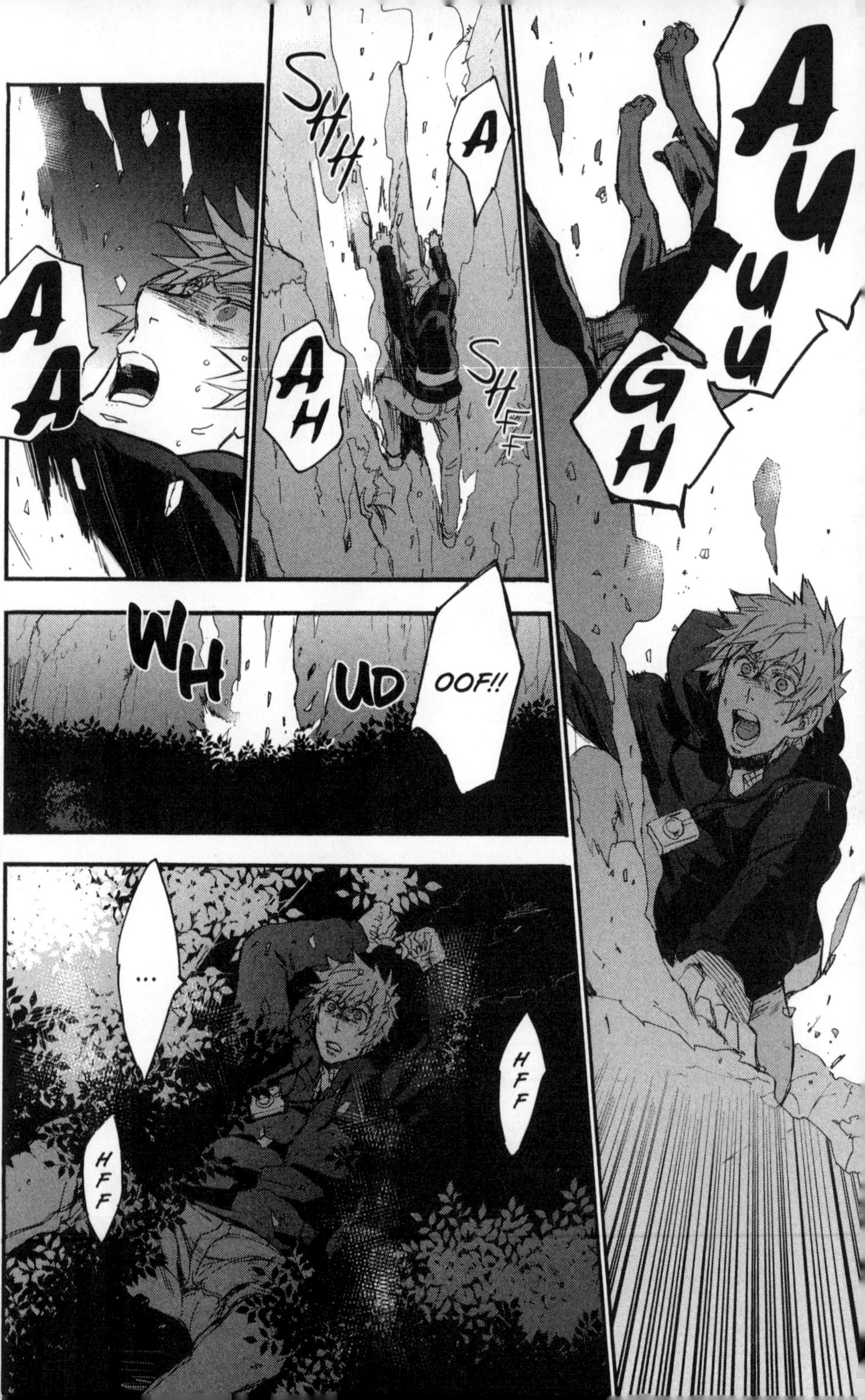
AUUUGH
A
SHHH
SHFF
AH
AA
OOF!!
WHUD
...
HFF
HFF

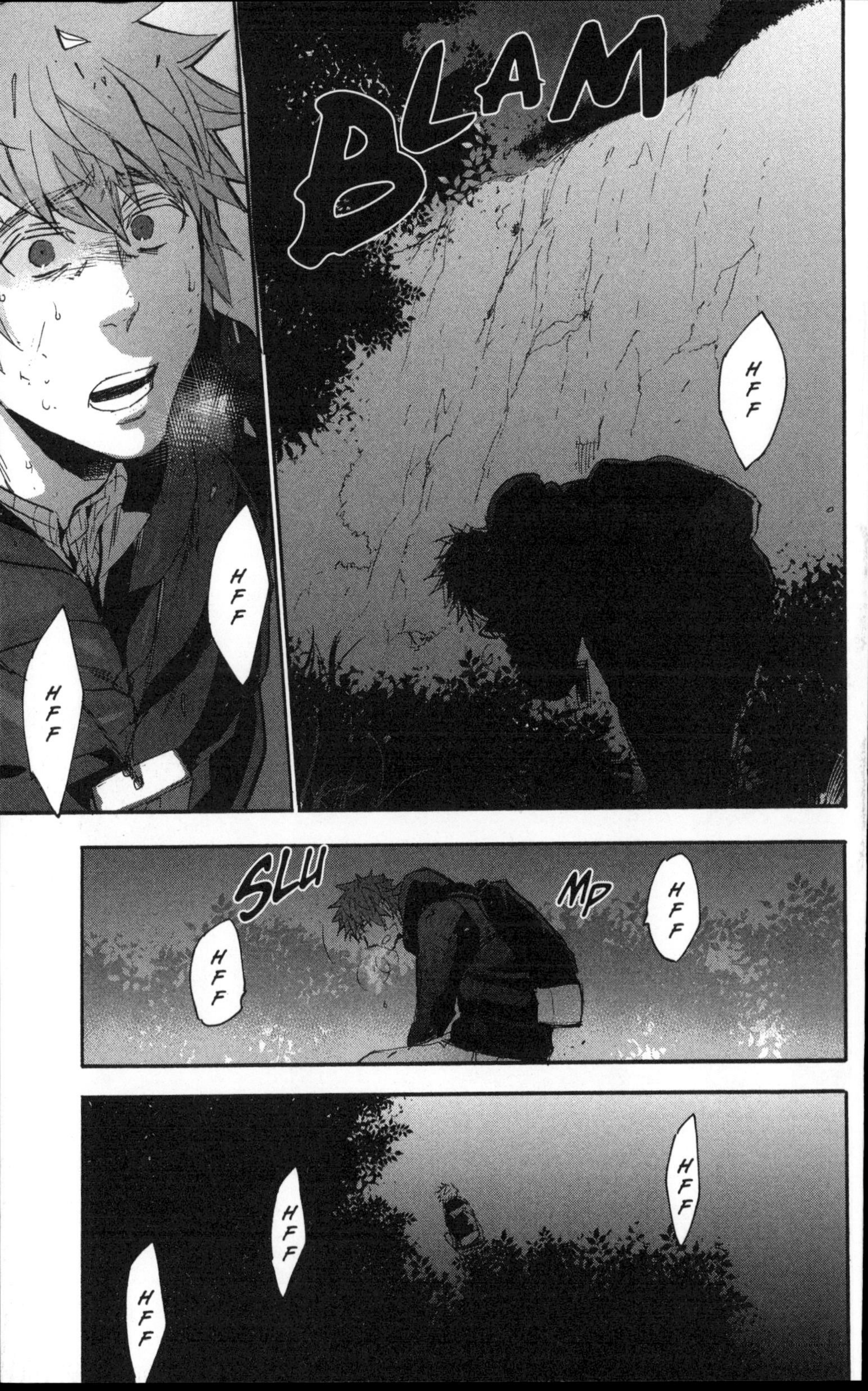
BLAM
HFF
HFF
HFF
SLUMP
HFF
HFF
HFF
HFF
HFF

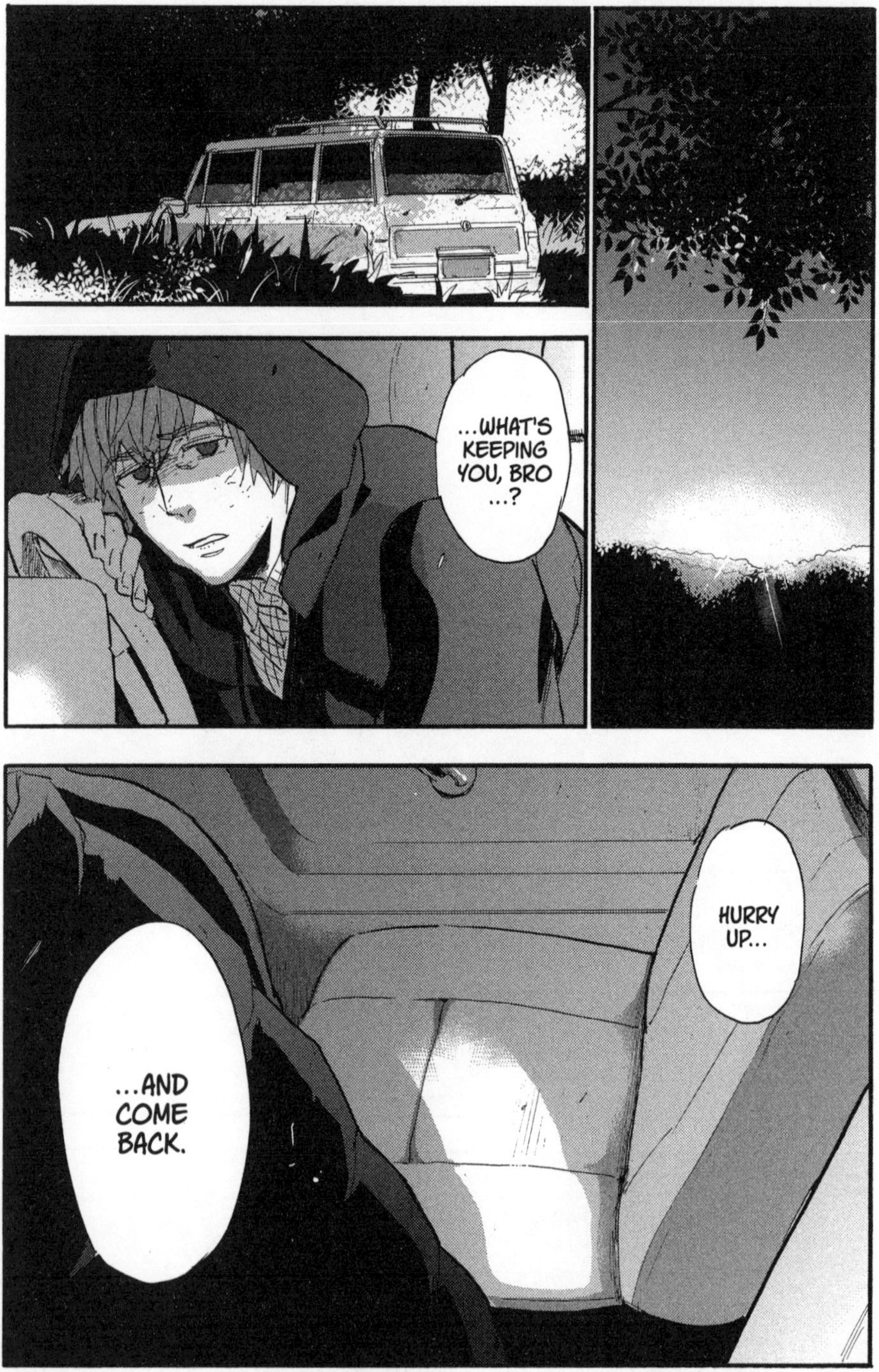
...WHAT'S KEEPING YOU, BRO ...?
HURRY UP...
...AND COME BACK.

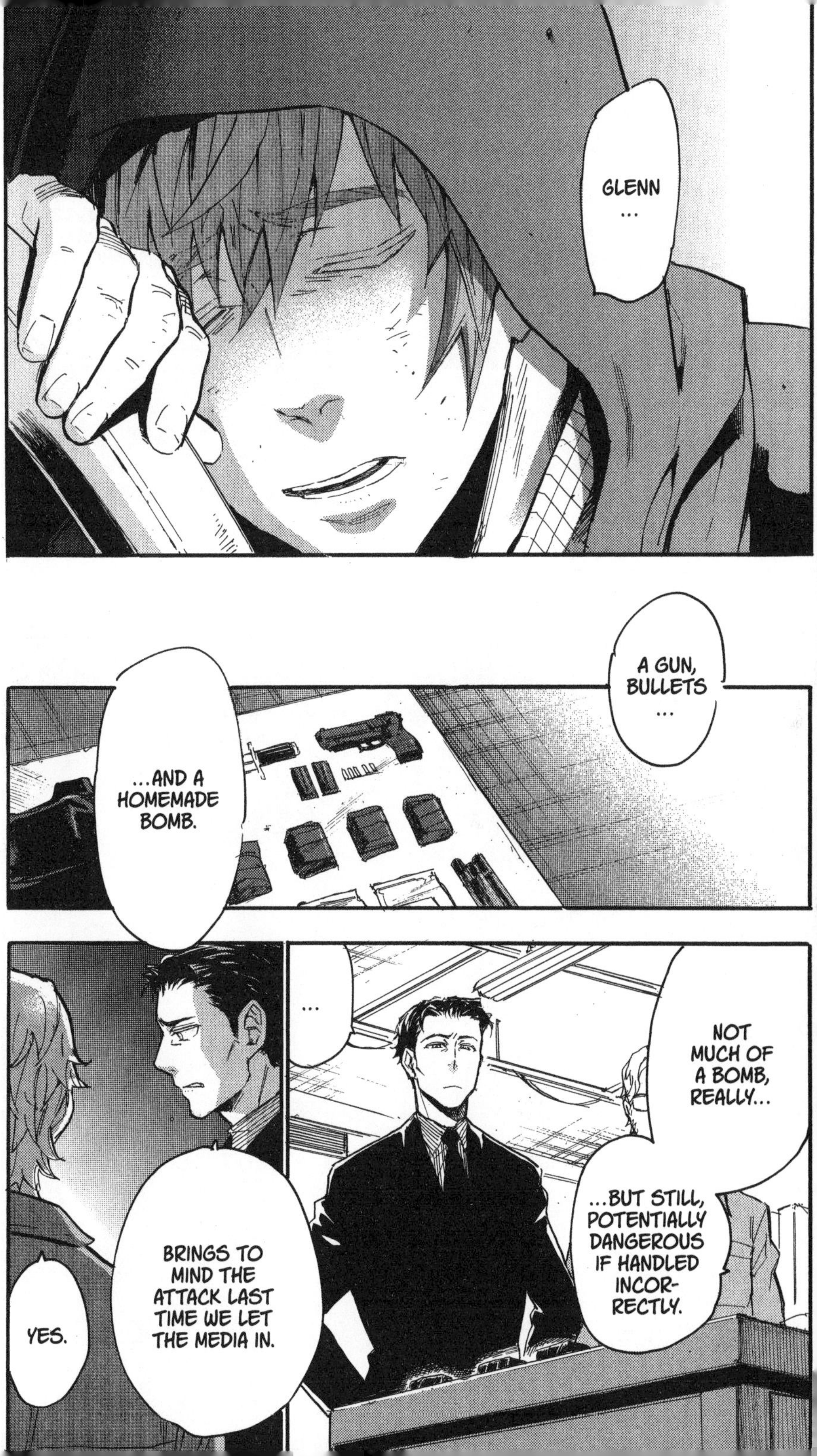
GLENN …
A GUN, BULLETS …
…AND A HOMEMADE BOMB.
NOT MUCH OF A BOMB, REALLY…
…BUT STILL, POTENTIALLY DANGEROUS IF HANDLED INCOR-RECTLY.
…
BRINGS TO MIND THE ATTACK LAST TIME WE LET THE MEDIA IN.
YES.

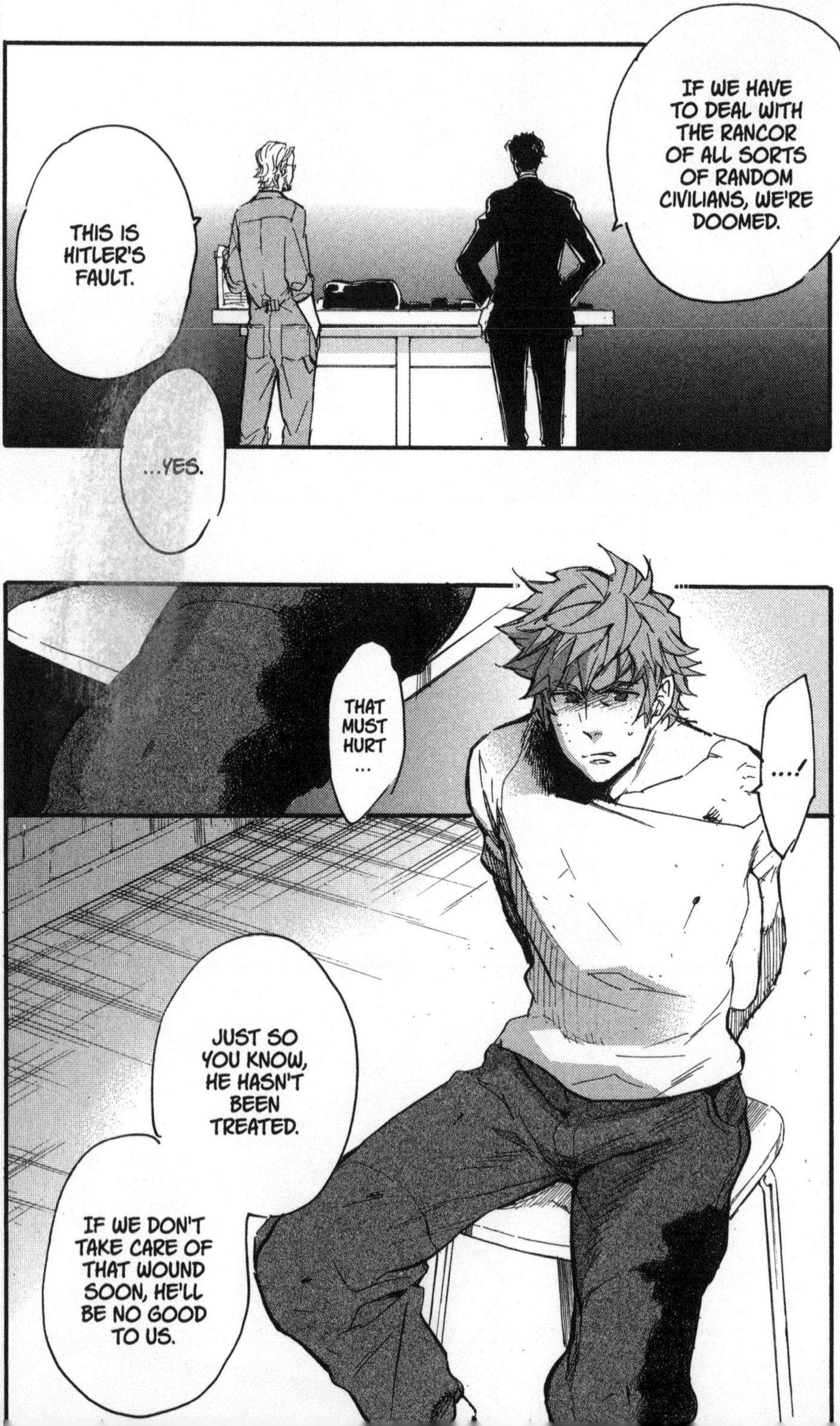
IF WE HAVE TO DEAL WITH THE RANCOR OF ALL SORTS OF RANDOM CIVILIANS, WE'RE DOOMED.
THIS IS HITLER'S FAULT.
...YES.
THAT MUST HURT ...
...!
JUST SO YOU KNOW, HE HASN'T BEEN TREATED.
IF WE DON'T TAKE CARE OF THAT WOUND SOON, HE'LL BE NO GOOD TO US.

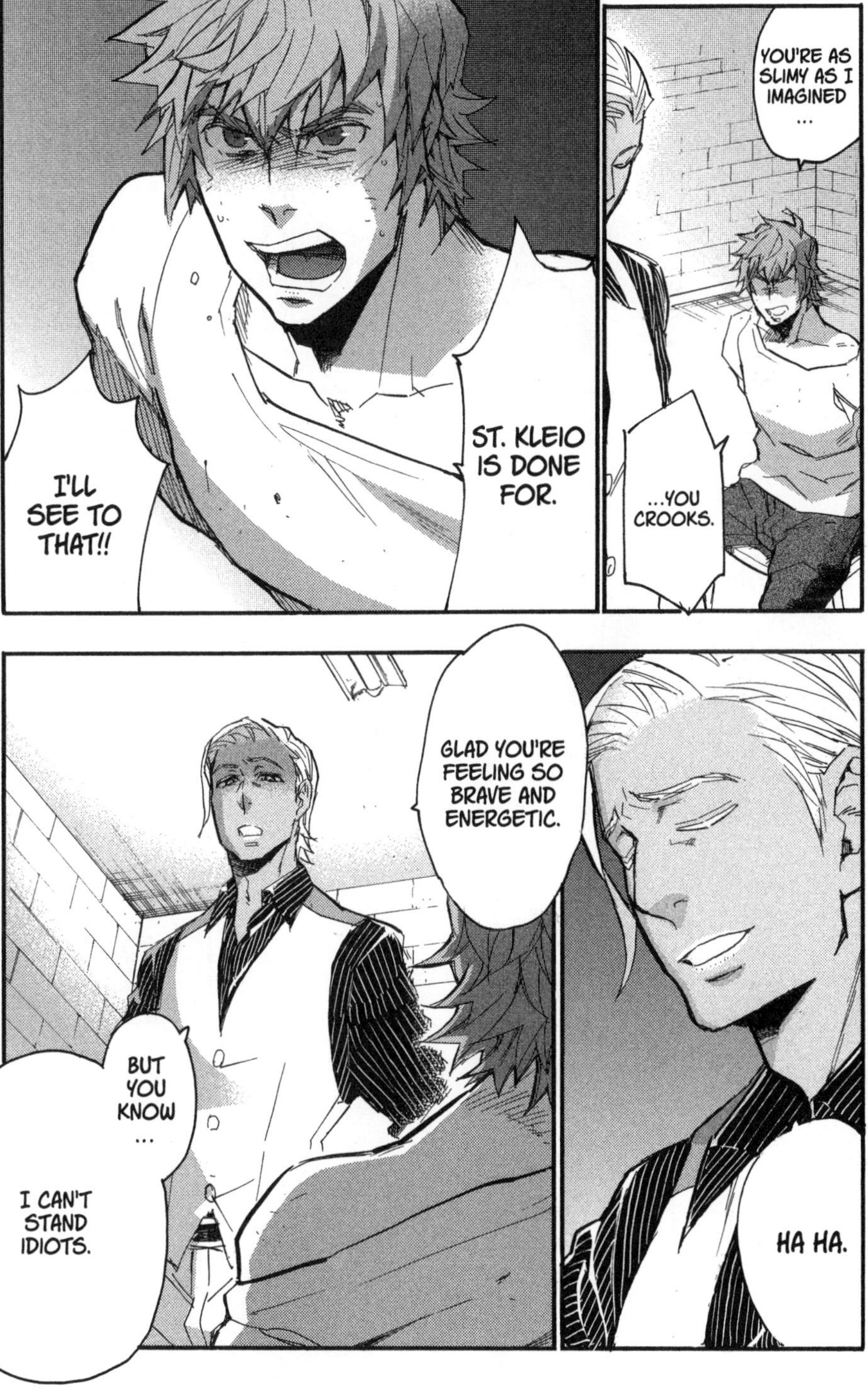
YOU'RE AS SLIMY AS I IMAGINED ...
...YOU CROOKS.
ST. KLEIO IS DONE FOR.
I'LL SEE TO THAT!!
GLAD YOU'RE FEELING SO BRAVE AND ENERGETIC.
HA HA.
BUT YOU KNOW ...
I CAN'T STAND IDIOTS.

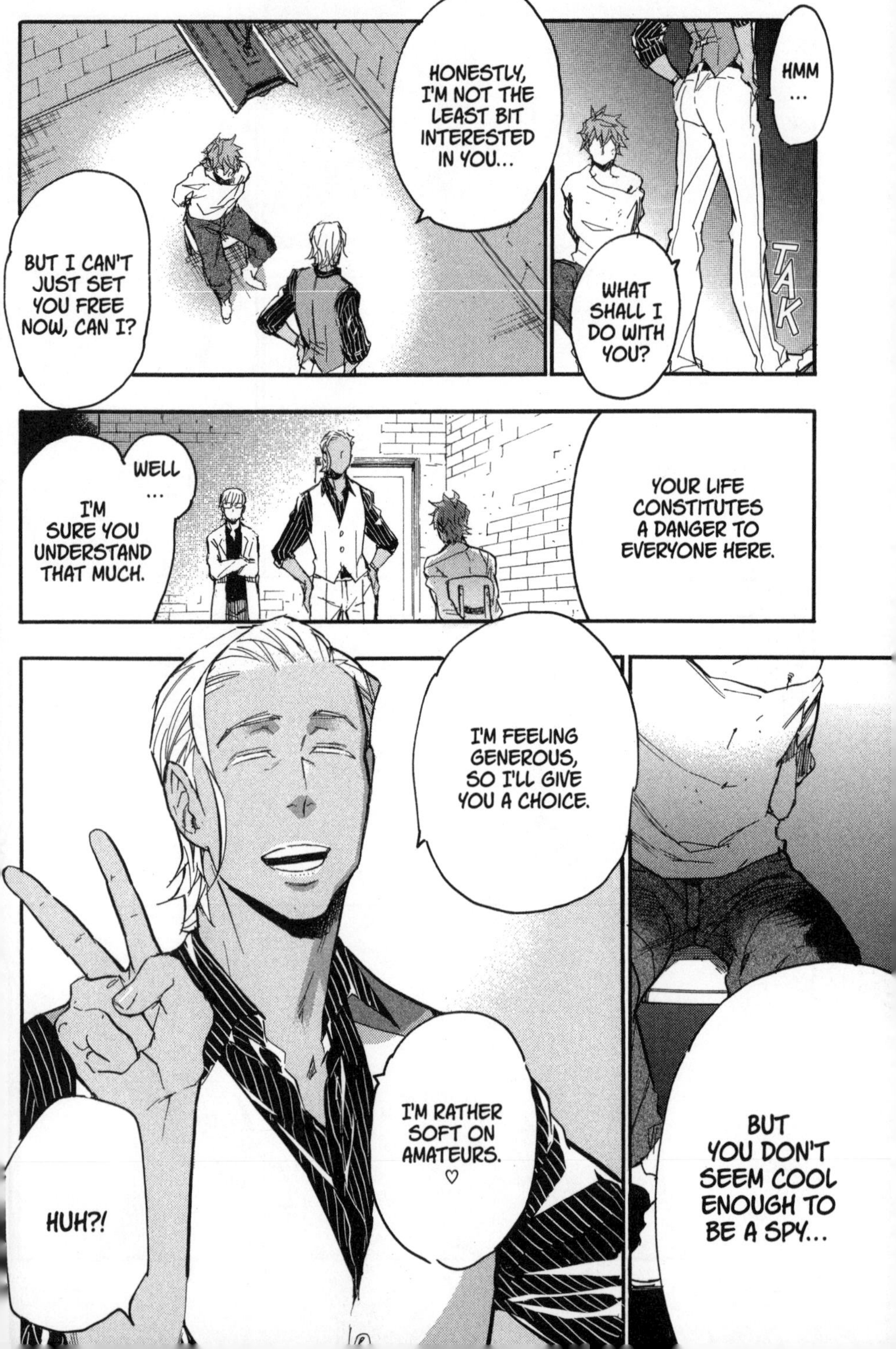
HMM ...
TAK
WHAT SHALL I DO WITH YOU?
HONESTLY, I'M NOT THE LEAST BIT INTERESTED IN YOU...
BUT I CAN'T JUST SET YOU FREE NOW, CAN I?
YOUR LIFE CONSTITUTES A DANGER TO EVERYONE HERE.
WELL ...
I'M SURE YOU UNDERSTAND THAT MUCH.
BUT YOU DON'T SEEM COOL ENOUGH TO BE A SPY...
I'M FEELING GENEROUS, SO I'LL GIVE YOU A CHOICE.
I'M RATHER SOFT ON AMATEURS. ♡
HUH?!

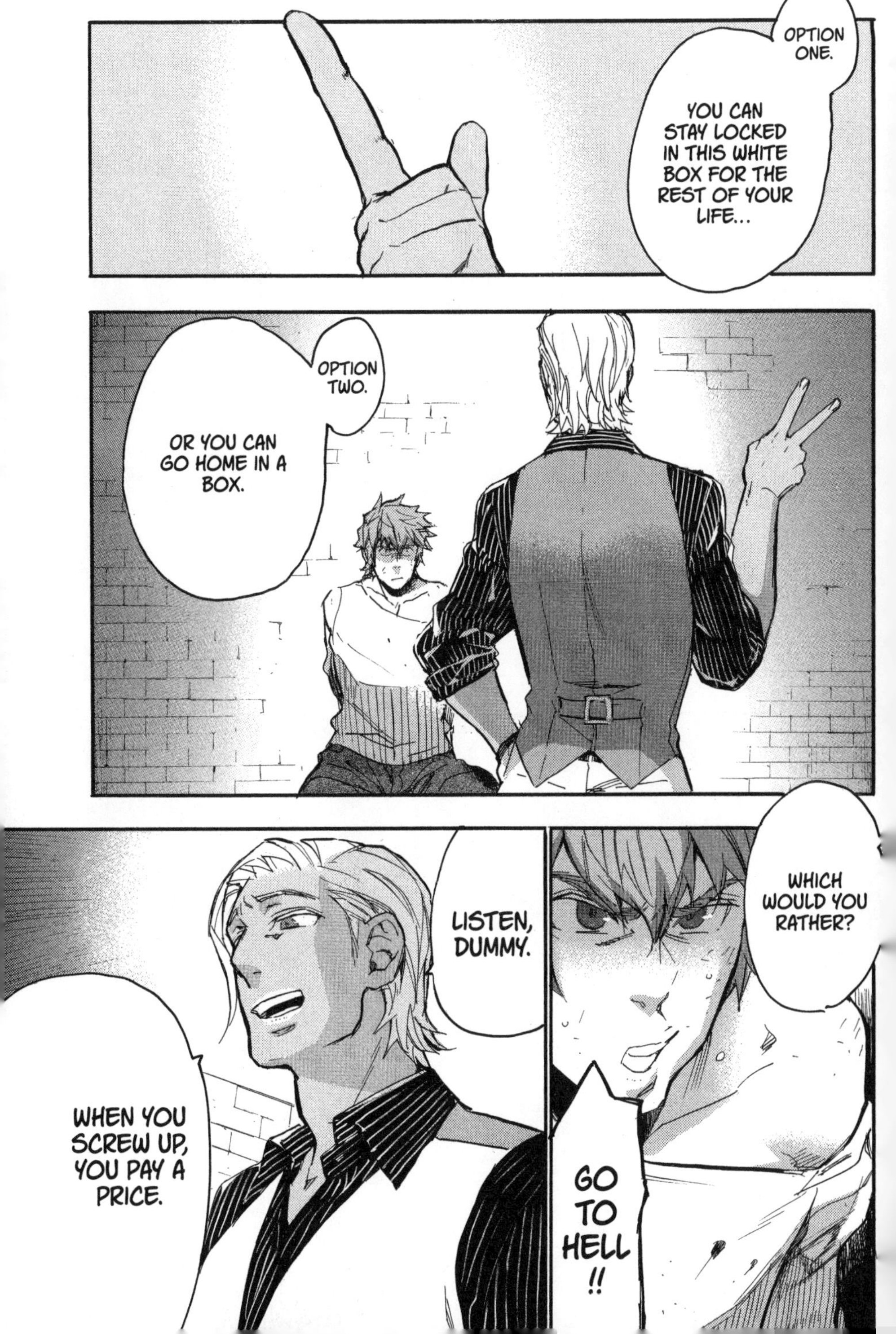
OPTION ONE.
YOU CAN STAY LOCKED IN THIS WHITE BOX FOR THE REST OF YOUR LIFE...
OPTION TWO.
OR YOU CAN GO HOME IN A BOX.
WHICH WOULD YOU RATHER?
GO TO HELL!!
LISTEN, DUMMY.
WHEN YOU SCREW UP, YOU PAY A PRICE.

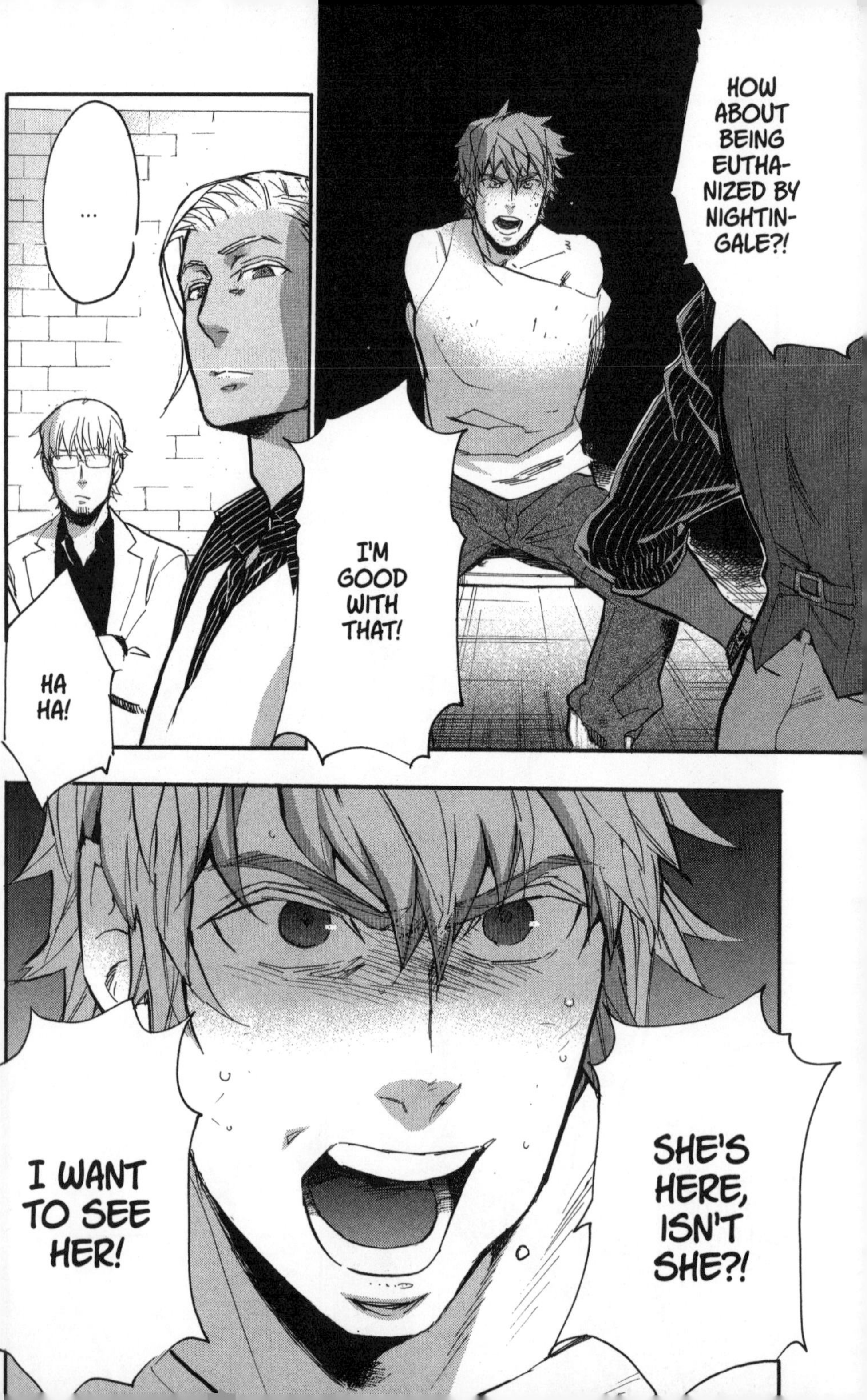
HOW ABOUT BEING EUTHA- NIZED BY NIGHTIN- GALE?!
I'M GOOD WITH THAT!
...
HA HA!
SHE'S HERE, ISN'T SHE?!
I WANT TO SEE HER!

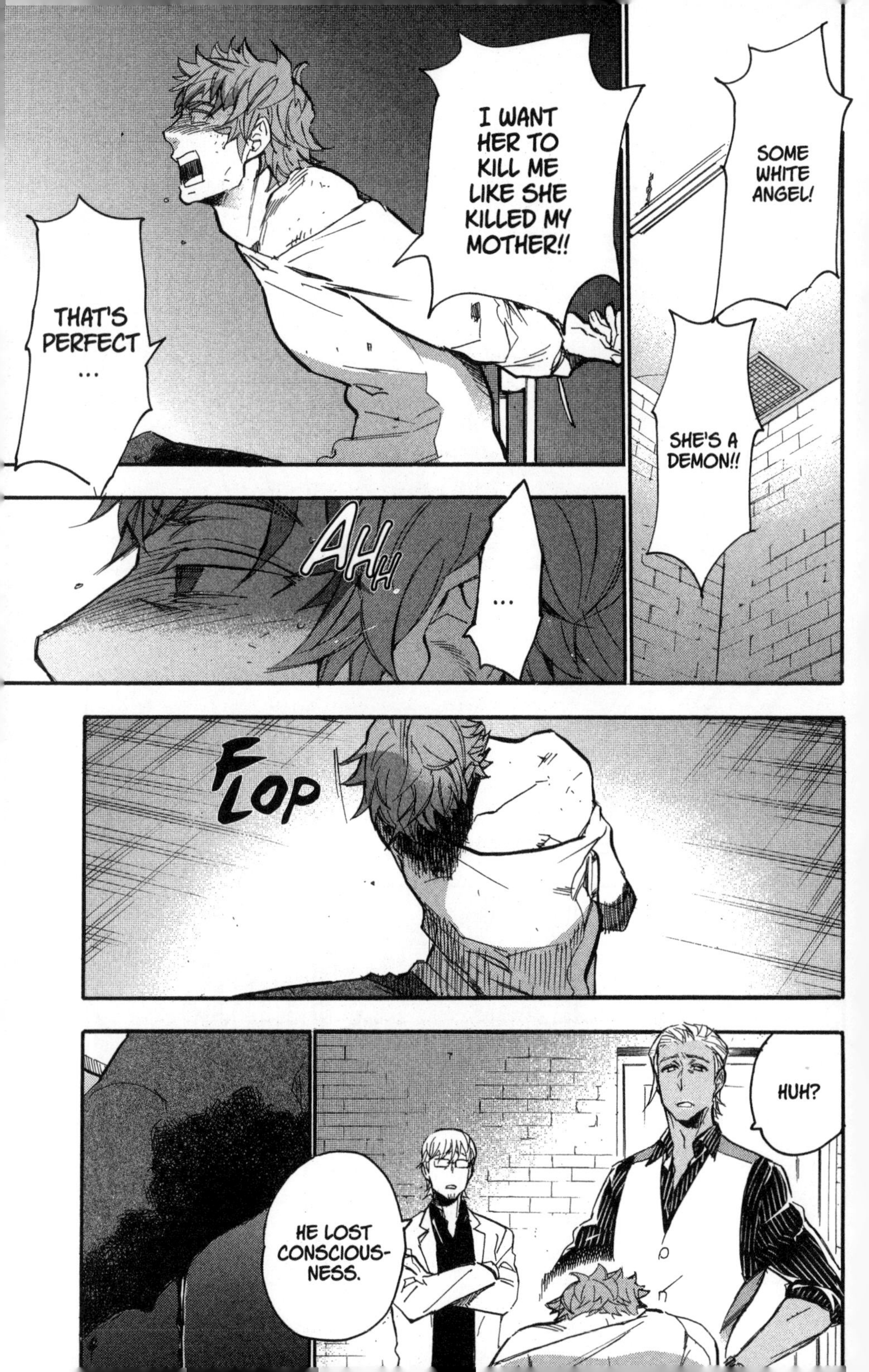
SOME WHITE ANGEL!
SHE'S A DEMON!!
I WANT HER TO KILL ME LIKE SHE KILLED MY MOTHER!!
THAT'S PERFECT ...
...
AHH
FLOP
HUH?
HE LOST CONSCIOUS-NESS.

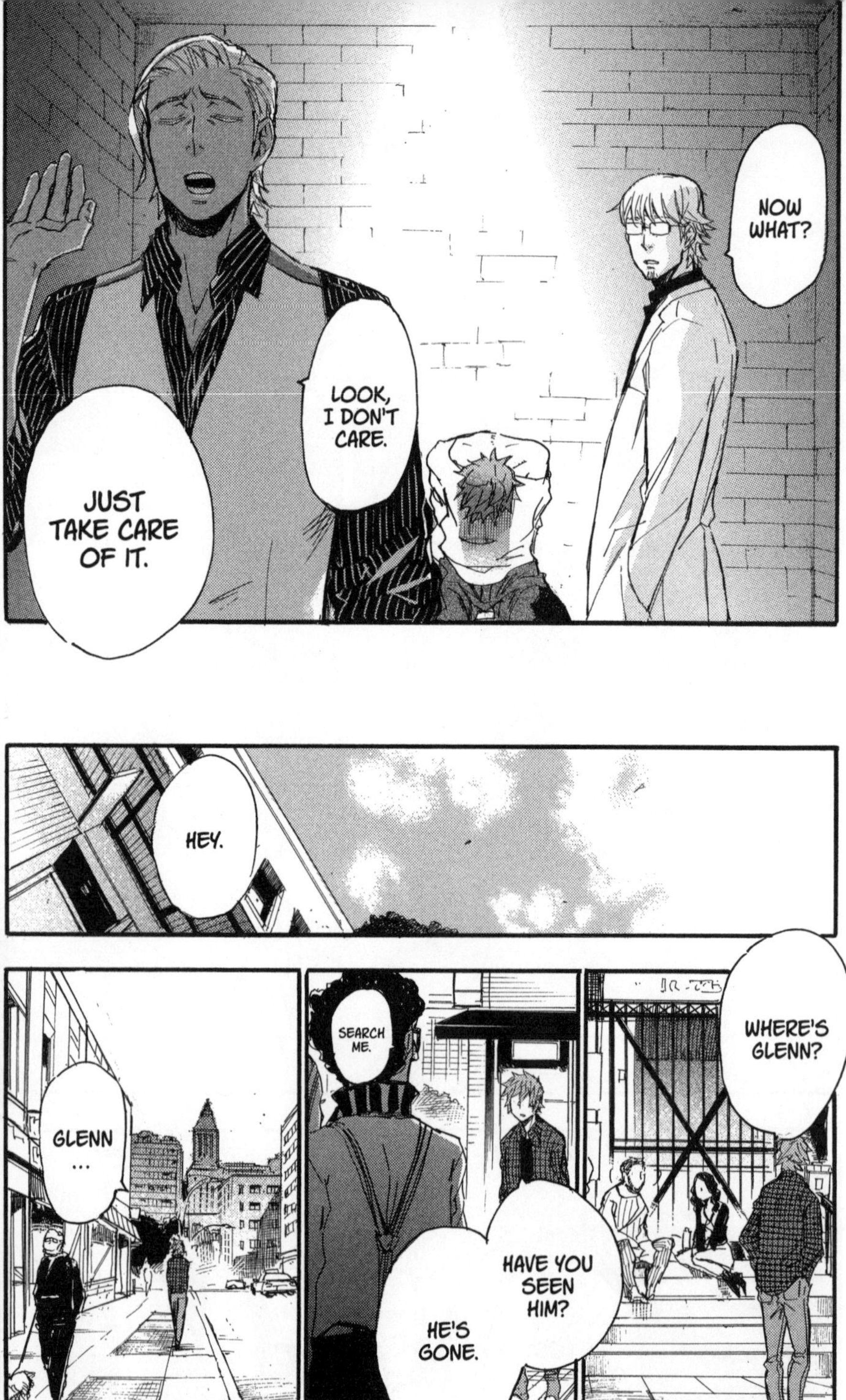
NOW WHAT?
LOOK, I DON'T CARE.
JUST TAKE CARE OF IT.
HEY.
WHERE'S GLENN?
HAVE YOU SEEN HIM?
SEARCH ME.
HE'S GONE.
GLENN ...

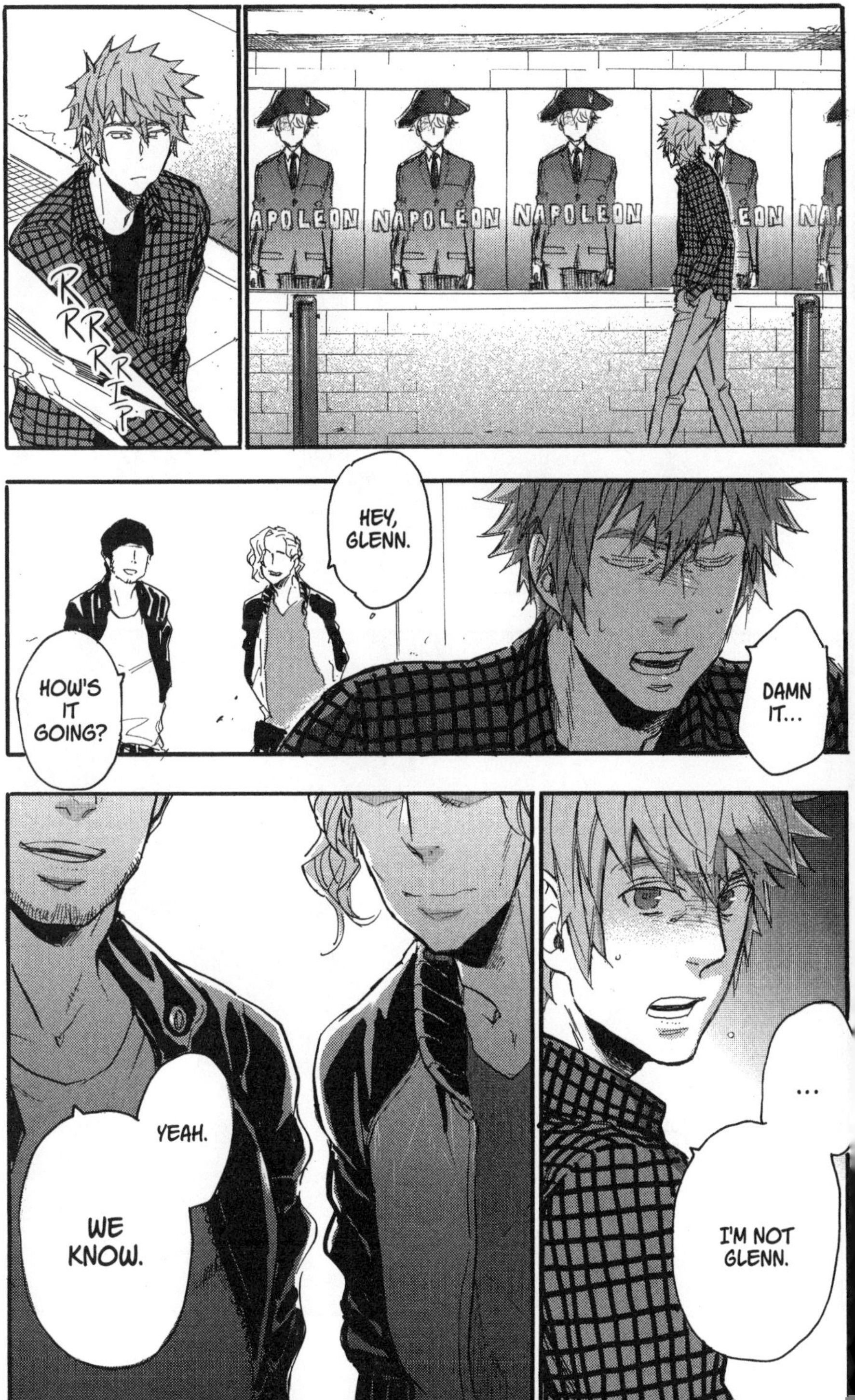
NAPOLEON
NAPOLEON
NAPOLEON
RRRRRIP
HEY, GLENN.
DAMN IT...
HOW'S IT GOING?
...
I'M NOT GLENN.
YEAH.
WE KNOW.

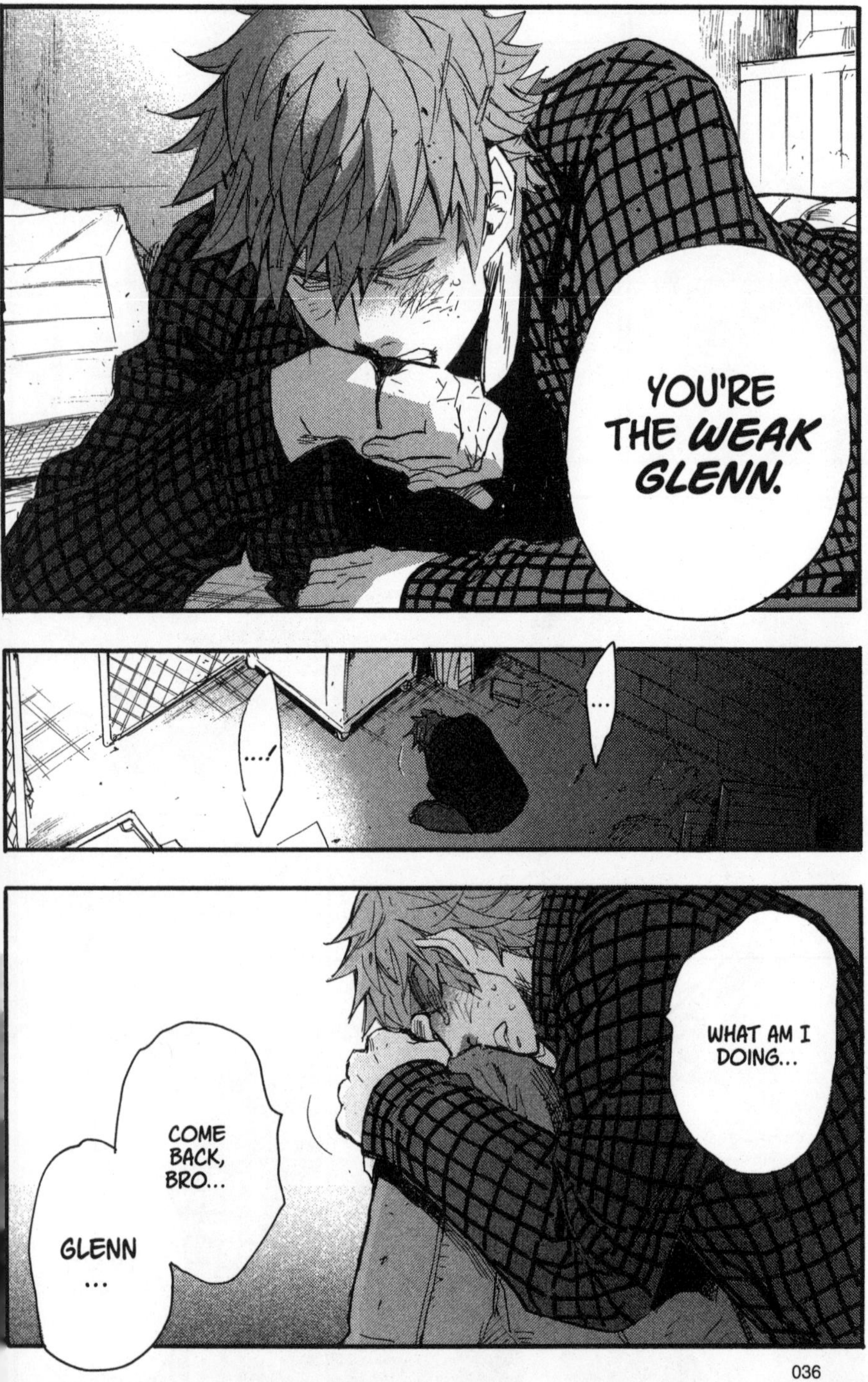
YOU'RE THE WEAK GLENN.
...
...!
WHAT AM I DOING...
COME BACK, BRO...
GLENN ...

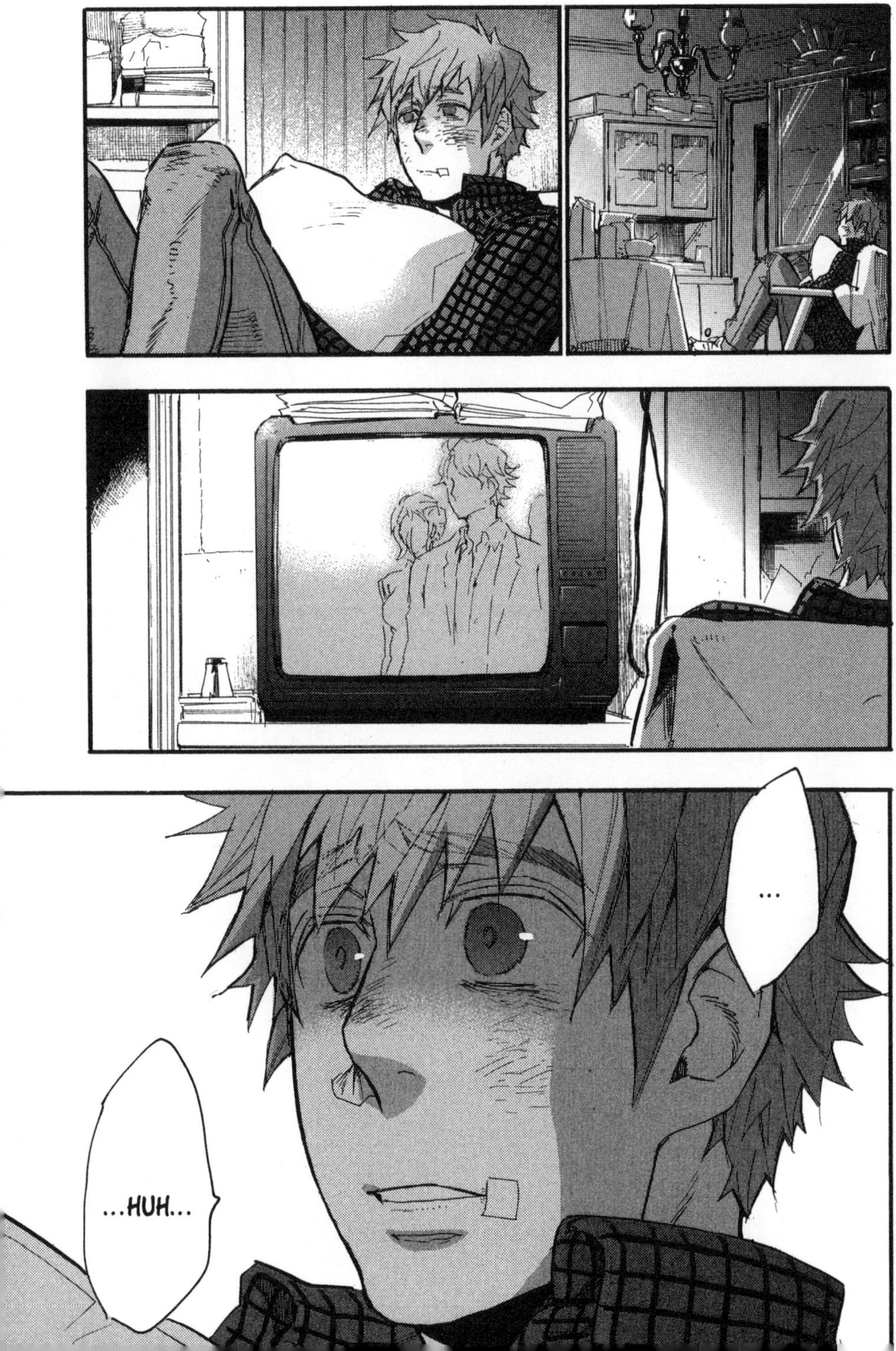
...
...HUH...

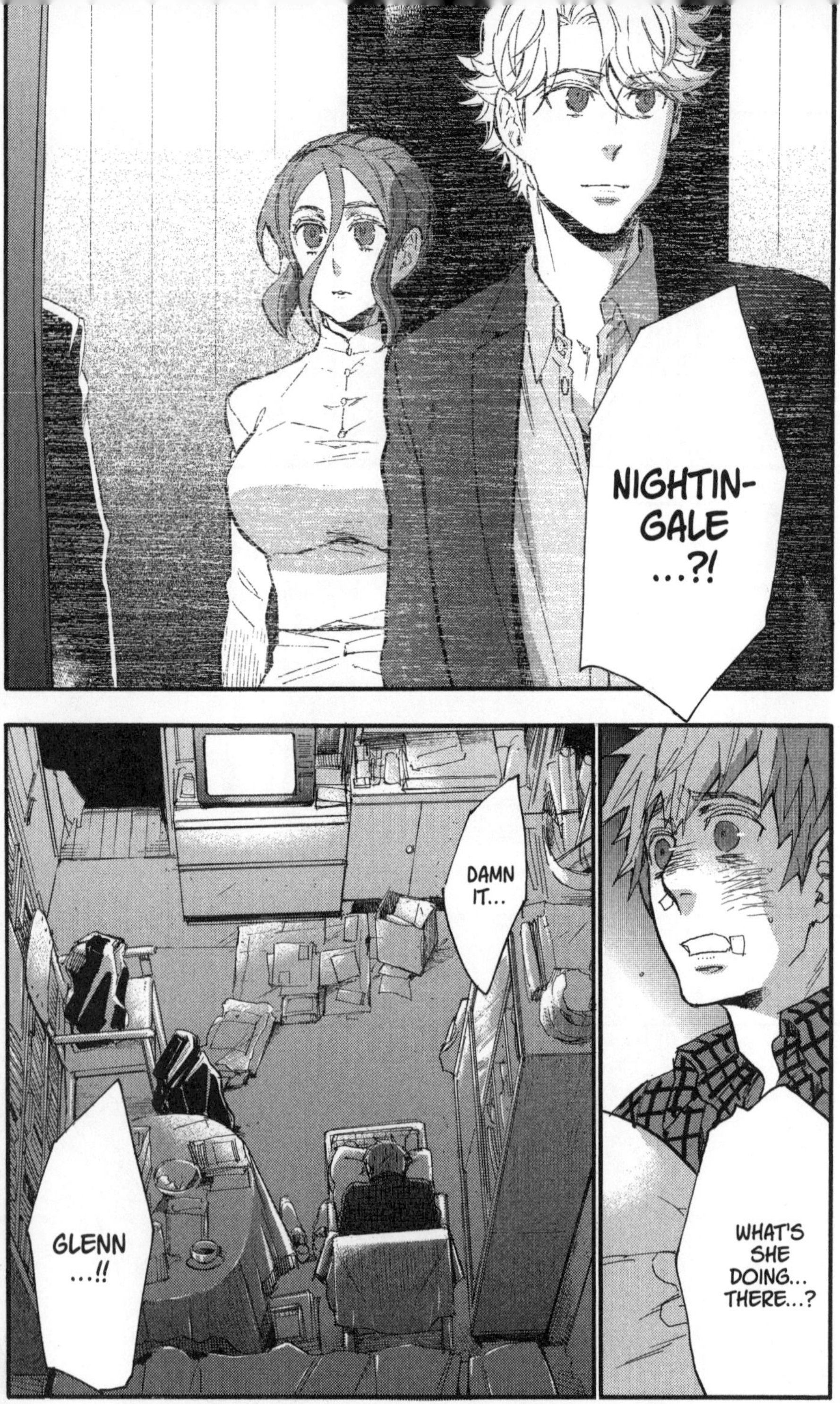
NIGHTIN-GALE ...?!
WHAT'S SHE DOING... THERE...?
DAMN IT...
GLENN ...!!

# CHAPTER sixty-two

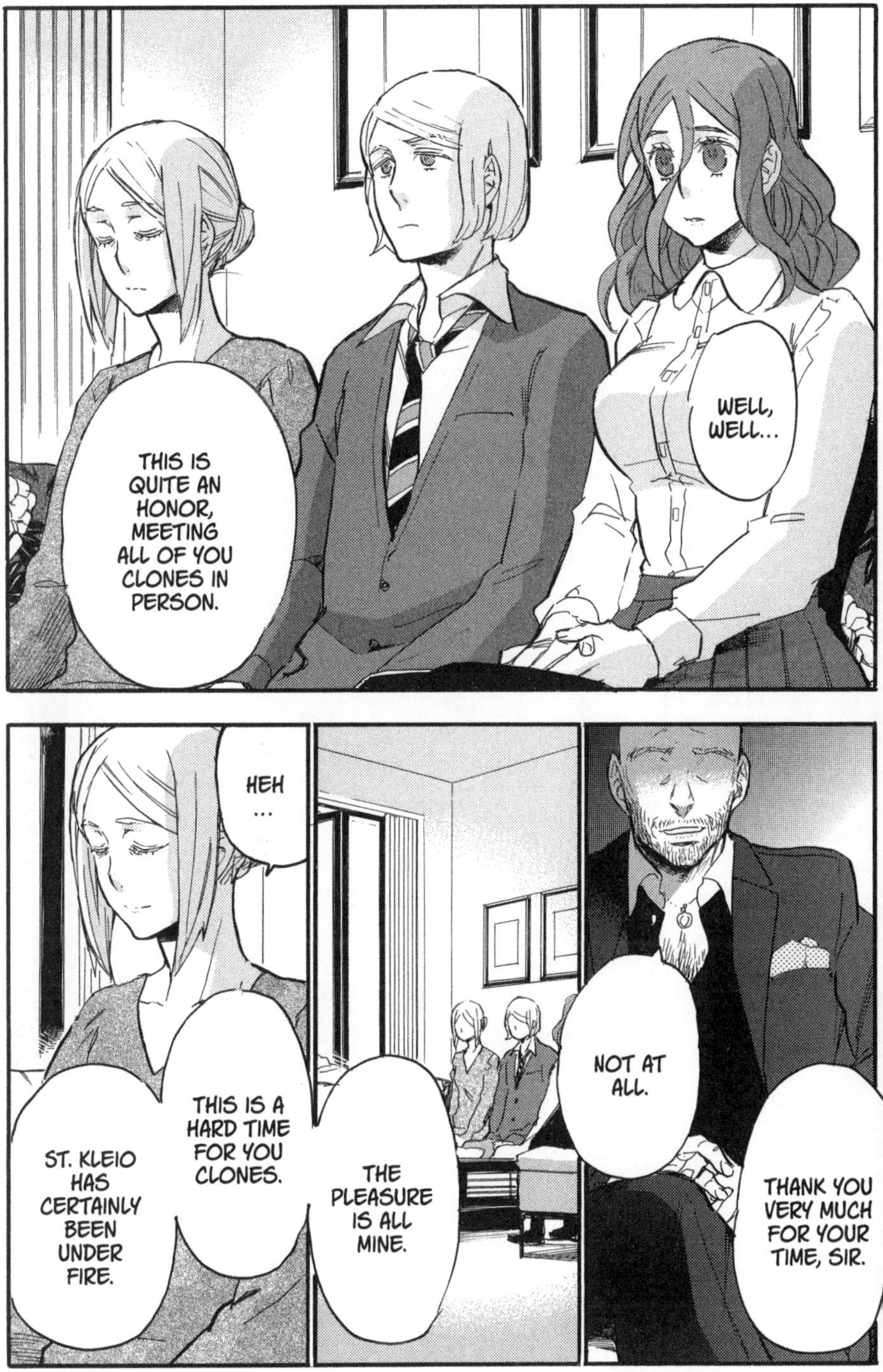
WELL, WELL...
THIS IS QUITE AN HONOR, MEETING ALL OF YOU CLONES IN PERSON.
THANK YOU VERY MUCH FOR YOUR TIME, SIR.
NOT AT ALL.
THE PLEASURE IS ALL MINE.
HEH ...
THIS IS A HARD TIME FOR YOU CLONES.
ST. KLEIO HAS CERTAINLY BEEN UNDER FIRE.

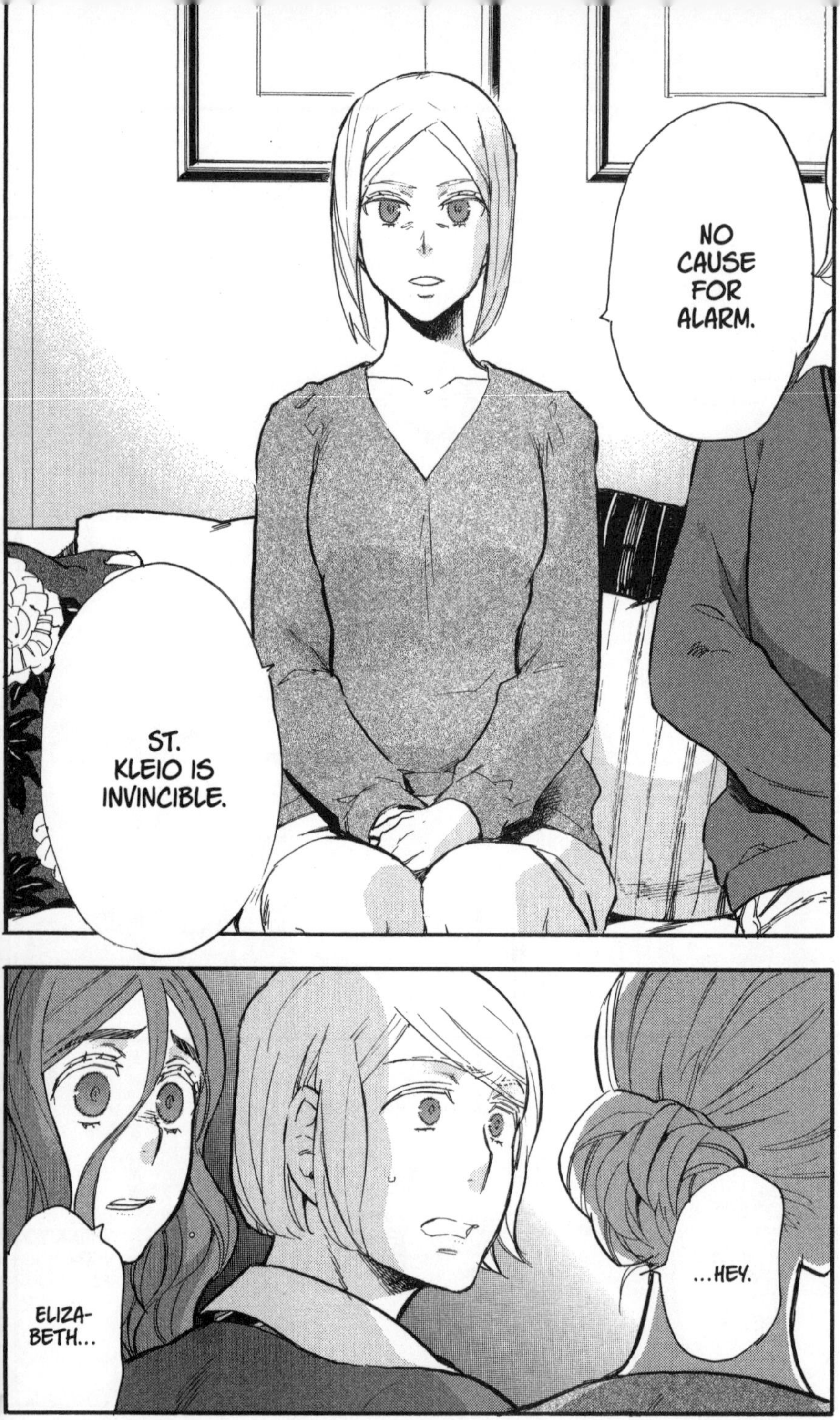
NO CAUSE FOR ALARM.
ST. KLEIO IS INVINCIBLE.
...HEY.
ELIZA-BETH...

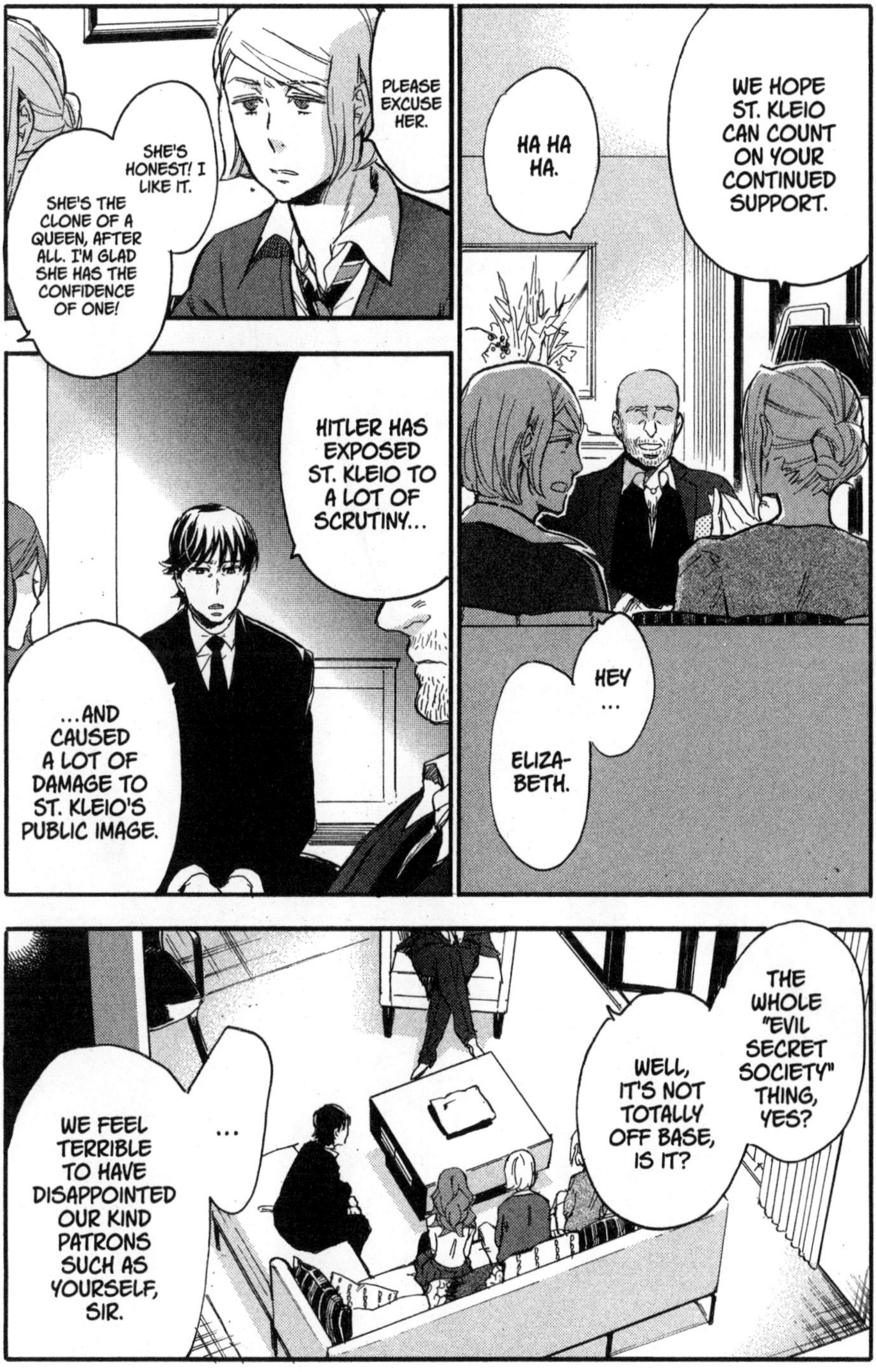
WE HOPE ST. KLEIO CAN COUNT ON YOUR CONTINUED SUPPORT.
HA HA HA.
PLEASE EXCUSE HER.
SHE'S HONEST! I LIKE IT.
SHE'S THE CLONE OF A QUEEN, AFTER ALL. I'M GLAD SHE HAS THE CONFIDENCE OF ONE!
HITLER HAS EXPOSED ST. KLEIO TO A LOT OF SCRUTINY...
...AND CAUSED A LOT OF DAMAGE TO ST. KLEIO'S PUBLIC IMAGE.
HEY...
ELIZABETH.
THE WHOLE "EVIL SECRET SOCIETY" THING, YES?
WELL, IT'S NOT TOTALLY OFF BASE, IS IT?
...
WE FEEL TERRIBLE TO HAVE DISAPPOINTED OUR KIND PATRONS SUCH AS YOURSELF, SIR.

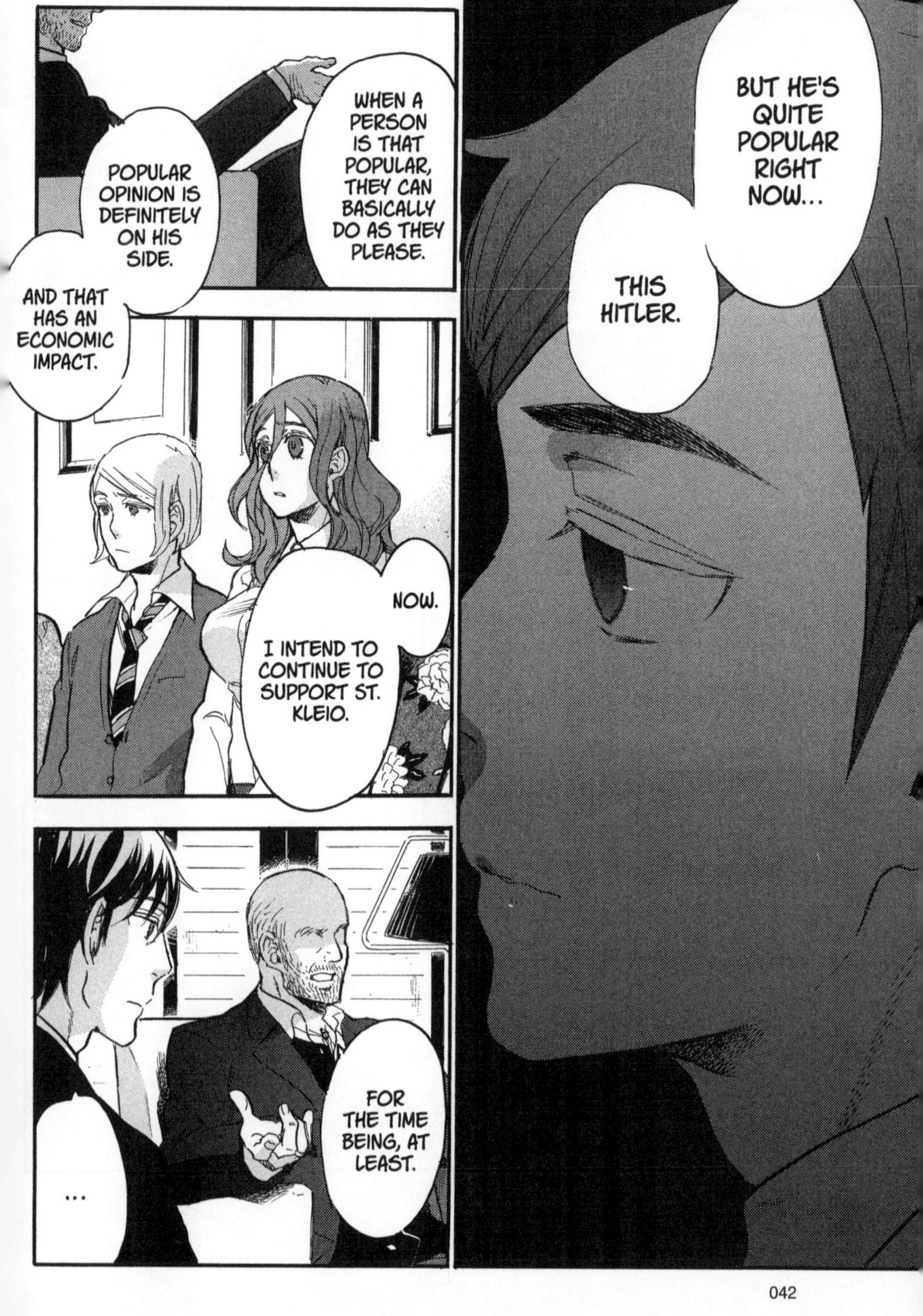
BUT HE'S QUITE POPULAR RIGHT NOW...
THIS HITLER.
WHEN A PERSON IS THAT POPULAR, THEY CAN BASICALLY DO AS THEY PLEASE.
POPULAR OPINION IS DEFINITELY ON HIS SIDE.
AND THAT HAS AN ECONOMIC IMPACT.
NOW.
I INTEND TO CONTINUE TO SUPPORT ST. KLEIO.
FOR THE TIME BEING, AT LEAST.
...

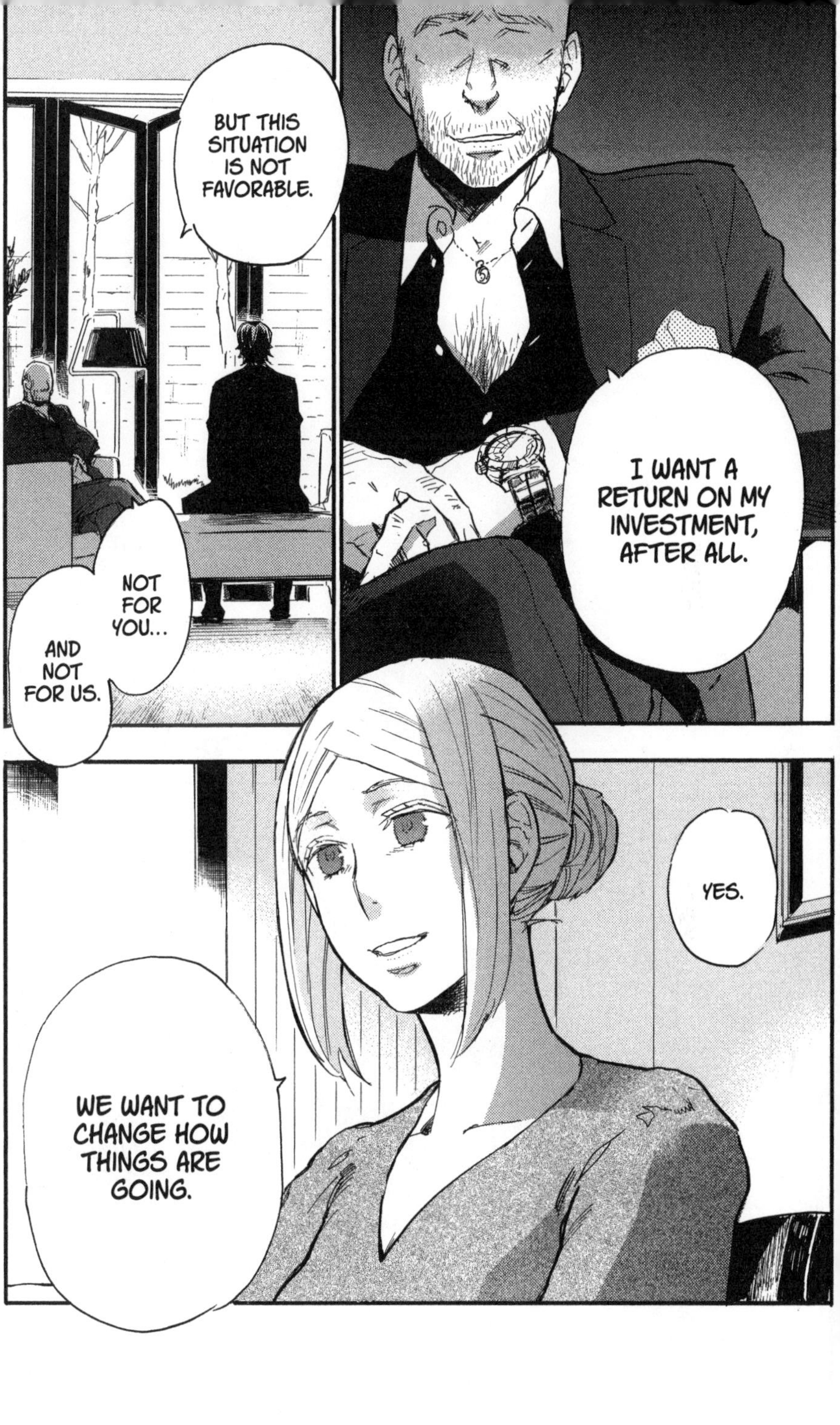
I WANT A RETURN ON MY INVESTMENT, AFTER ALL.
BUT THIS SITUATION IS NOT FAVORABLE.
NOT FOR YOU... AND NOT FOR US.
YES.
WE WANT TO CHANGE HOW THINGS ARE GOING.

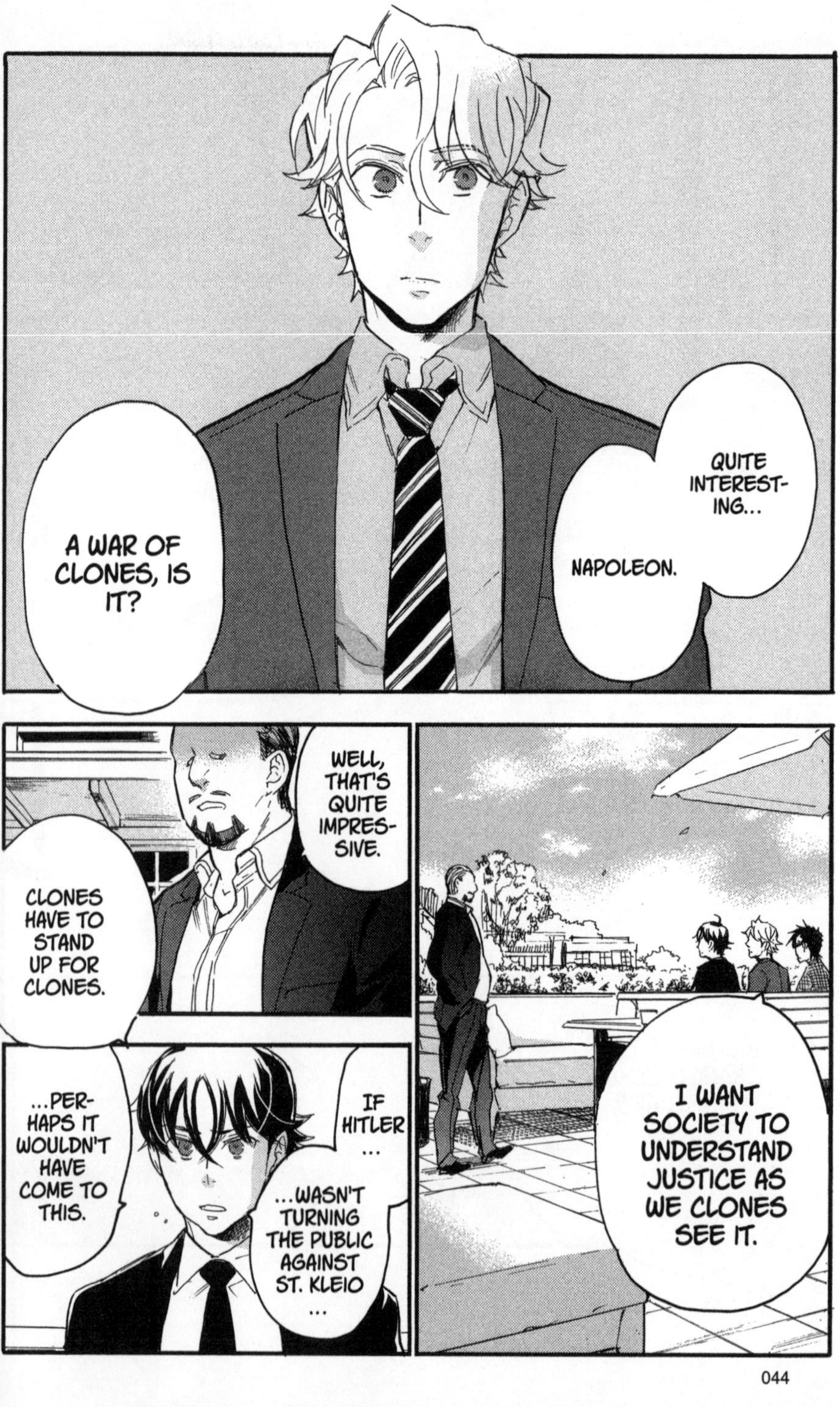
QUITE INTEREST-ING...
NAPOLEON.
A WAR OF CLONES, IS IT?
I WANT SOCIETY TO UNDERSTAND JUSTICE AS WE CLONES SEE IT.
WELL, THAT'S QUITE IMPRES-SIVE.
CLONES HAVE TO STAND UP FOR CLONES.
IF HITLER ...
...WASN'T TURNING THE PUBLIC AGAINST ST. KLEIO ...
...PER-HAPS IT WOULDN'T HAVE COME TO THIS.

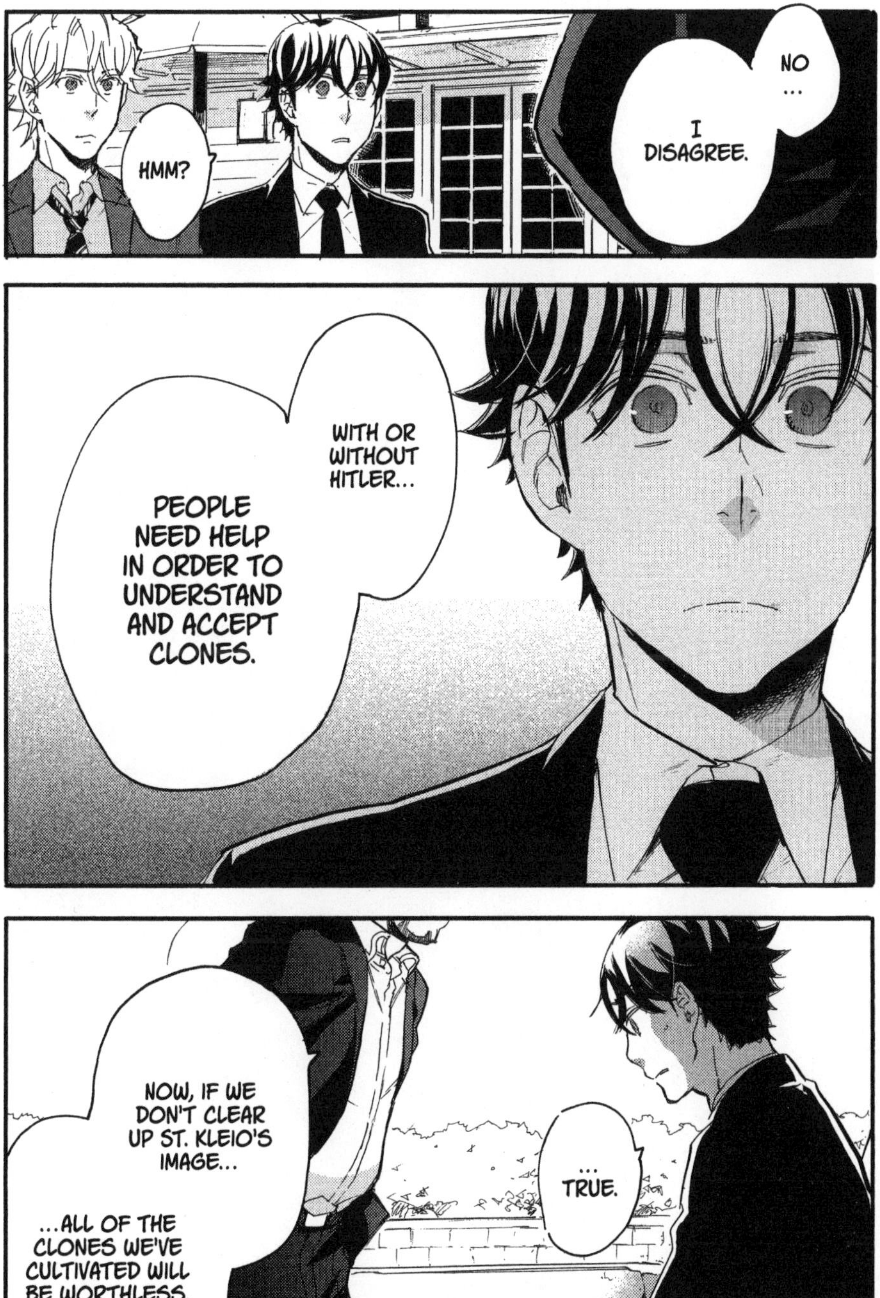
NO ...
I DISAGREE.
HMM?
WITH OR WITHOUT HITLER...
PEOPLE NEED HELP IN ORDER TO UNDERSTAND AND ACCEPT CLONES.
NOW, IF WE DON'T CLEAR UP ST. KLEIO'S IMAGE...
...ALL OF THE CLONES WE'VE CULTIVATED WILL BE WORTHLESS.
... TRUE.

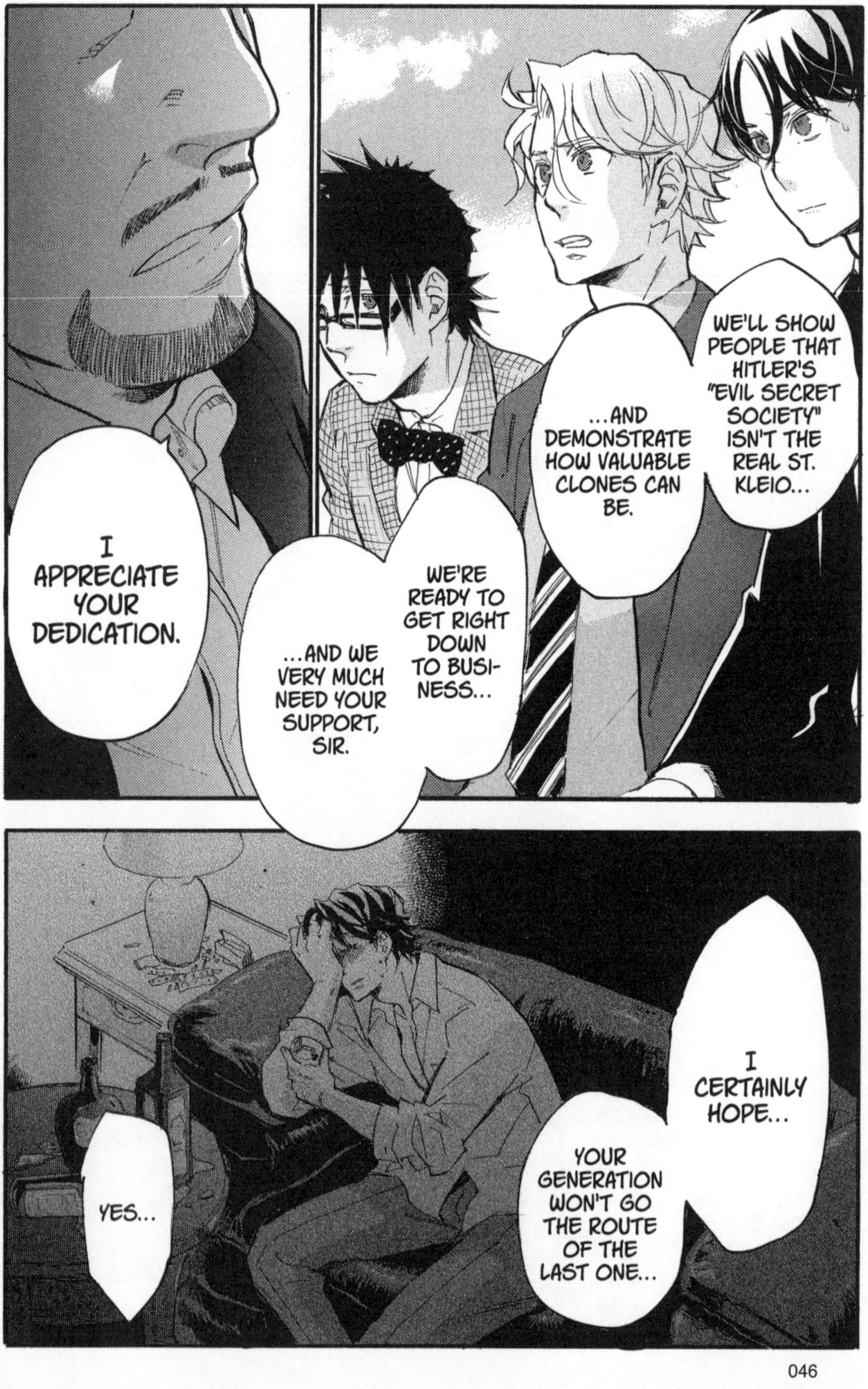
WE'LL SHOW PEOPLE THAT HITLER'S "EVIL SECRET SOCIETY" ISN'T THE REAL ST. KLEIO...
...AND DEMONSTRATE HOW VALUABLE CLONES CAN BE.
WE'RE READY TO GET RIGHT DOWN TO BUSI-NESS...
...AND WE VERY MUCH NEED YOUR SUPPORT, SIR.
I APPRECIATE YOUR DEDICATION.
I CERTAINLY HOPE...
YOUR GENERATION WON'T GO THE ROUTE OF THE LAST ONE...
YES...

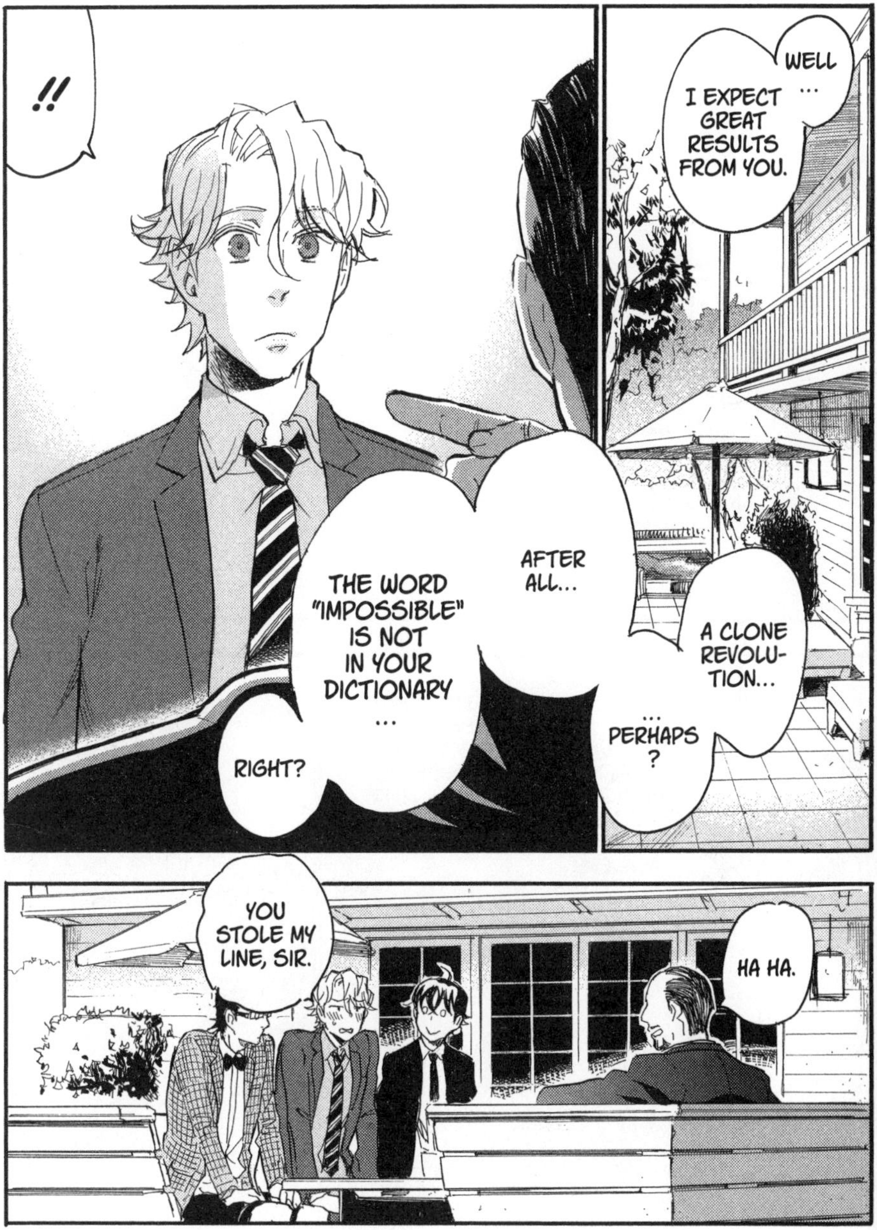
WELL ...
I EXPECT GREAT RESULTS FROM YOU.
A CLONE REVOLUTION...
... PERHAPS?
AFTER ALL...
THE WORD "IMPOSSIBLE" IS NOT IN YOUR DICTIONARY ...
RIGHT?
!!
HA HA.
YOU STOLE MY LINE, SIR.

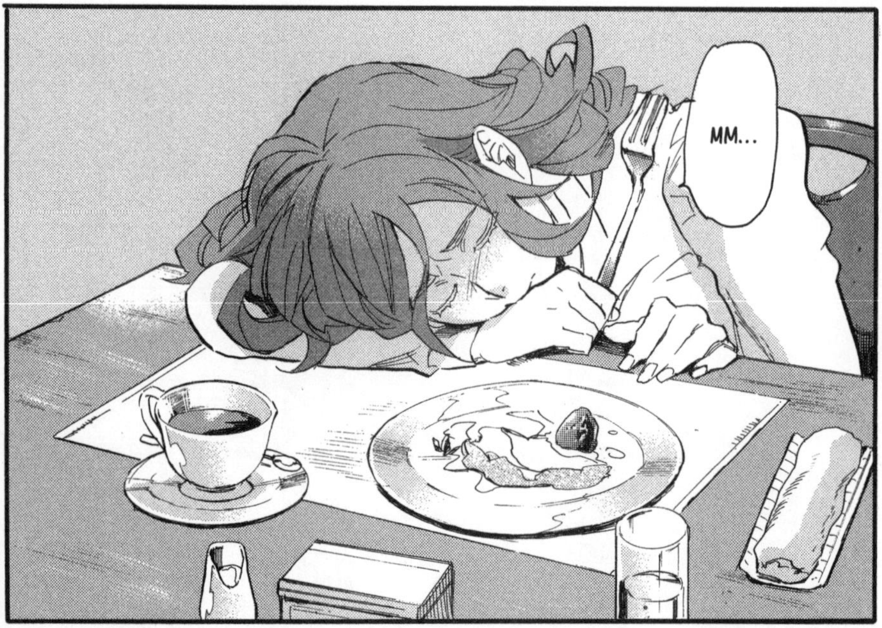
MM...

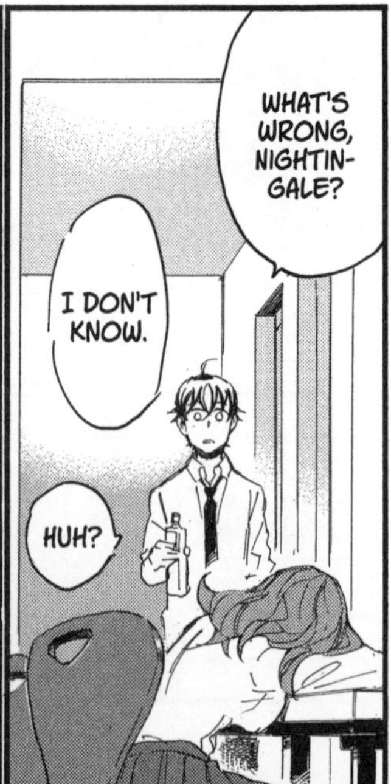
WHAT'S WRONG, NIGHTIN-GALE?
I DON'T KNOW.
HUH?

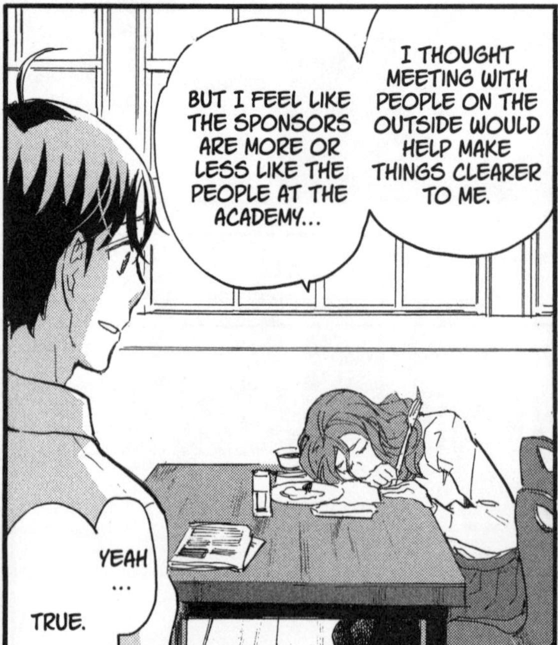
I THOUGHT MEETING WITH PEOPLE ON THE OUTSIDE WOULD HELP MAKE THINGS CLEARER TO ME.
BUT I FEEL LIKE THE SPONSORS ARE MORE OR LESS LIKE THE PEOPLE AT THE ACADEMY...
YEAH ... TRUE.

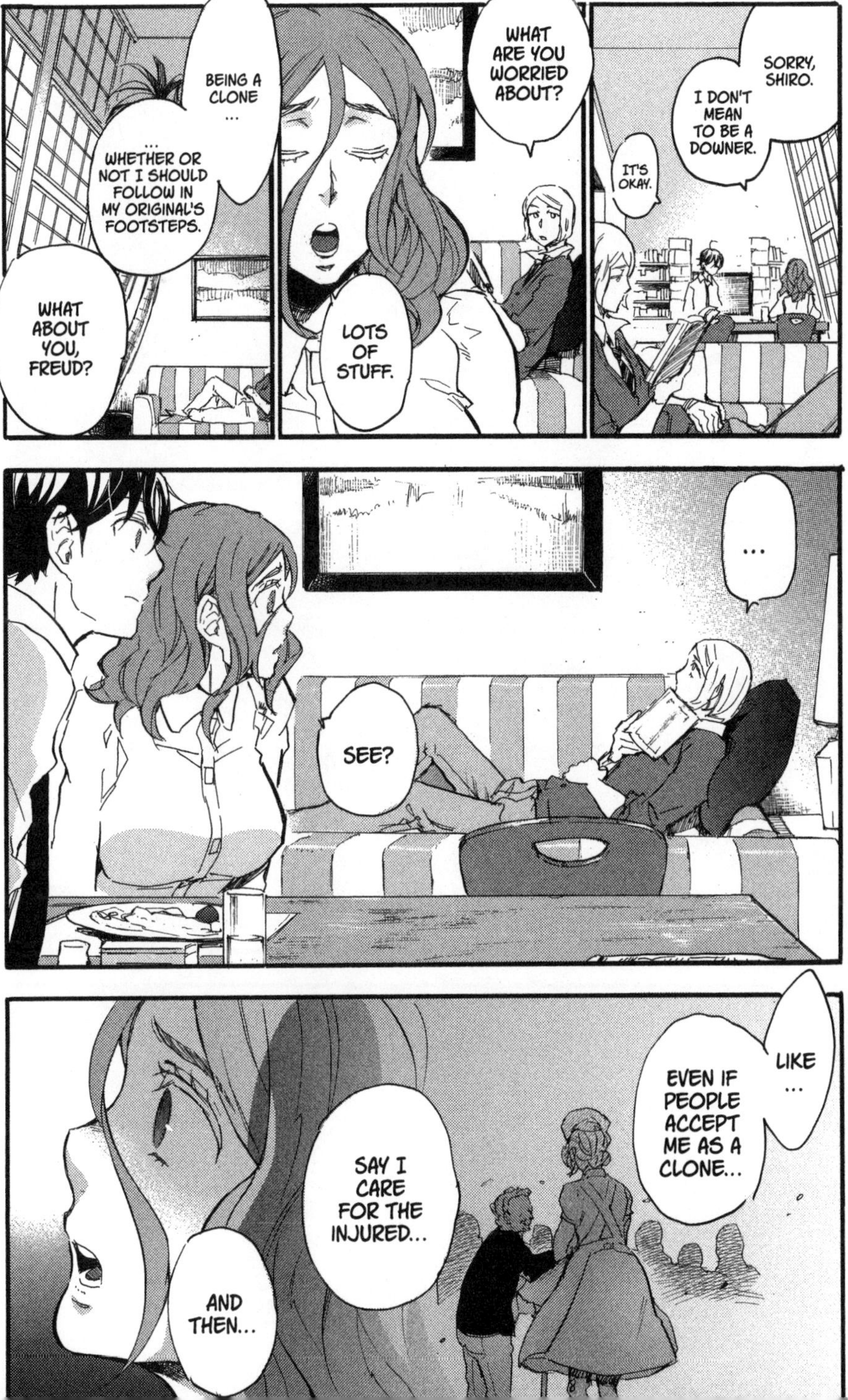
SORRY, SHIRO.
I DON'T MEAN TO BE A DOWNER.
IT'S OKAY.
WHAT ARE YOU WORRIED ABOUT?
LOTS OF STUFF.
BEING A CLONE ...
... WHETHER OR NOT I SHOULD FOLLOW IN MY ORIGINAL'S FOOTSTEPS.
WHAT ABOUT YOU, FREUD?
...
SEE?
LIKE ...
EVEN IF PEOPLE ACCEPT ME AS A CLONE...
SAY I CARE FOR THE INJURED...
AND THEN...

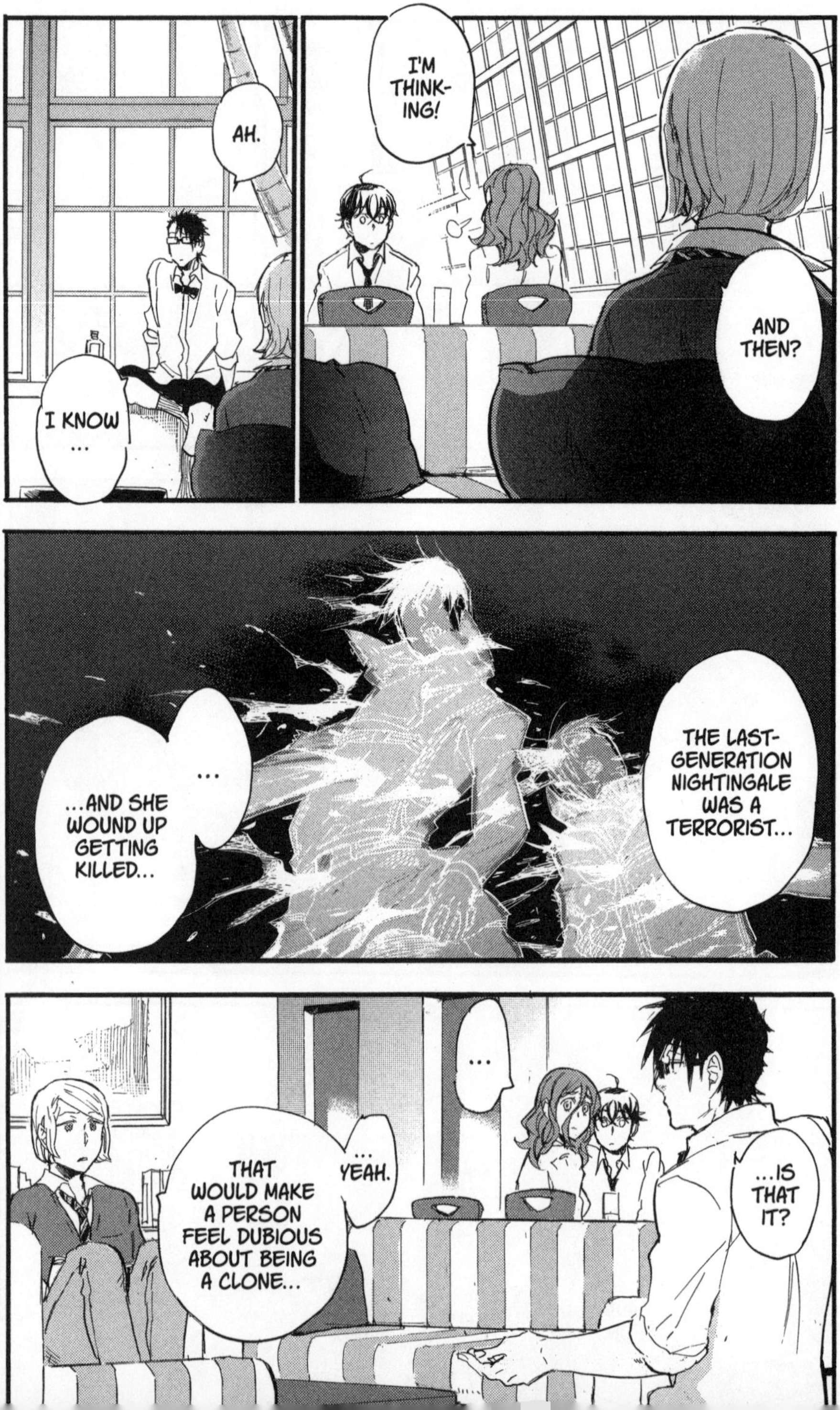
AND THEN?
I'M THINKING!
AH.
I KNOW ...
THE LAST-GENERATION NIGHTINGALE WAS A TERRORIST...
...
...AND SHE WOUND UP GETTING KILLED...
...IS THAT IT?
...
... YEAH.
THAT WOULD MAKE A PERSON FEEL DUBIOUS ABOUT BEING A CLONE...

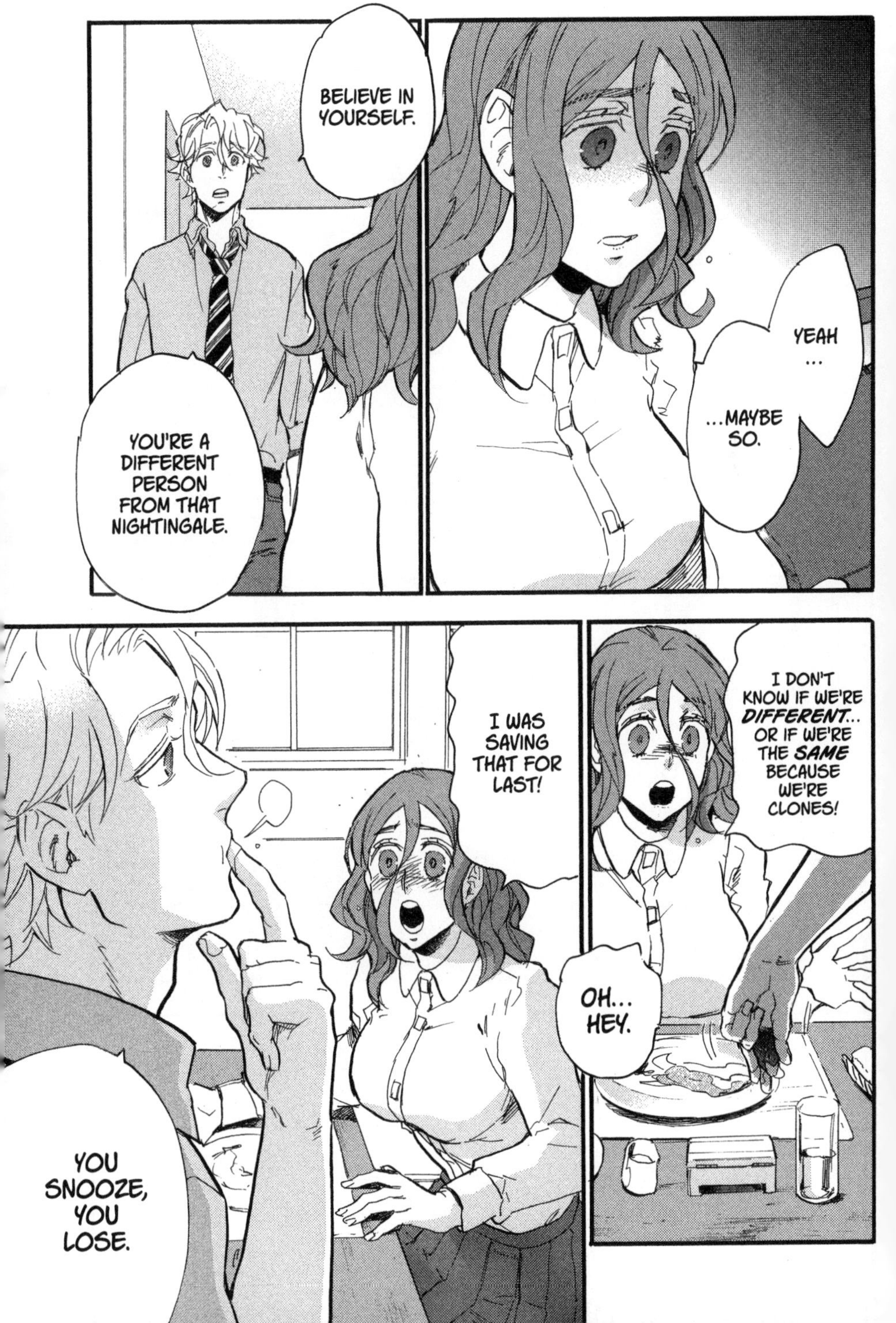
BELIEVE IN YOURSELF.
YEAH ...
...MAYBE SO.
YOU'RE A DIFFERENT PERSON FROM THAT NIGHTINGALE.
I DON'T KNOW IF WE'RE *DIFFERENT*... OR IF WE'RE THE *SAME* BECAUSE WE'RE CLONES!
OH... HEY.
I WAS SAVING THAT FOR LAST!
YOU SNOOZE, YOU LOSE.

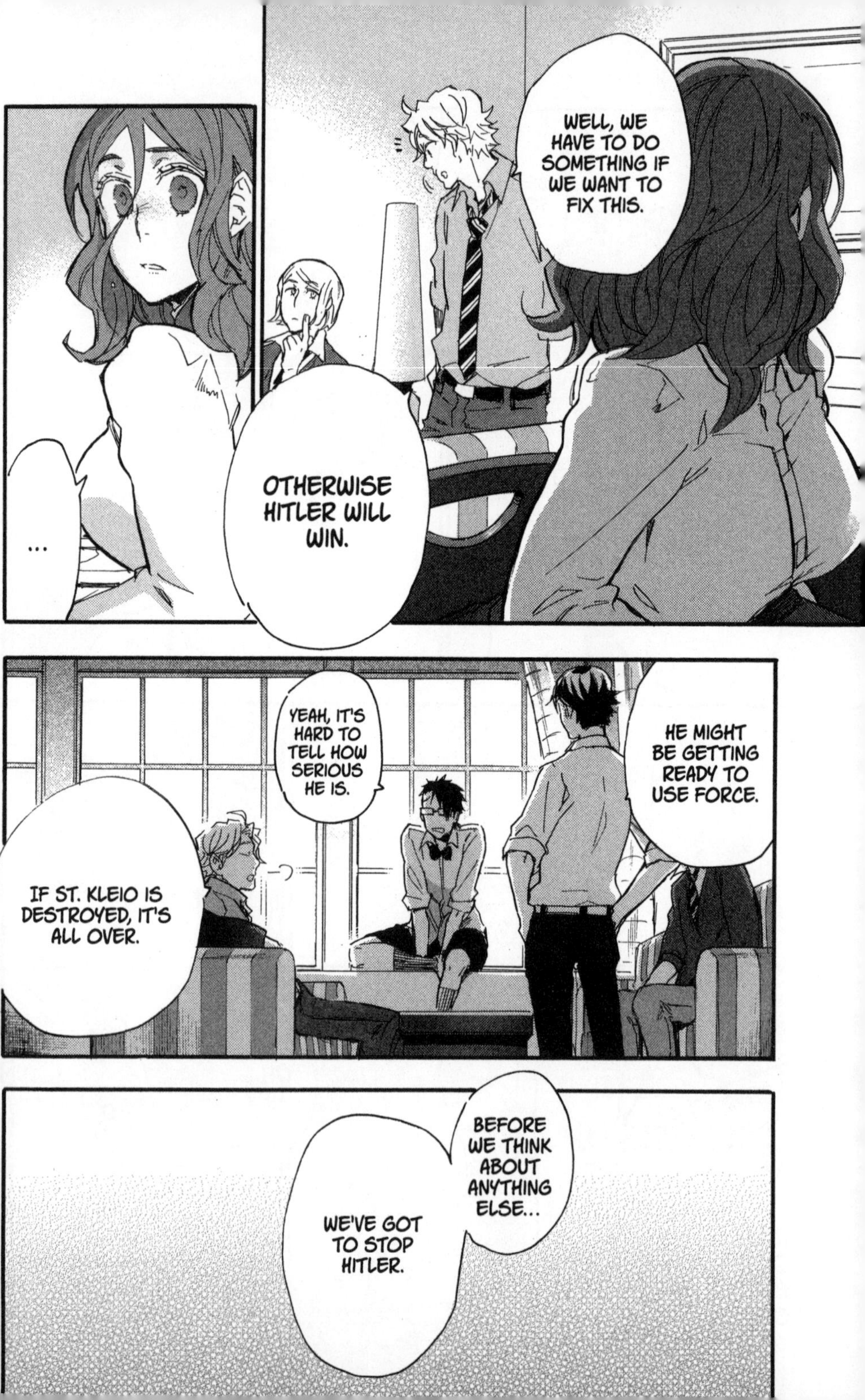
WELL, WE HAVE TO DO SOMETHING IF WE WANT TO FIX THIS.
OTHERWISE HITLER WILL WIN.
...
HE MIGHT BE GETTING READY TO USE FORCE.
YEAH, IT'S HARD TO TELL HOW SERIOUS HE IS.
IF ST. KLEIO IS DESTROYED, IT'S ALL OVER.
BEFORE WE THINK ABOUT ANYTHING ELSE...
WE'VE GOT TO STOP HITLER.

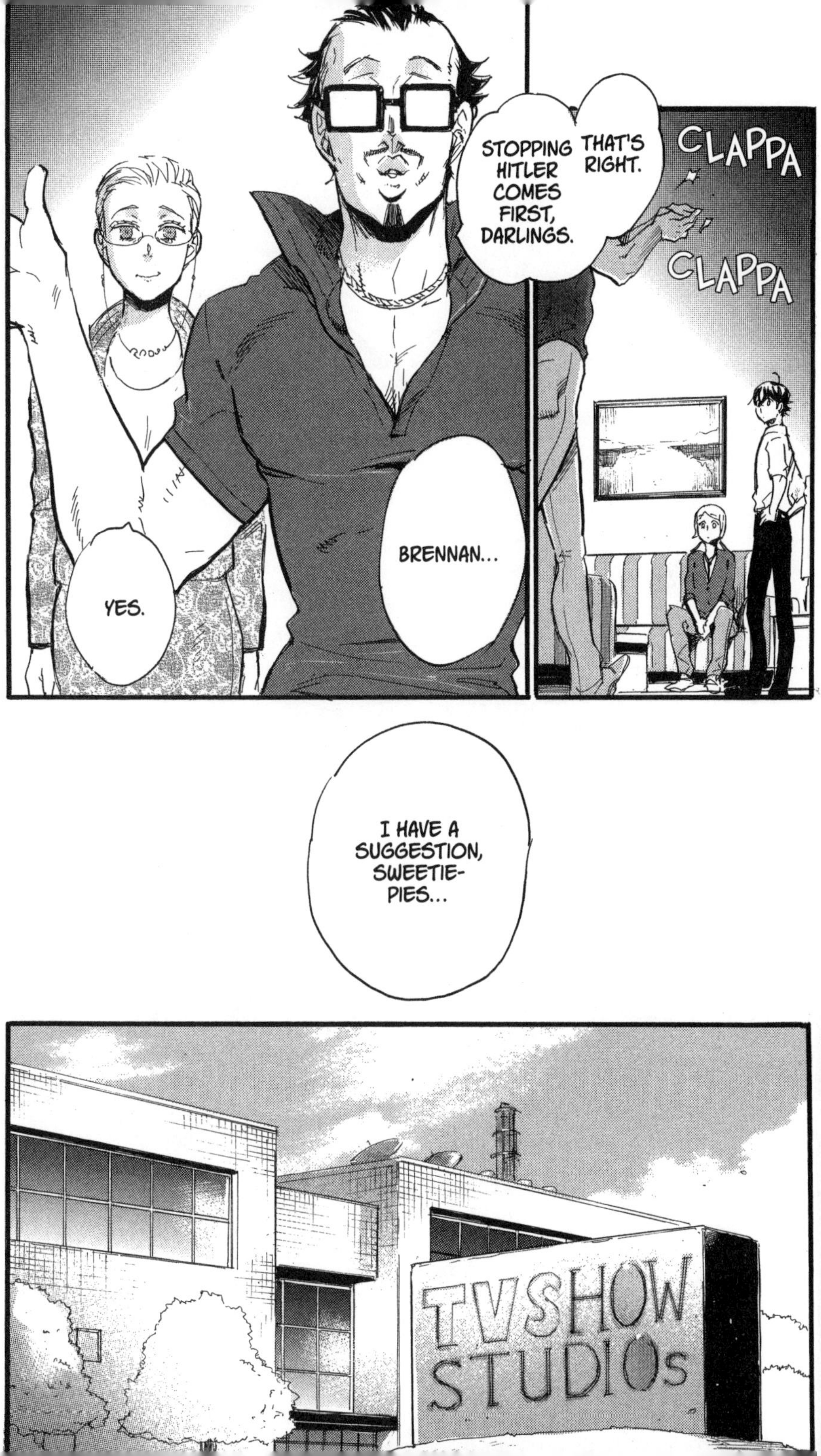
CLAPPA
CLAPPA
THAT'S RIGHT.
STOPPING HITLER COMES FIRST, DARLINGS.
BRENNAN...
YES.
I HAVE A SUGGESTION, SWEETIE-PIES...
TVSHOW STUDIOs

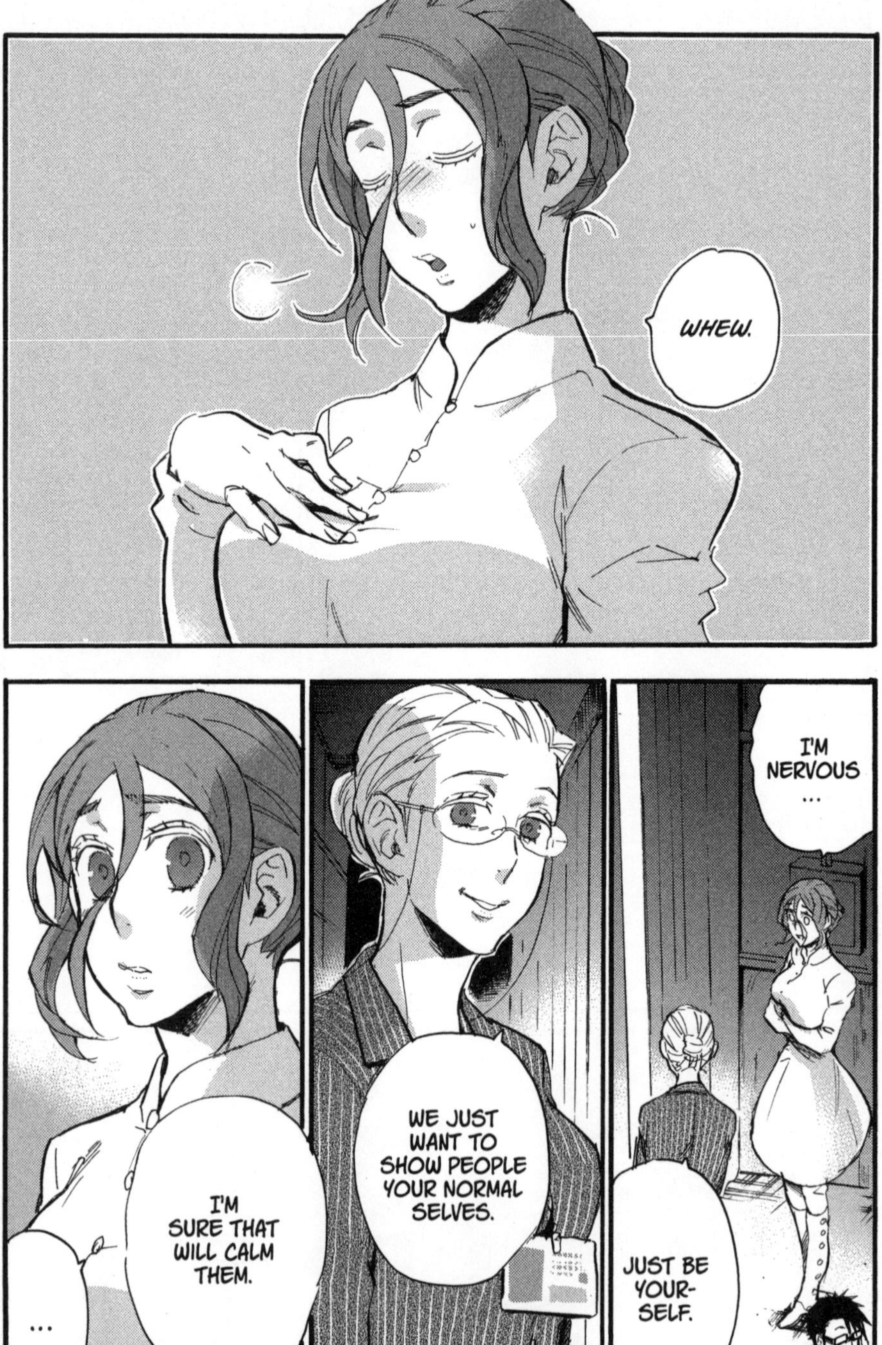
WHEW.
I'M NERVOUS ...
JUST BE YOUR-SELF.
WE JUST WANT TO SHOW PEOPLE YOUR NORMAL SELVES.
I'M SURE THAT WILL CALM THEM.
...

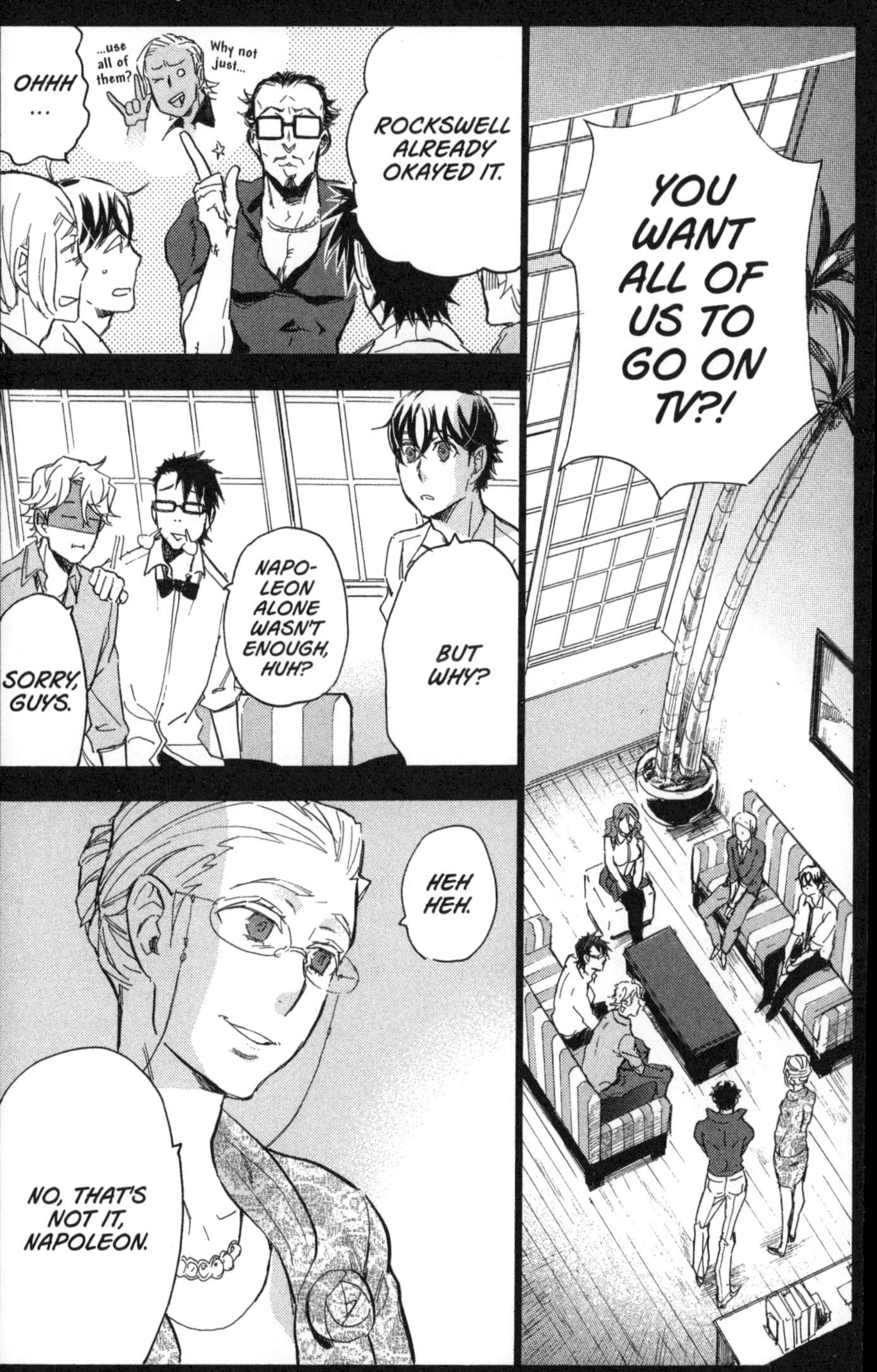
YOU WANT ALL OF US TO GO ON TV?!
ROCKSWELL ALREADY OKAYED IT.
Why not just...
...use all of them?
OHHH ...
BUT WHY?
NAPOLEON ALONE WASN'T ENOUGH, HUH?
SORRY, GUYS.
HEH HEH.
NO, THAT'S NOT IT, NAPOLEON.

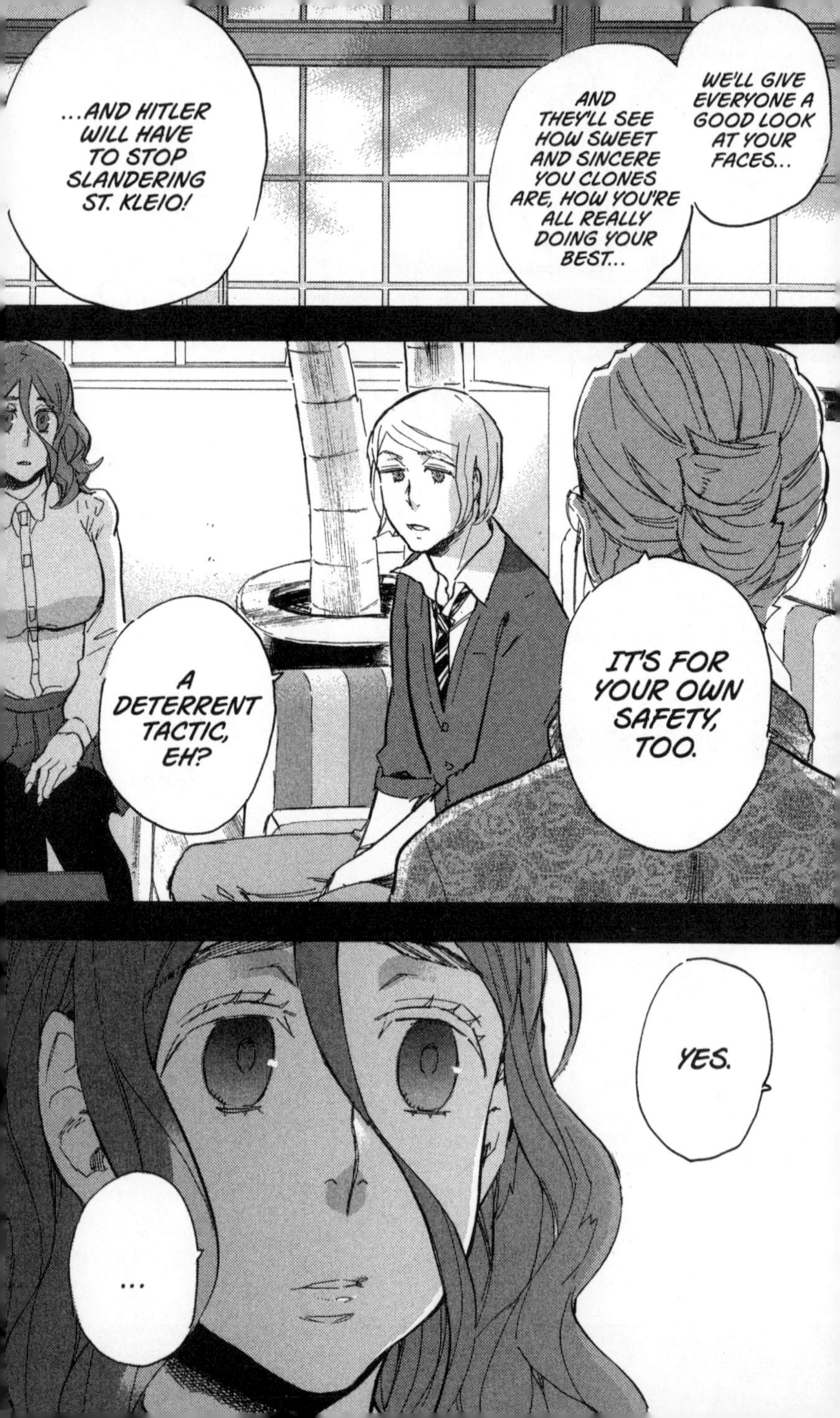
WE'LL GIVE EVERYONE A GOOD LOOK AT YOUR FACES...
AND THEY'LL SEE HOW SWEET AND SINCERE YOU CLONES ARE, HOW YOU'RE ALL REALLY DOING YOUR BEST...
...AND HITLER WILL HAVE TO STOP SLANDERING ST. KLEIO!
IT'S FOR YOUR OWN SAFETY, TOO.
A DETERRENT TACTIC, EH?
YES.
...

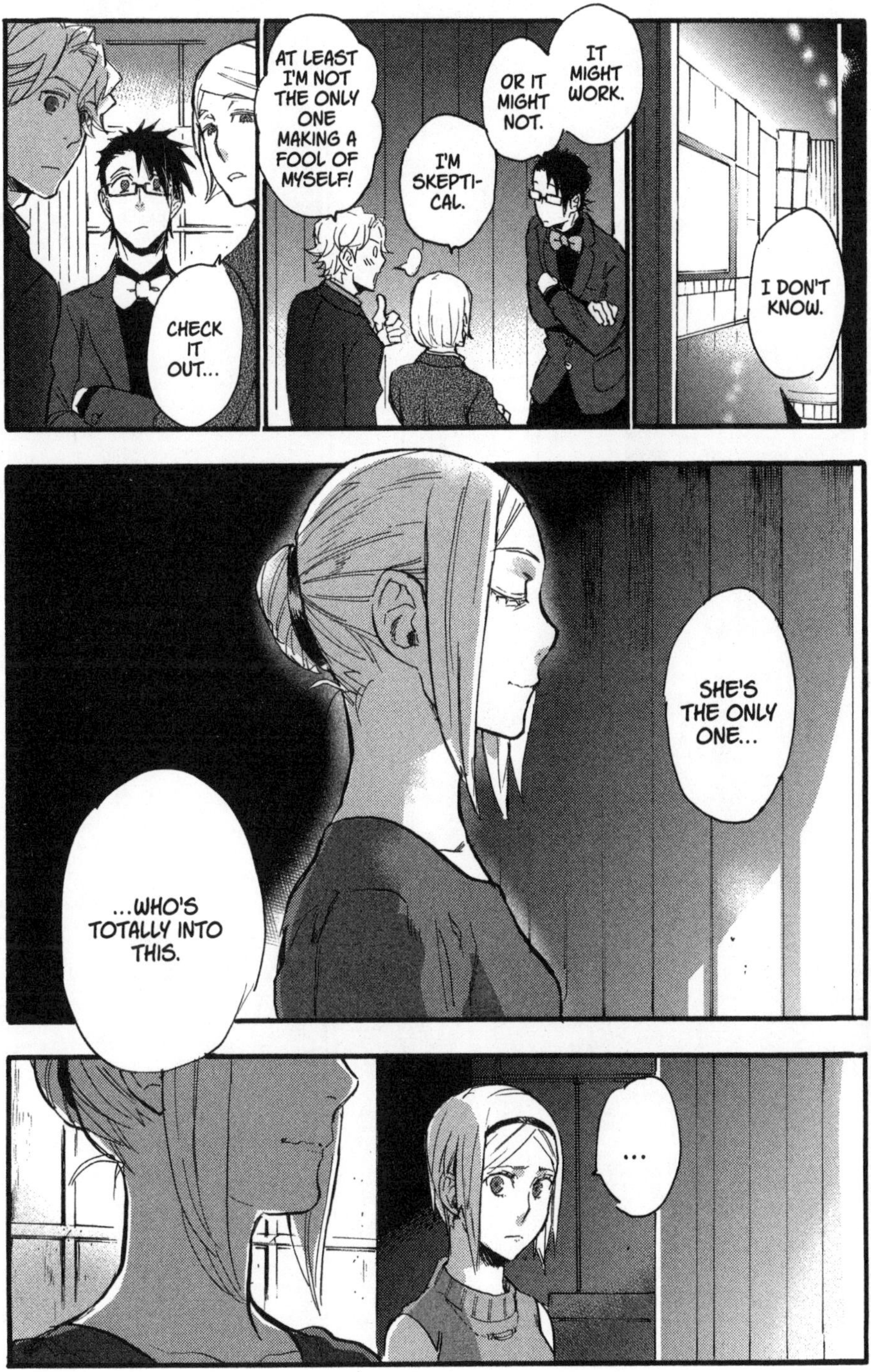
I DON'T KNOW.
IT MIGHT WORK.
OR IT MIGHT NOT.
I'M SKEPTI-CAL.
AT LEAST I'M NOT THE ONLY ONE MAKING A FOOL OF MYSELF!
CHECK IT OUT...
SHE'S THE ONLY ONE...
...WHO'S TOTALLY INTO THIS.
...

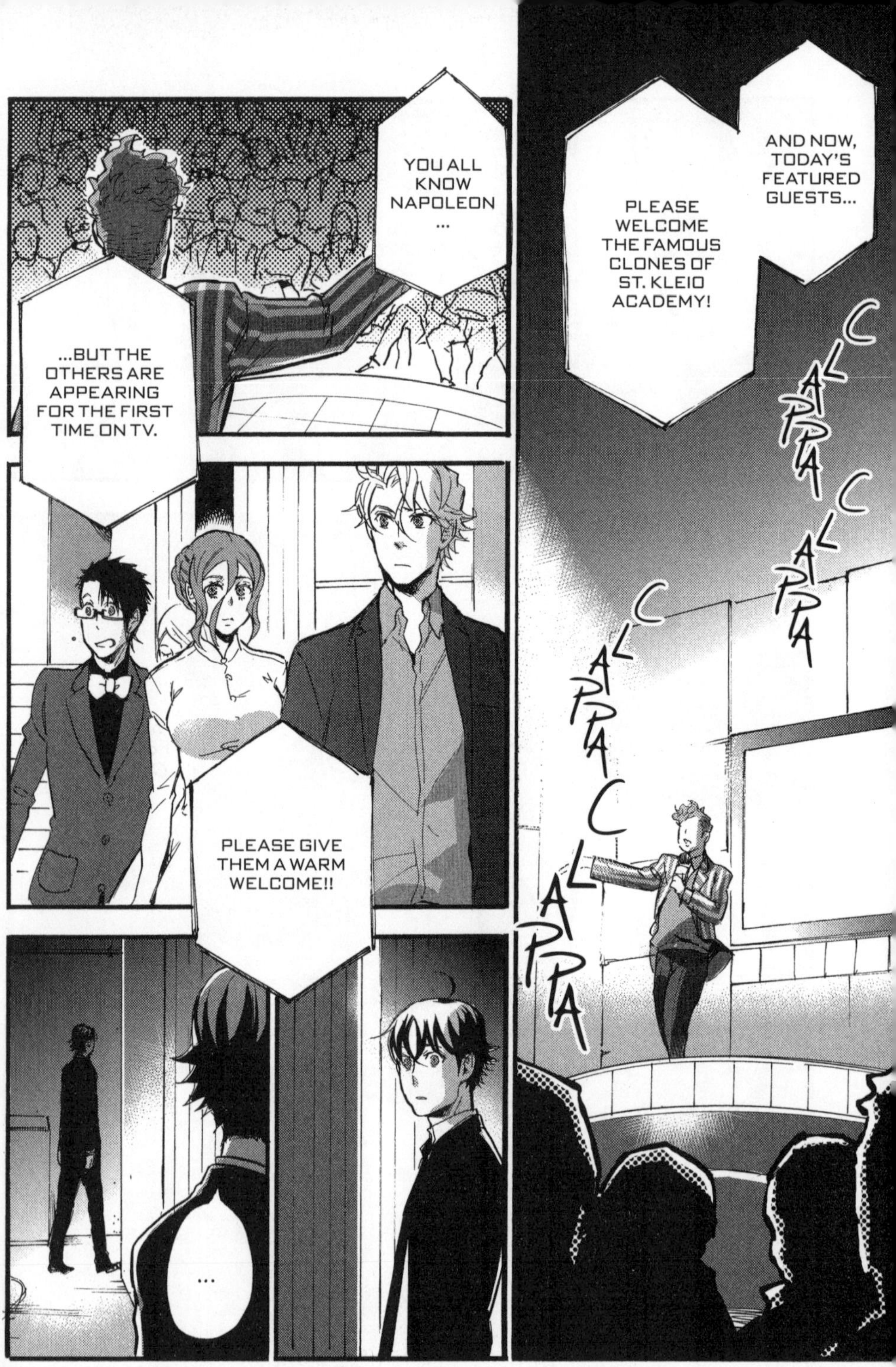
AND NOW, TODAY'S FEATURED GUESTS...
PLEASE WELCOME THE FAMOUS CLONES OF ST. KLEIO ACADEMY!
CLAPPA CLAPPA
CLAPPA CLAPPA
YOU ALL KNOW NAPOLEON ...
...BUT THE OTHERS ARE APPEARING FOR THE FIRST TIME ON TV.
PLEASE GIVE THEM A WARM WELCOME!!
...

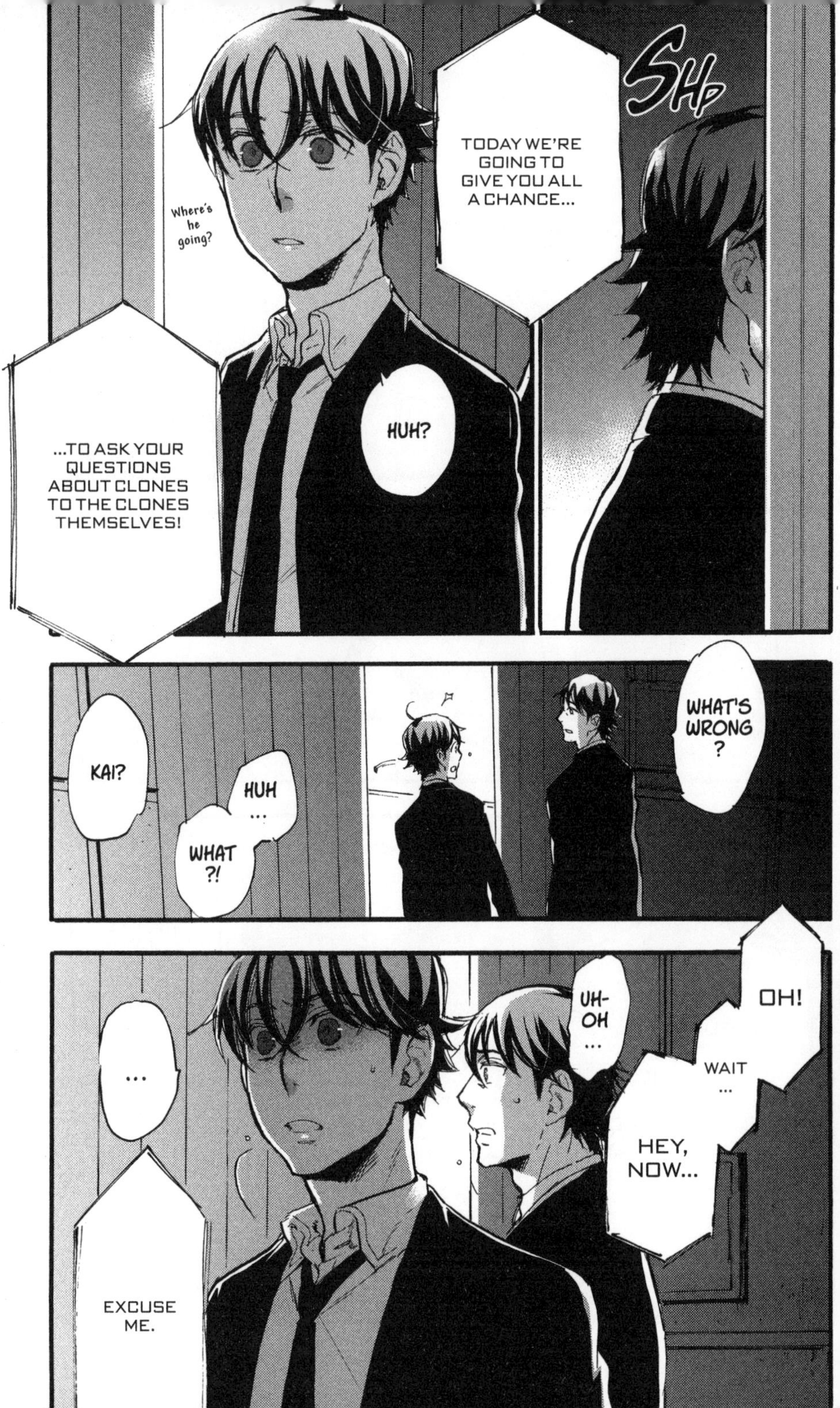
SHp
TODAY WE'RE GOING TO GIVE YOU ALL A CHANCE...
HUH?
Where's he going?
...TO ASK YOUR QUESTIONS ABOUT CLONES TO THE CLONES THEMSELVES!
WHAT'S WRONG?
KAI?
HUH...
WHAT?!
OH!
UH-OH...
WAIT...
HEY, NOW...
...
EXCUSE ME.

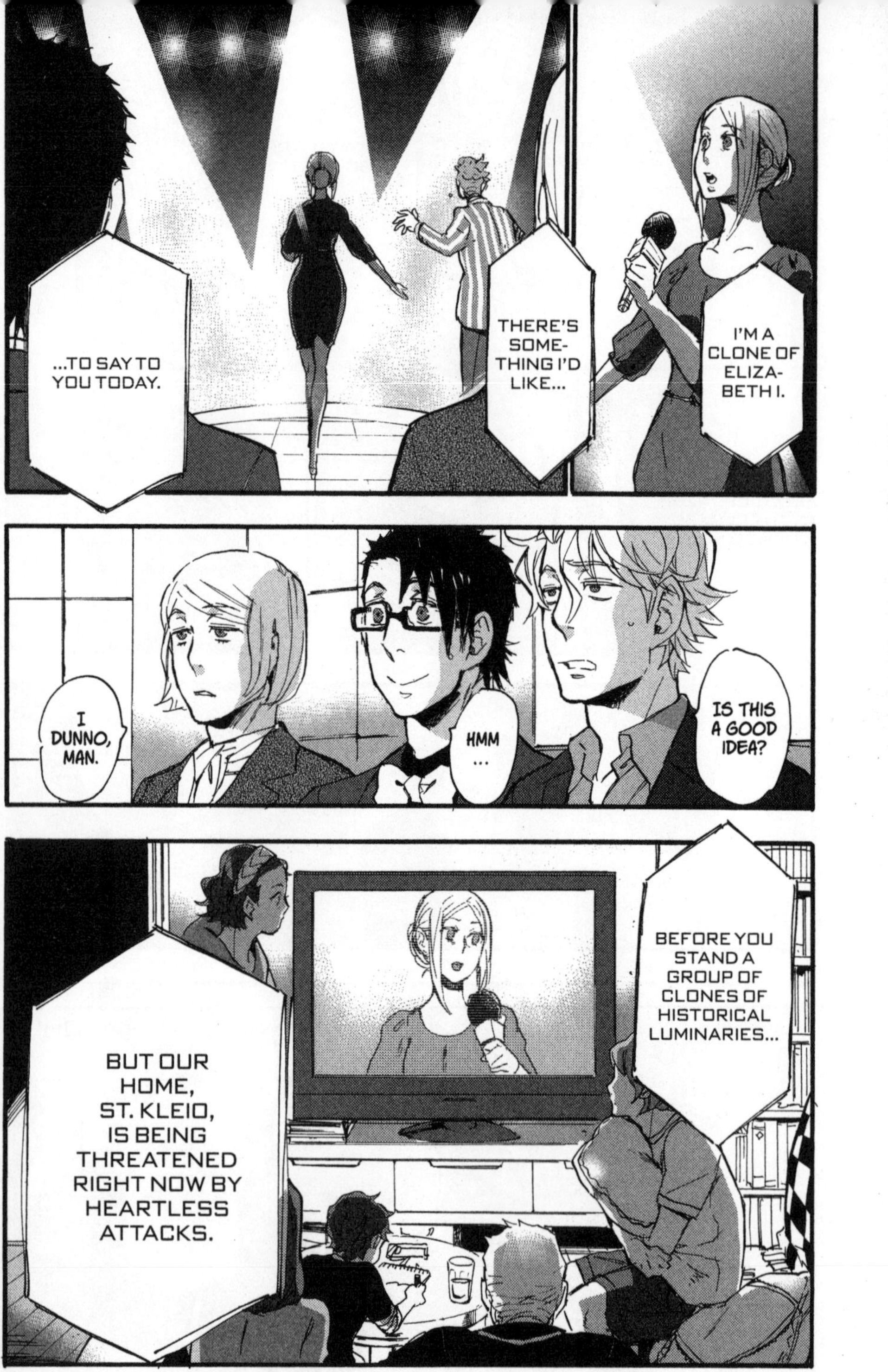

I'M A CLONE OF ELIZA-BETH I.
THERE'S SOME-THING I'D LIKE...
...TO SAY TO YOU TODAY.
IS THIS A GOOD IDEA?
HMM ...
I DUNNO, MAN.
BEFORE YOU STAND A GROUP OF CLONES OF HISTORICAL LUMINARIES...
BUT OUR HOME, ST. KLEIO, IS BEING THREATENED RIGHT NOW BY HEARTLESS ATTACKS.

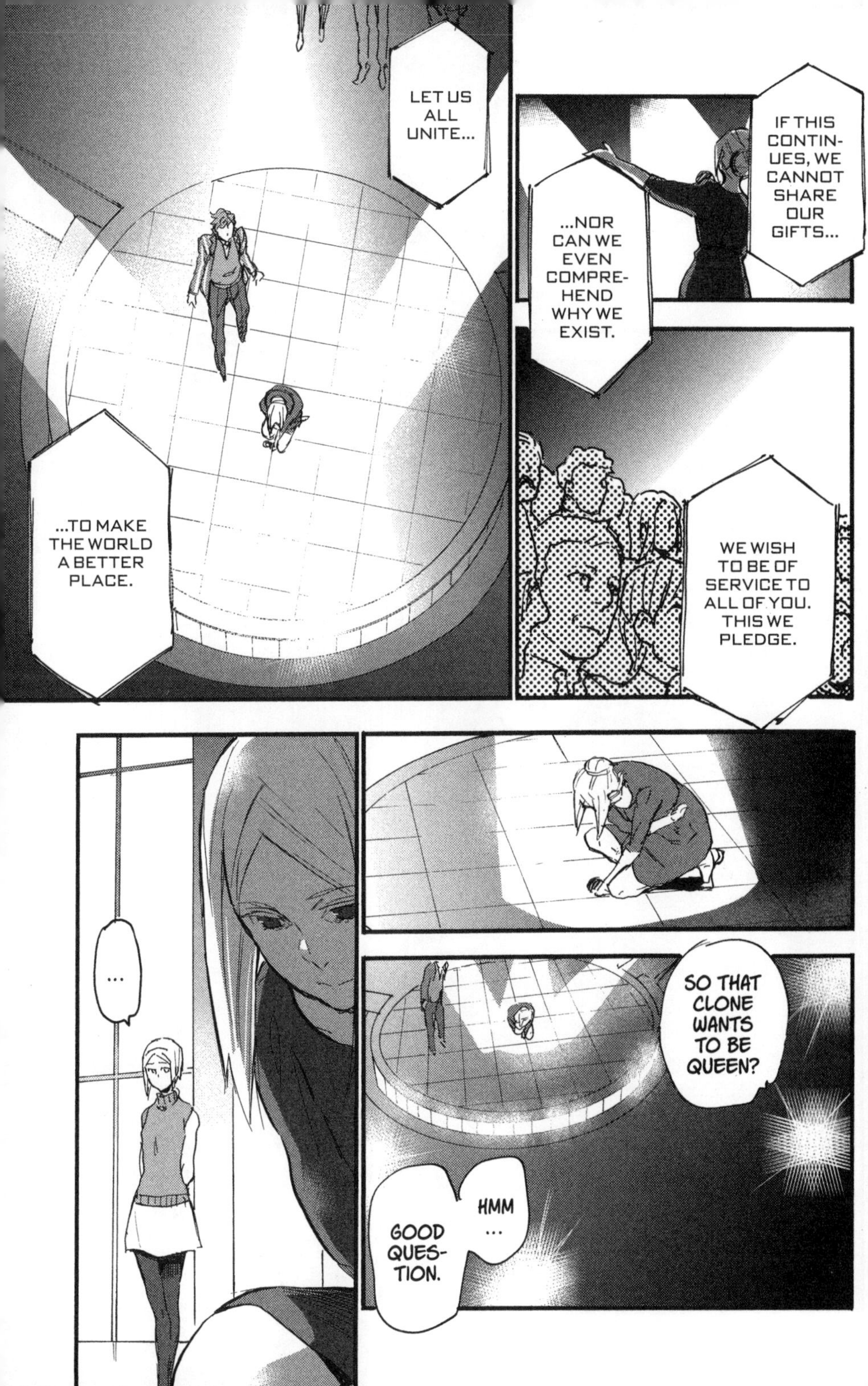
IF THIS CONTINUES, WE CANNOT SHARE OUR GIFTS...
...NOR CAN WE EVEN COMPREHEND WHY WE EXIST.
WE WISH TO BE OF SERVICE TO ALL OF YOU. THIS WE PLEDGE.
LET US ALL UNITE...
...TO MAKE THE WORLD A BETTER PLACE.
SO THAT CLONE WANTS TO BE QUEEN?
HMM...
GOOD QUESTION.
...

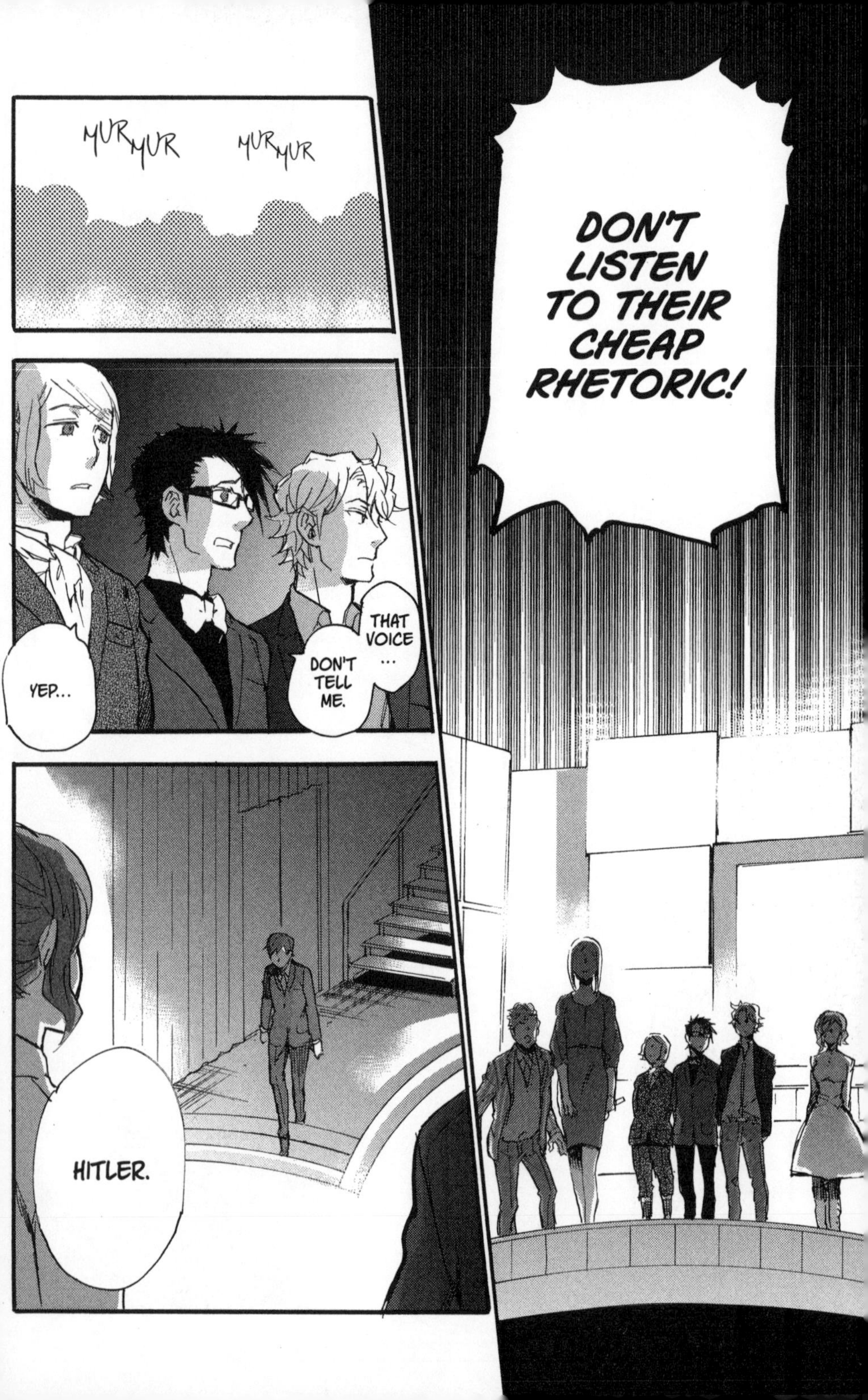
DON'T LISTEN TO THEIR CHEAP RHETORIC!
MUR MUR
MUR MUR
THAT VOICE ...
DON'T TELL ME.
YEP...
HITLER.

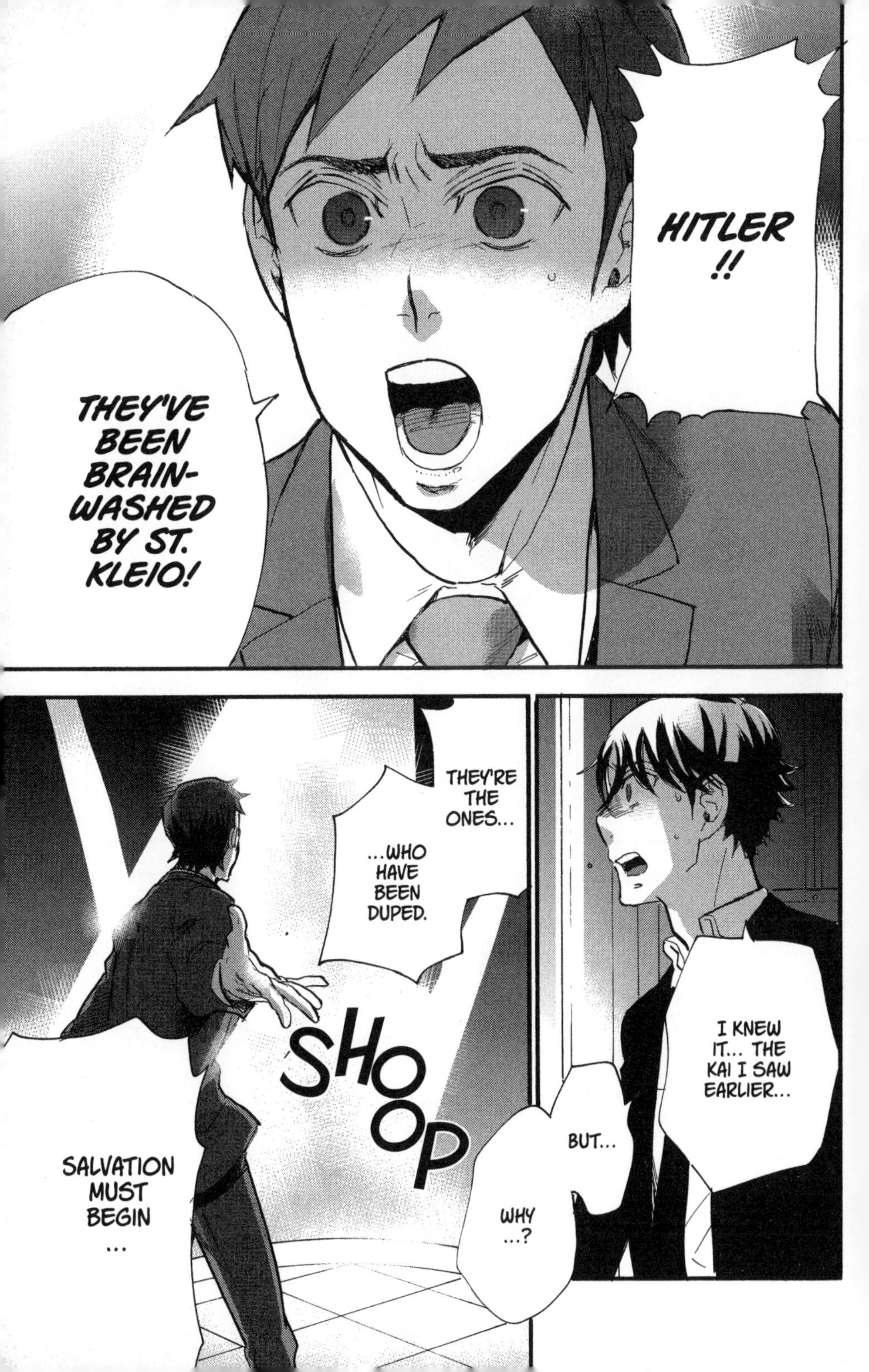
HITLER!!
THEY'VE BEEN BRAIN-WASHED BY ST. KLEIO!
I KNEW IT... THE KAI I SAW EARLIER...
BUT...
WHY...?
THEY'RE THE ONES...
...WHO HAVE BEEN DUPED.
SHOOP
SALVATION MUST BEGIN...

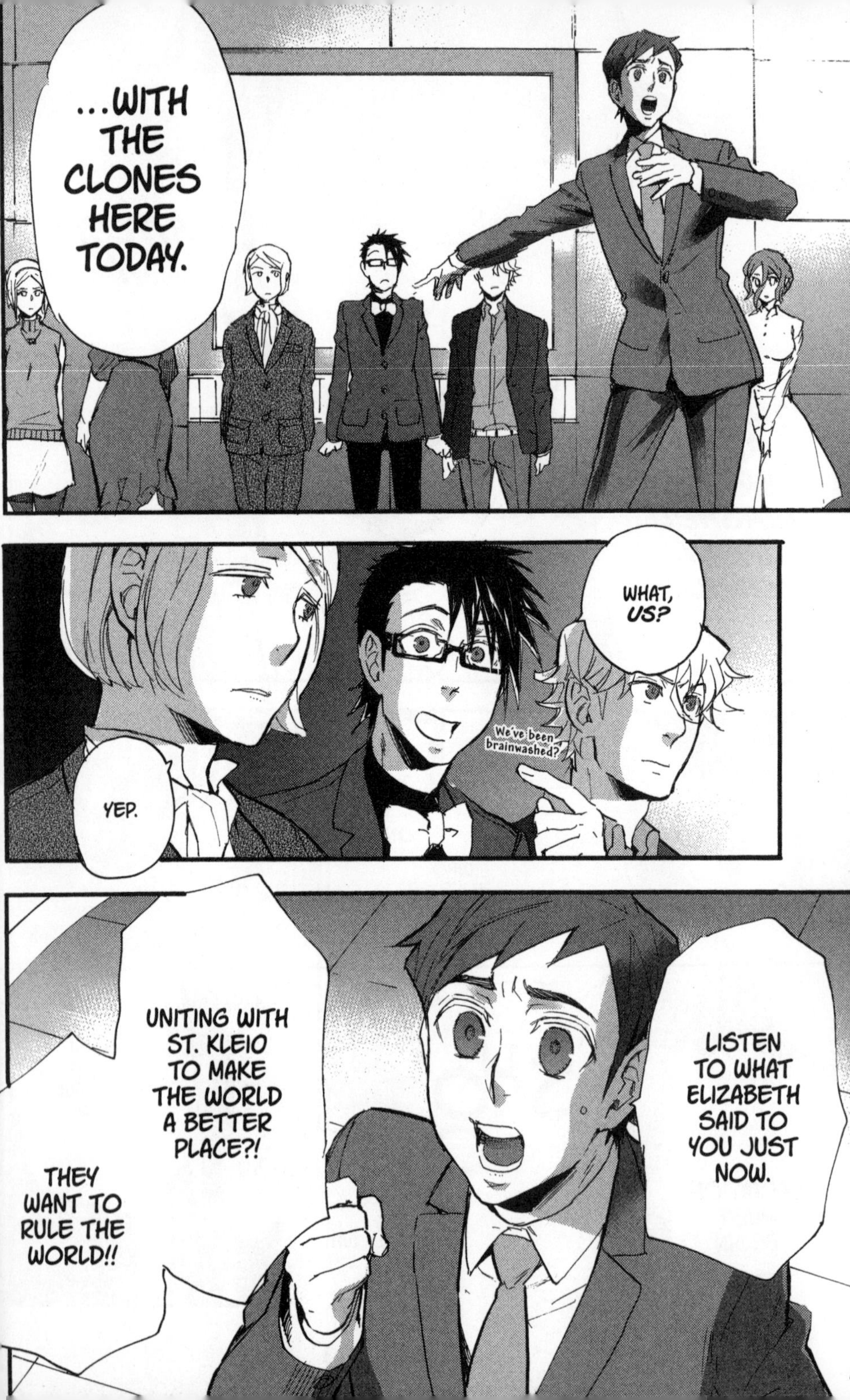
...WITH THE CLONES HERE TODAY.
WHAT, US?
We've been brainwashed?
YEP.
LISTEN TO WHAT ELIZABETH SAID TO YOU JUST NOW.
UNITING WITH ST. KLEIO TO MAKE THE WORLD A BETTER PLACE?!
THEY WANT TO RULE THE WORLD!!

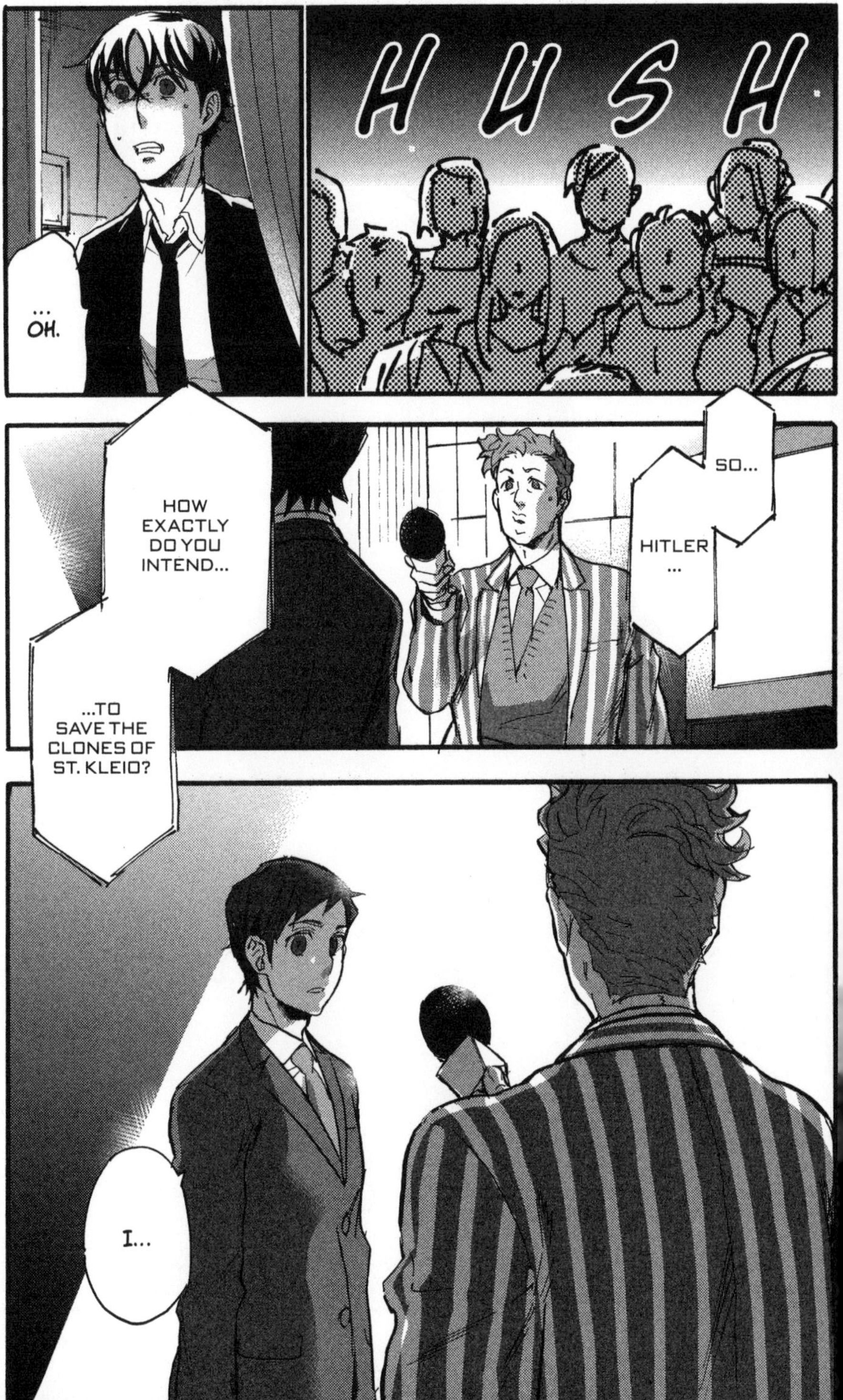
HUSH
...OH.
SO...
HITLER...
HOW EXACTLY DO YOU INTEND...
...TO SAVE THE CLONES OF ST. KLEIO?
I...

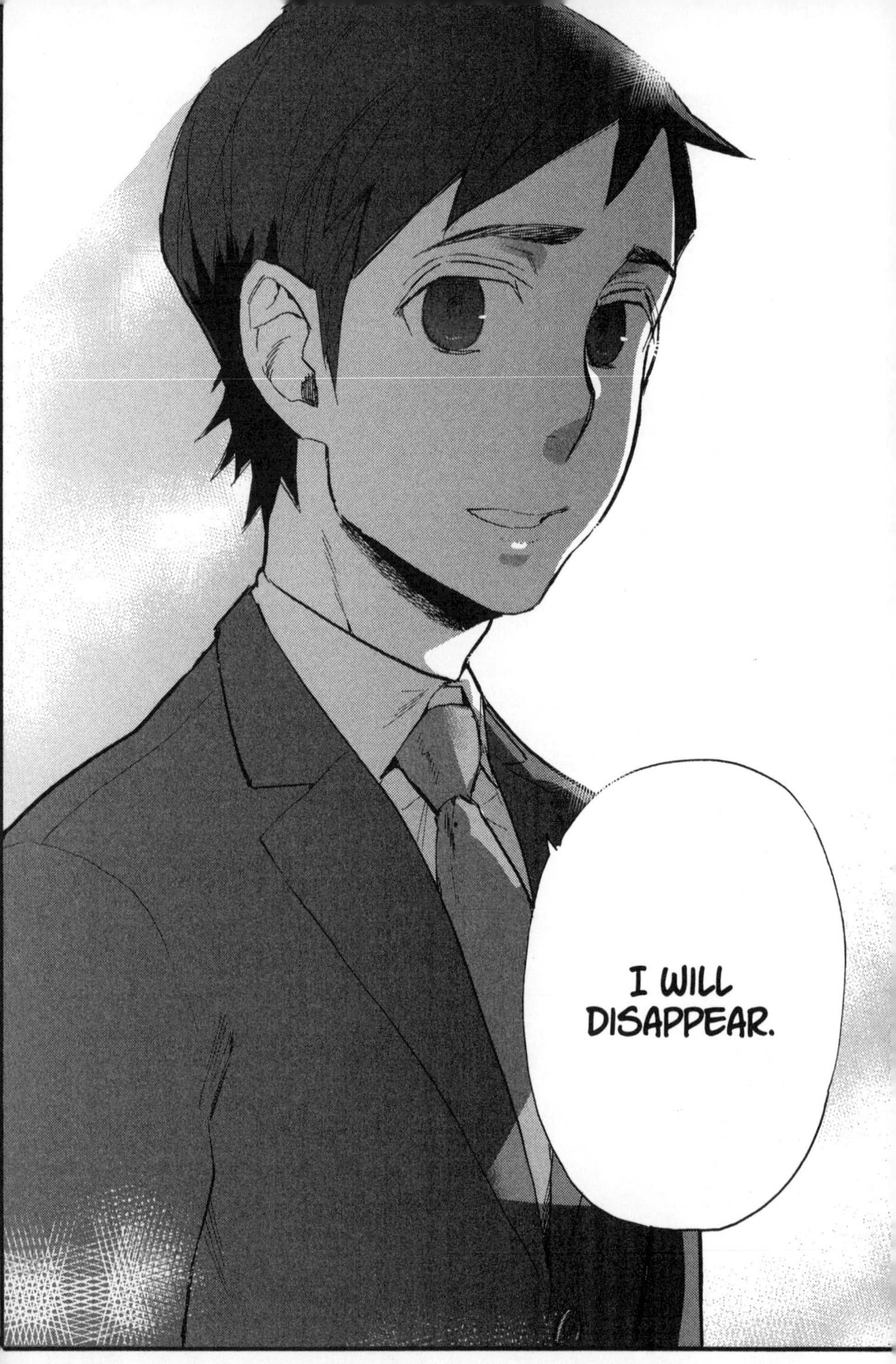
I WILL DISAPPEAR.

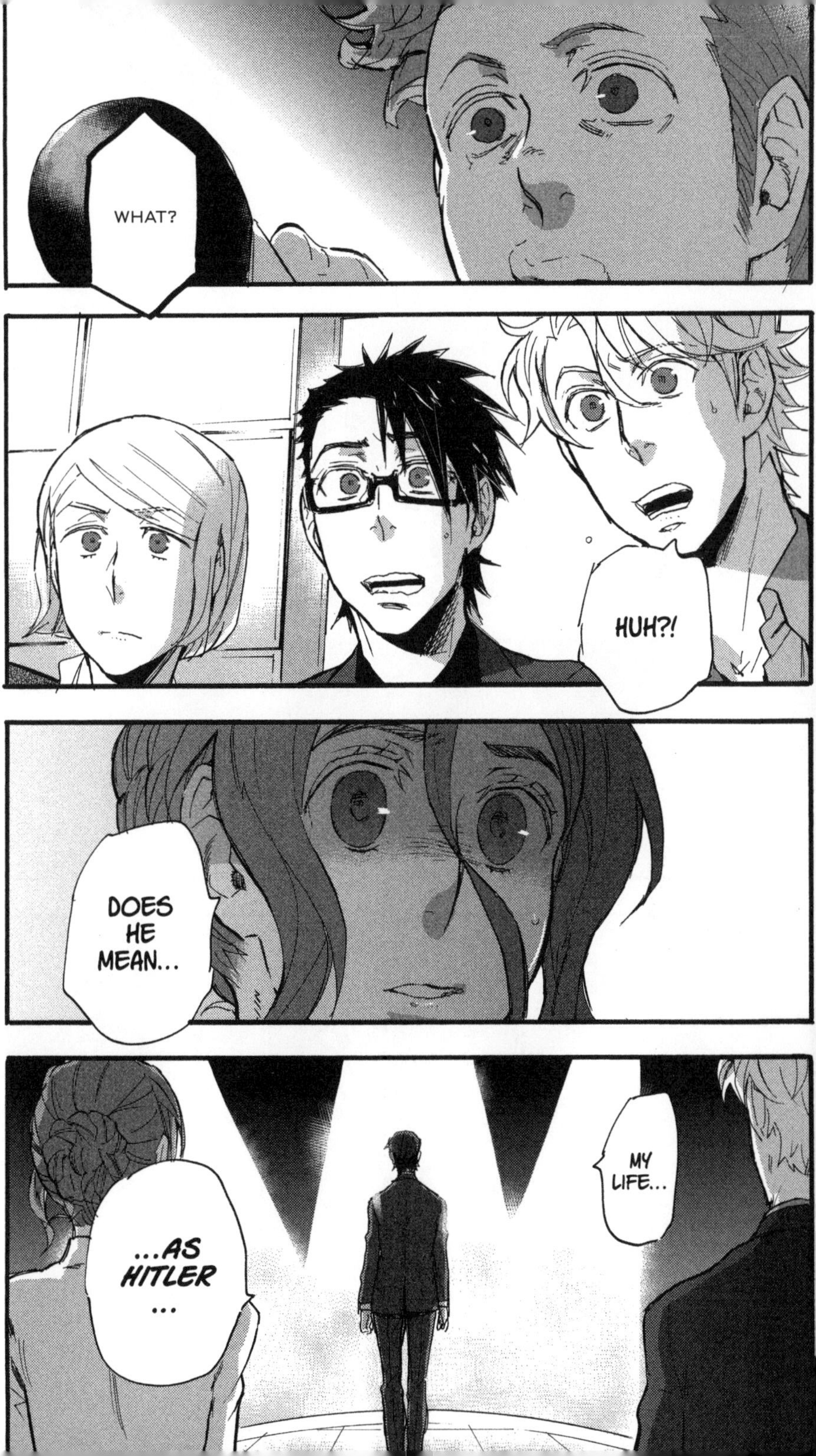
WHAT?
HUH?!
DOES HE MEAN...
MY LIFE...
...AS HITLER ...

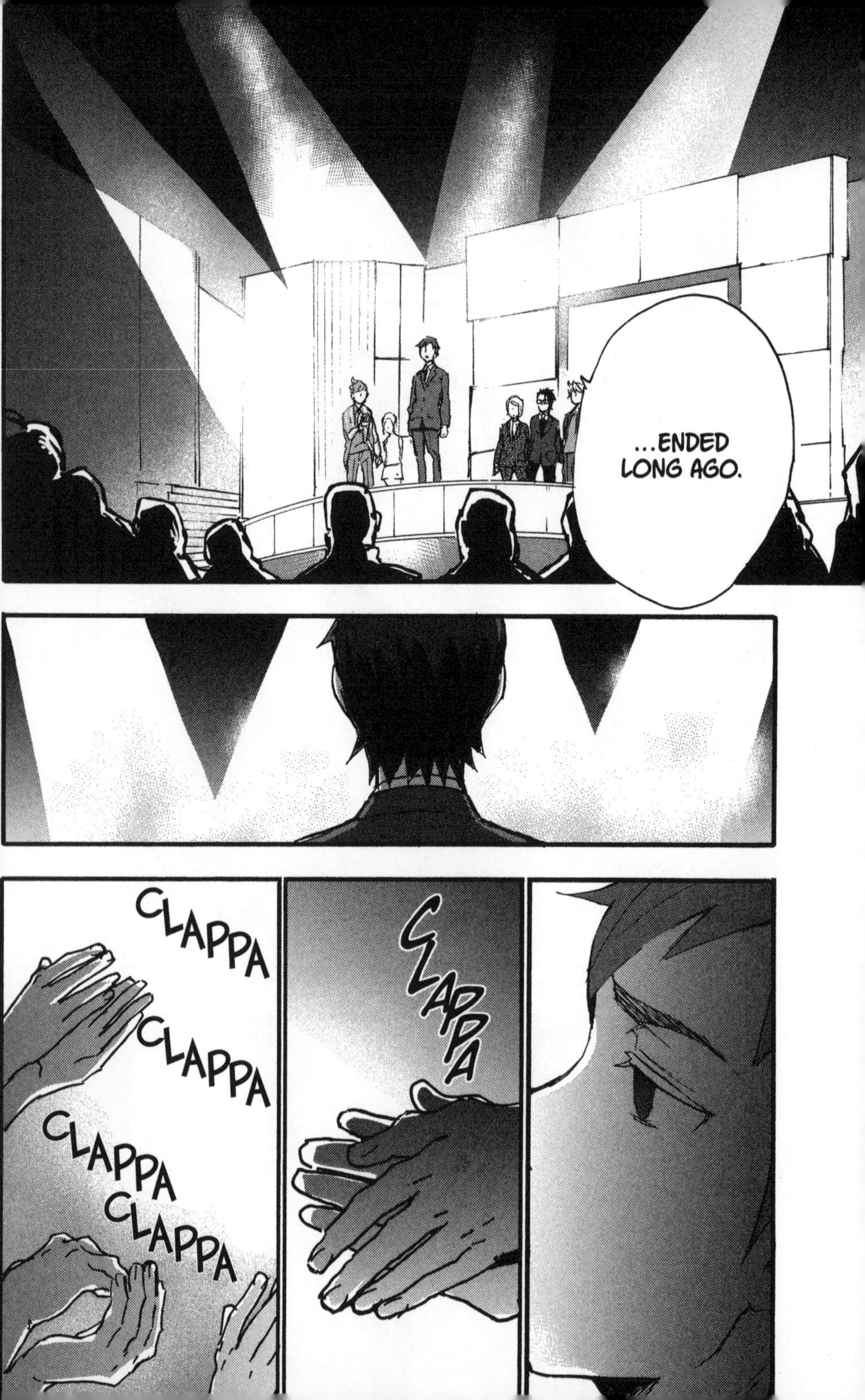
...ENDED LONG AGO.
CLAPPA
CLAPPA
CLAPPA
CLAPPA
CLAPPA

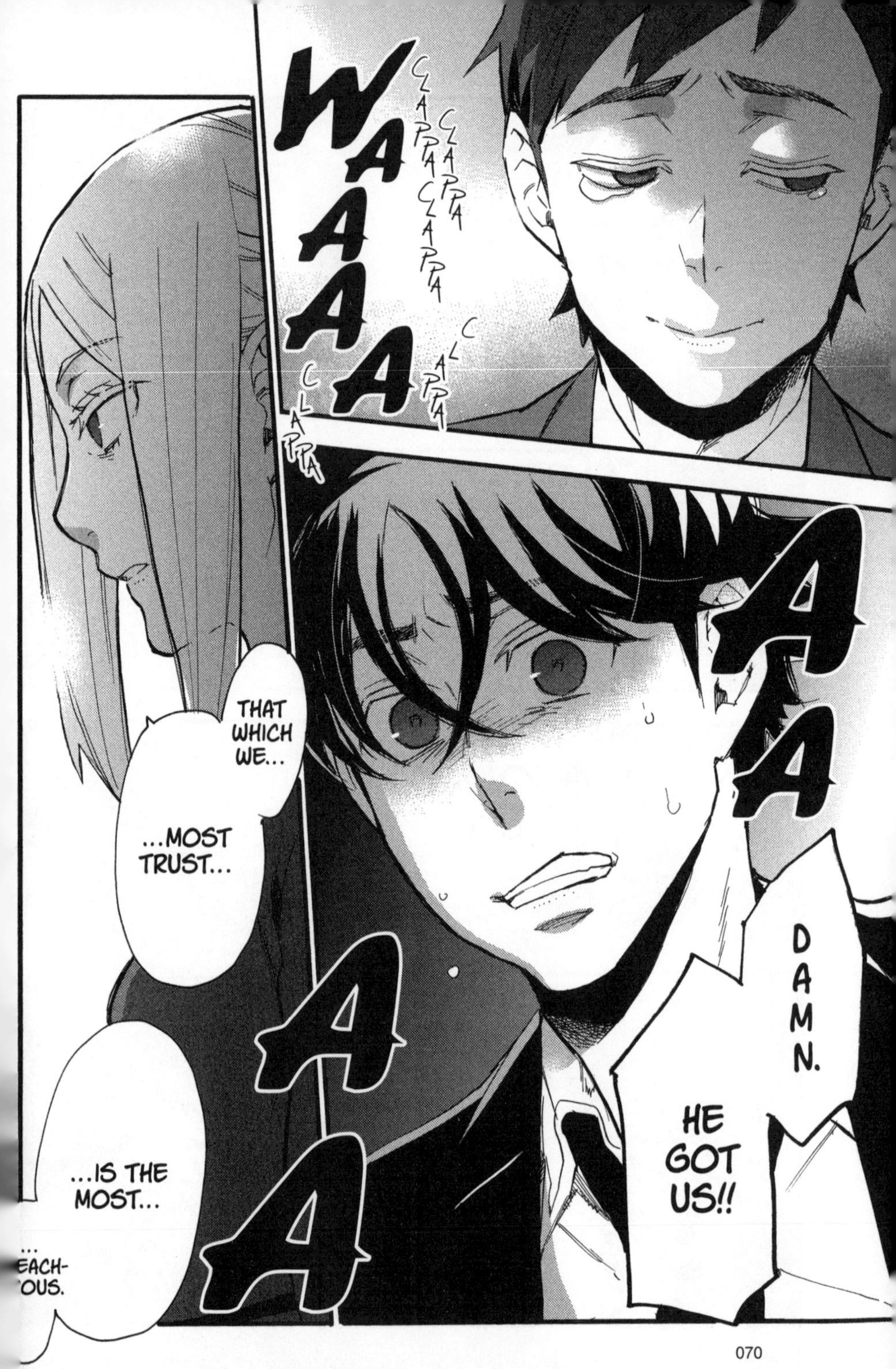
WAAAAA
CLAPPA CLAPPA CLAPPA CLAPPA
CLAPPA
AAAAA
DAMN.
HE GOT US!!
THAT WHICH WE...
...MOST TRUST...
...IS THE MOST...
... EACH- OUS.

CHAPTER sixty-three

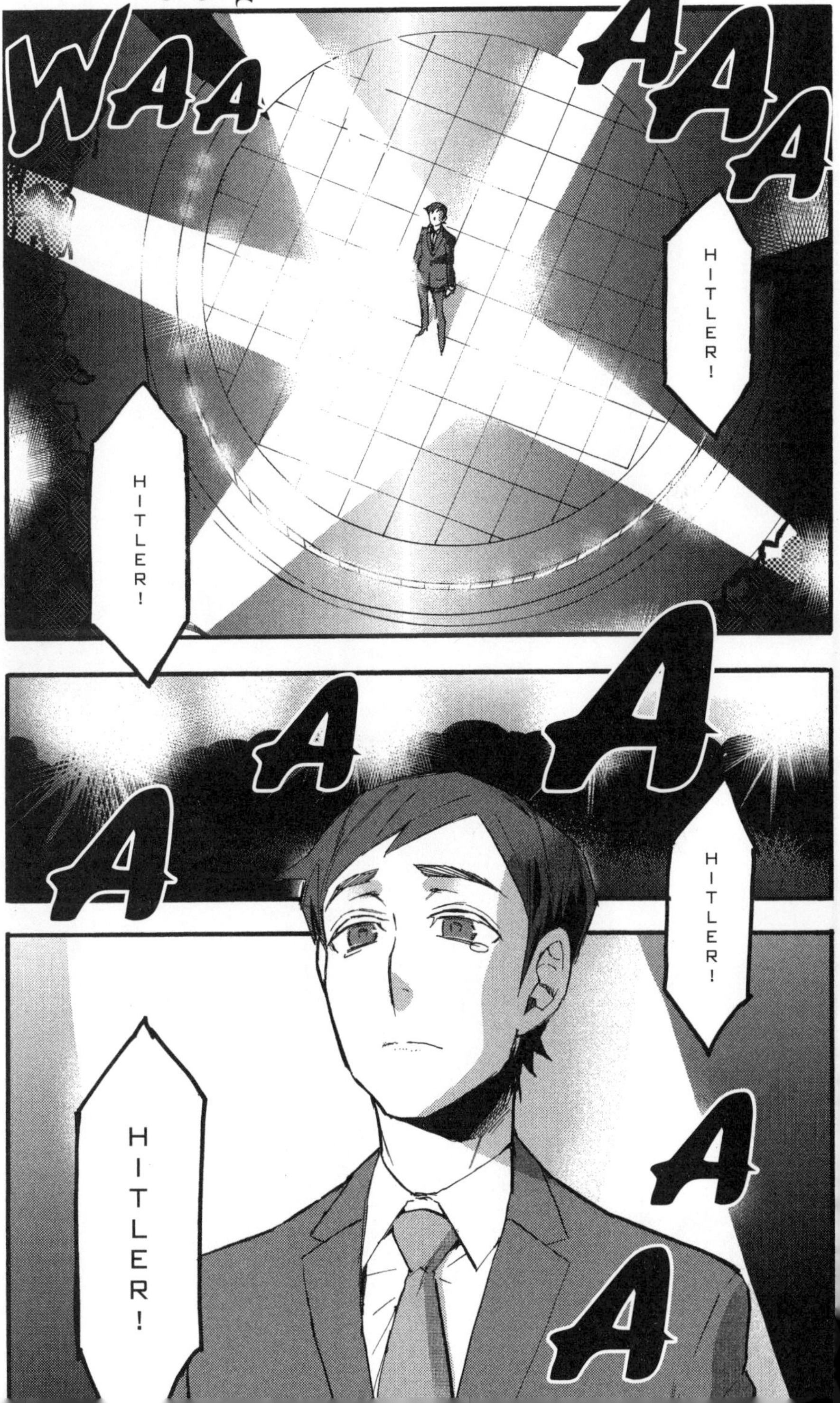
WAAAAAA
HITLER!
HITLER!
AAA
HITLER!
HITLER!
AA

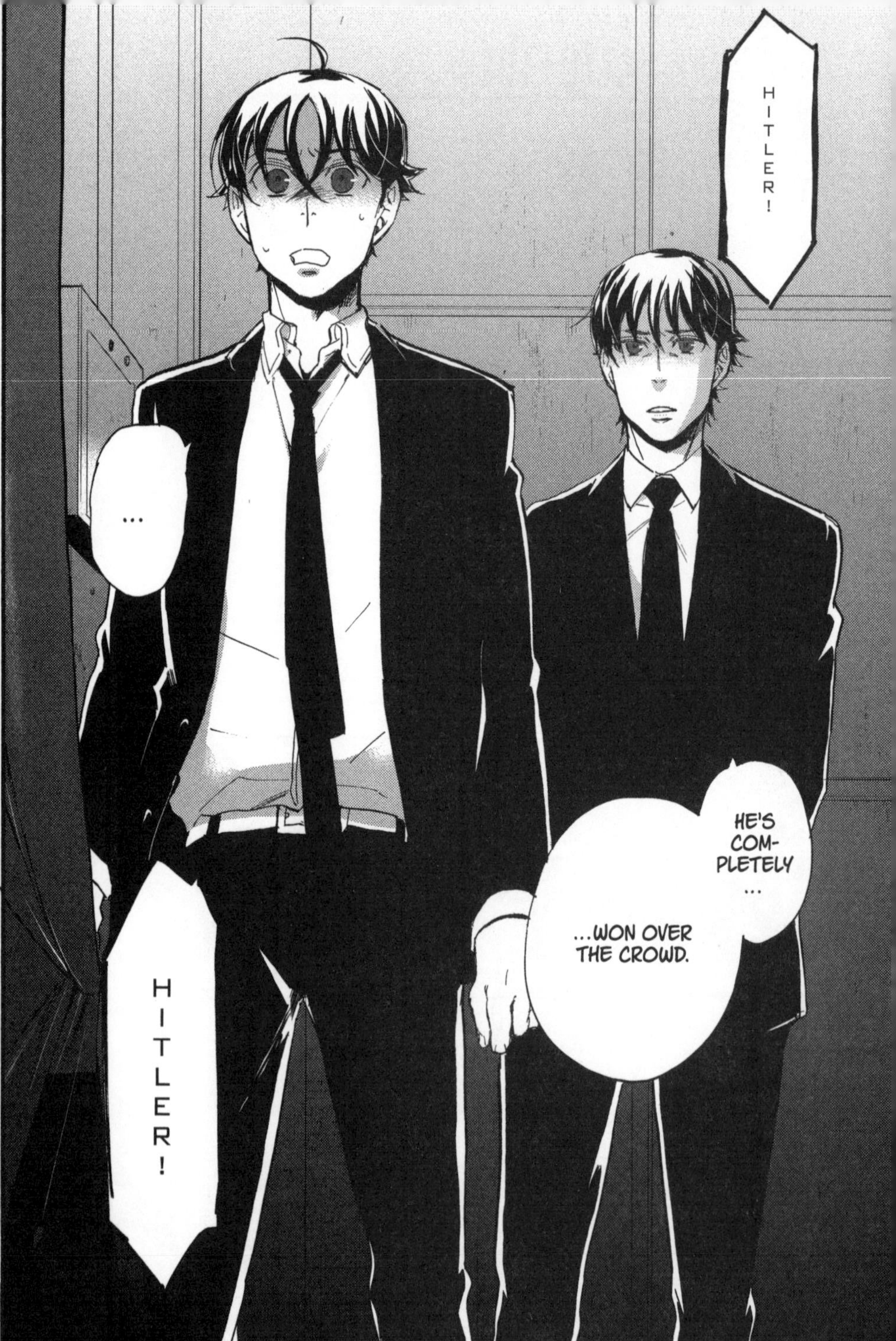
HITLER!
...
HE'S COMPLETELY...
...WON OVER THE CROWD.
HITLER!

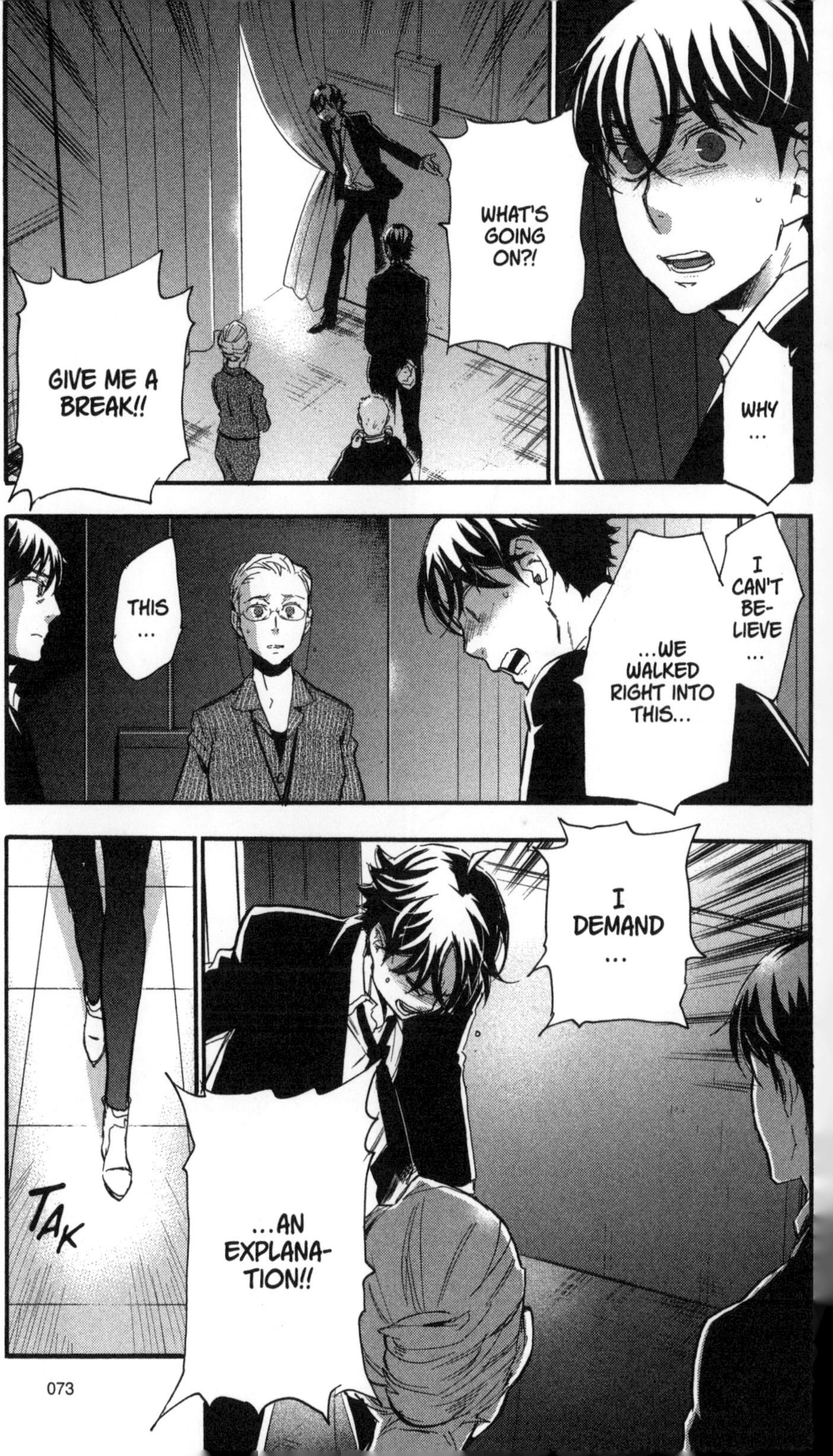
WHAT'S GOING ON?!
WHY ...
GIVE ME A BREAK!!
I CAN'T BE-LIEVE ...
...WE WALKED RIGHT INTO THIS...
THIS ...
I DEMAND ...
...AN EXPLANATION!!
TAK

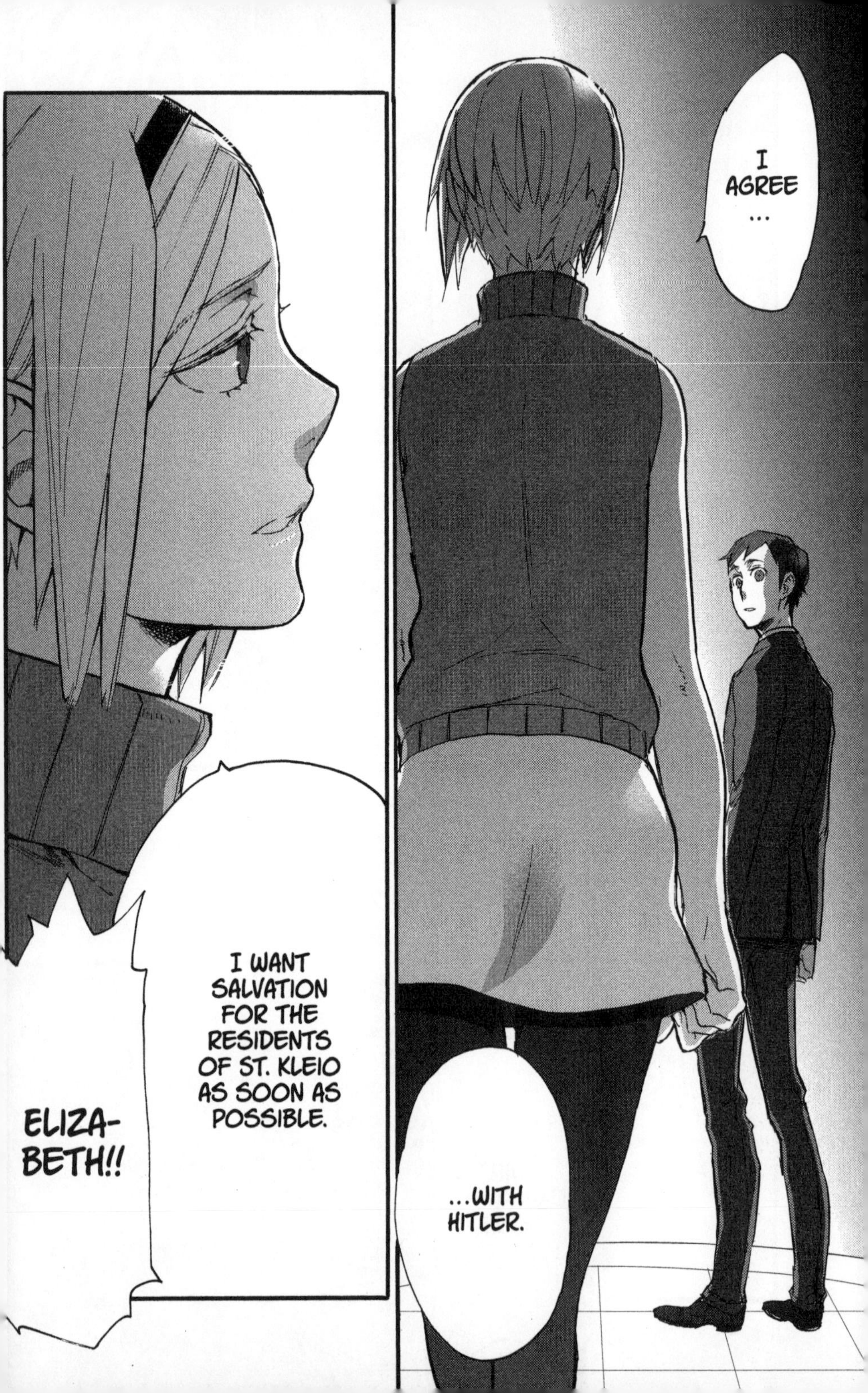
I AGREE ...
...WITH HITLER.
I WANT SALVATION FOR THE RESIDENTS OF ST. KLEIO AS SOON AS POSSIBLE.
ELIZA-BETH!!

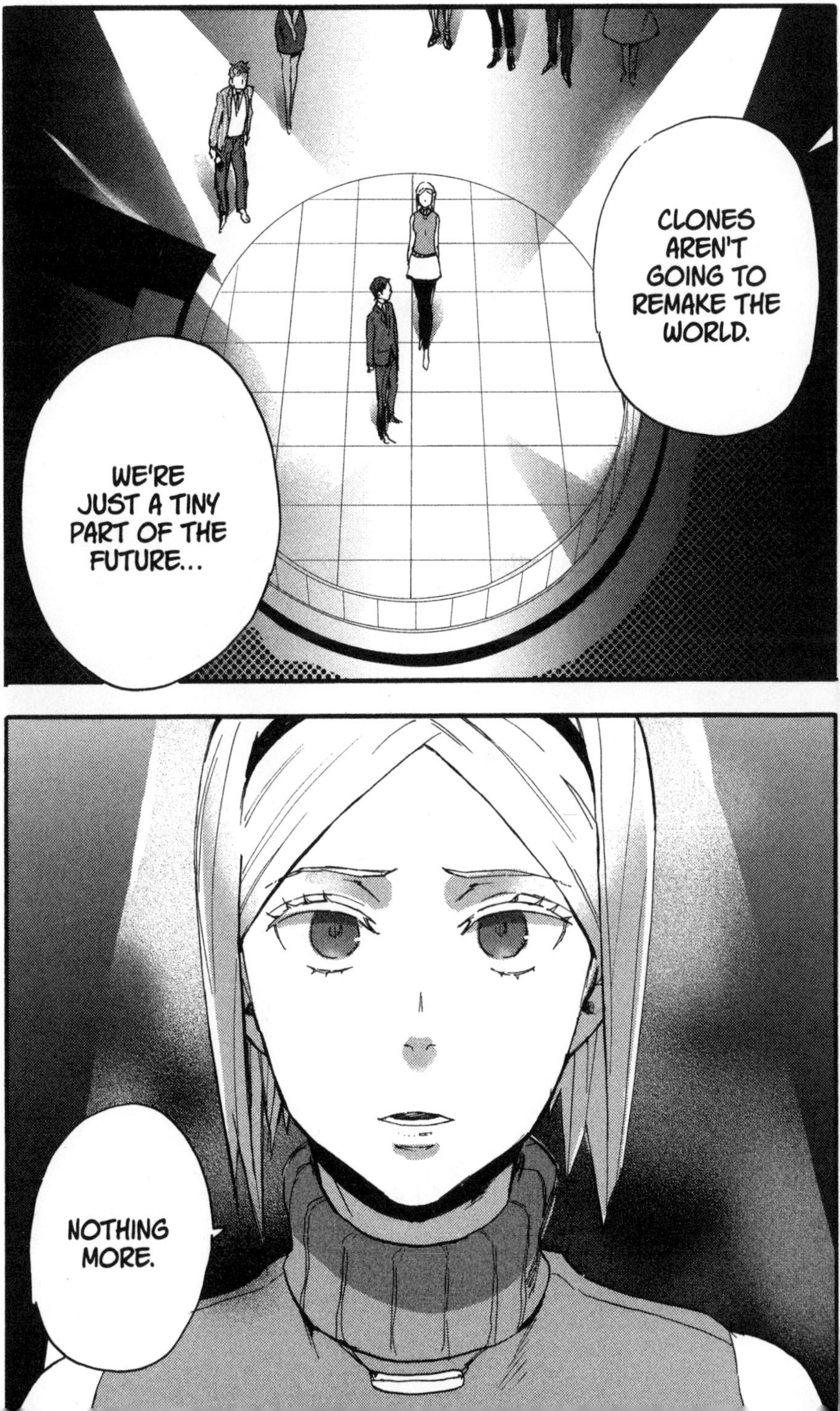
CLONES AREN'T GOING TO REMAKE THE WORLD.
WE'RE JUST A TINY PART OF THE FUTURE...
NOTHING MORE.

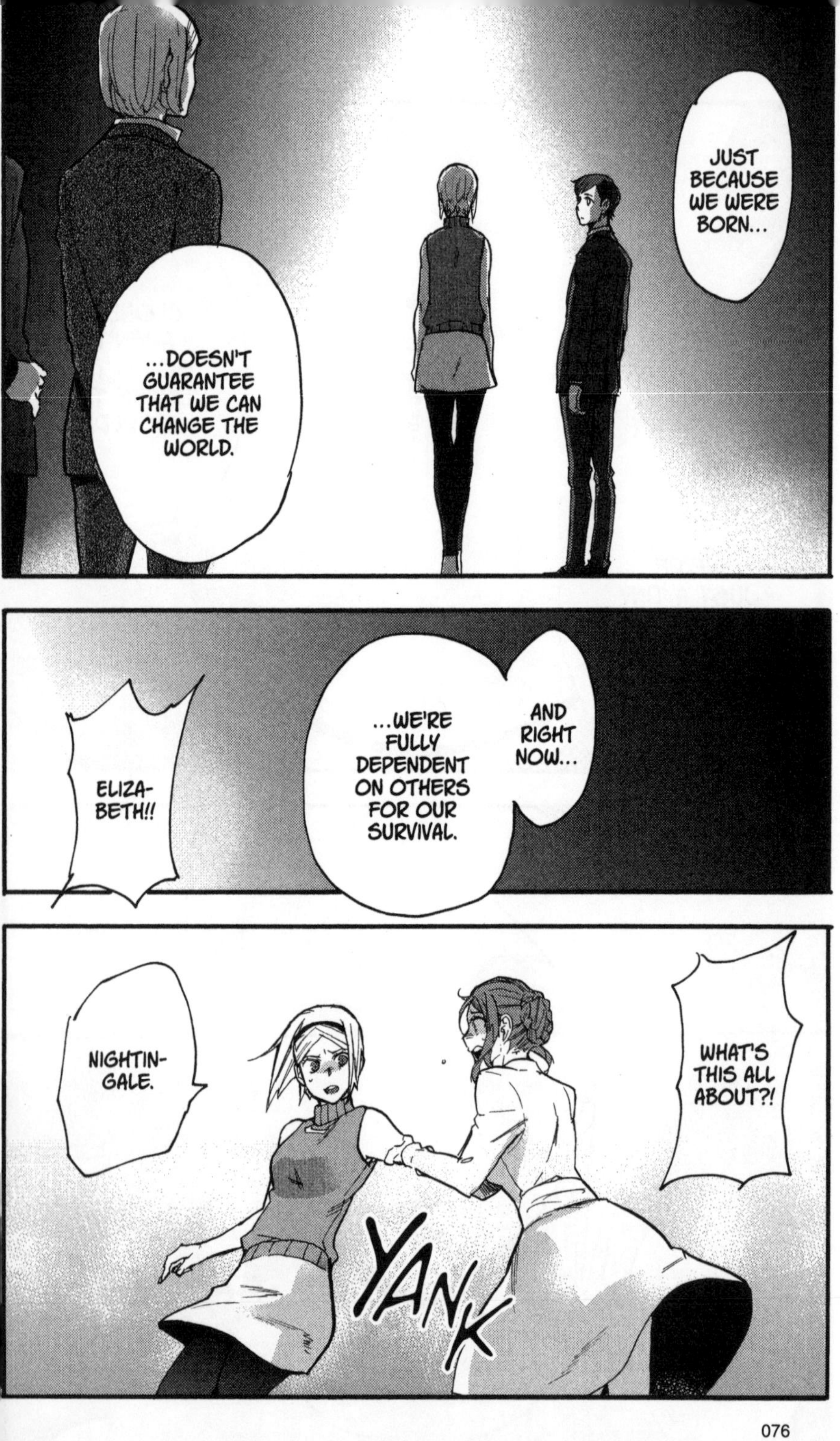
JUST BECAUSE WE WERE BORN...
...DOESN'T GUARANTEE THAT WE CAN CHANGE THE WORLD.
AND RIGHT NOW...
...WE'RE FULLY DEPENDENT ON OTHERS FOR OUR SURVIVAL.
ELIZA-BETH!!
WHAT'S THIS ALL ABOUT?!
YANK
NIGHTIN-GALE.

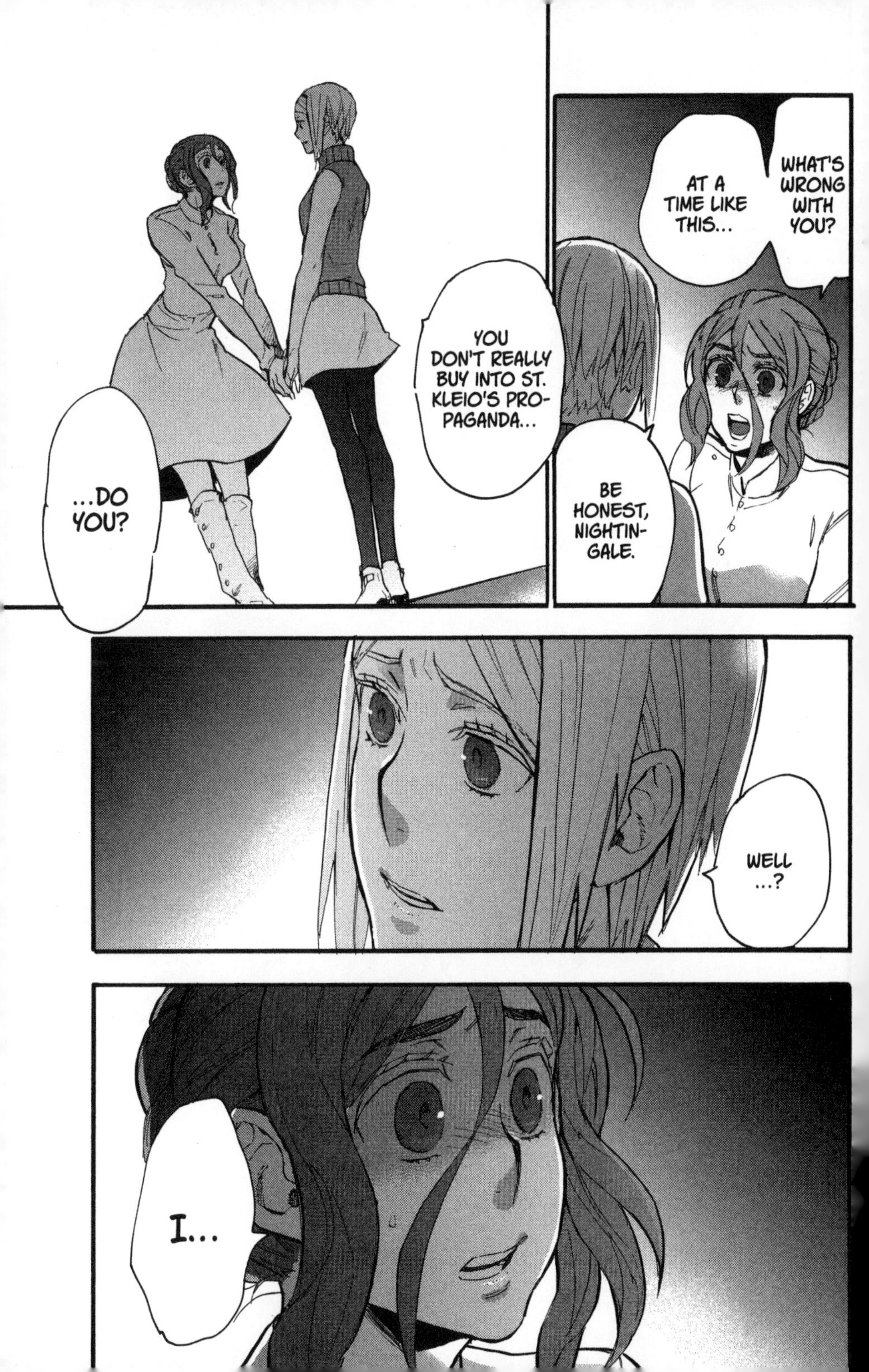
WHAT'S WRONG WITH YOU?
AT A TIME LIKE THIS...
BE HONEST, NIGHTINGALE.
YOU DON'T REALLY BUY INTO ST. KLEIO'S PRO-PAGANDA...
...DO YOU?
WELL ...?
I...

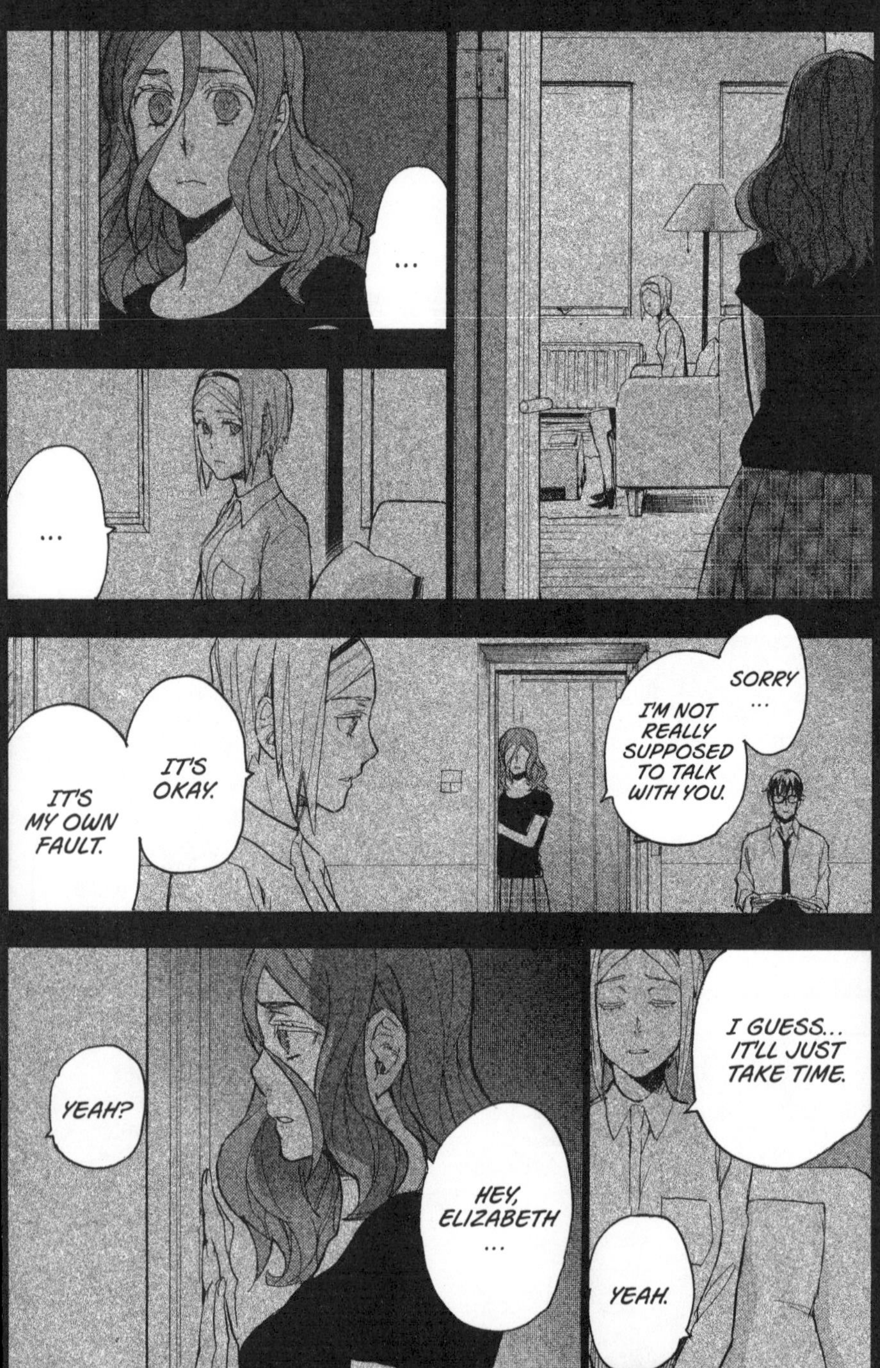
...
...
SORRY... I'M NOT REALLY SUPPOSED TO TALK WITH YOU.
IT'S OKAY.
IT'S MY OWN FAULT.
I GUESS... IT'LL JUST TAKE TIME.
YEAH.
HEY, ELIZABETH...
YEAH?

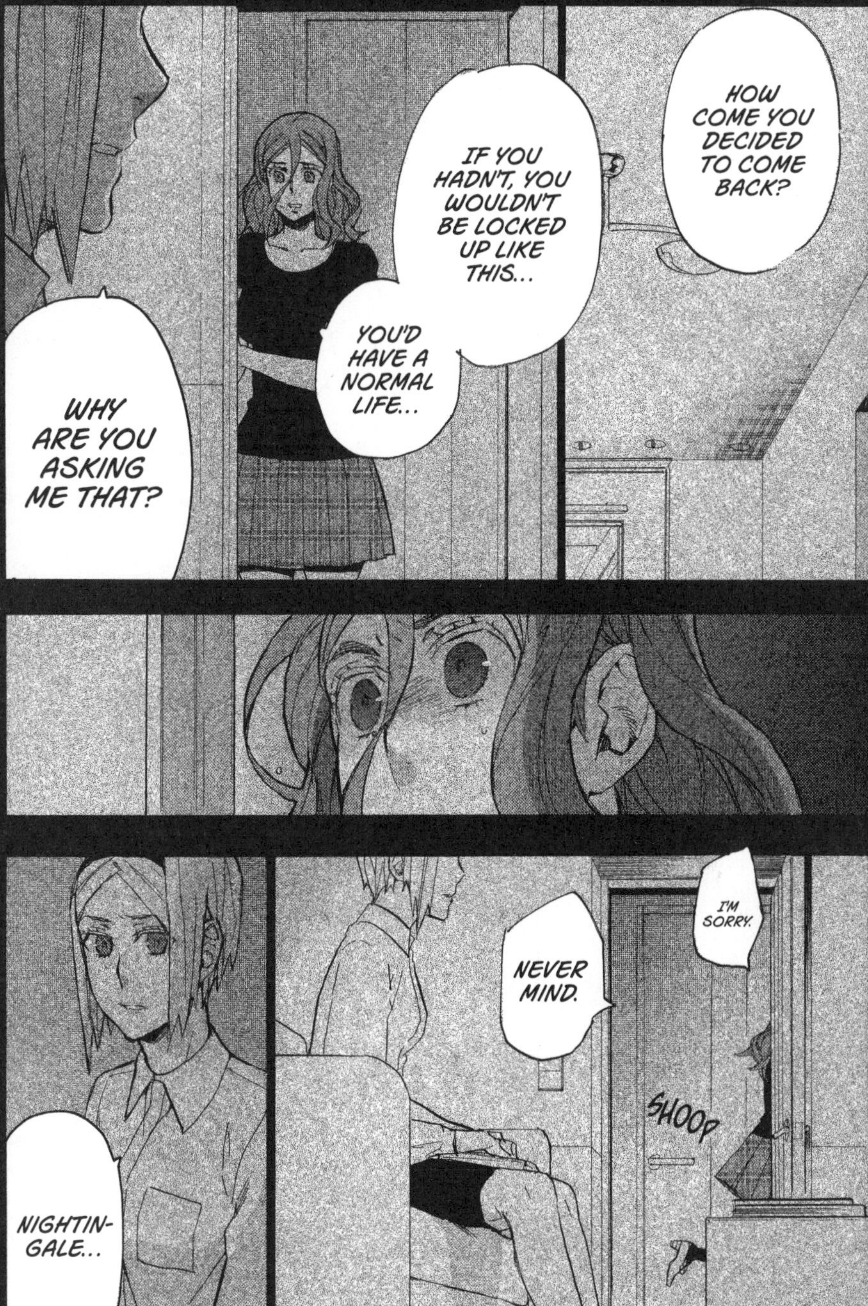
HOW COME YOU DECIDED TO COME BACK?
IF YOU HADN'T, YOU WOULDN'T BE LOCKED UP LIKE THIS...
YOU'D HAVE A NORMAL LIFE...
WHY ARE YOU ASKING ME THAT?
I'M SORRY.
NEVER MIND.
SHOOP
NIGHTIN-GALE...

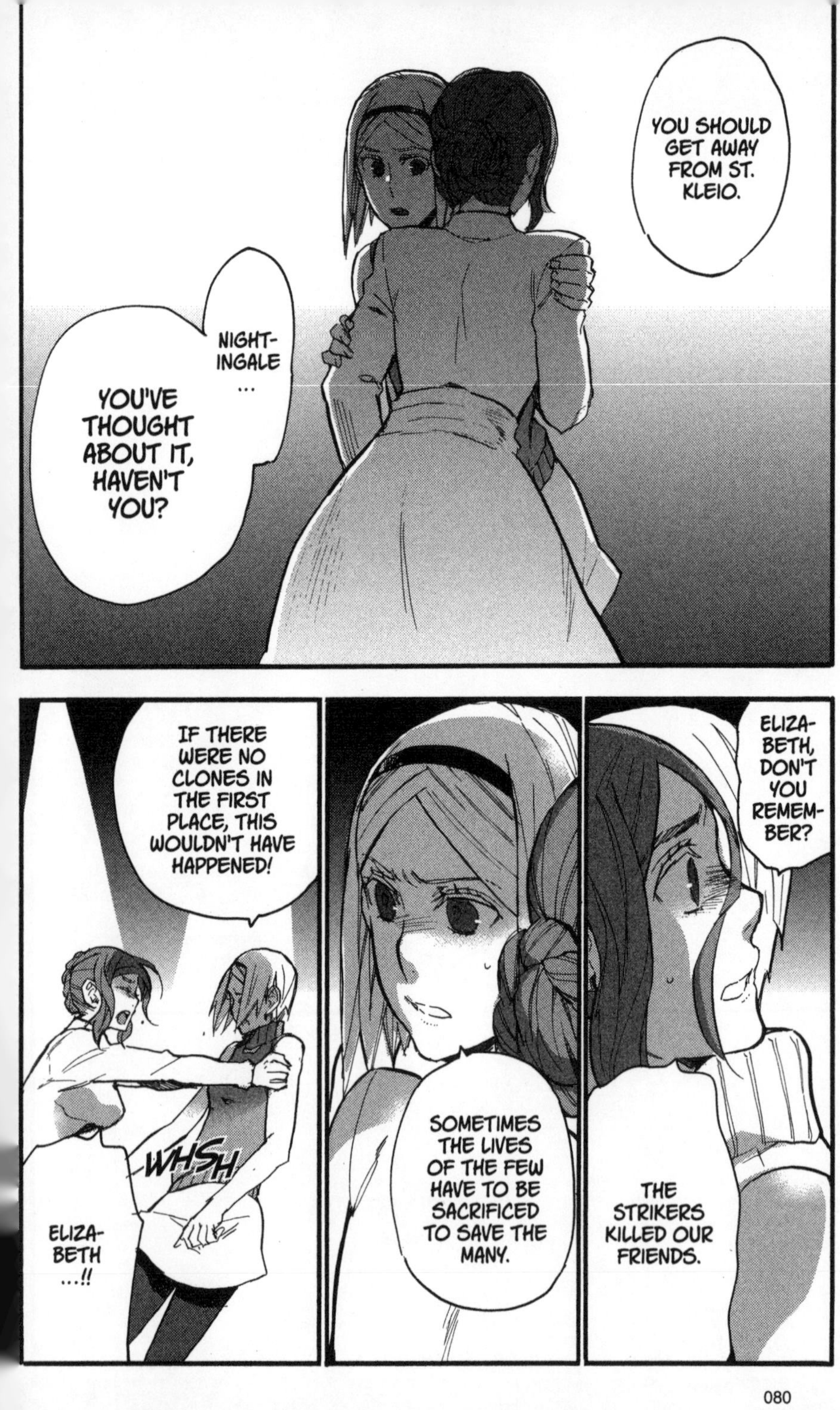
YOU SHOULD GET AWAY FROM ST. KLEIO.
NIGHT-INGALE ...
YOU'VE THOUGHT ABOUT IT, HAVEN'T YOU?
ELIZA-BETH, DON'T YOU REMEMBER?
THE STRIKERS KILLED OUR FRIENDS.
SOMETIMES THE LIVES OF THE FEW HAVE TO BE SACRIFICED TO SAVE THE MANY.
IF THERE WERE NO CLONES IN THE FIRST PLACE, THIS WOULDN'T HAVE HAPPENED!
WHSH
ELIZA-BETH ...!!

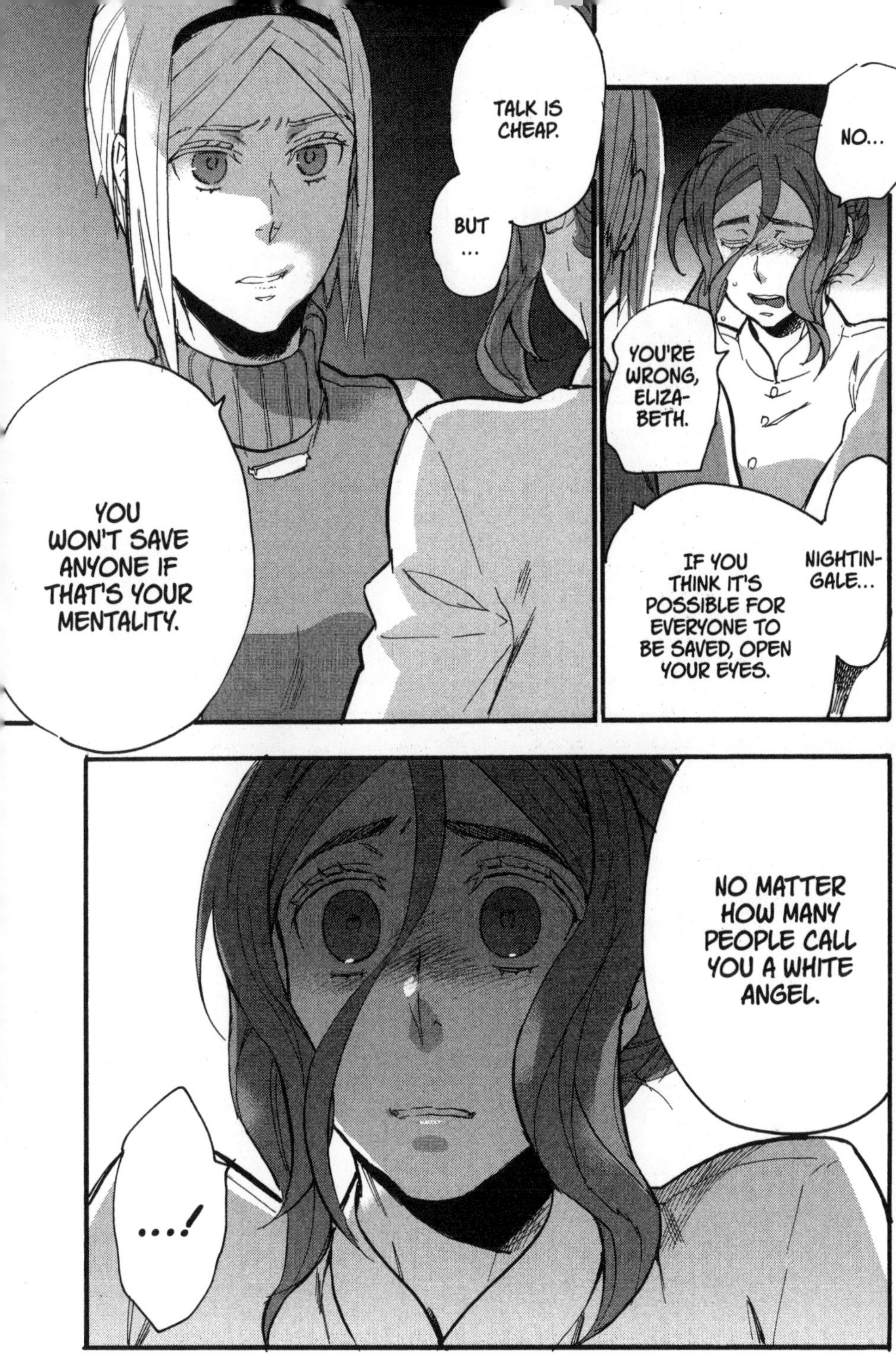
NO...
YOU'RE WRONG, ELIZA-BETH.
NIGHTIN-GALE...
IF YOU THINK IT'S POSSIBLE FOR EVERYONE TO BE SAVED, OPEN YOUR EYES.
TALK IS CHEAP.
BUT ...
YOU WON'T SAVE ANYONE IF THAT'S YOUR MENTALITY.
NO MATTER HOW MANY PEOPLE CALL YOU A WHITE ANGEL.
...!

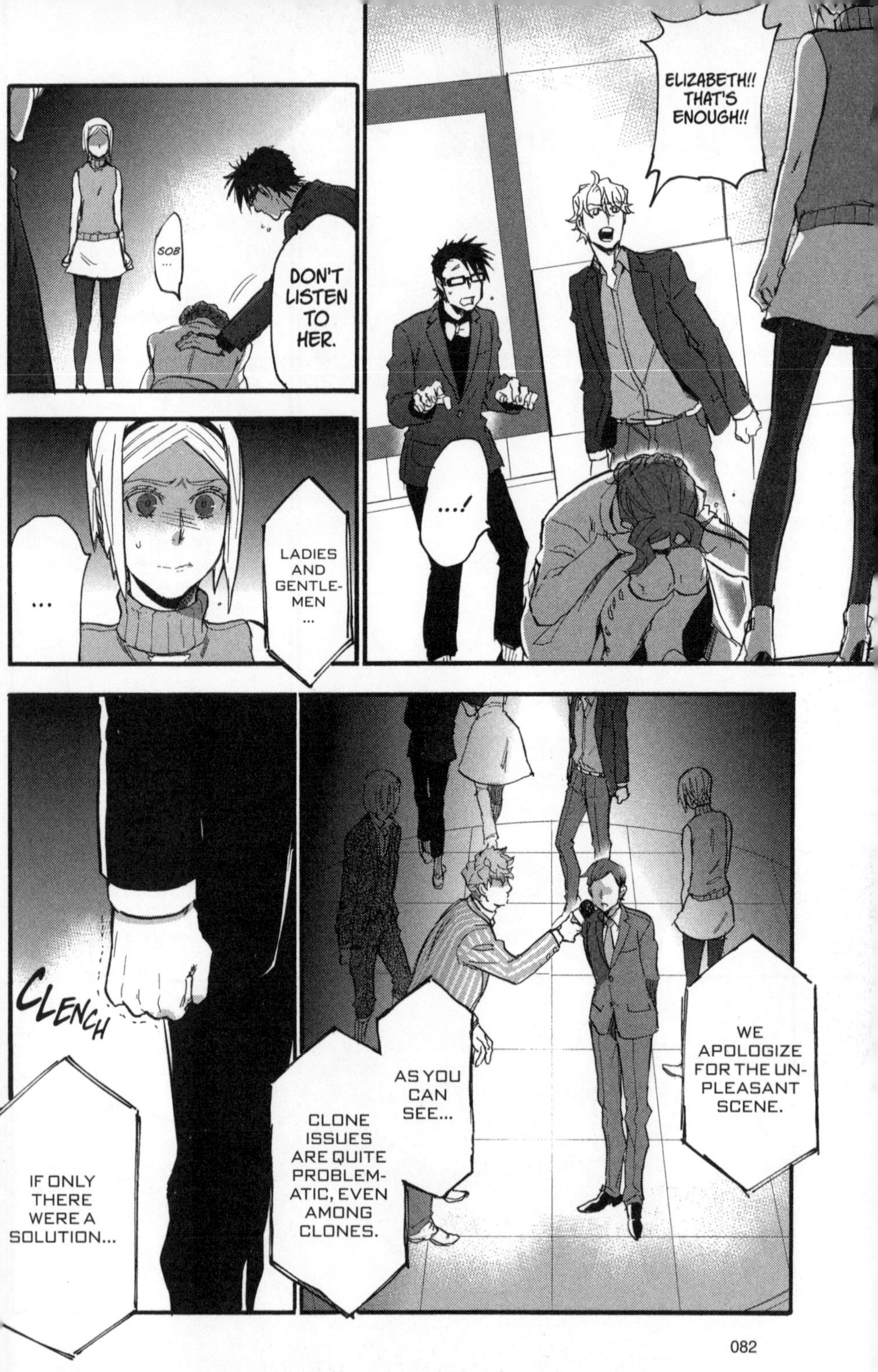
ELIZABETH!! THAT'S ENOUGH!!
...!
DON'T LISTEN TO HER.
SOB ...
LADIES AND GENTLEMEN ...
...
WE APOLOGIZE FOR THE UNPLEASANT SCENE.
AS YOU CAN SEE...
CLONE ISSUES ARE QUITE PROBLEMATIC, EVEN AMONG CLONES.
CLENCH
IF ONLY THERE WERE A SOLUTION...

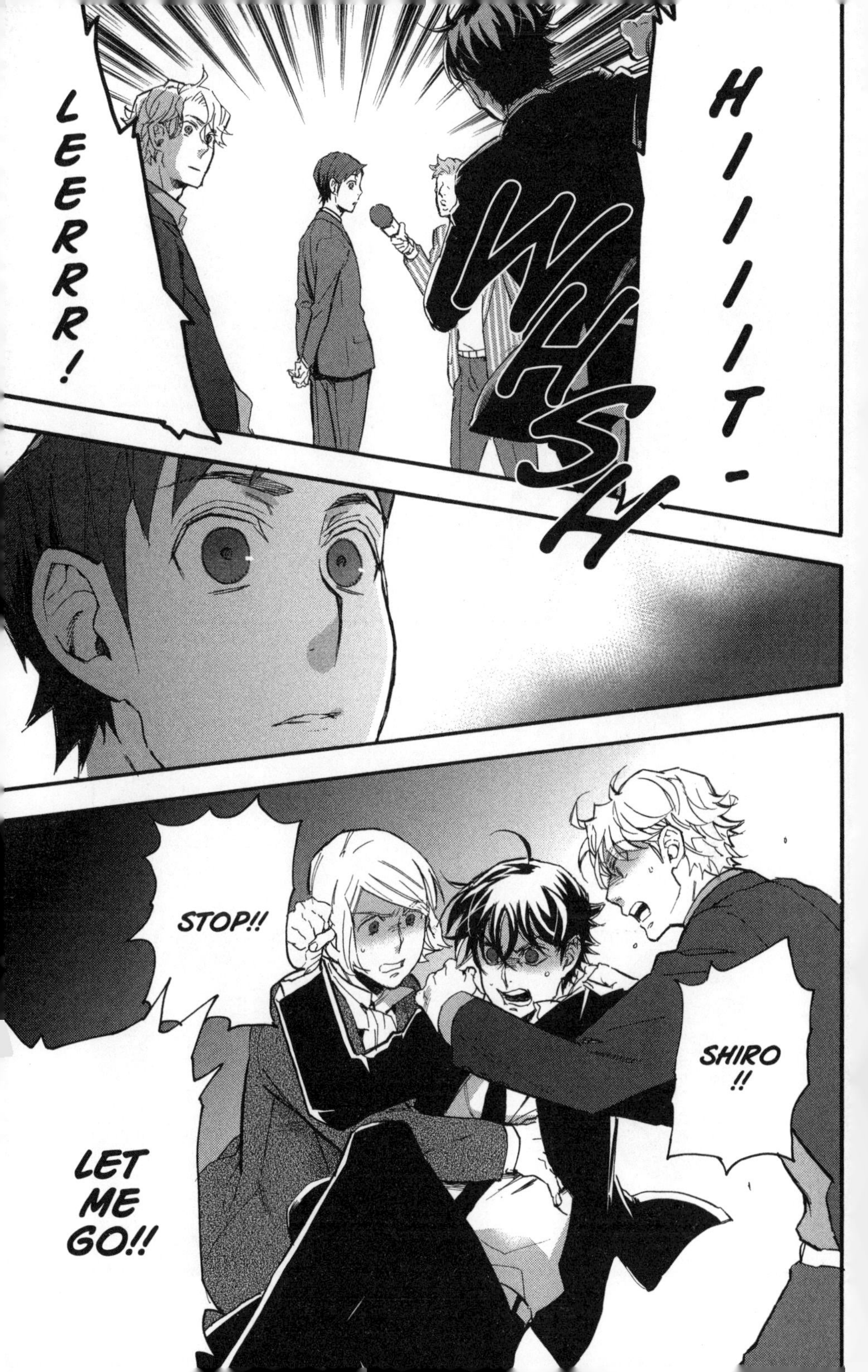
HIIIIT-
WHSH
LEEERRRR!
SHIRO!!
STOP!!
LET ME GO!!

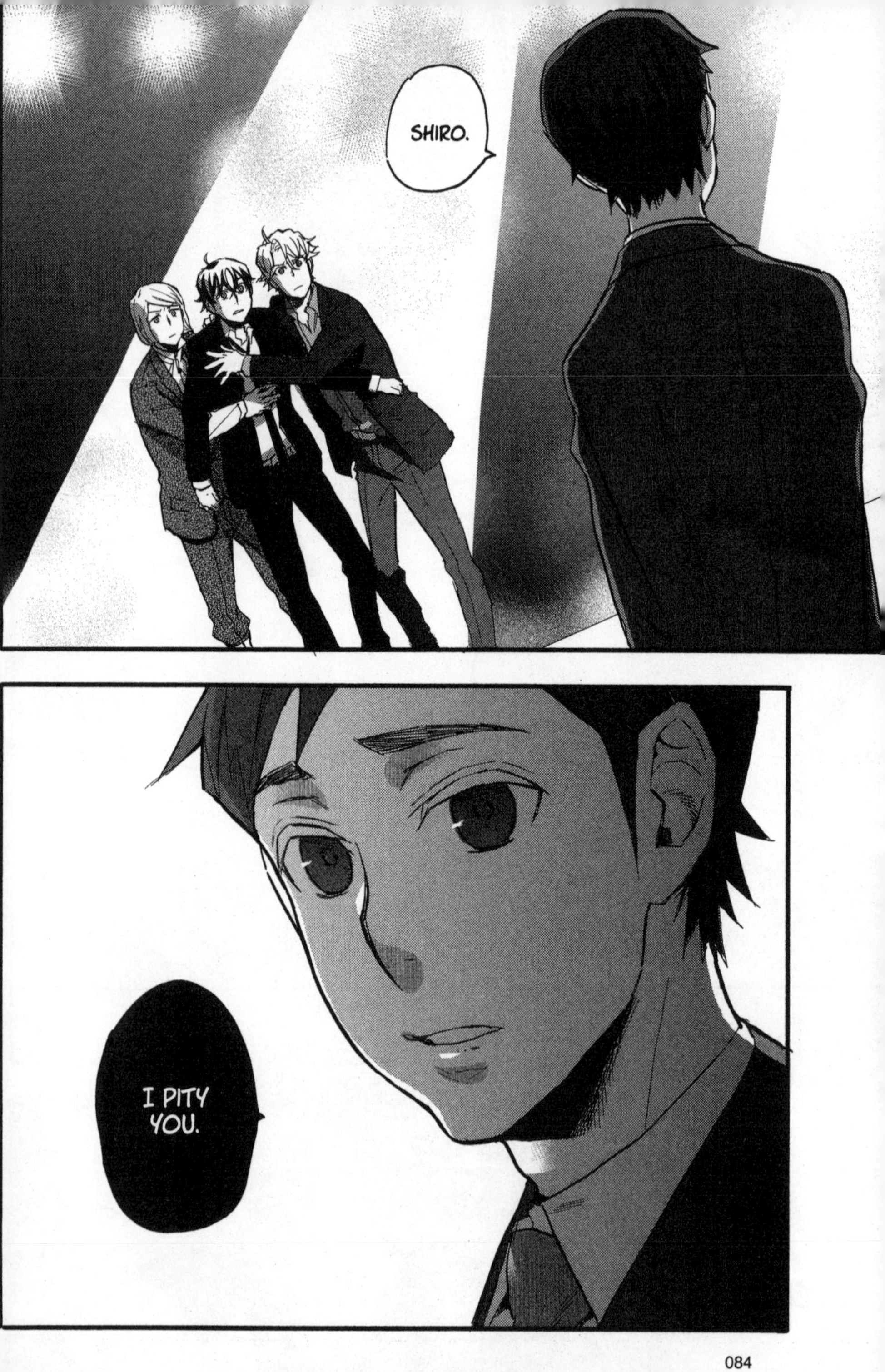
SHIRO.
I PITY YOU.

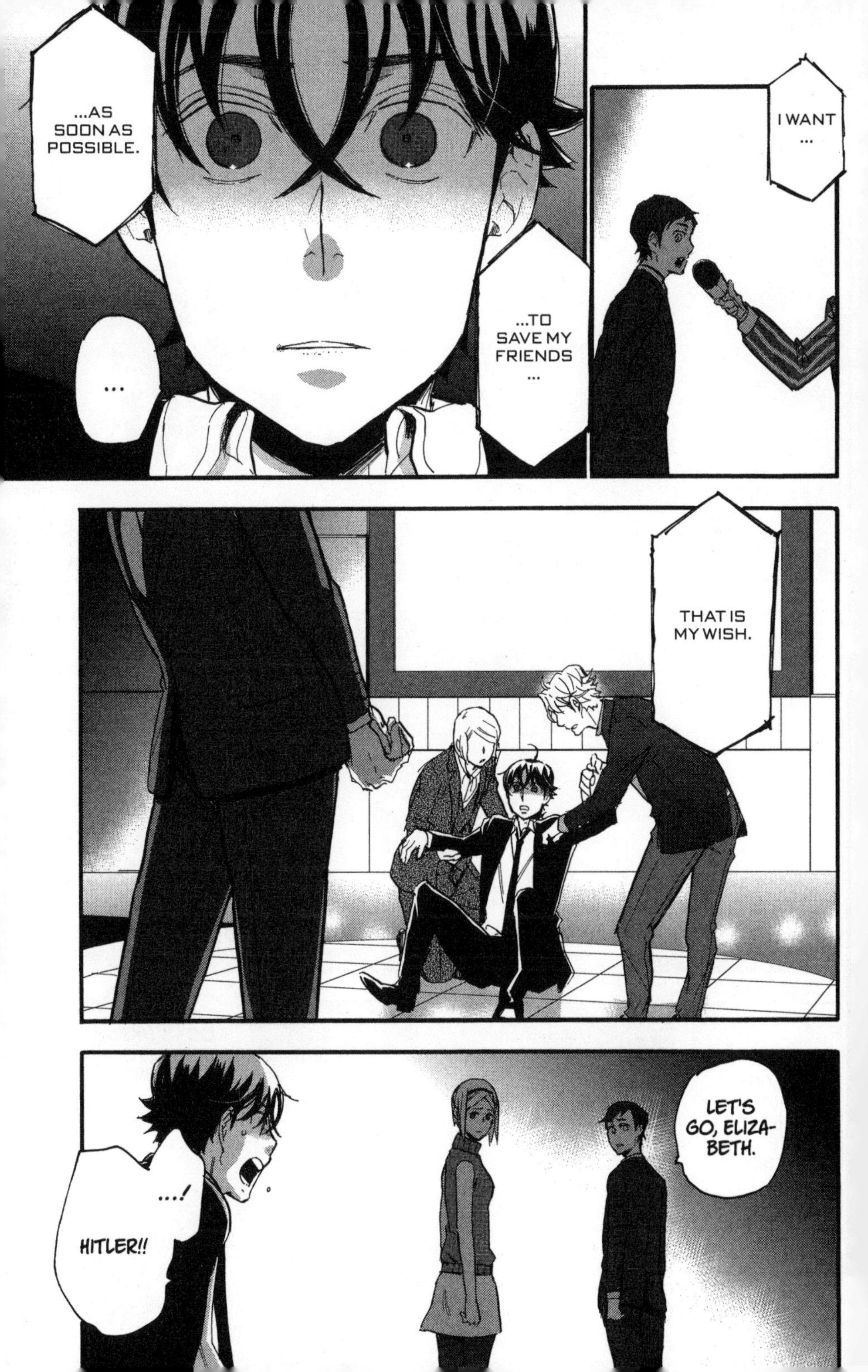
I WANT ...
...TO SAVE MY FRIENDS ...
...AS SOON AS POSSIBLE.
...
THAT IS MY WISH.
LET'S GO, ELIZA-BETH.
...!
HITLER!!

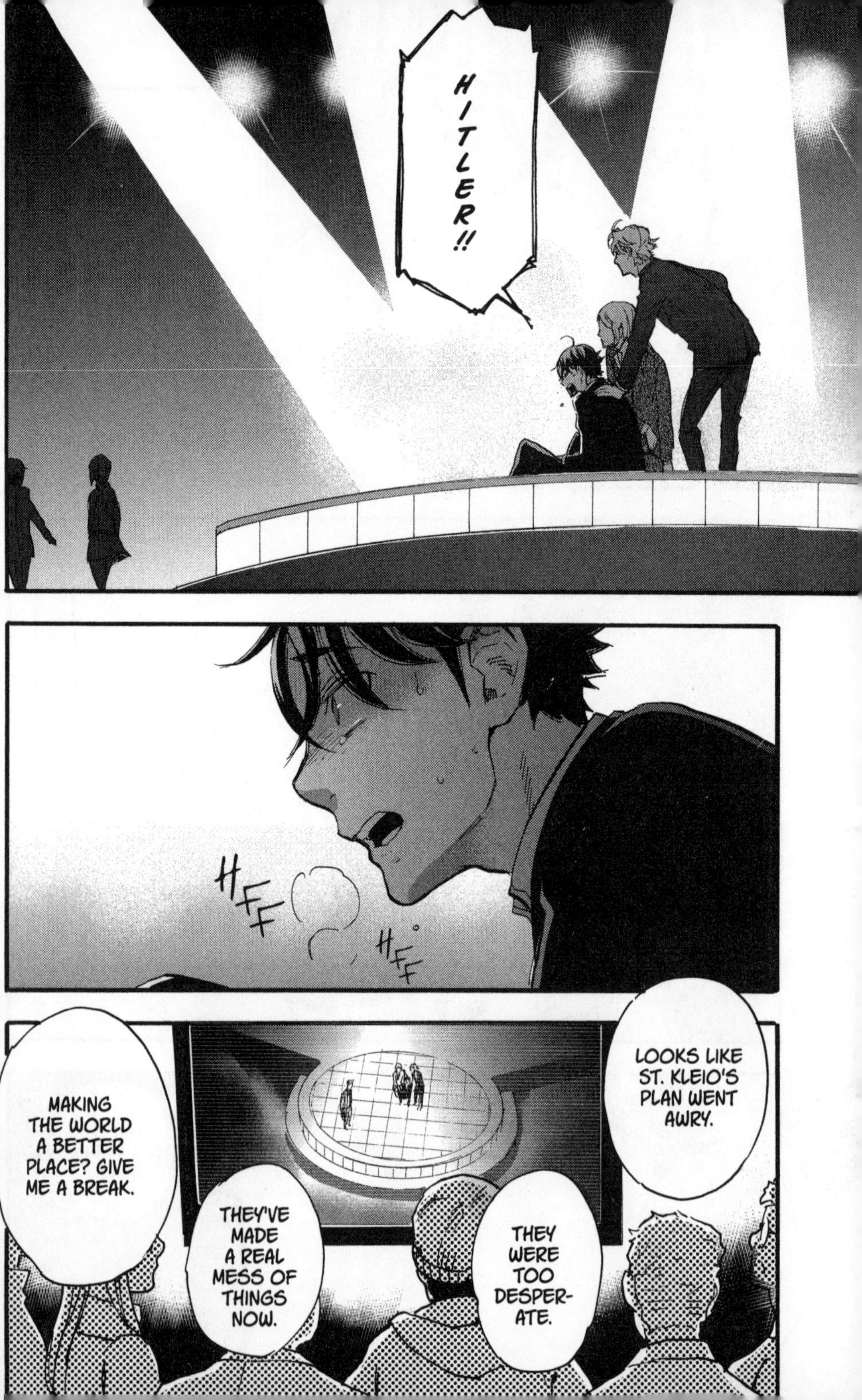
HITLER!!
HFF
HFF
LOOKS LIKE ST. KLEIO'S PLAN WENT AWRY.
THEY WERE TOO DESPERATE.
THEY'VE MADE A REAL MESS OF THINGS NOW.
MAKING THE WORLD A BETTER PLACE? GIVE ME A BREAK.

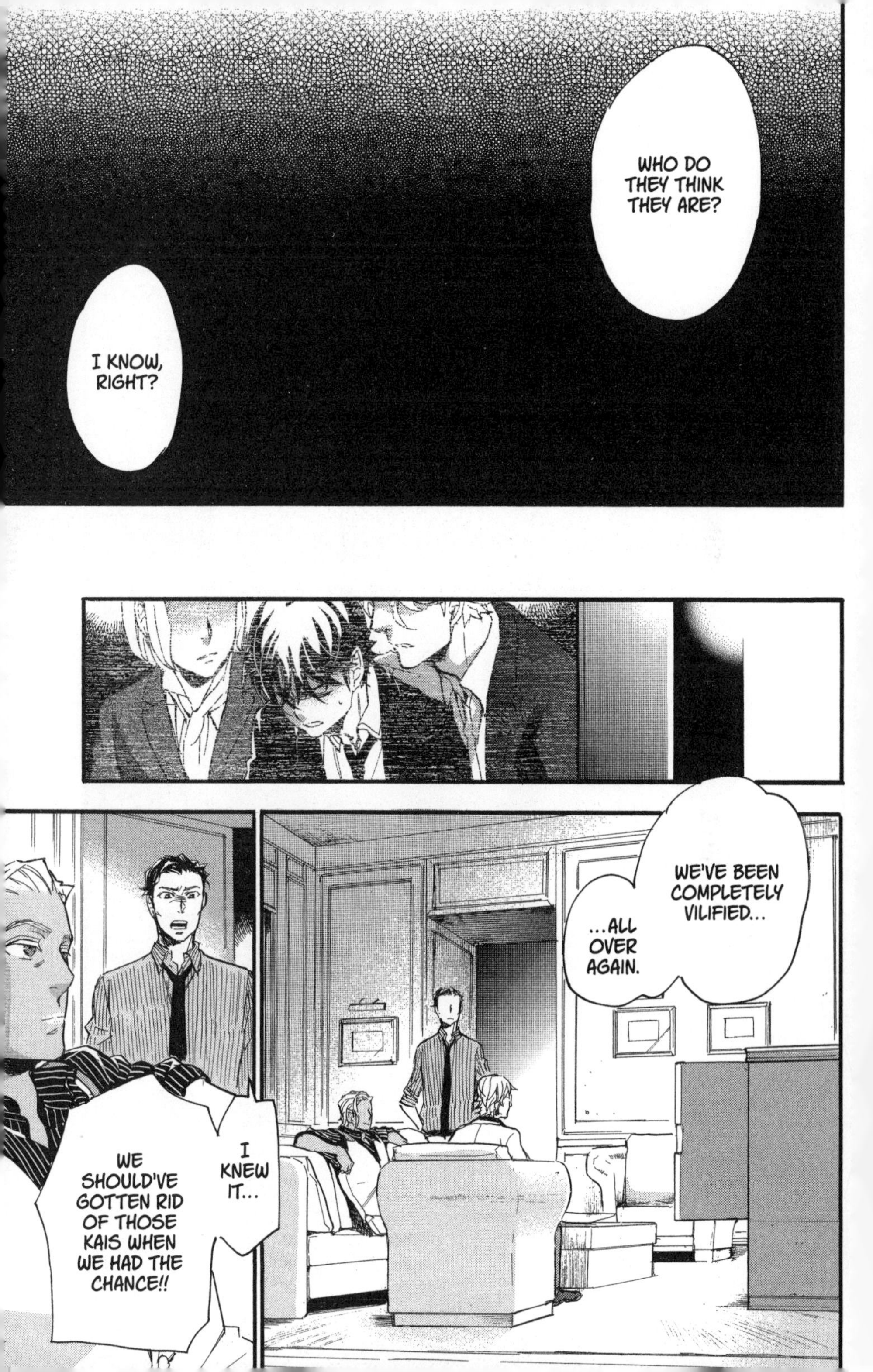
WHO DO THEY THINK THEY ARE?
I KNOW, RIGHT?
WE'VE BEEN COMPLETELY VILIFIED...
...ALL OVER AGAIN.
I KNEW IT...
WE SHOULD'VE GOTTEN RID OF THOSE KAIS WHEN WE HAD THE CHANCE!!

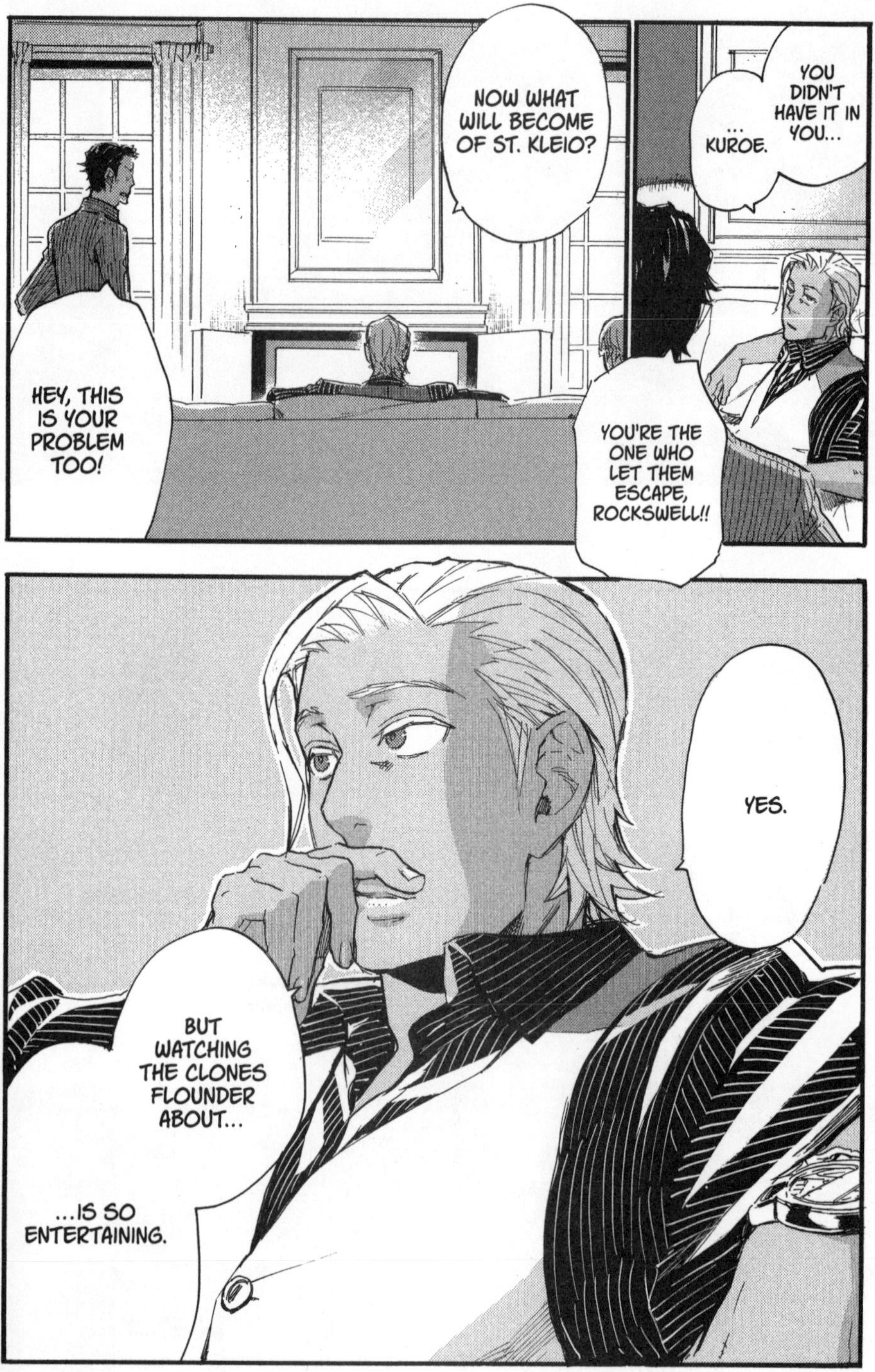
YOU DIDN'T HAVE IT IN YOU...
... KUROE.
YOU'RE THE ONE WHO LET THEM ESCAPE, ROCKSWELL!!
NOW WHAT WILL BECOME OF ST. KLEIO?
HEY, THIS IS YOUR PROBLEM TOO!
YES.
BUT WATCHING THE CLONES FLOUNDER ABOUT...
...IS SO ENTERTAINING.

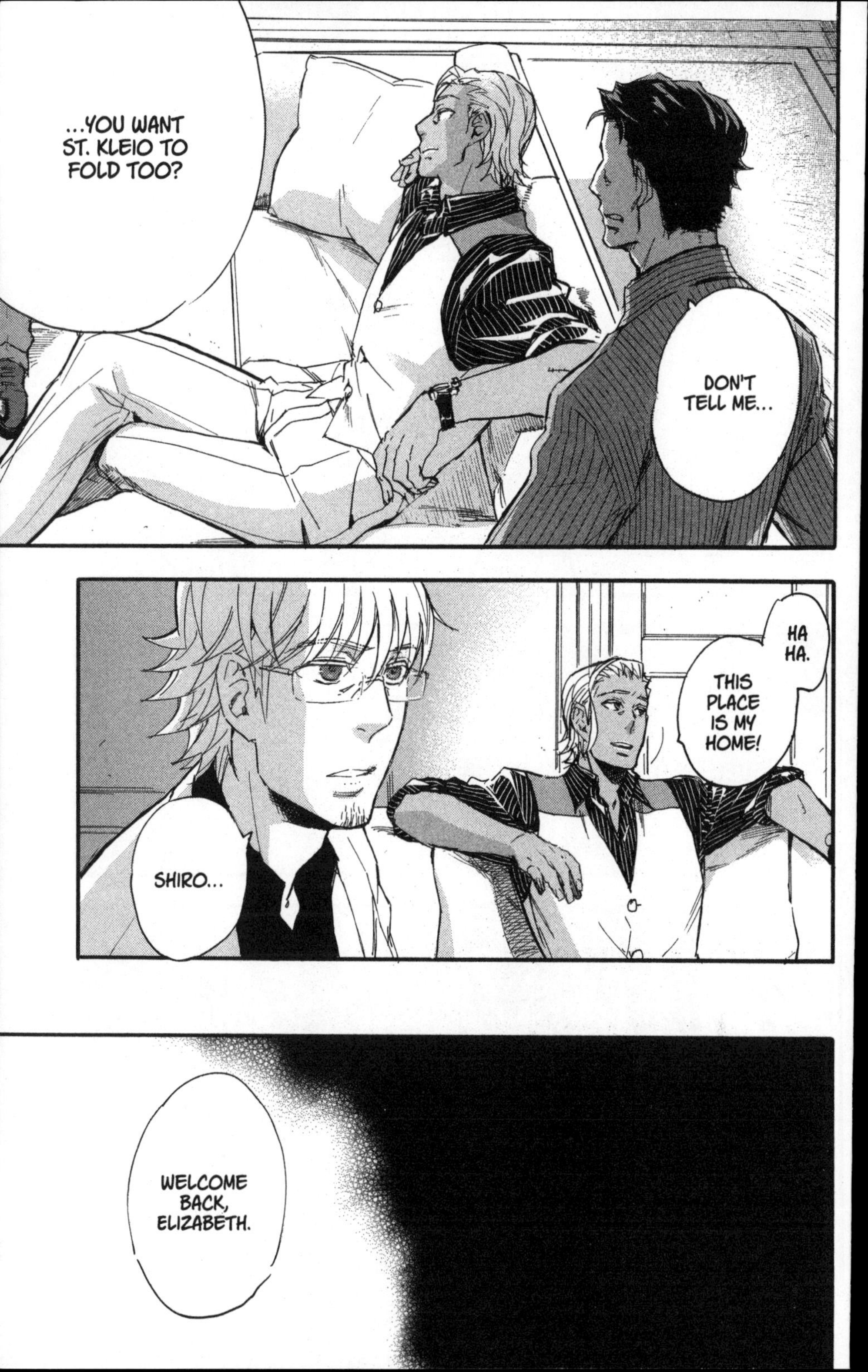
DON'T TELL ME...
...YOU WANT ST. KLEIO TO FOLD TOO?
HA HA.
THIS PLACE IS MY HOME!
SHIRO...
WELCOME BACK, ELIZABETH.

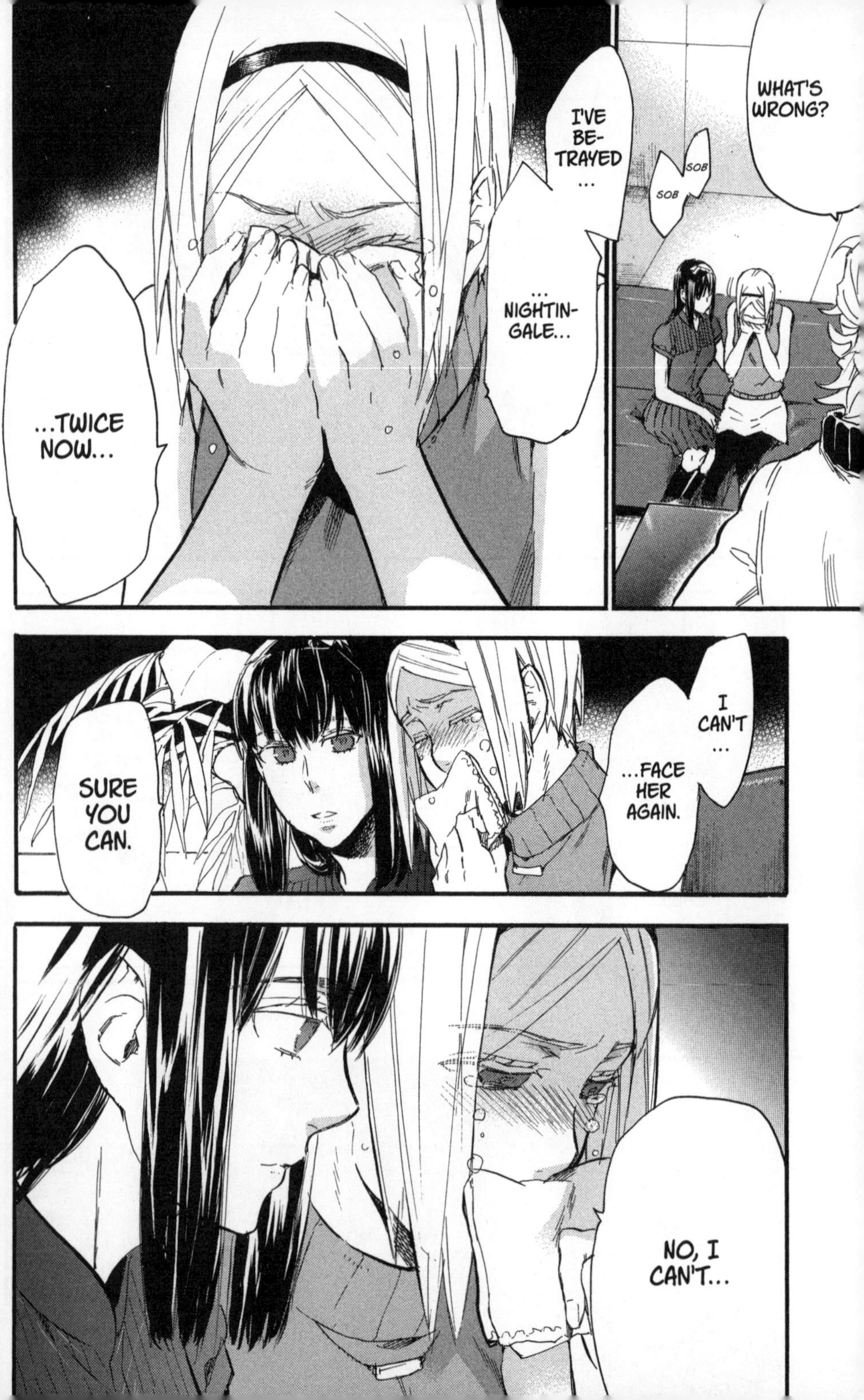
WHAT'S WRONG?
SOB
SOB
I'VE BE-TRAYED...
...NIGHTIN-GALE...
...TWICE NOW...
I CAN'T...
...FACE HER AGAIN.
SURE YOU CAN.
NO, I CAN'T...

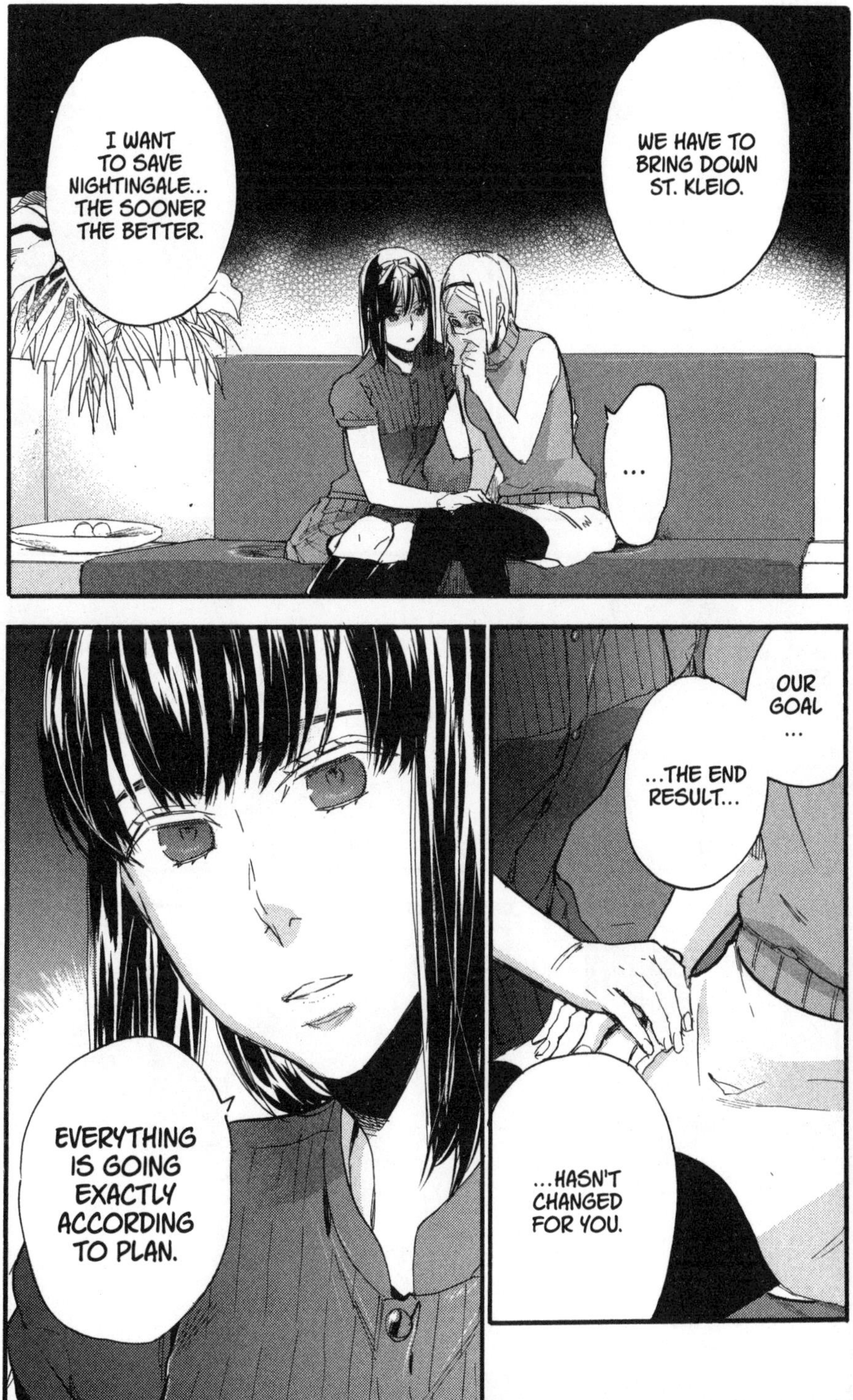
WE HAVE TO BRING DOWN ST. KLEIO.
I WANT TO SAVE NIGHTINGALE... THE SOONER THE BETTER.
...
OUR GOAL ...
...THE END RESULT...
...HASN'T CHANGED FOR YOU.
EVERYTHING IS GOING EXACTLY ACCORDING TO PLAN.

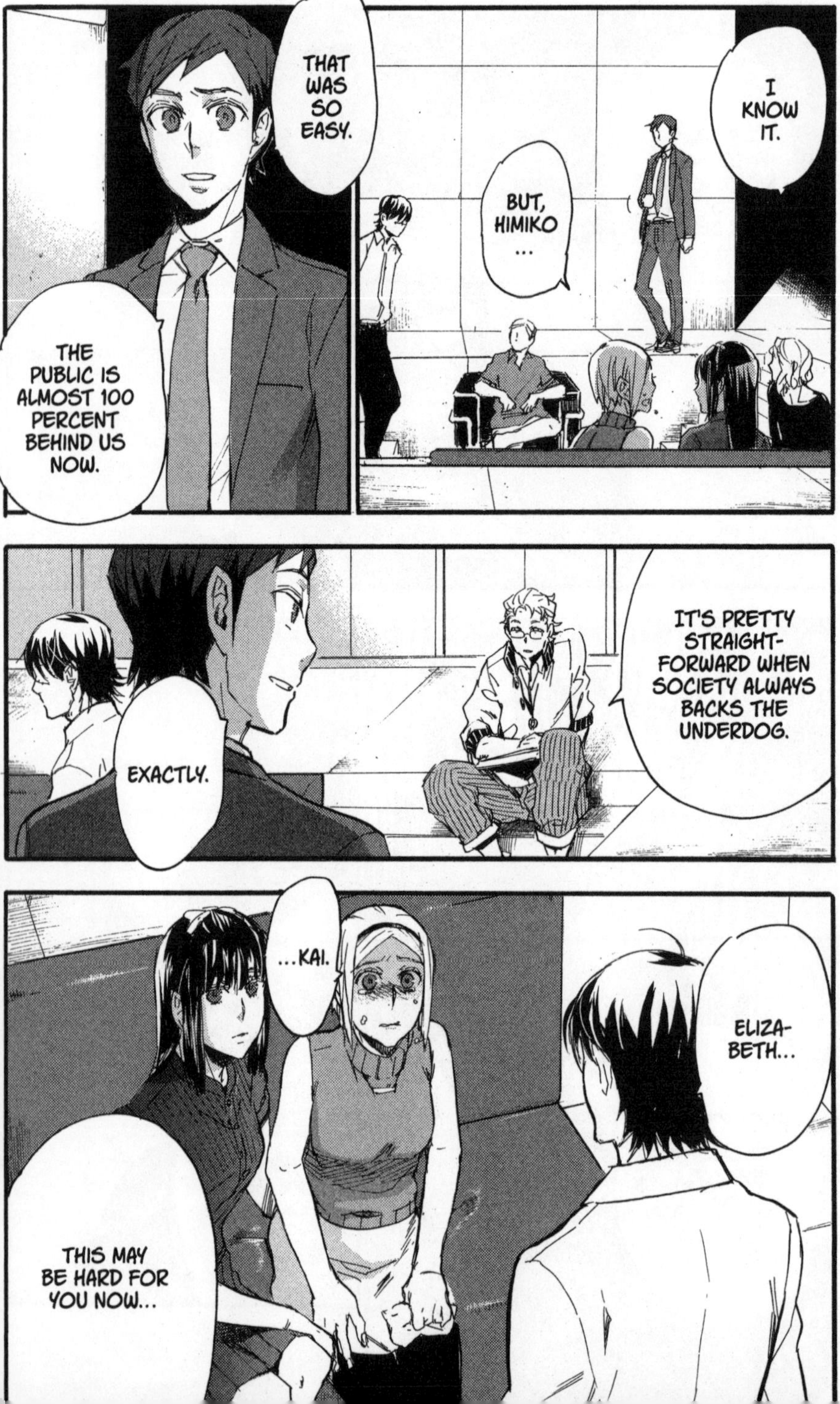
I KNOW IT.
BUT, HIMIKO...
THAT WAS SO EASY.
THE PUBLIC IS ALMOST 100 PERCENT BEHIND US NOW.
IT'S PRETTY STRAIGHT-FORWARD WHEN SOCIETY ALWAYS BACKS THE UNDERDOG.
EXACTLY.
ELIZA-BETH...
...KAI.
THIS MAY BE HARD FOR YOU NOW...

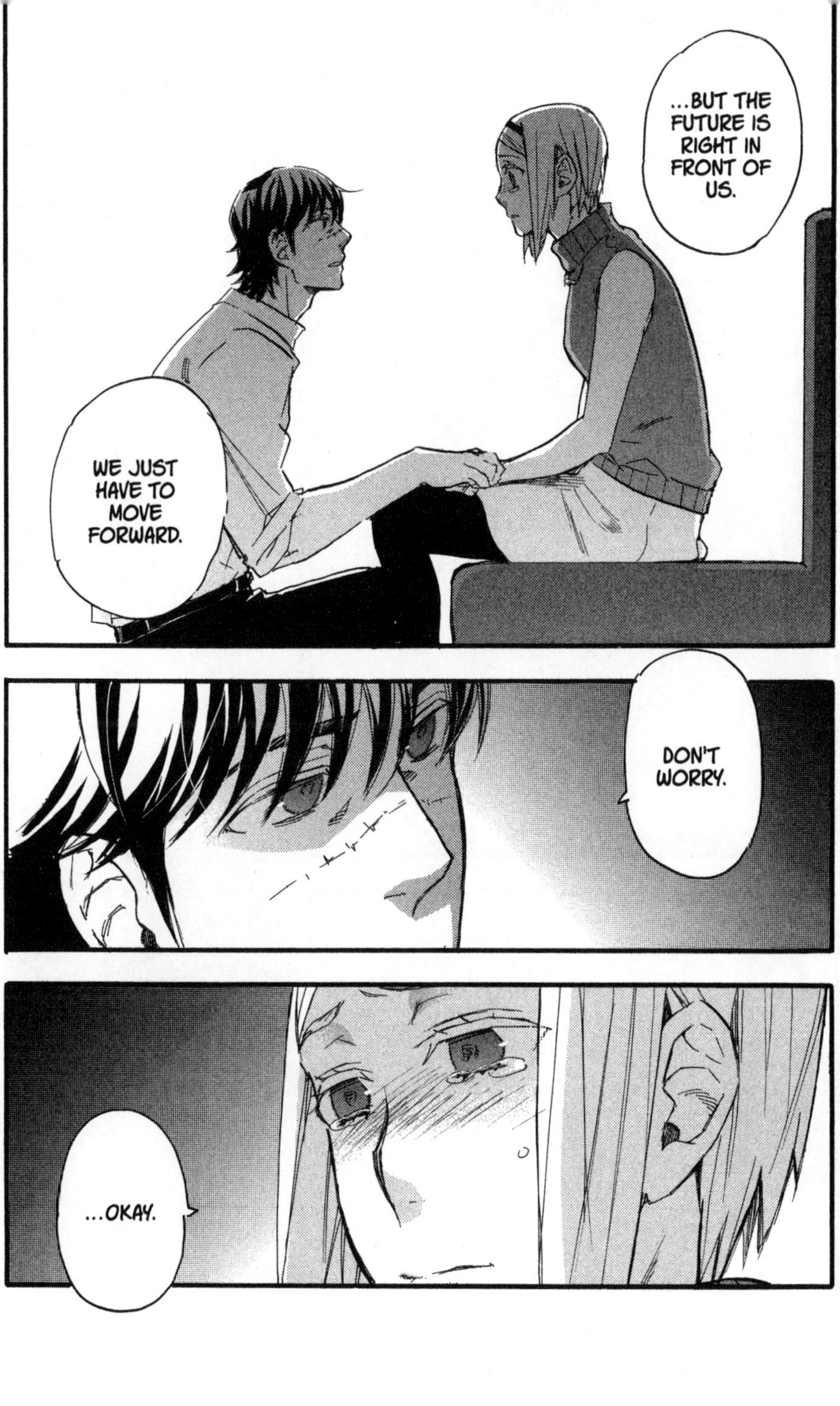
...BUT THE FUTURE IS RIGHT IN FRONT OF US.
WE JUST HAVE TO MOVE FORWARD.
DON'T WORRY.
...OKAY.

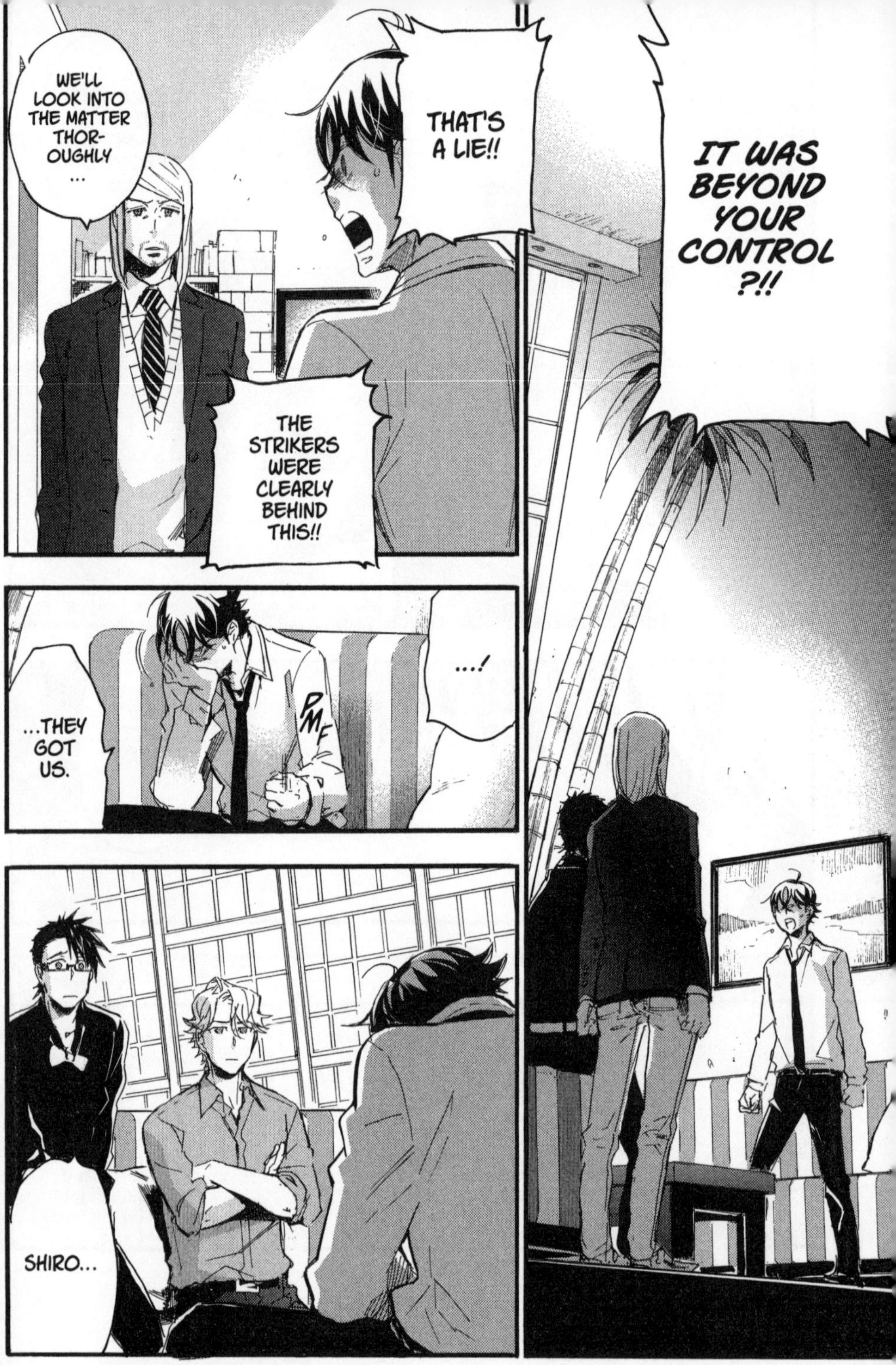
IT WAS BEYOND YOUR CONTROL ?!!
WE'LL LOOK INTO THE MATTER THOR-OUGHLY ...
THAT'S A LIE!!
THE STRIKERS WERE CLEARLY BEHIND THIS!!
...!
PMF
...THEY GOT US.
SHIRO...

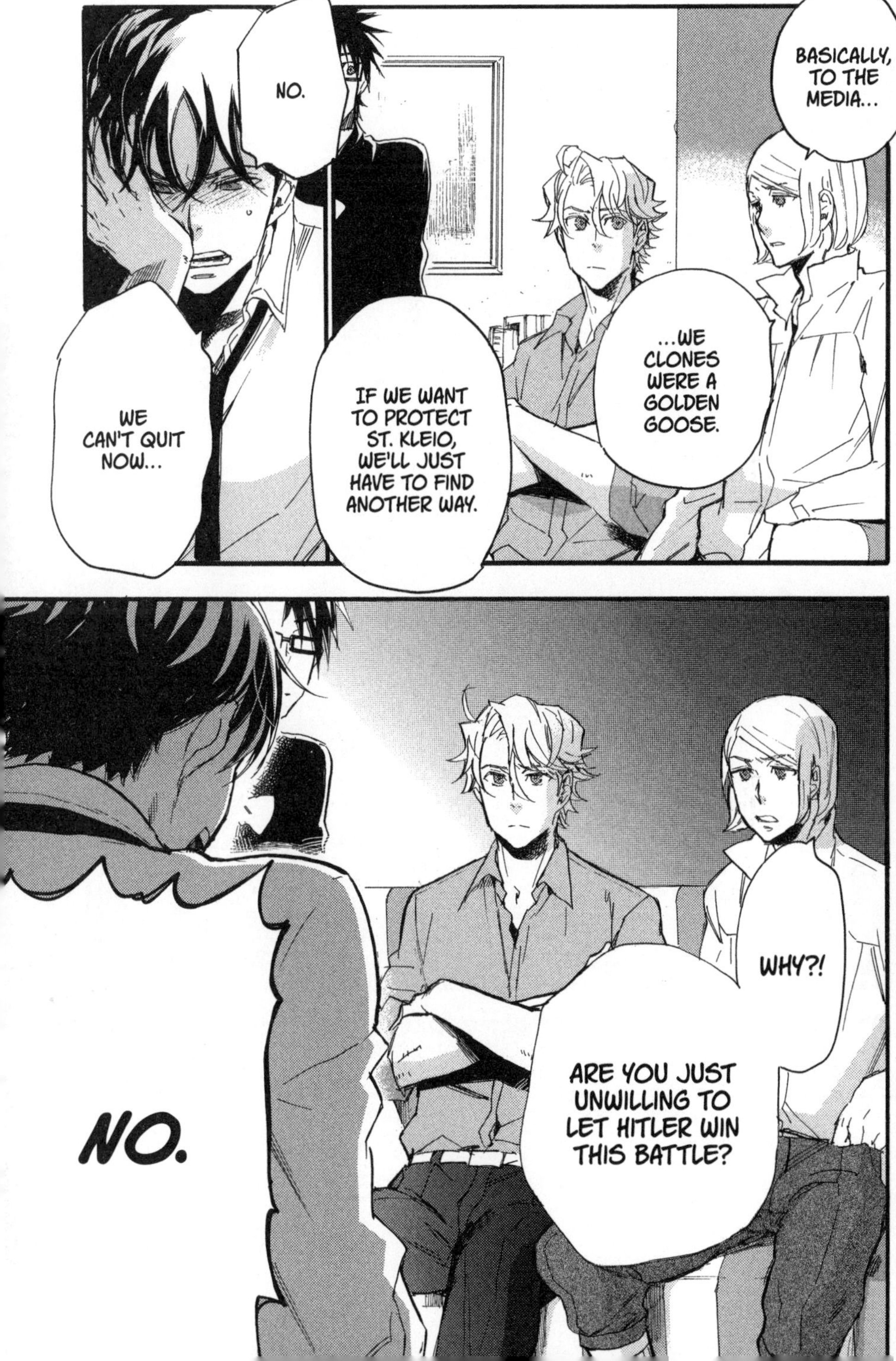
BASICALLY, TO THE MEDIA...
...WE CLONES WERE A GOLDEN GOOSE.
IF WE WANT TO PROTECT ST. KLEIO, WE'LL JUST HAVE TO FIND ANOTHER WAY.
NO.
WE CAN'T QUIT NOW...
WHY?!
ARE YOU JUST UNWILLING TO LET HITLER WIN THIS BATTLE?
NO.

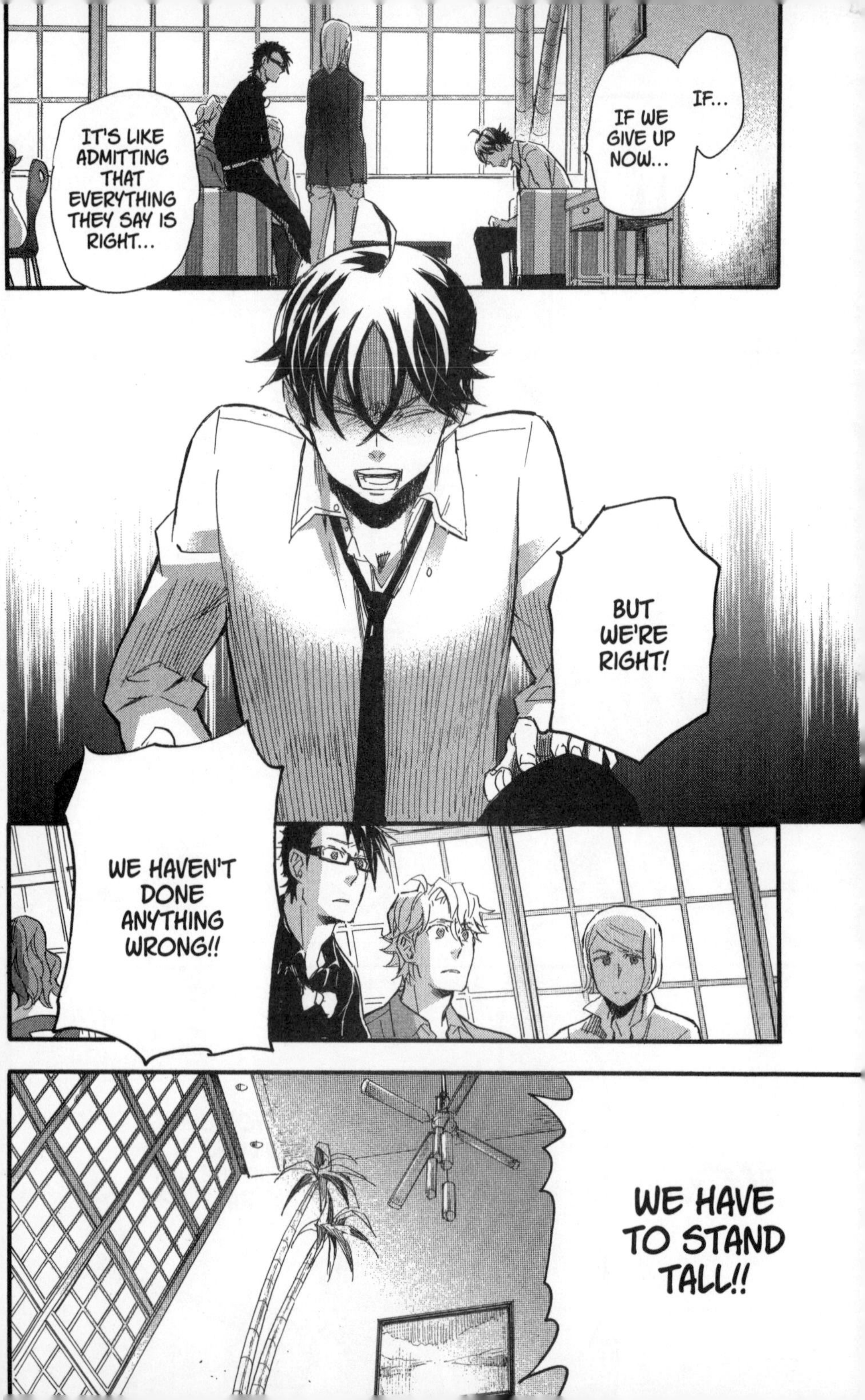
IF...
IF WE GIVE UP NOW...
IT'S LIKE ADMITTING THAT EVERYTHING THEY SAY IS RIGHT...
BUT WE'RE RIGHT!
WE HAVEN'T DONE ANYTHING WRONG!!
WE HAVE TO STAND TALL!!

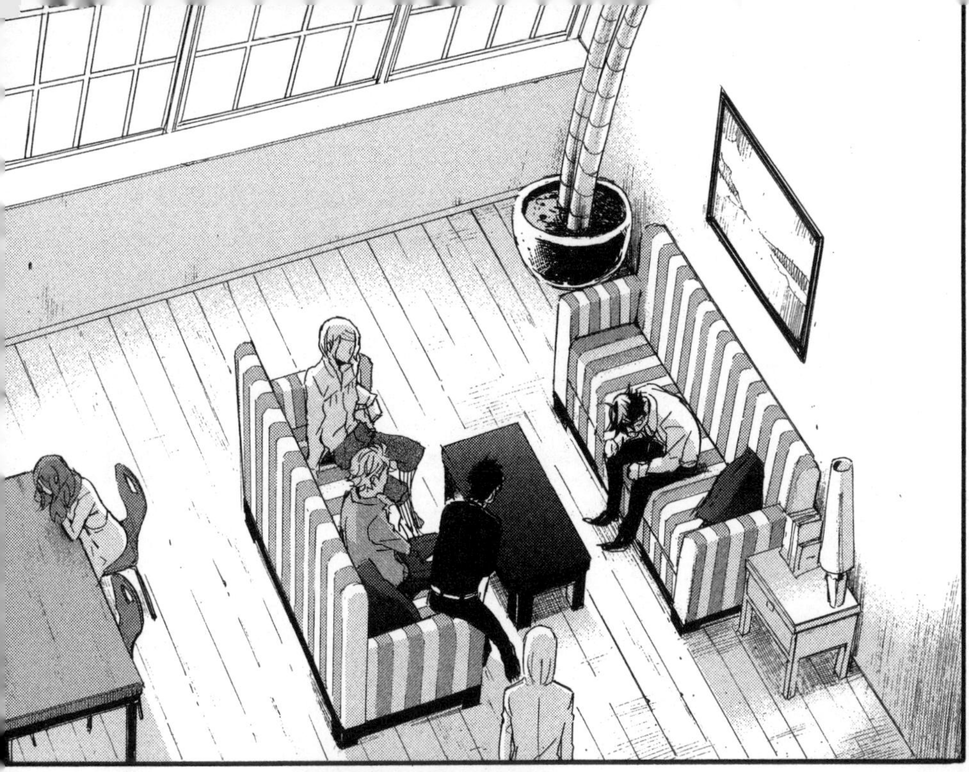

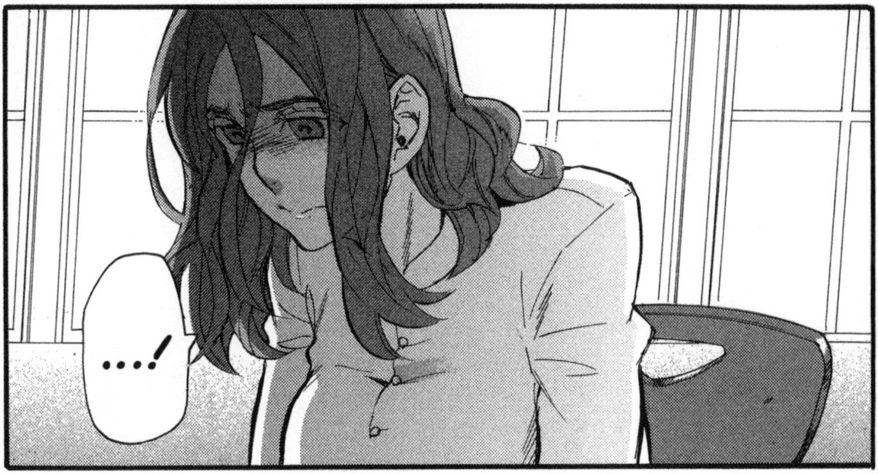
...!

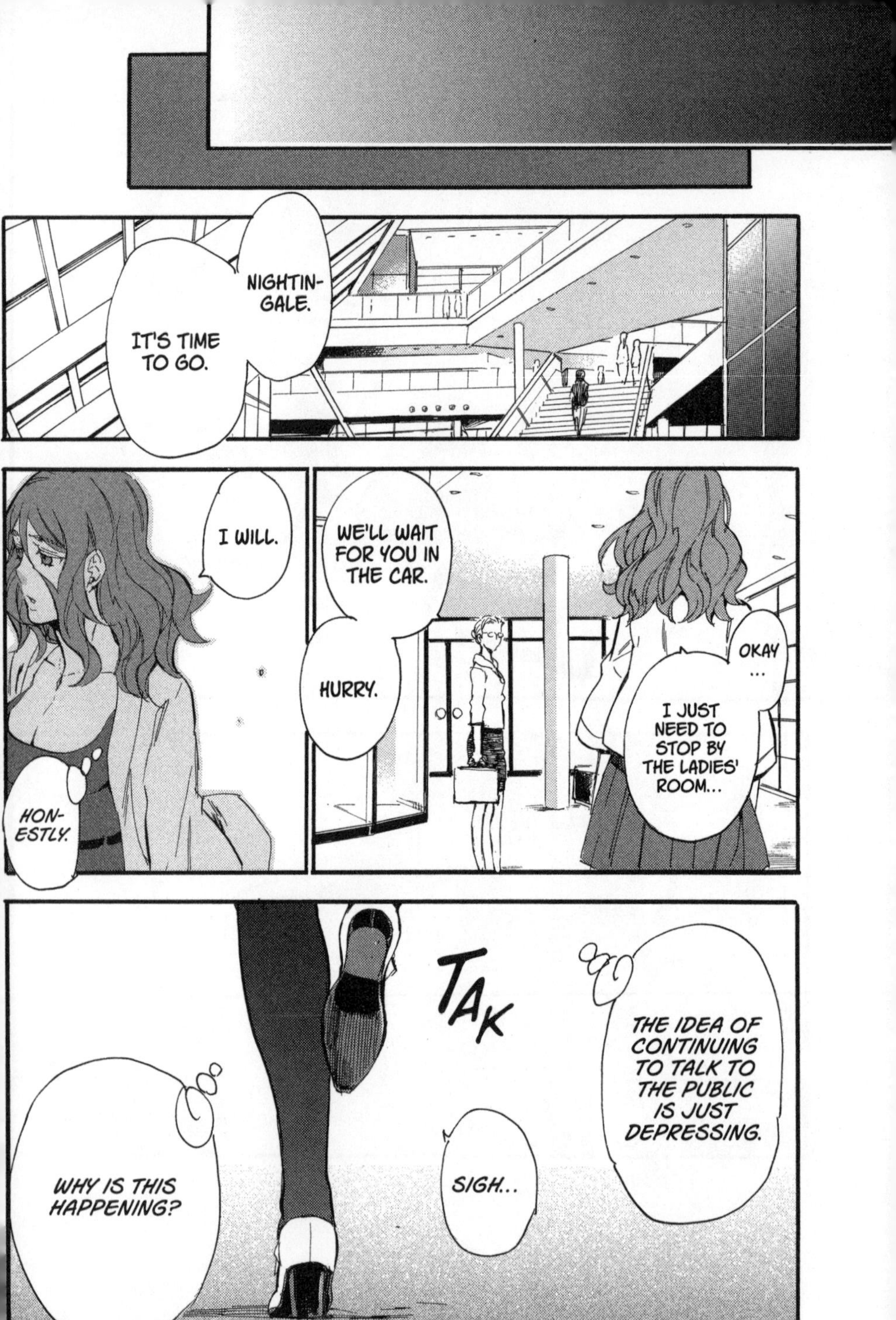
NIGHTIN-GALE.
IT'S TIME TO GO.
WE'LL WAIT FOR YOU IN THE CAR.
HURRY.
OKAY... I JUST NEED TO STOP BY THE LADIES' ROOM...
I WILL.
HON-ESTLY.
THE IDEA OF CONTINUING TO TALK TO THE PUBLIC IS JUST DEPRESSING.
TAK
SIGH...
WHY IS THIS HAPPENING?

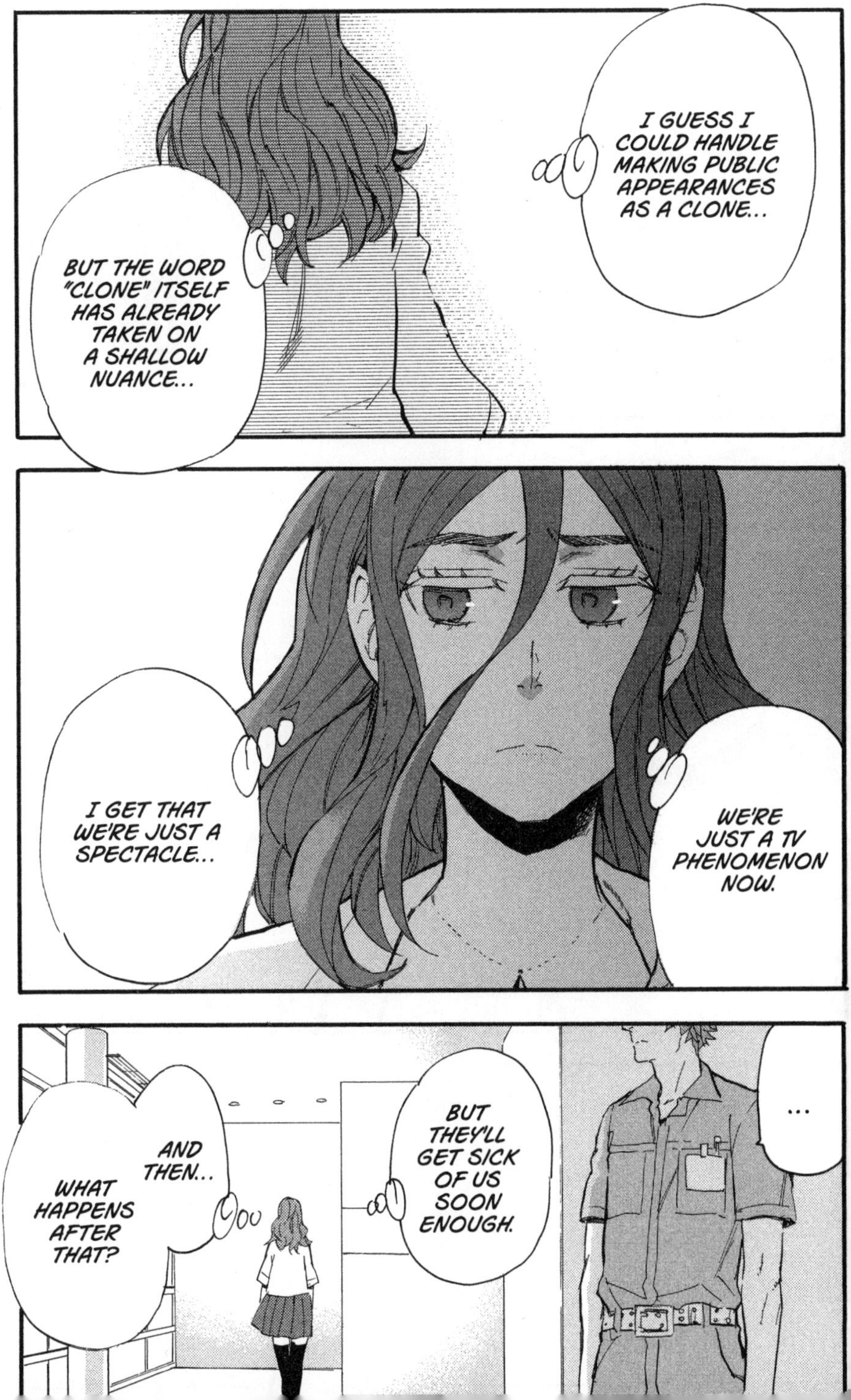
I GUESS I COULD HANDLE MAKING PUBLIC APPEARANCES AS A CLONE...
BUT THE WORD "CLONE" ITSELF HAS ALREADY TAKEN ON A SHALLOW NUANCE...
WE'RE JUST A TV PHENOMENON NOW.
I GET THAT WE'RE JUST A SPECTACLE...
...
BUT THEY'LL GET SICK OF US SOON ENOUGH.
AND THEN...
WHAT HAPPENS AFTER THAT?

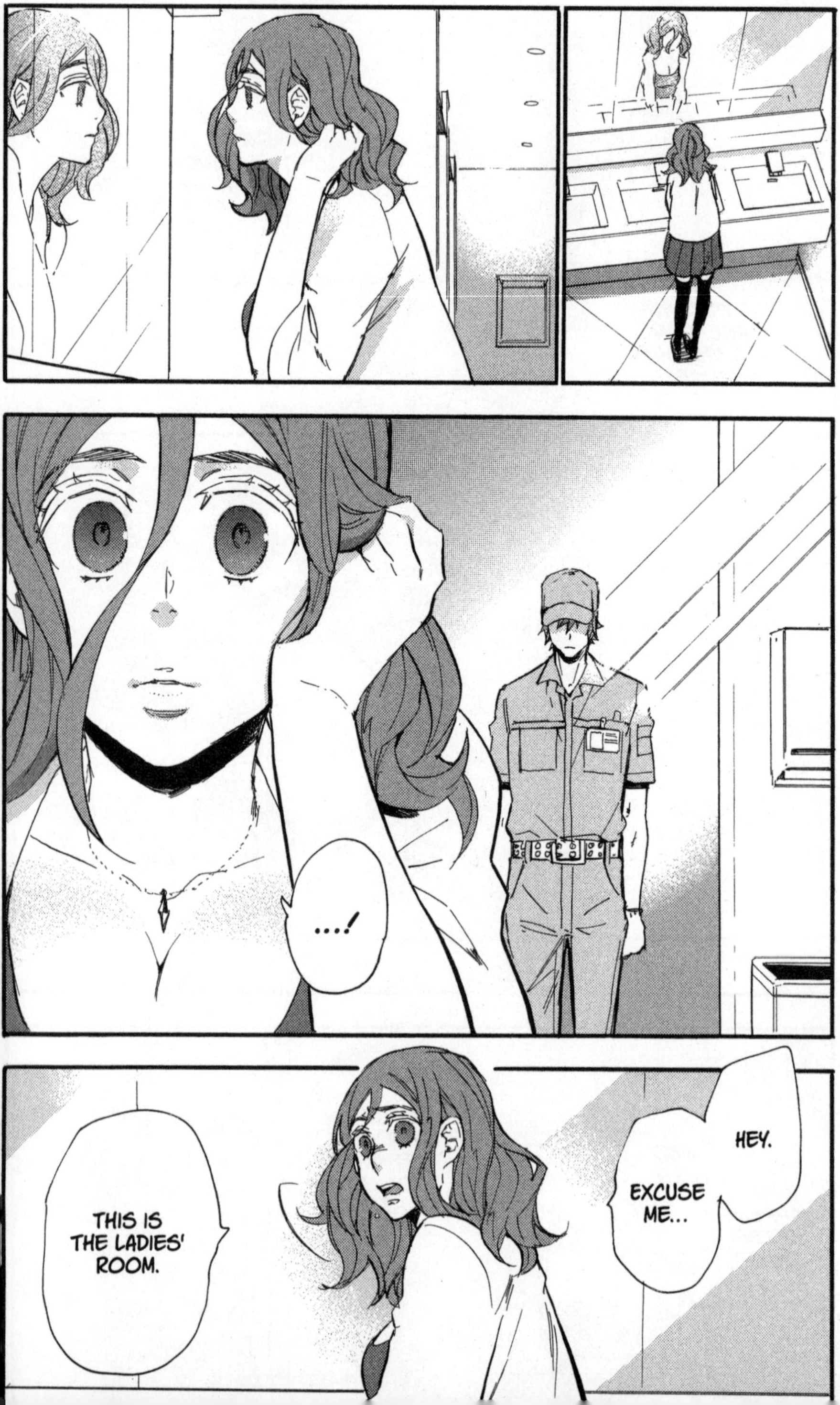
...!
HEY.
EXCUSE ME...
THIS IS THE LADIES' ROOM.

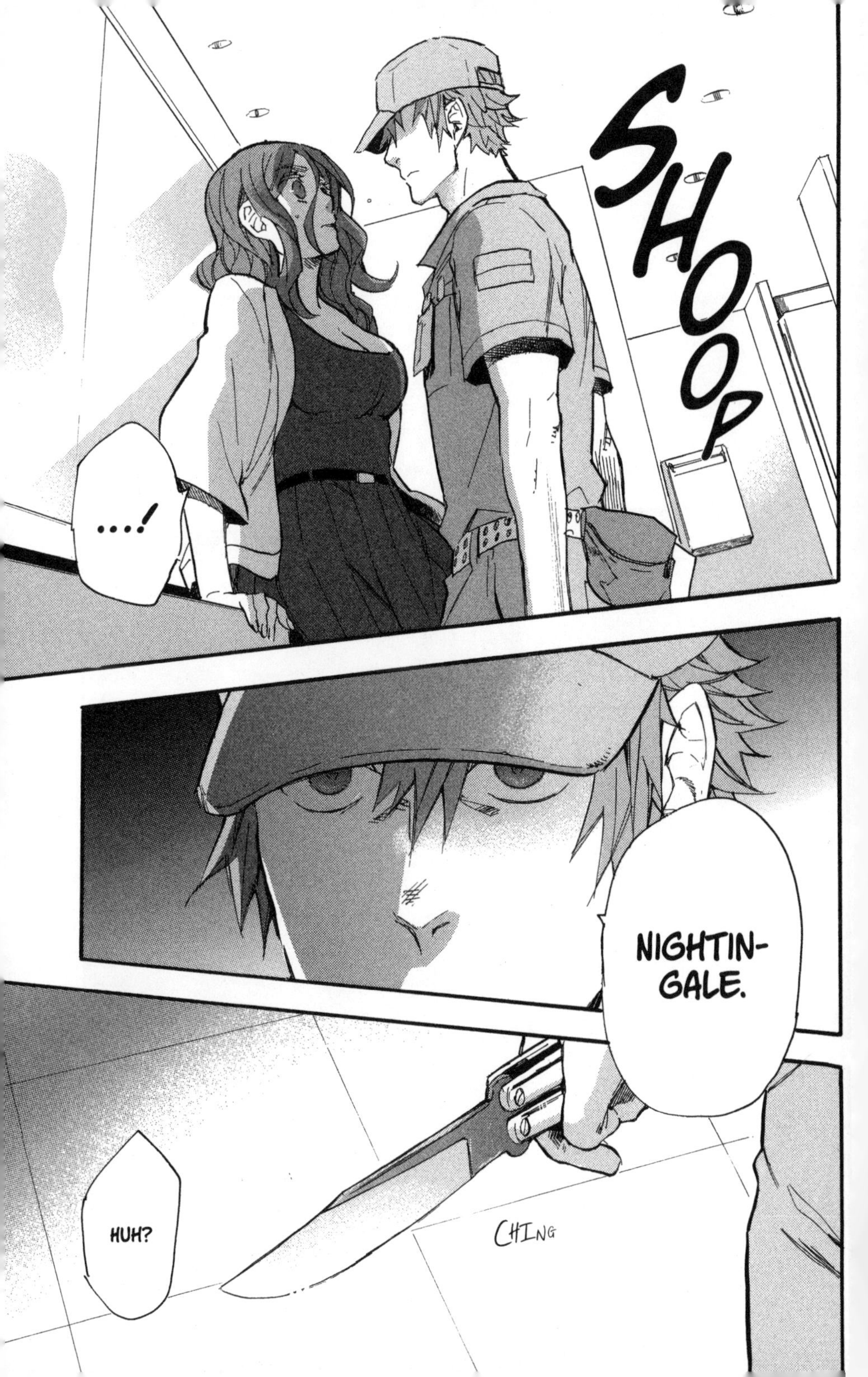
SHOOP
...!
NIGHTIN-GALE.
CHING
HUH?

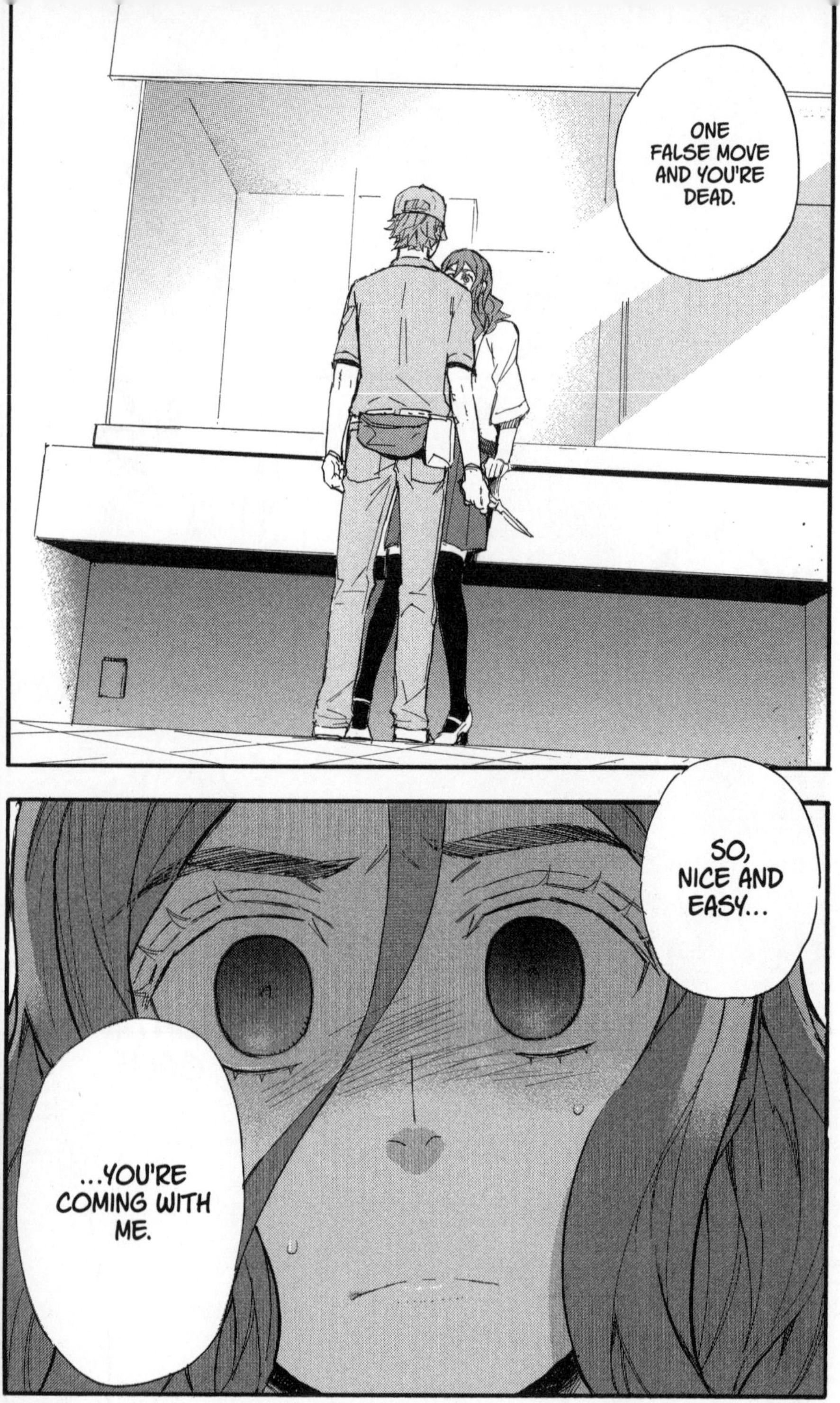
ONE FALSE MOVE AND YOU'RE DEAD.
SO, NICE AND EASY...
...YOU'RE COMING WITH ME.

# CHAPTER sixty-four

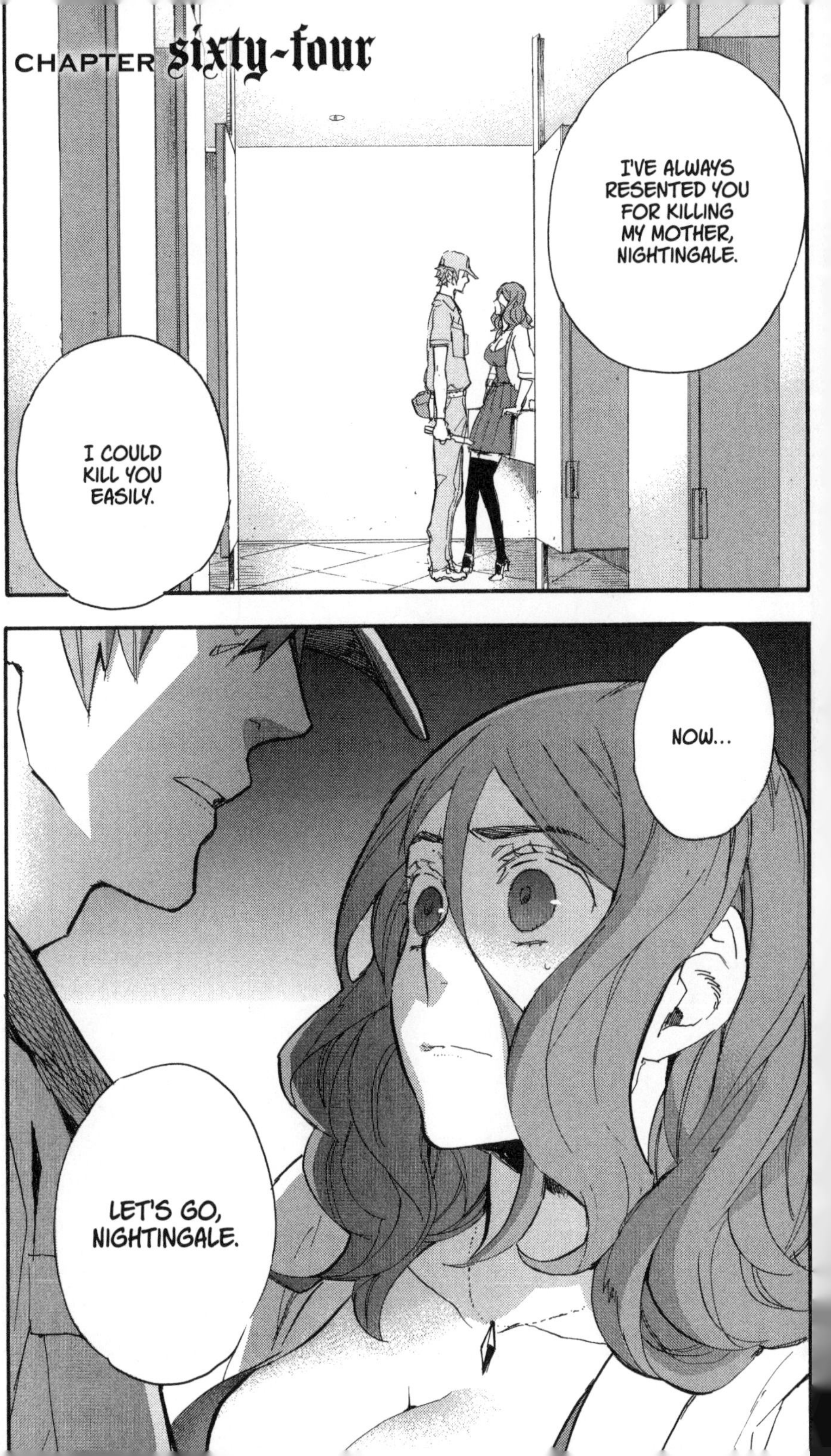
I'VE ALWAYS RESENTED YOU FOR KILLING MY MOTHER, NIGHTINGALE.
I COULD KILL YOU EASILY.
NOW...
LET'S GO, NIGHTINGALE.

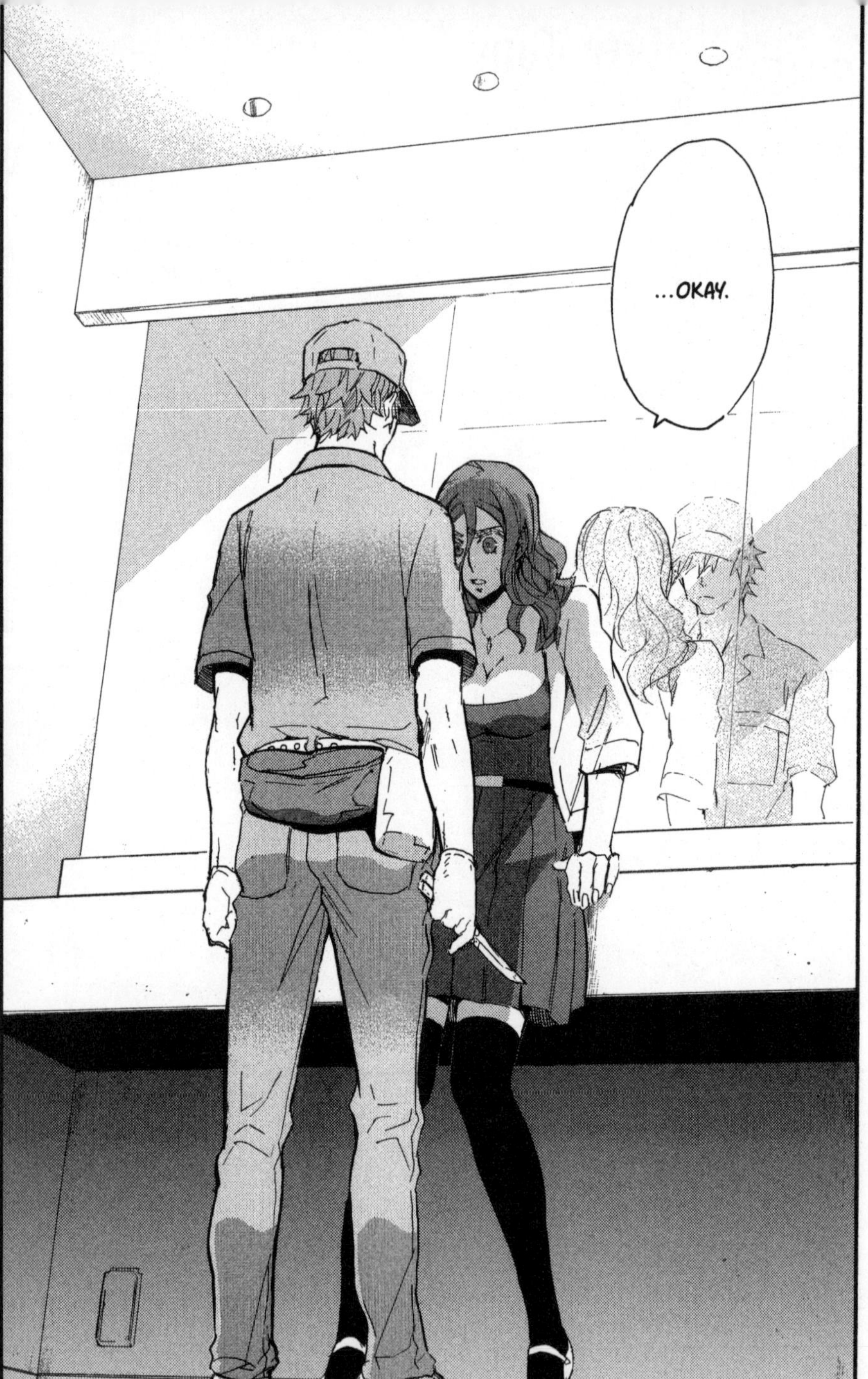
...OKAY.

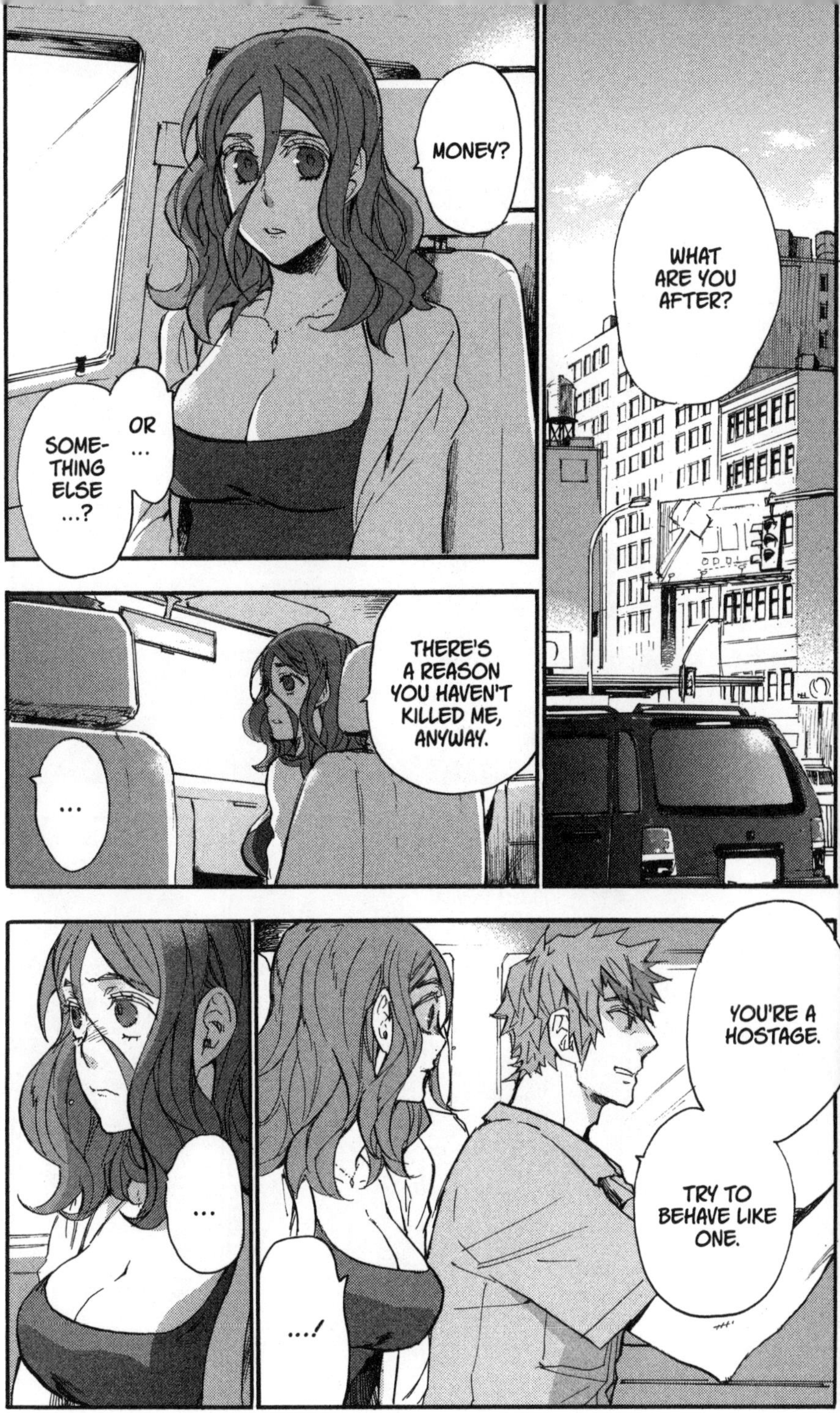
WHAT ARE YOU AFTER?
MONEY?
OR ...
SOME-THING ELSE ...?
THERE'S A REASON YOU HAVEN'T KILLED ME, ANYWAY.
...
YOU'RE A HOSTAGE.
TRY TO BEHAVE LIKE ONE.
...!
...

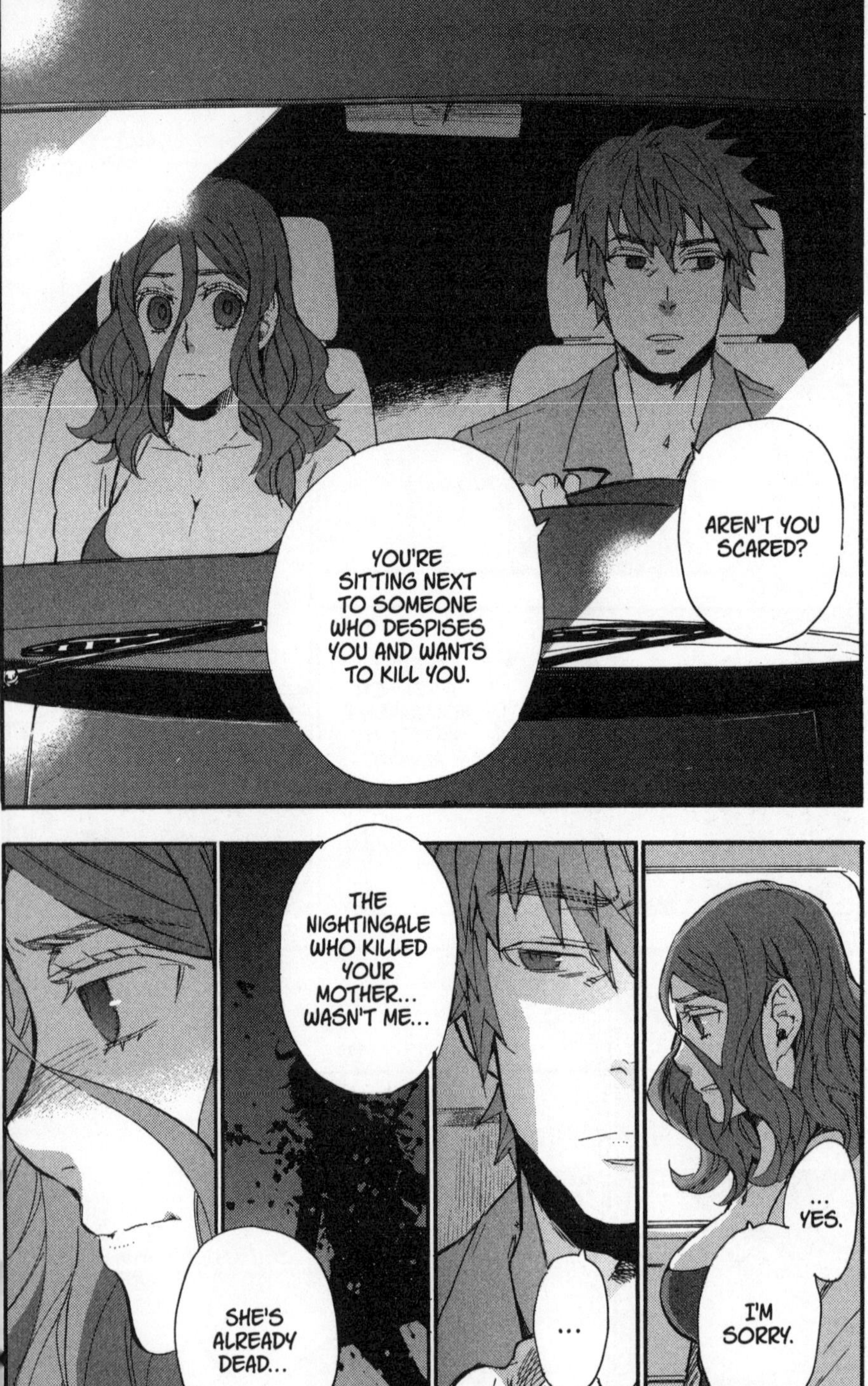
AREN'T YOU SCARED?
YOU'RE SITTING NEXT TO SOMEONE WHO DESPISES YOU AND WANTS TO KILL YOU.
...YES.
I'M SORRY.
THE NIGHTINGALE WHO KILLED YOUR MOTHER... WASN'T ME...
...
SHE'S ALREADY DEAD...

YEAH, BUT YOU'RE CLONES. WHAT DO I CARE WHICH NIGHTINGALE YOU ARE?

IT DOESN'T MATTER.

IF YOU'RE NIGHTINGALE, YOU'RE GUILTY!

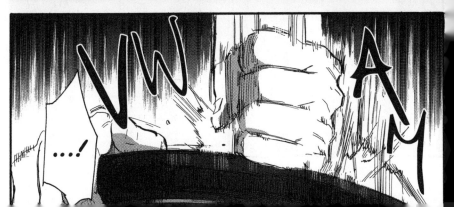

VW

AM

....!

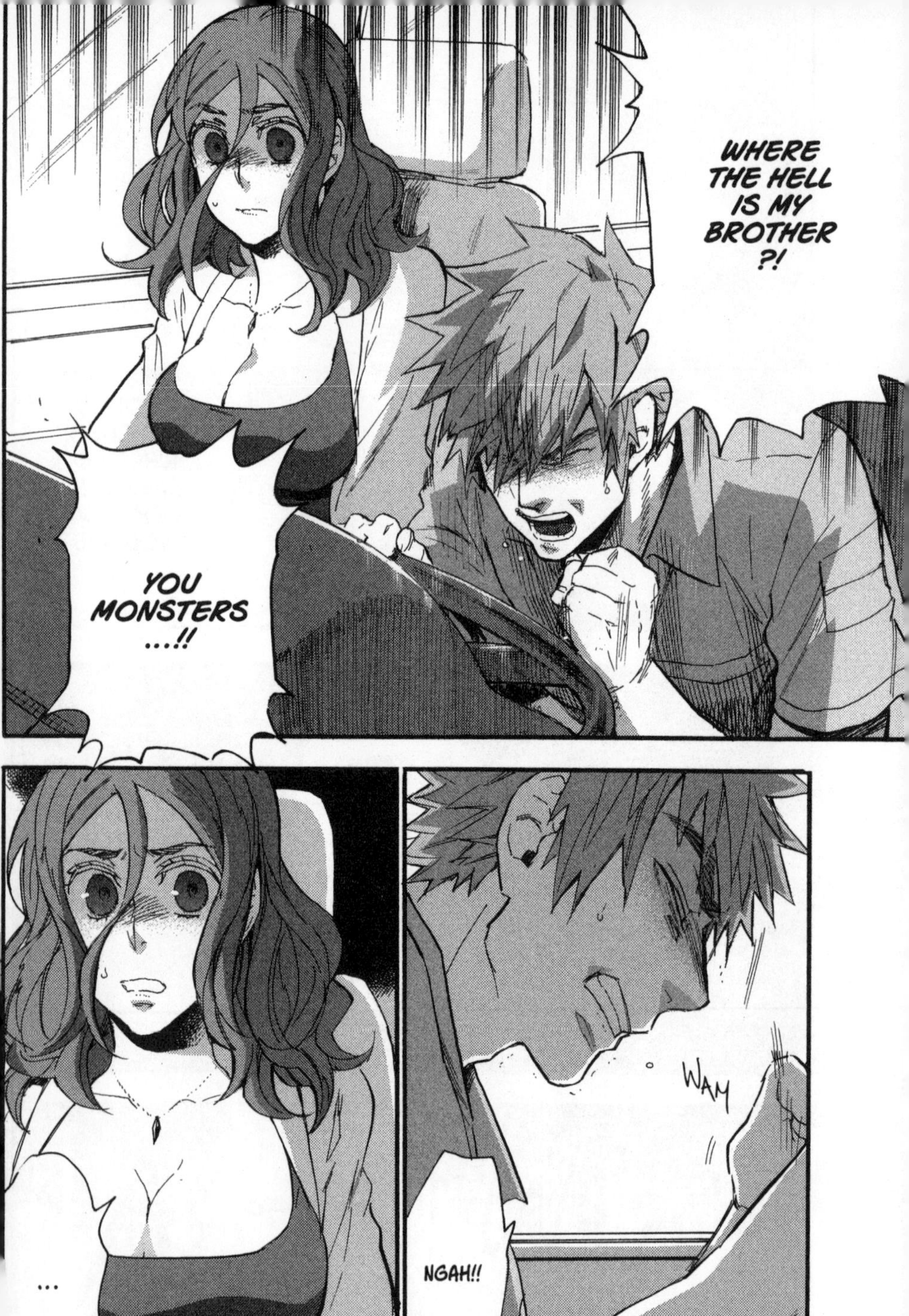
WHERE THE HELL IS MY BROTHER ?!
YOU MONSTERS ...!!
WAM
NGAH!!
...

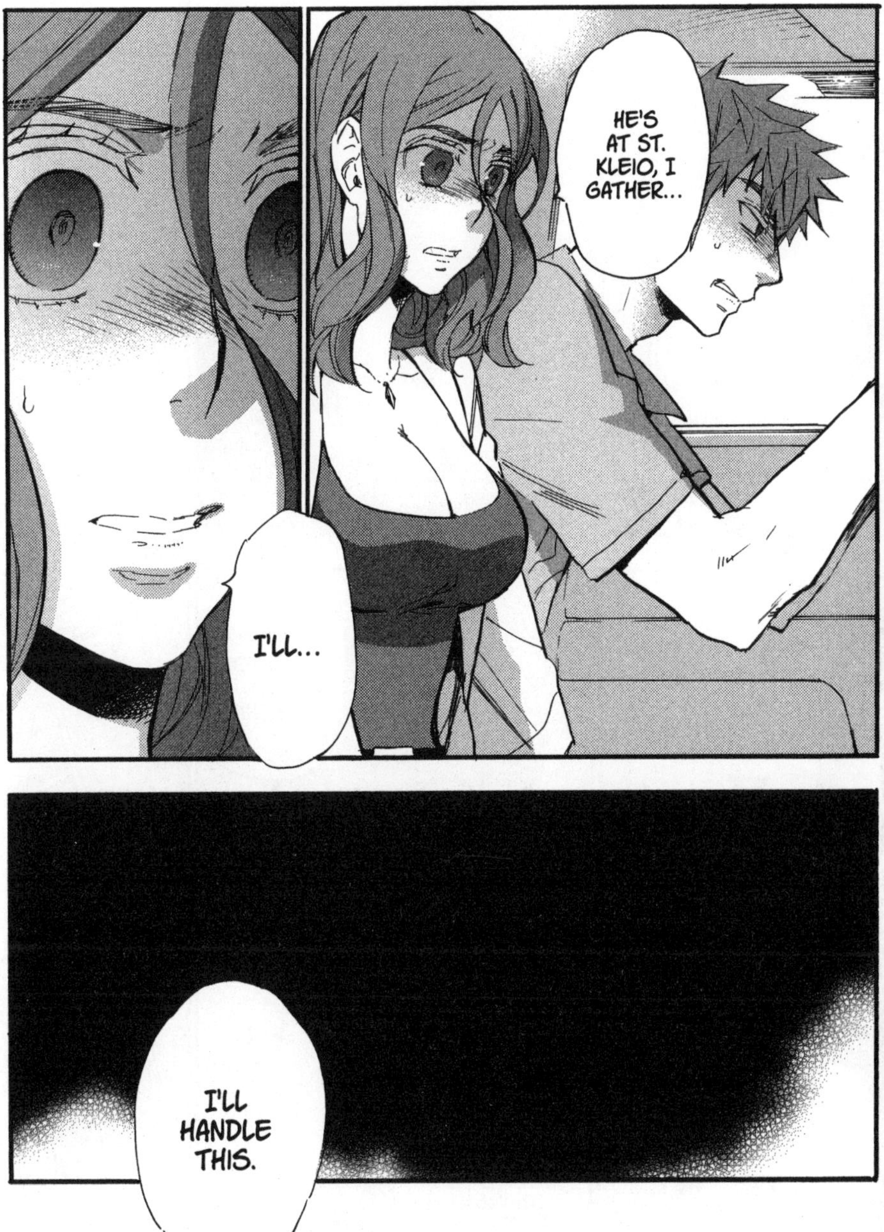
HE'S AT ST. KLEIO, I GATHER...
I'LL...
I'LL HANDLE THIS.

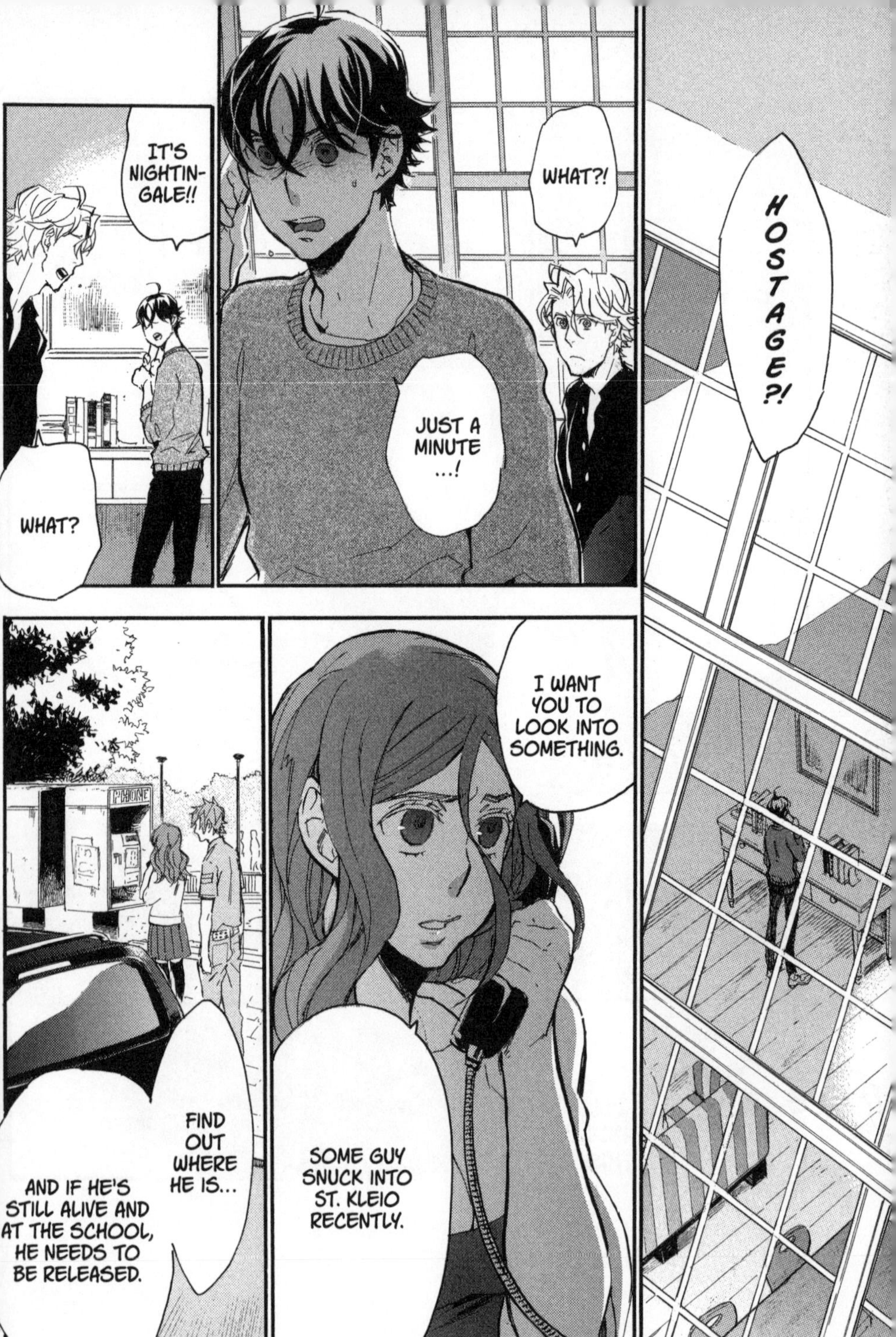
HOSTAGE?!
WHAT?!
JUST A MINUTE ...!
IT'S NIGHTIN-GALE!!
WHAT?
I WANT YOU TO LOOK INTO SOMETHING.
SOME GUY SNUCK INTO ST. KLEIO RECENTLY.
FIND OUT WHERE HE IS...
AND IF HE'S STILL ALIVE AND AT THE SCHOOL, HE NEEDS TO BE RELEASED.

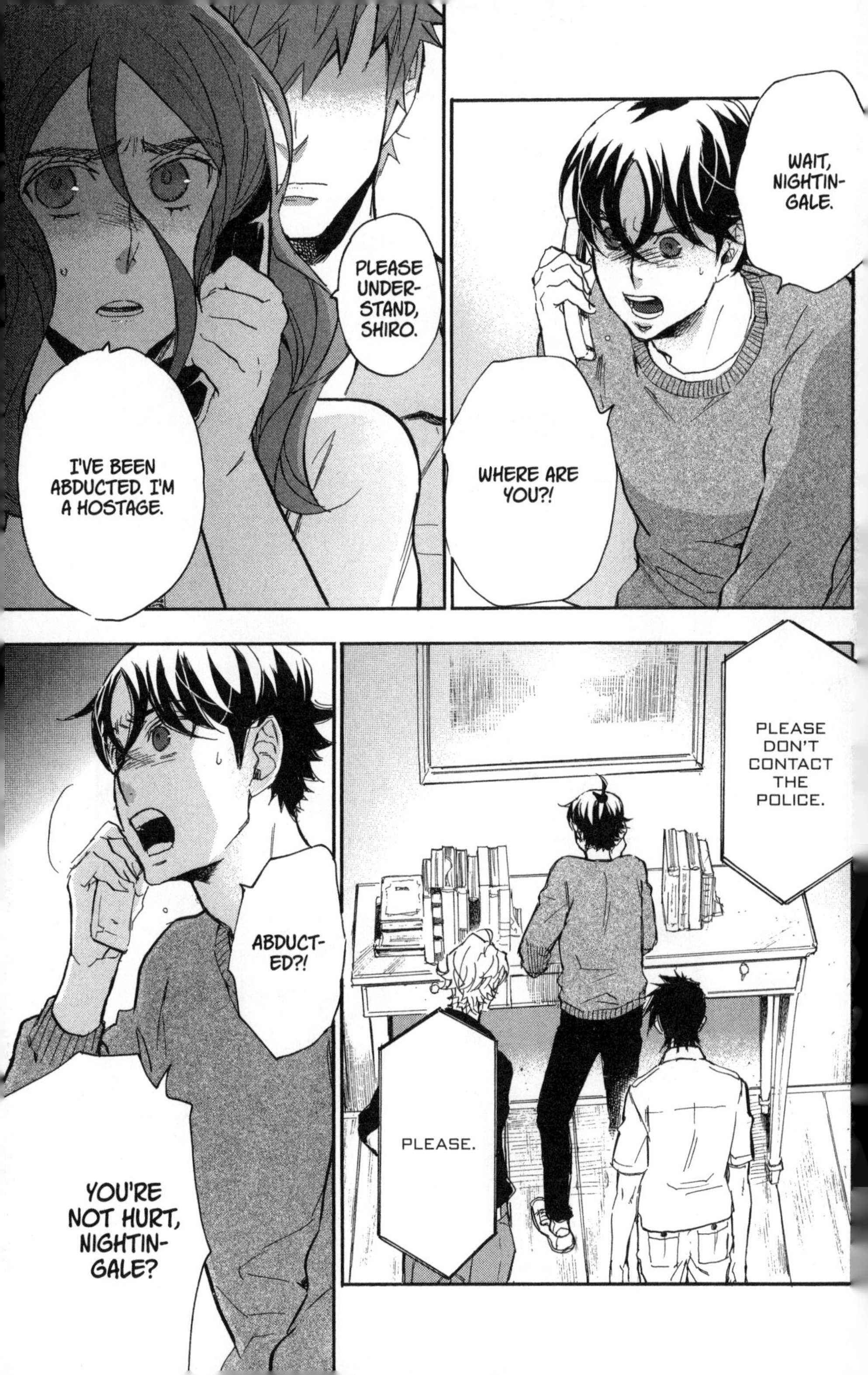
WAIT, NIGHTINGALE.
WHERE ARE YOU?!
PLEASE UNDERSTAND, SHIRO.
I'VE BEEN ABDUCTED. I'M A HOSTAGE.
PLEASE DON'T CONTACT THE POLICE.
PLEASE.
ABDUCTED?!
YOU'RE NOT HURT, NIGHTINGALE?

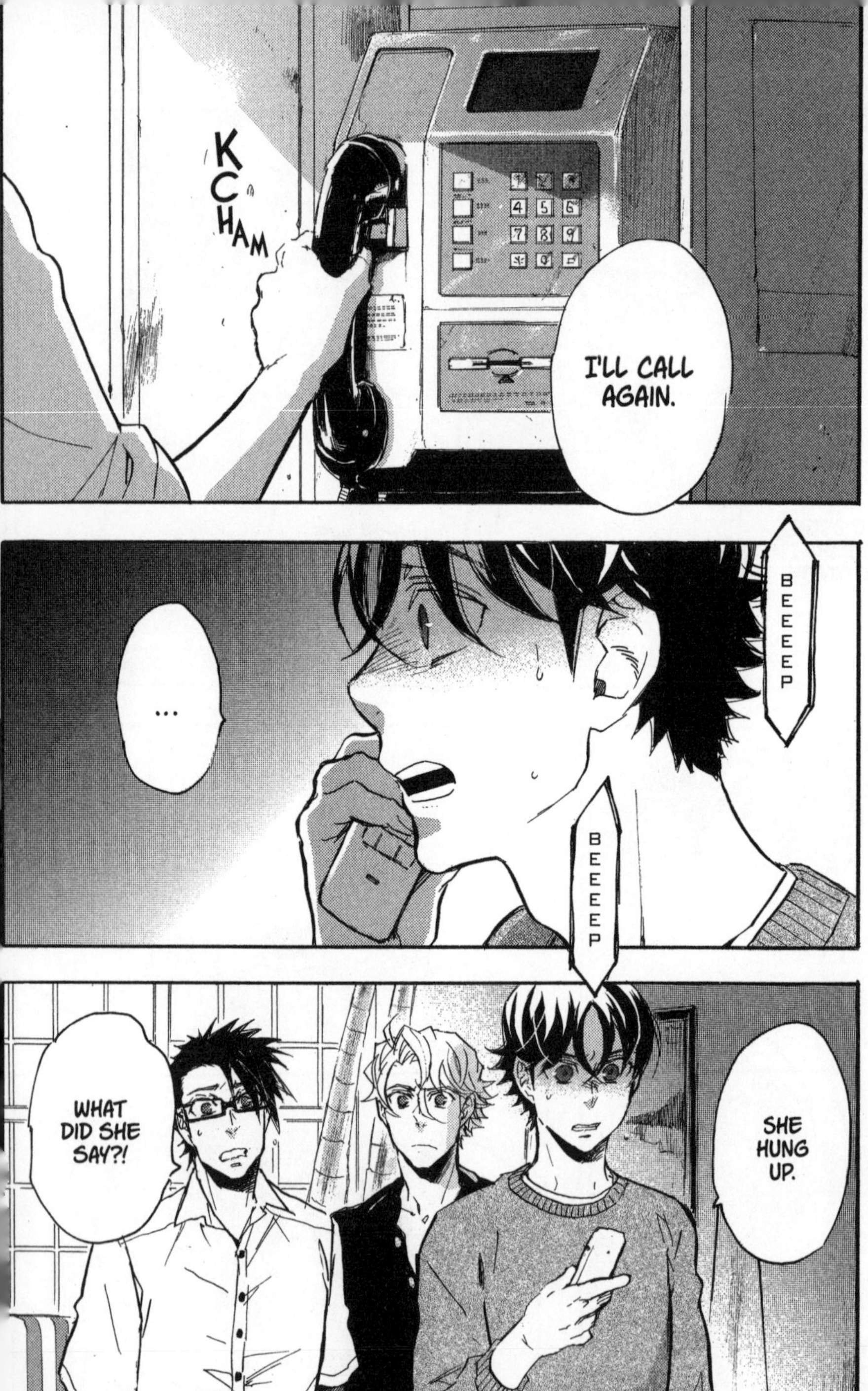
I'LL CALL AGAIN.
KCHAM
BEEEEP
...
BEEEEP
SHE HUNG UP.
WHAT DID SHE SAY?!

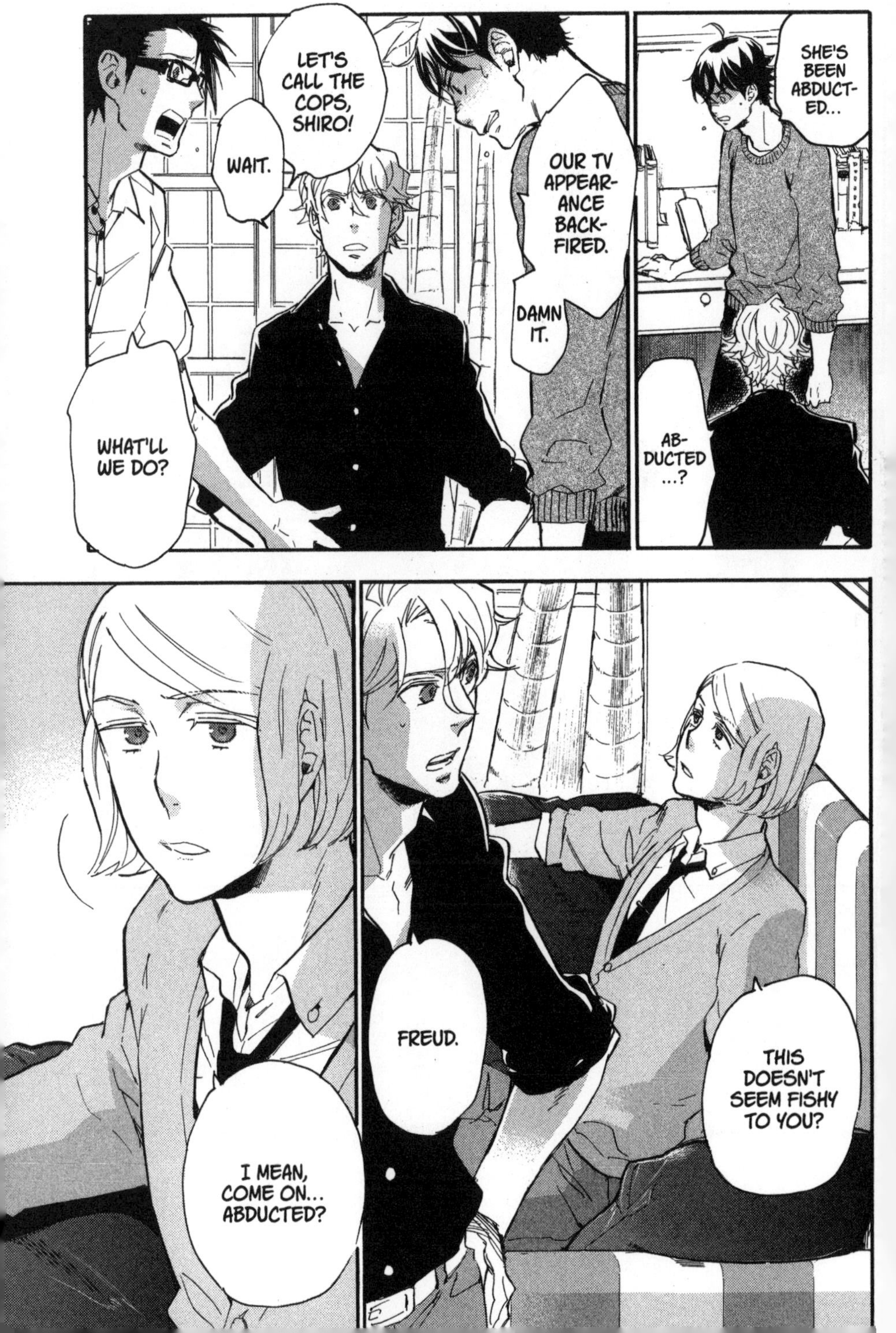
SHE'S BEEN ABDUCTED...
ABDUCTED...?
OUR TV APPEARANCE BACKFIRED.
DAMN IT.
WHAT'LL WE DO?
LET'S CALL THE COPS, SHIRO!
WAIT.
THIS DOESN'T SEEM FISHY TO YOU?
FREUD.
I MEAN, COME ON... ABDUCTED?

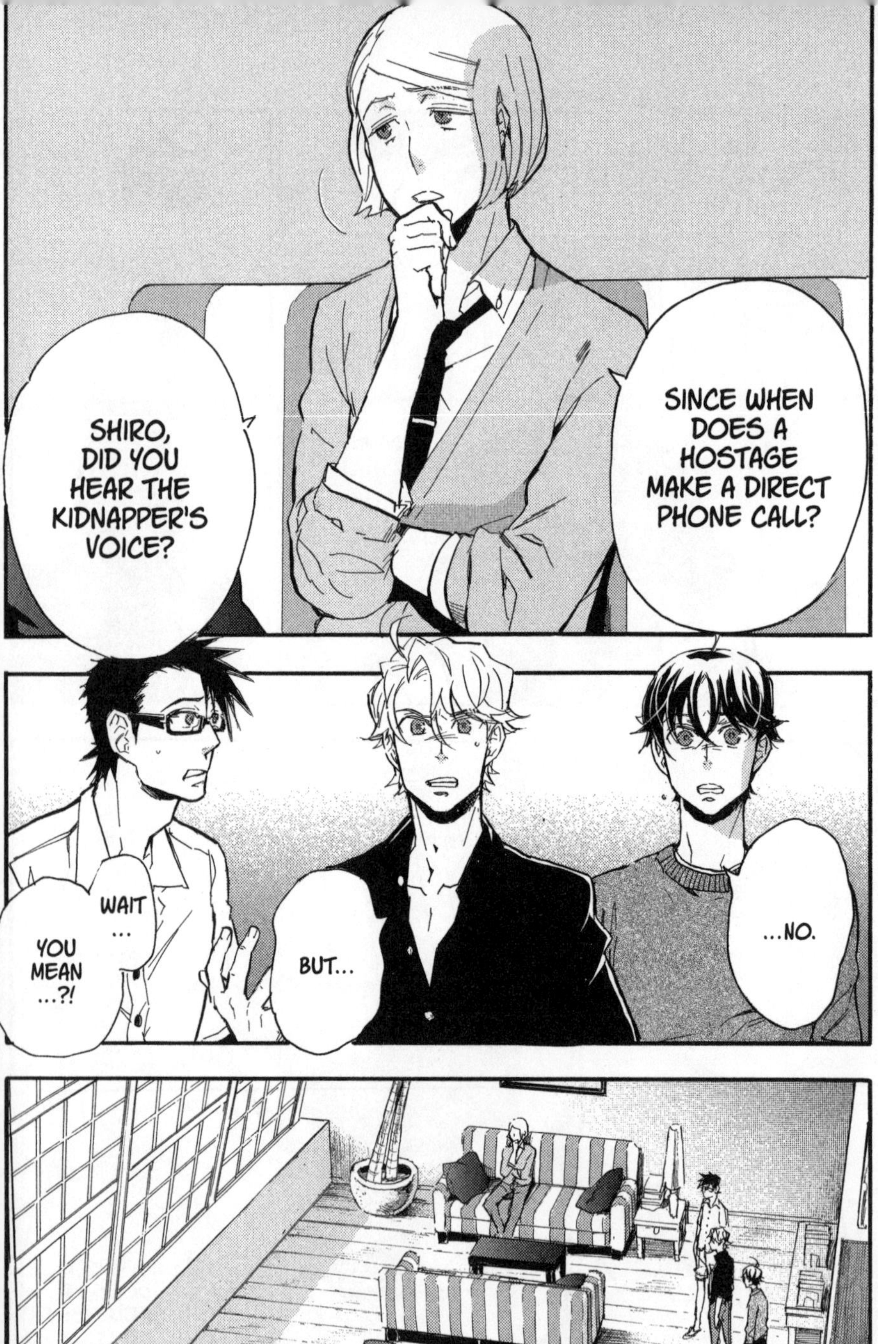
SINCE WHEN DOES A HOSTAGE MAKE A DIRECT PHONE CALL?
SHIRO, DID YOU HEAR THE KIDNAPPER'S VOICE?
...NO.
BUT...
WAIT...
YOU MEAN...?!

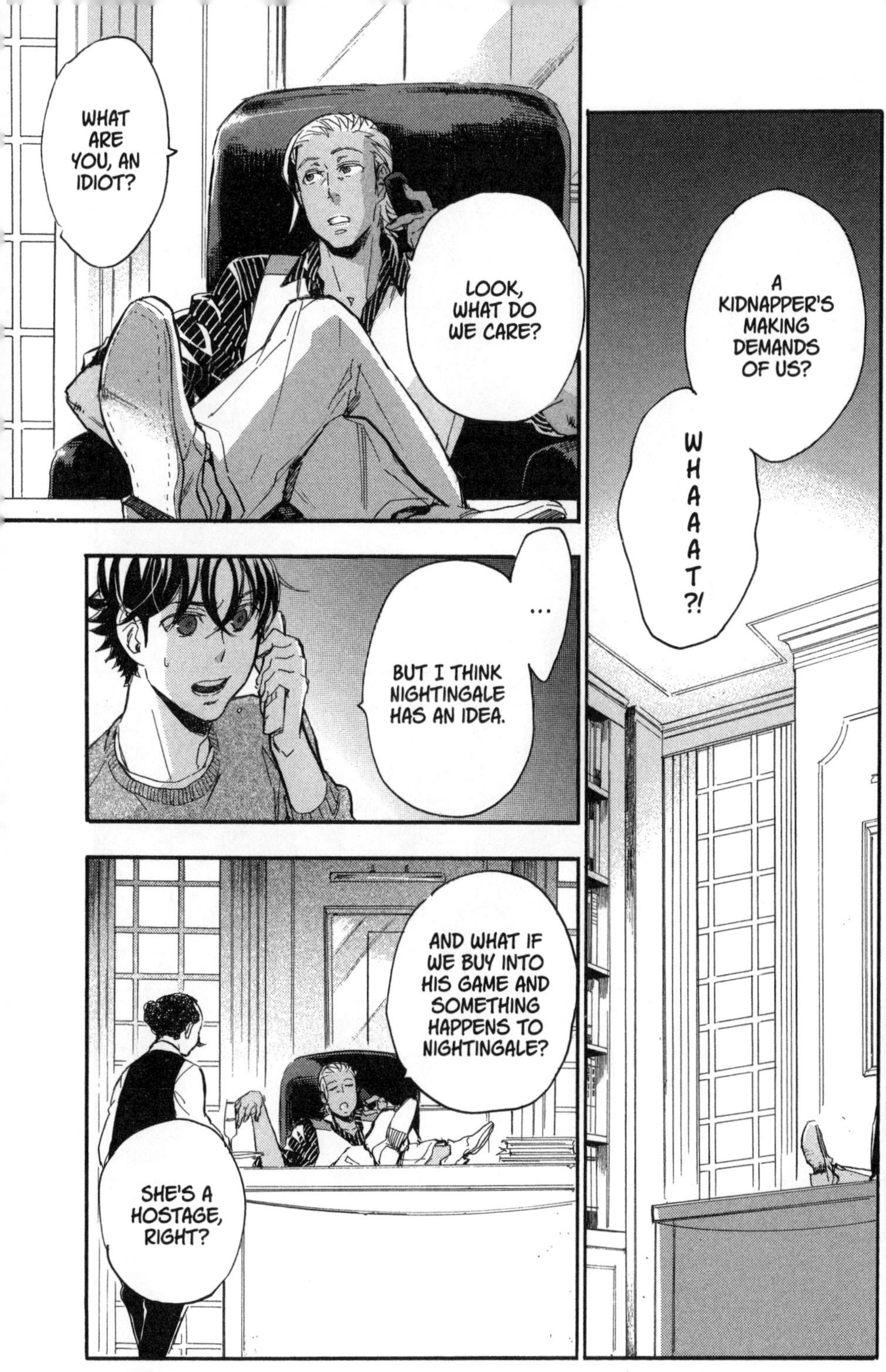
A KIDNAPPER'S MAKING DEMANDS OF US?
WHAAAAT?!
LOOK, WHAT DO WE CARE?
WHAT ARE YOU, AN IDIOT?
...
BUT I THINK NIGHTINGALE HAS AN IDEA.
AND WHAT IF WE BUY INTO HIS GAME AND SOMETHING HAPPENS TO NIGHTINGALE?
SHE'S A HOSTAGE, RIGHT?

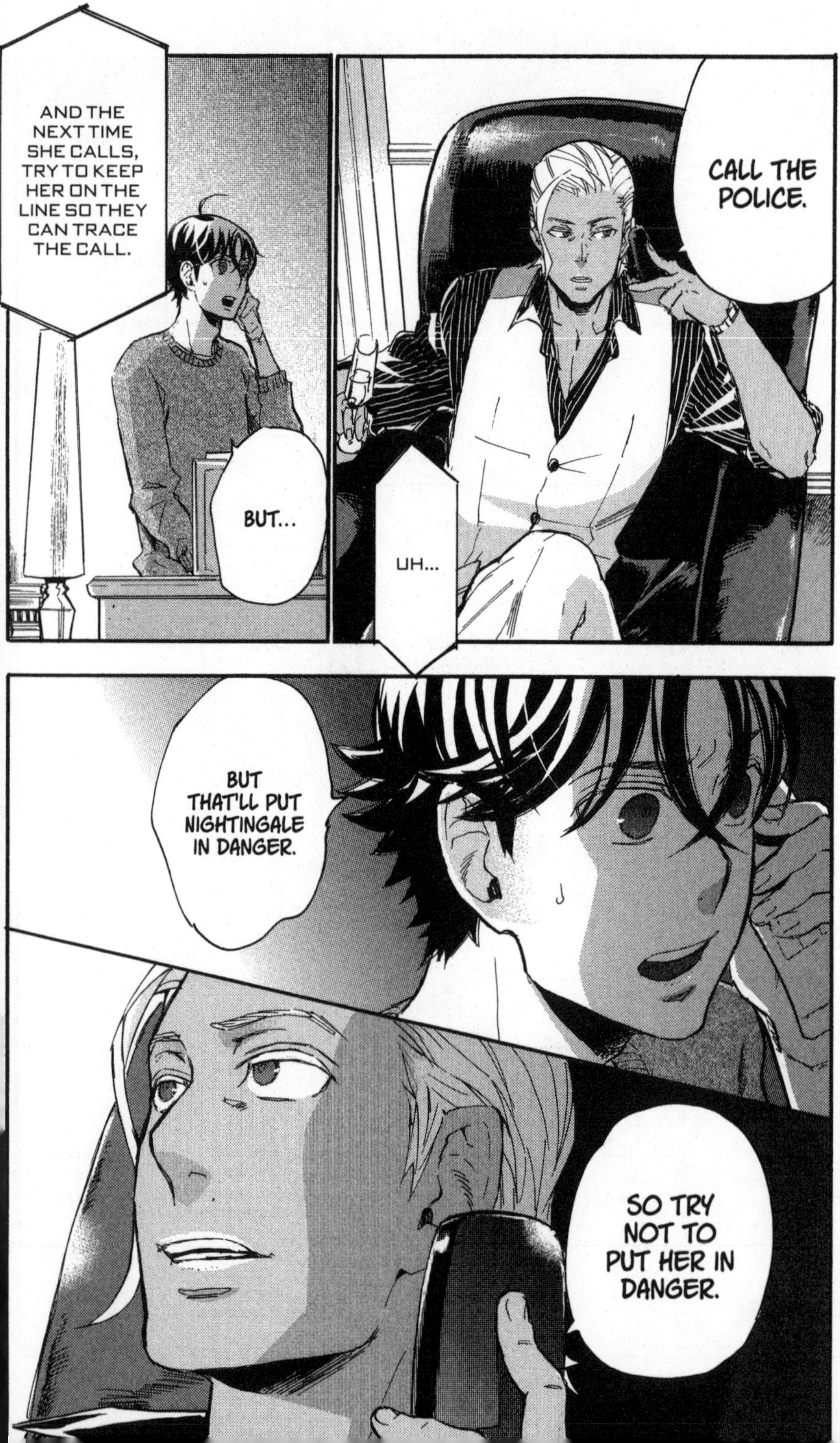
CALL THE POLICE.
UH...
AND THE NEXT TIME SHE CALLS, TRY TO KEEP HER ON THE LINE SO THEY CAN TRACE THE CALL.
BUT...
BUT THAT'LL PUT NIGHTINGALE IN DANGER.
SO TRY NOT TO PUT HER IN DANGER.

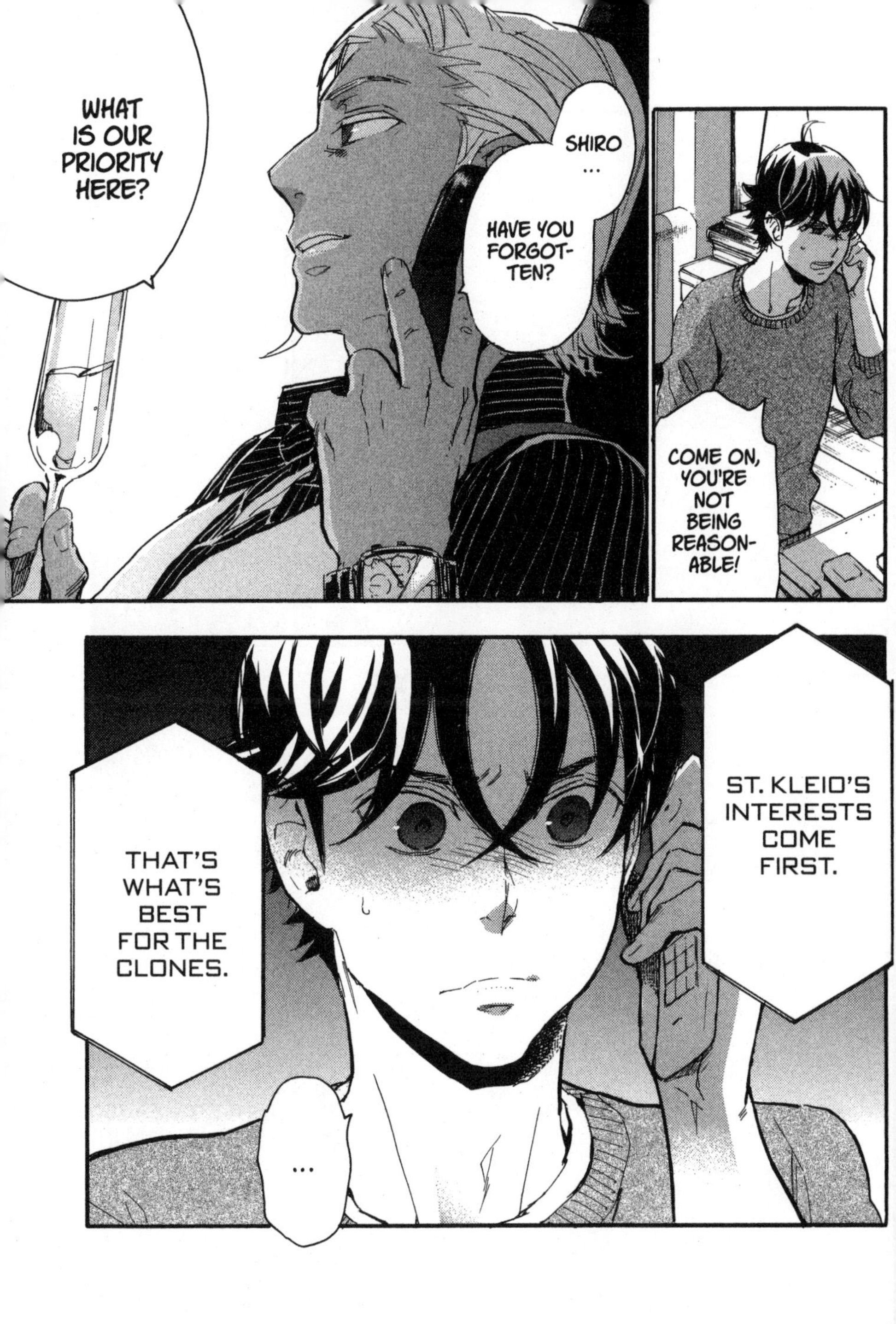
COME ON, YOU'RE NOT BEING REASON-ABLE!
SHIRO ...
HAVE YOU FORGOT-TEN?
WHAT IS OUR PRIORITY HERE?
ST. KLEIO'S INTERESTS COME FIRST.
THAT'S WHAT'S BEST FOR THE CLONES.
...

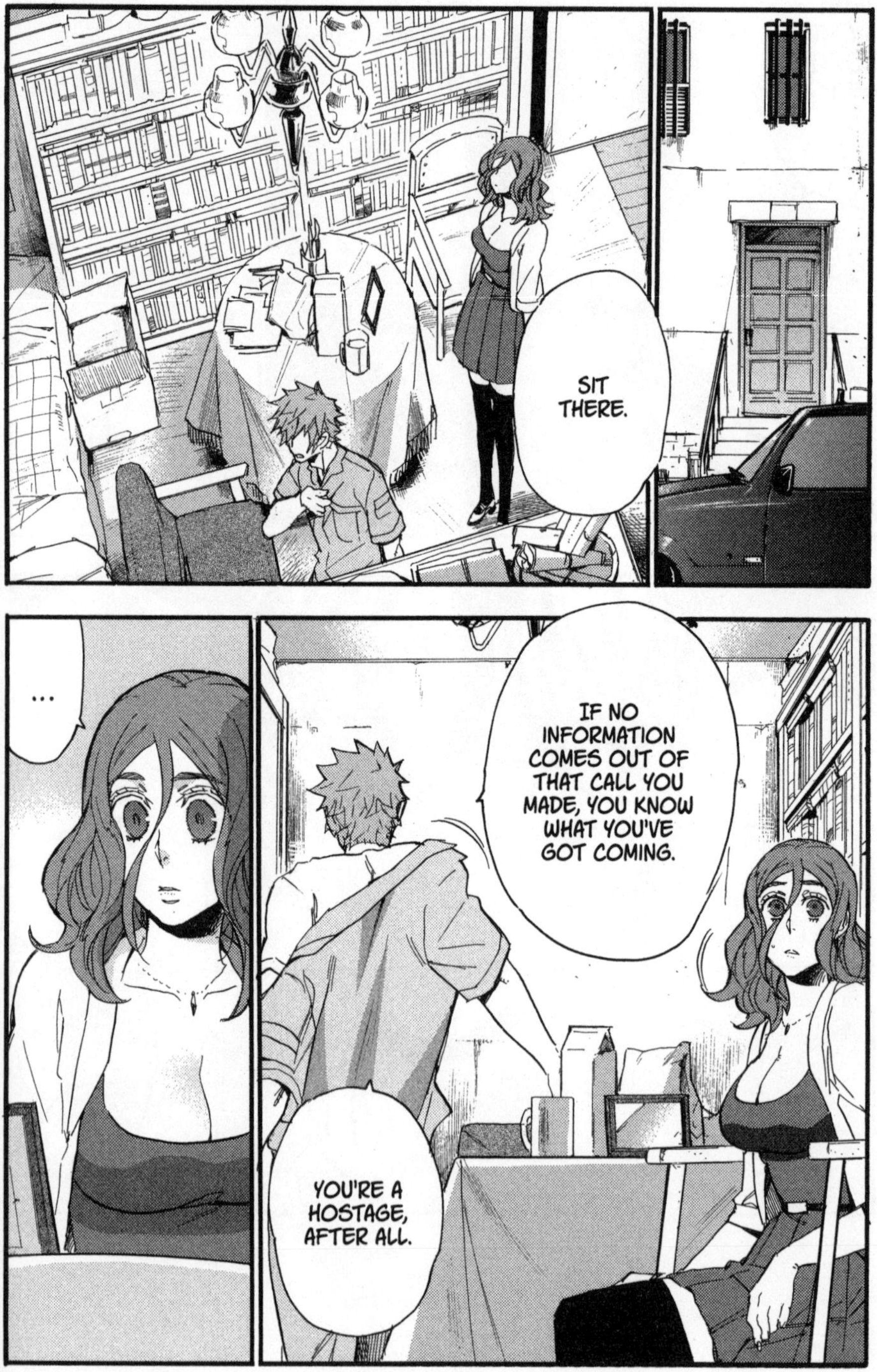
SIT THERE.
IF NO INFORMATION COMES OUT OF THAT CALL YOU MADE, YOU KNOW WHAT YOU'VE GOT COMING.
YOU'RE A HOSTAGE, AFTER ALL.
...

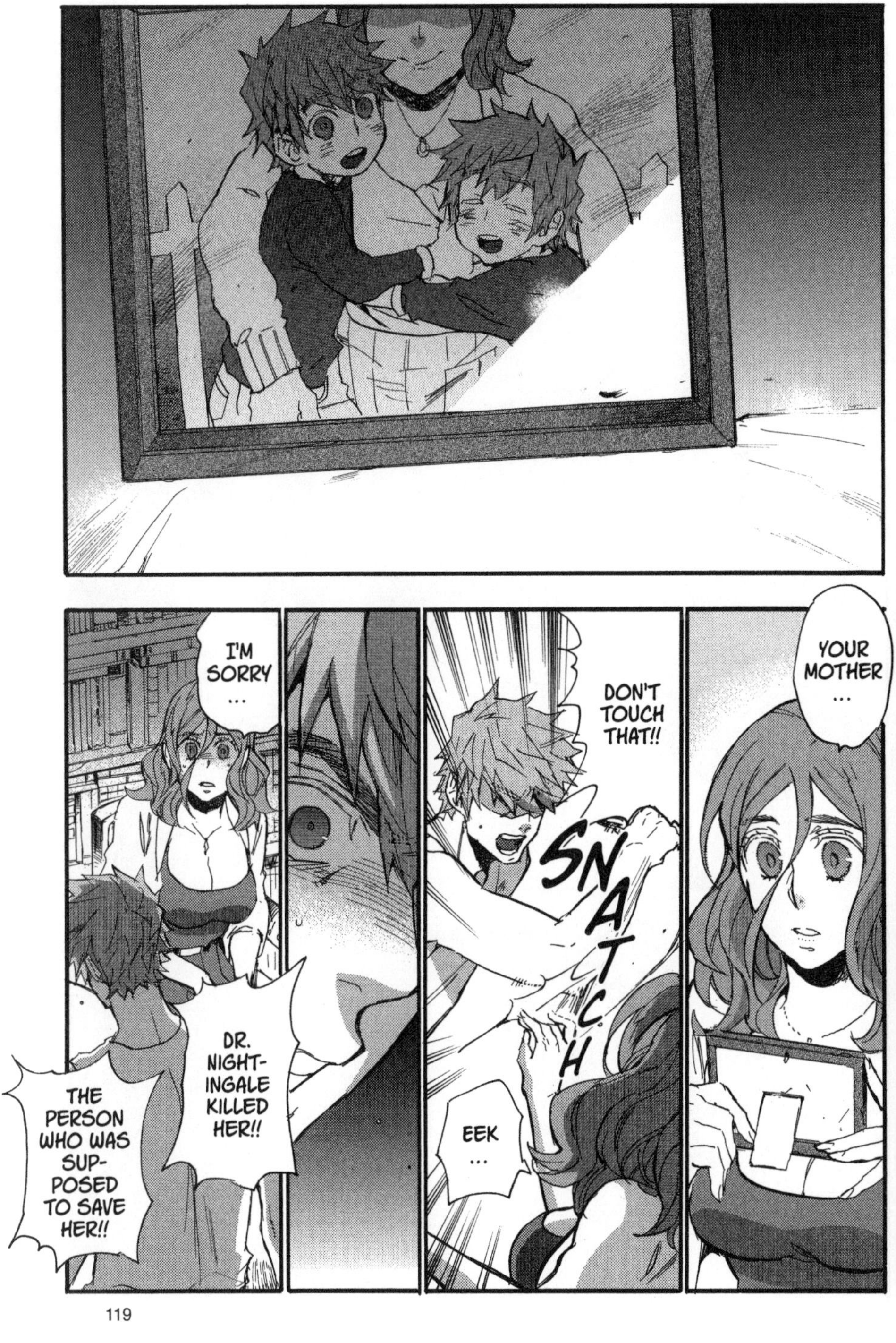
YOUR MOTHER ...
DON'T TOUCH THAT!!
SNATCH
EEK ...
I'M SORRY ...
DR. NIGHT-INGALE KILLED HER!!
THE PERSON WHO WAS SUP-POSED TO SAVE HER!!

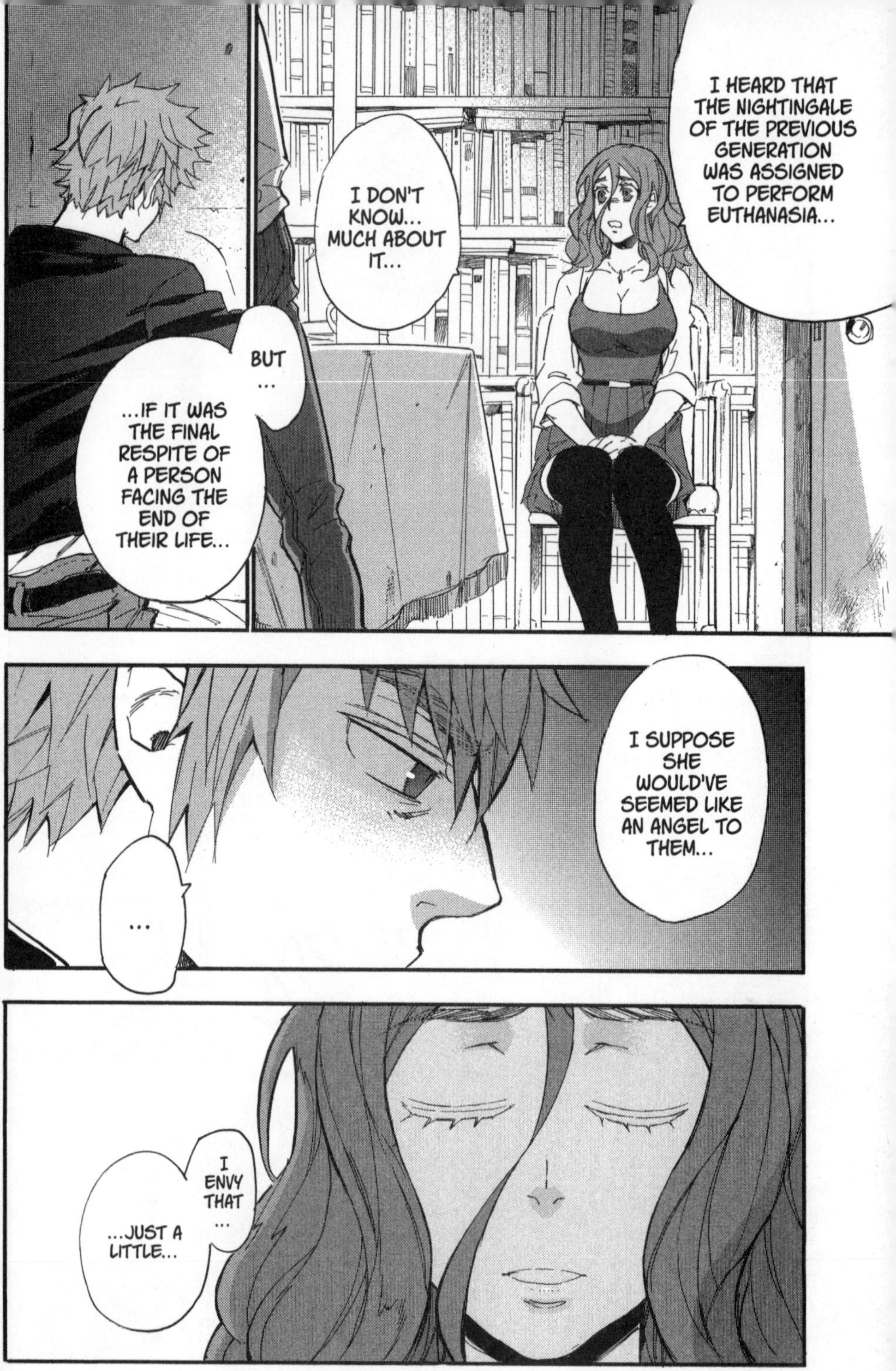
I HEARD THAT THE NIGHTINGALE OF THE PREVIOUS GENERATION WAS ASSIGNED TO PERFORM EUTHANASIA...
I DON'T KNOW... MUCH ABOUT IT...
BUT...
...IF IT WAS THE FINAL RESPITE OF A PERSON FACING THE END OF THEIR LIFE...
I SUPPOSE SHE WOULD'VE SEEMED LIKE AN ANGEL TO THEM...
...
I ENVY THAT...
...JUST A LITTLE...

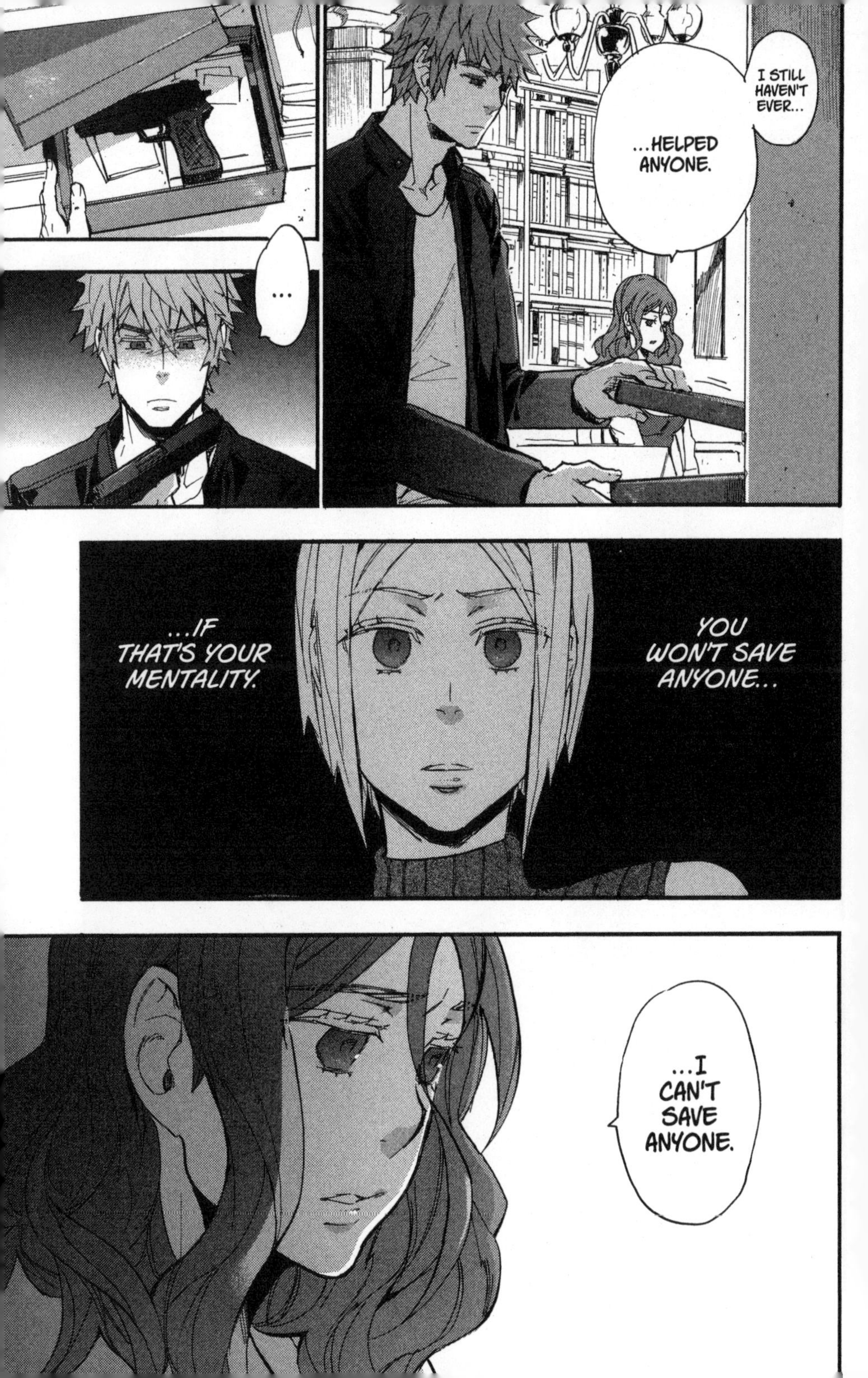
I STILL HAVEN'T EVER...
...HELPED ANYONE.
...
YOU WON'T SAVE ANYONE...
...IF THAT'S YOUR MENTALITY.
...I CAN'T SAVE ANYONE.

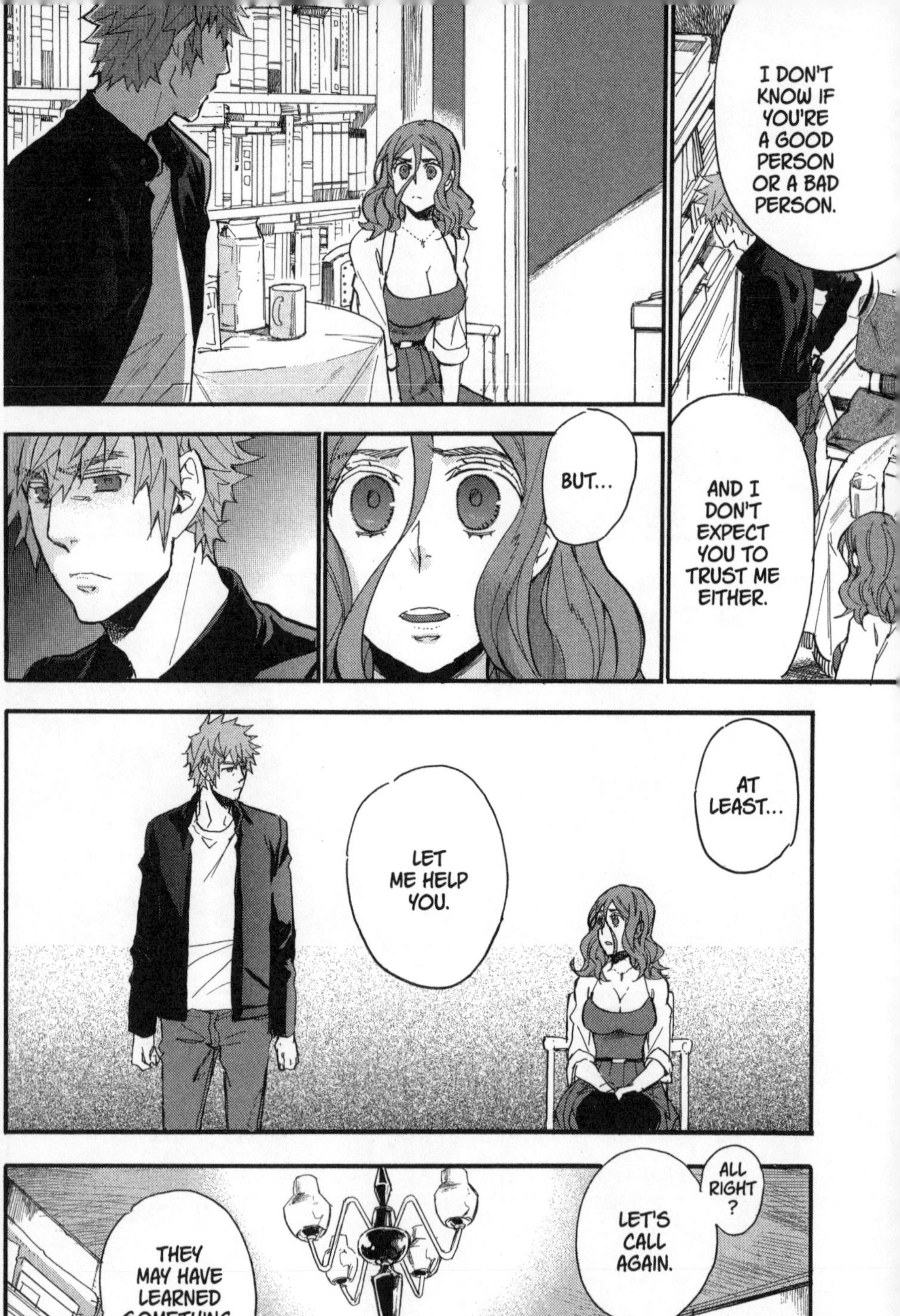
I DON'T KNOW IF YOU'RE A GOOD PERSON OR A BAD PERSON.
AND I DON'T EXPECT YOU TO TRUST ME EITHER.
BUT...
AT LEAST...
LET ME HELP YOU.
ALL RIGHT?
LET'S CALL AGAIN.
THEY MAY HAVE LEARNED SOMETHING.

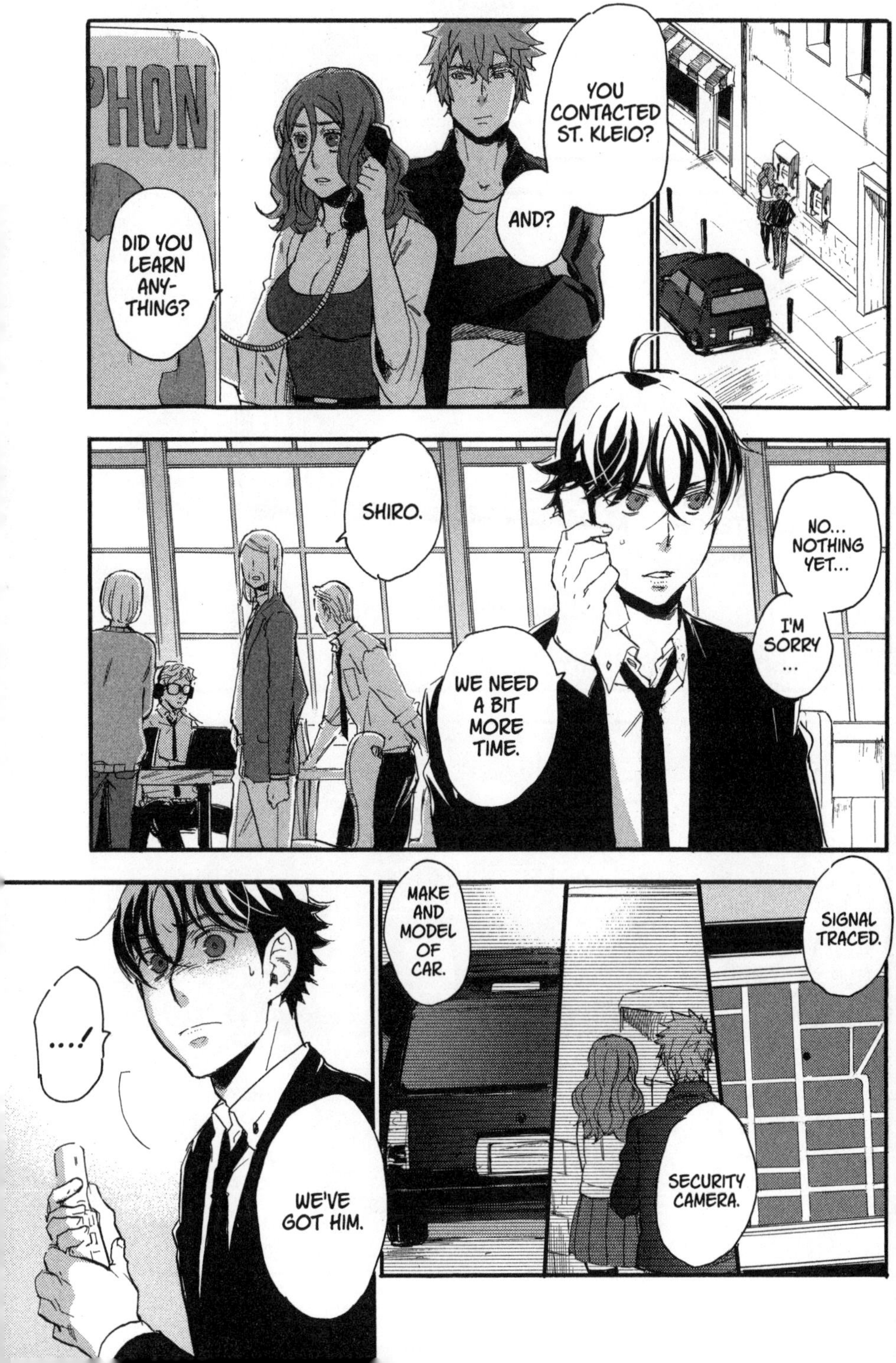
YOU CONTACTED ST. KLEIO?
AND?
PHON
DID YOU LEARN ANY-THING?
NO... NOTHING YET...
I'M SORRY...
SHIRO.
WE NEED A BIT MORE TIME.
SIGNAL TRACED.
MAKE AND MODEL OF CAR.
SECURITY CAMERA.
...!
WE'VE GOT HIM.

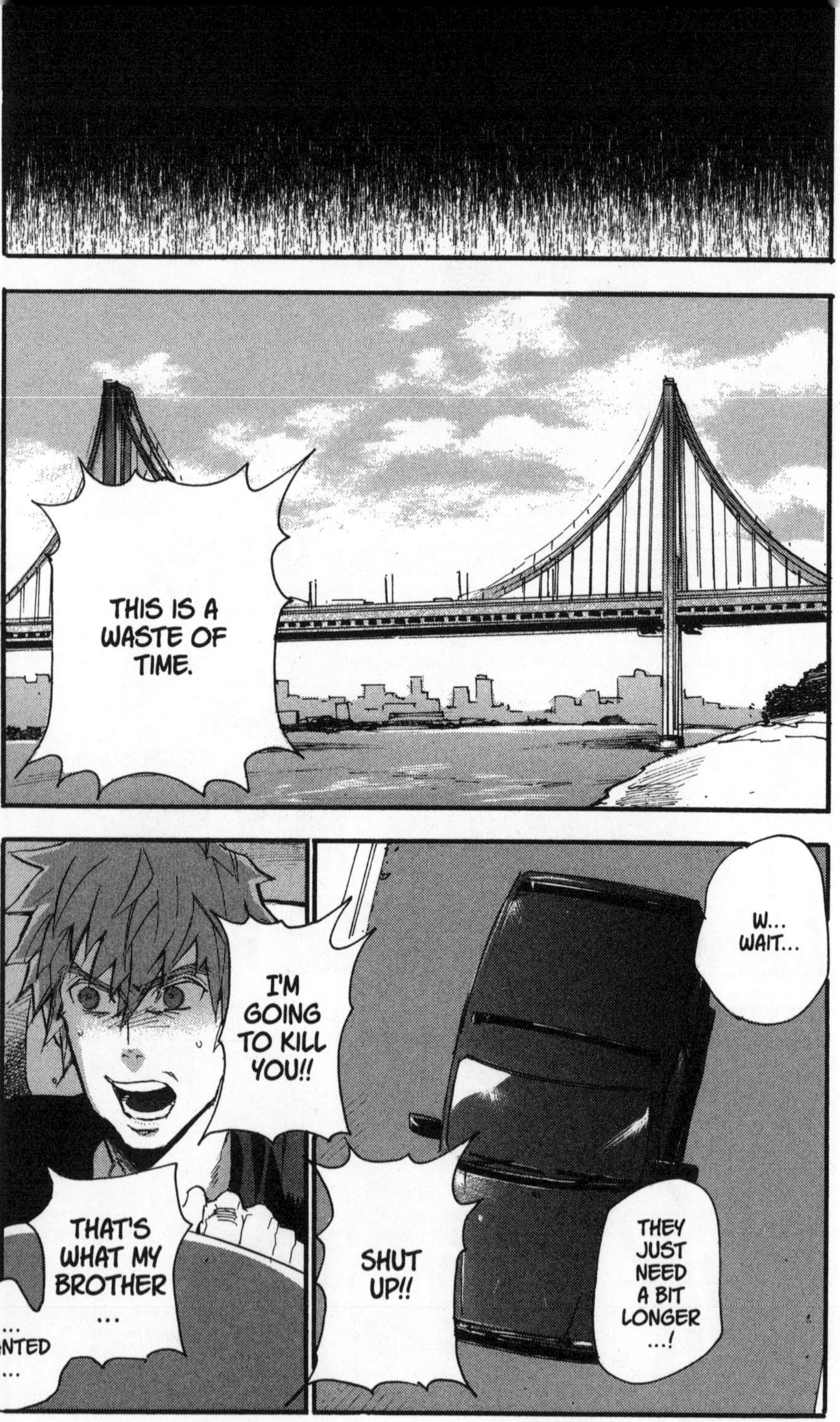
THIS IS A WASTE OF TIME.
W... WAIT...
THEY JUST NEED A BIT LONGER ...!
SHUT UP!!
I'M GOING TO KILL YOU!!
THAT'S WHAT MY BROTHER ...
... ANTED ...

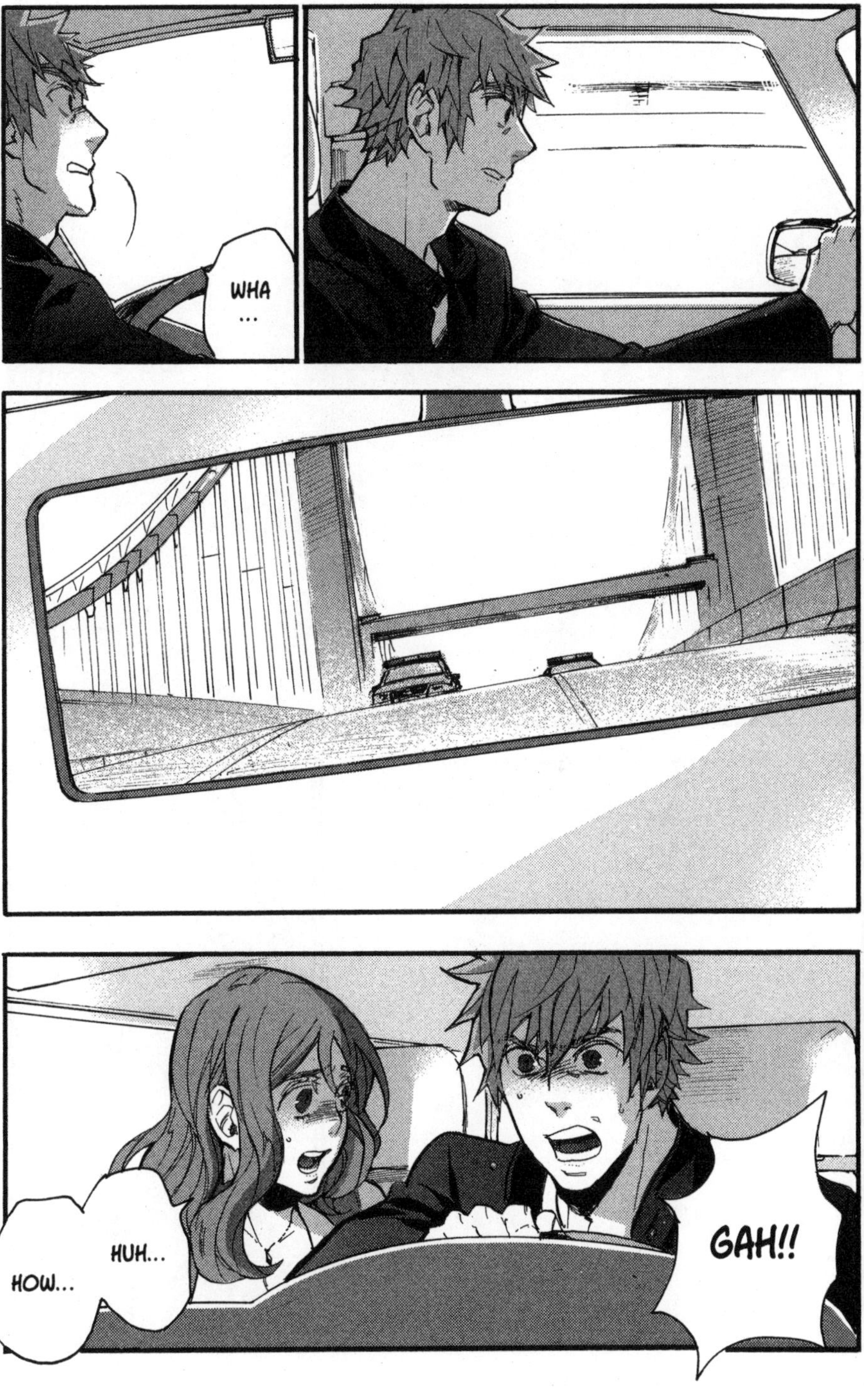
WHA ...
GAH!!
HUH... HOW...

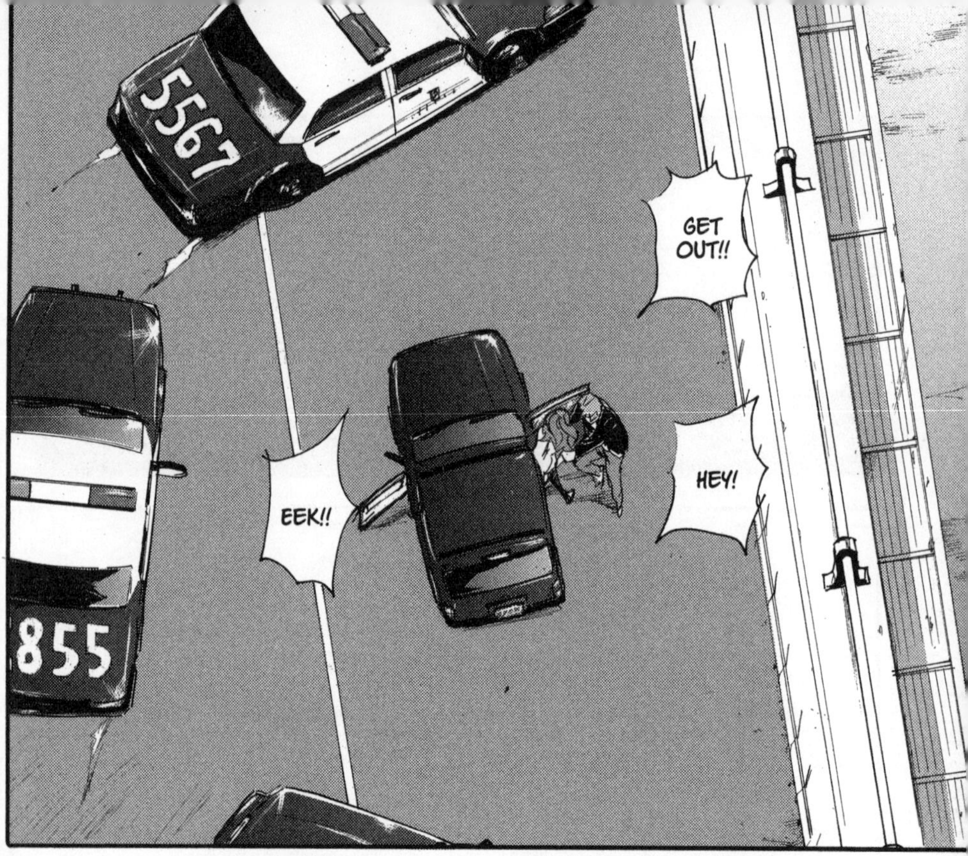
GET OUT!!
HEY!
5567
EEK!!
855

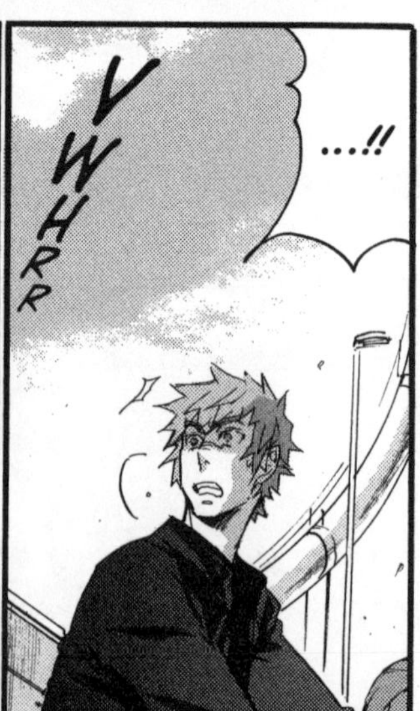
...!!
VWHRR

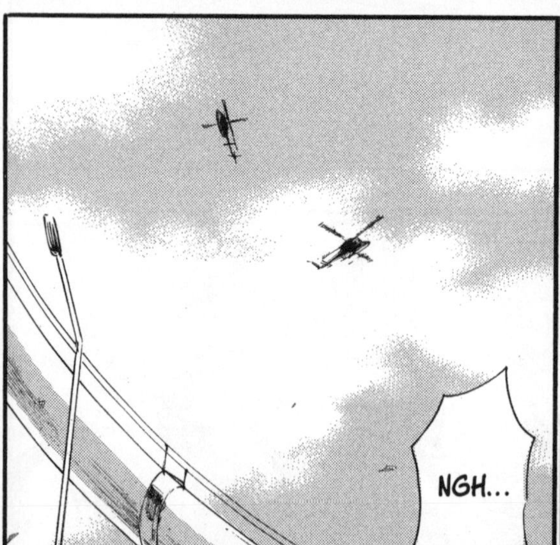
NGH...

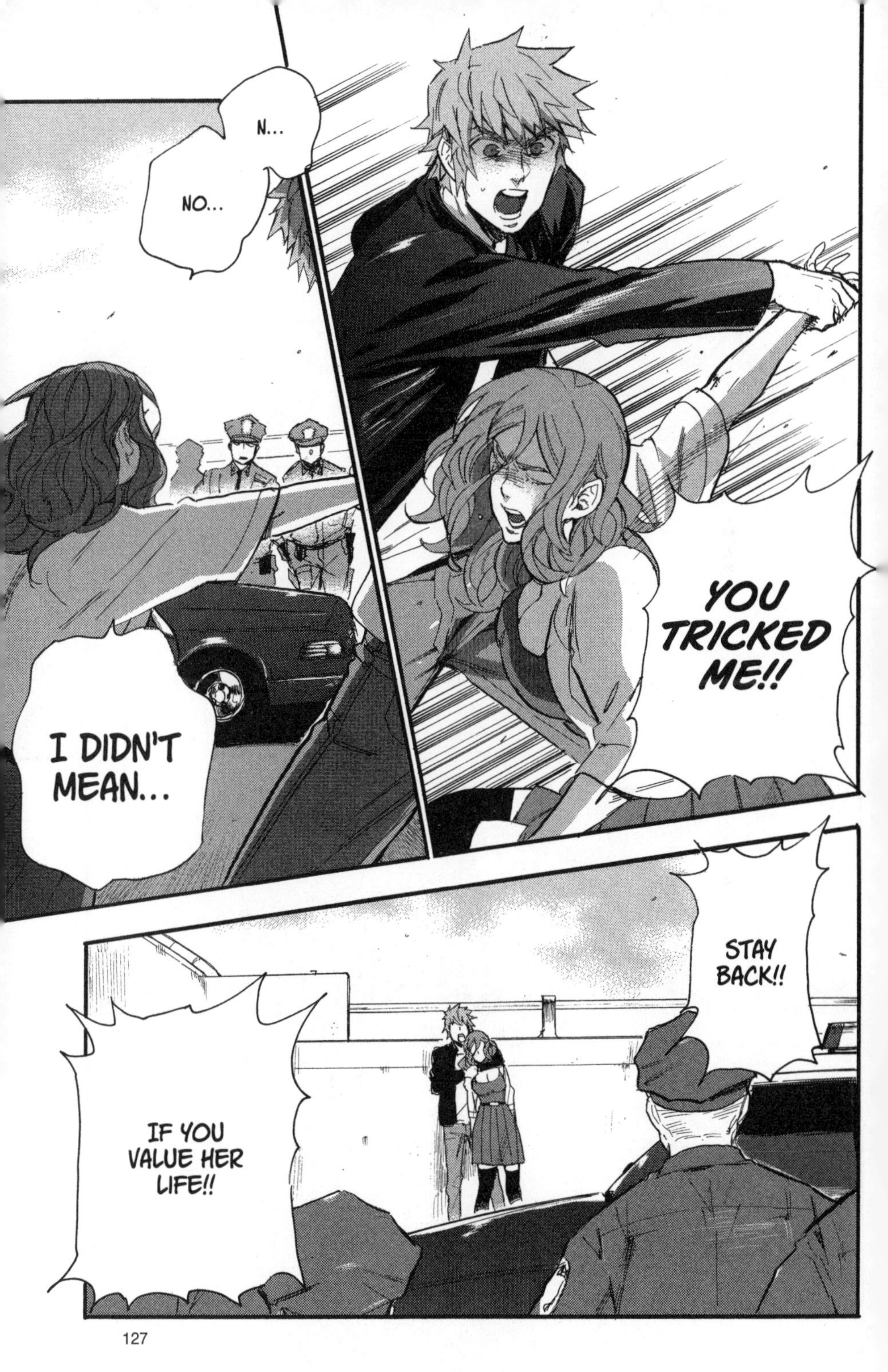
YOU TRICKED ME!!
N...
NO...
I DIDN'T MEAN...
STAY BACK!!
IF YOU VALUE HER LIFE!!

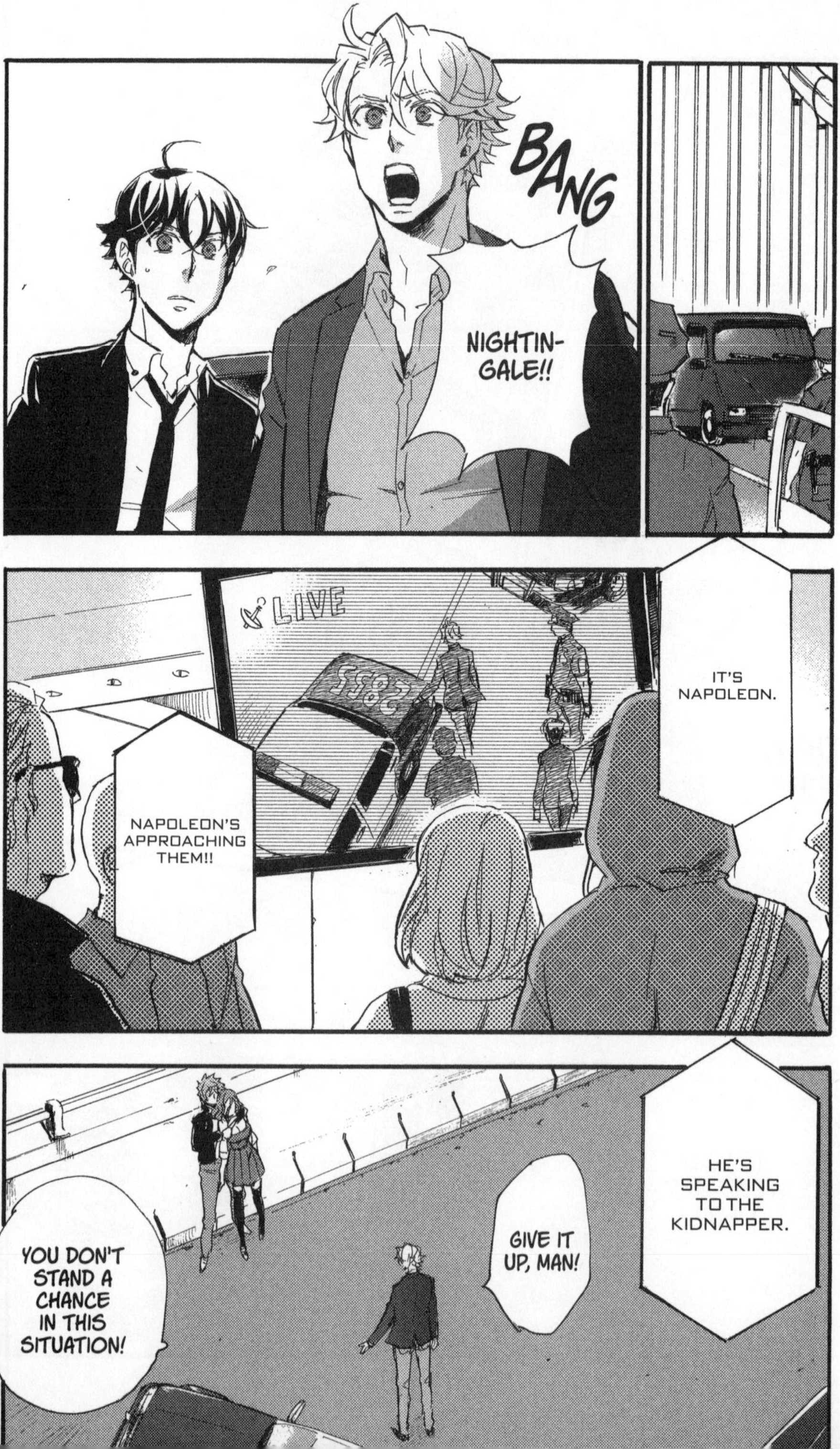
BANG
NIGHTIN-GALE!!
IT'S NAPOLEON.
LIVE
NAPOLEON'S APPROACHING THEM!!
HE'S SPEAKING TO THE KIDNAPPER.
GIVE IT UP, MAN!
YOU DON'T STAND A CHANCE IN THIS SITUATION!

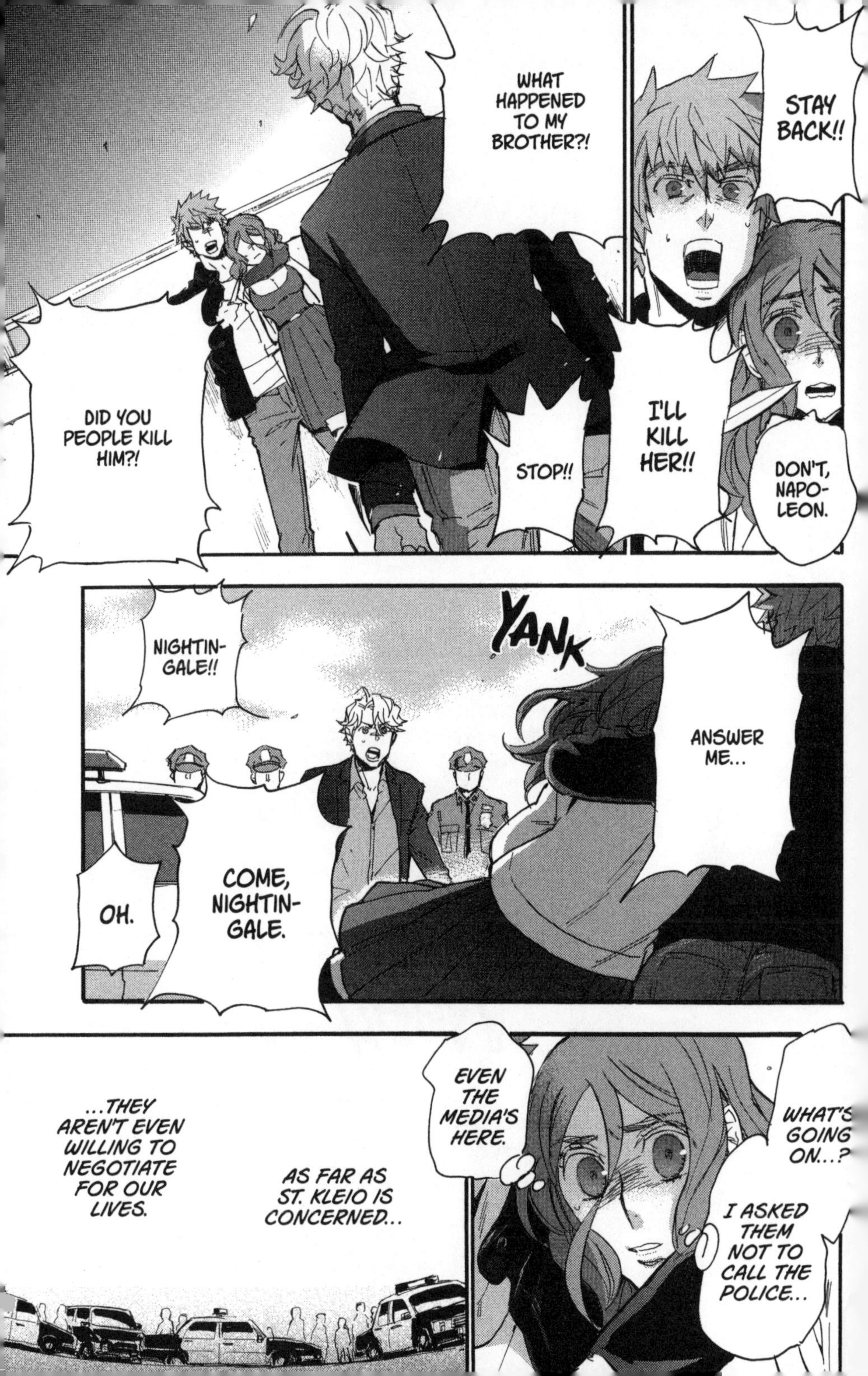
STAY BACK!!
I'LL KILL HER!!
DON'T, NAPO-LEON.
WHAT HAPPENED TO MY BROTHER?!
STOP!!
DID YOU PEOPLE KILL HIM?!
ANSWER ME...
YANK
NIGHTIN-GALE!!
COME, NIGHTIN-GALE.
OH.
WHAT'S GOING ON...?
EVEN THE MEDIA'S HERE.
I ASKED THEM NOT TO CALL THE POLICE...
AS FAR AS ST. KLEIO IS CONCERNED...
...THEY AREN'T EVEN WILLING TO NEGOTIATE FOR OUR LIVES.

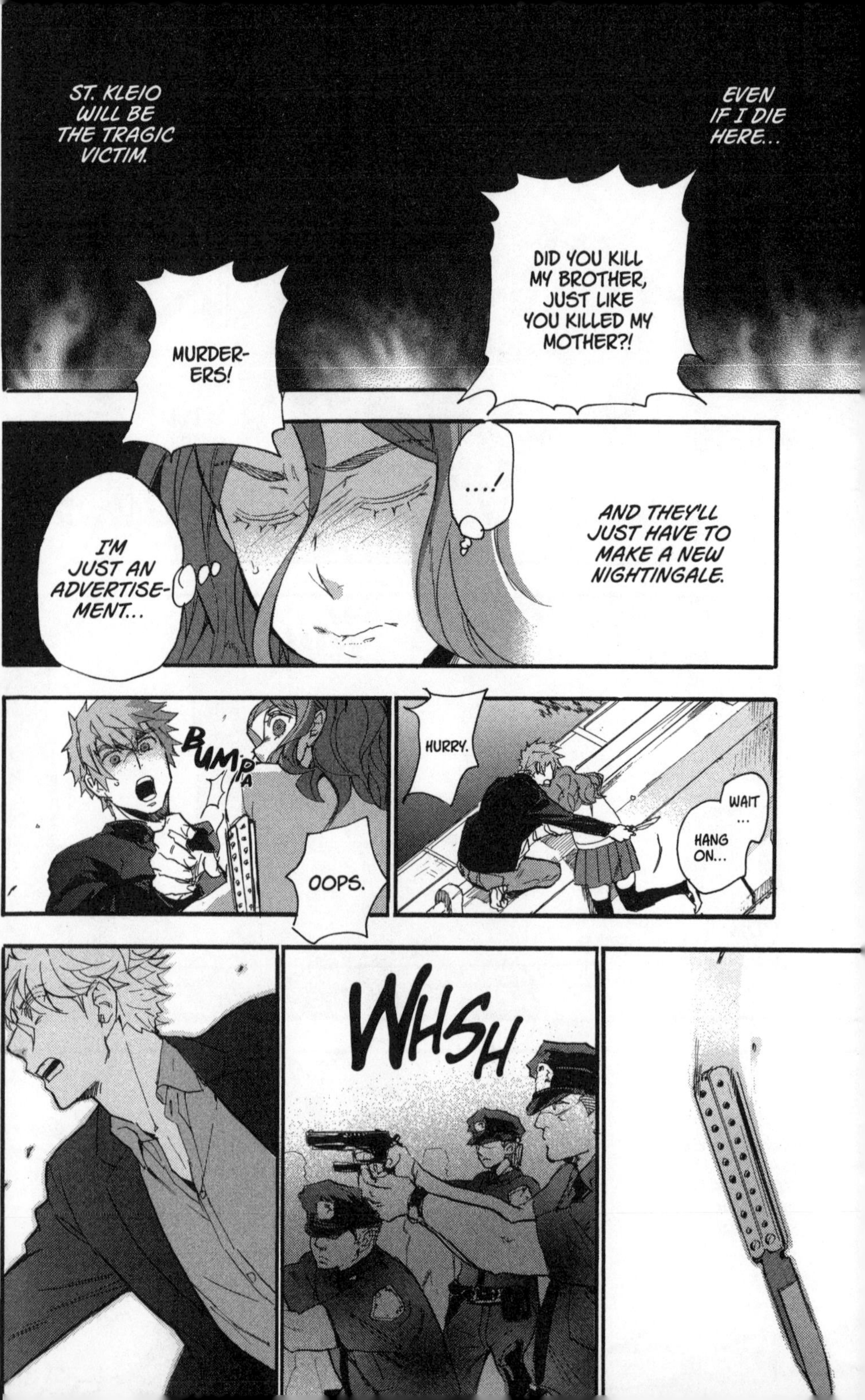

EVEN IF I DIE HERE...
ST. KLEIO WILL BE THE TRAGIC VICTIM.
DID YOU KILL MY BROTHER, JUST LIKE YOU KILLED MY MOTHER?!
MURDER-ERS!
AND THEY'LL JUST HAVE TO MAKE A NEW NIGHTINGALE.
....!
I'M JUST AN ADVERTISE-MENT...
HURRY.
WAIT ...
HANG ON...
BUMPA
OOPS.
WHSH

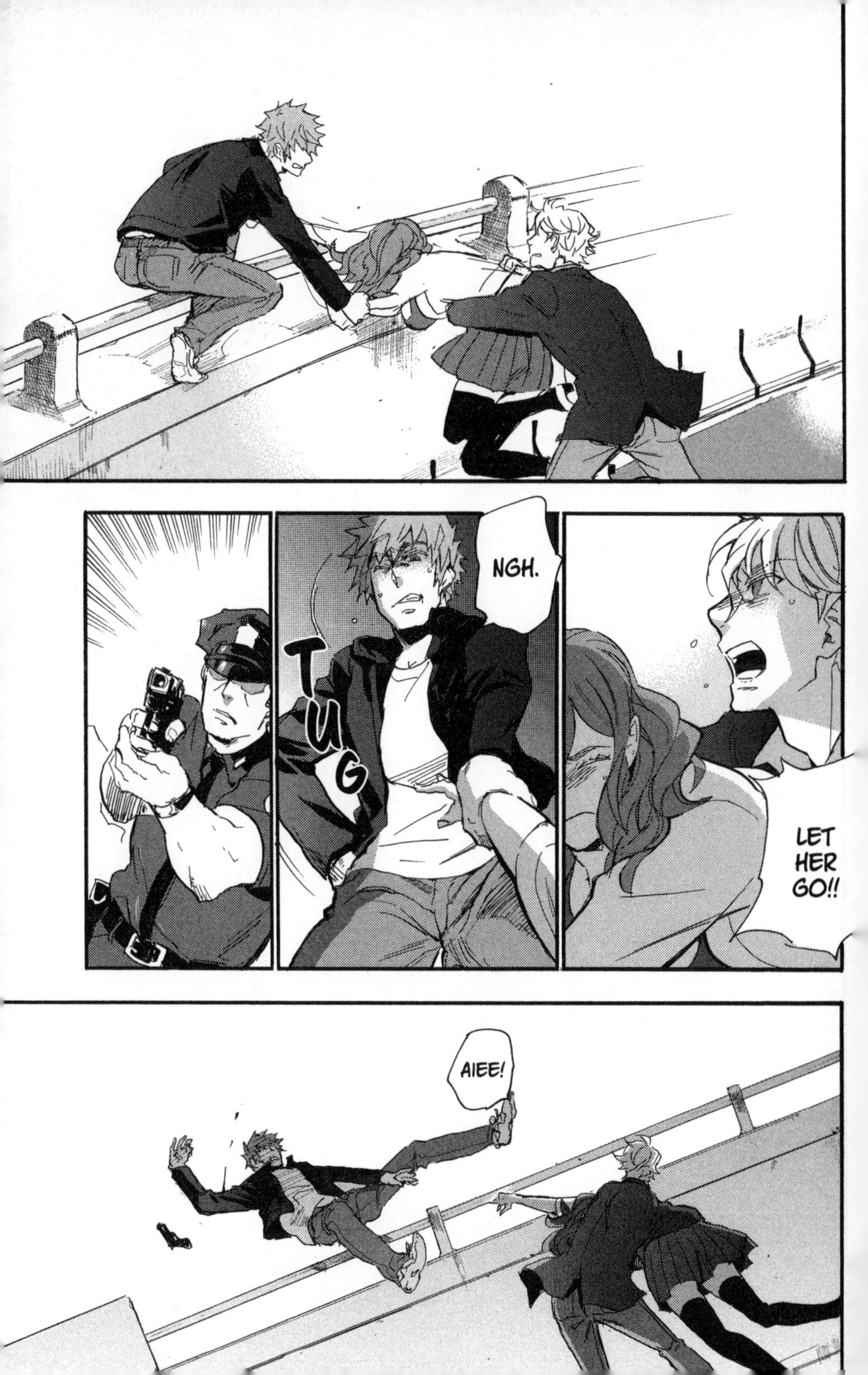
LET HER GO!!
NGH.
TUG
AIEE!

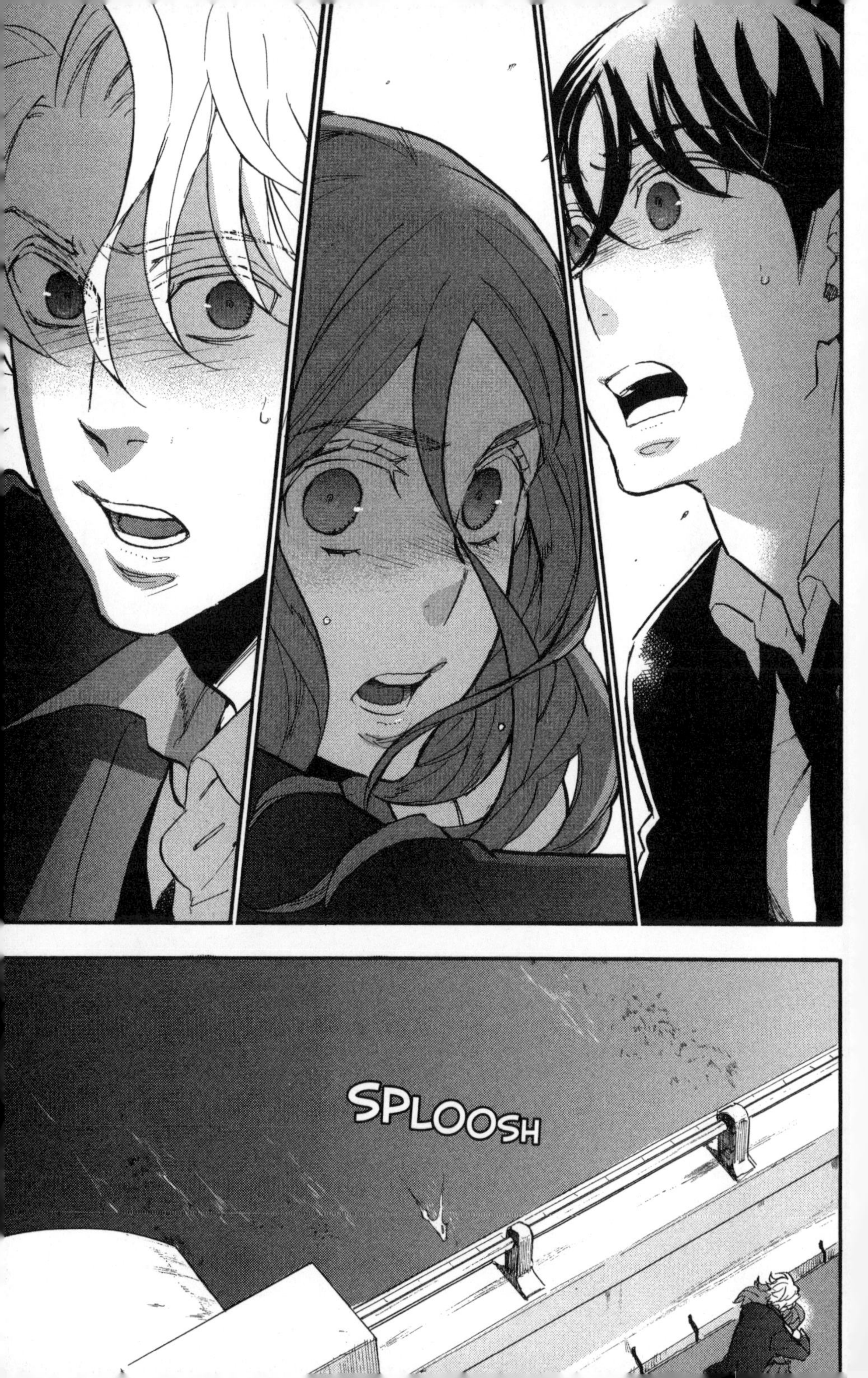
SPLOOSH

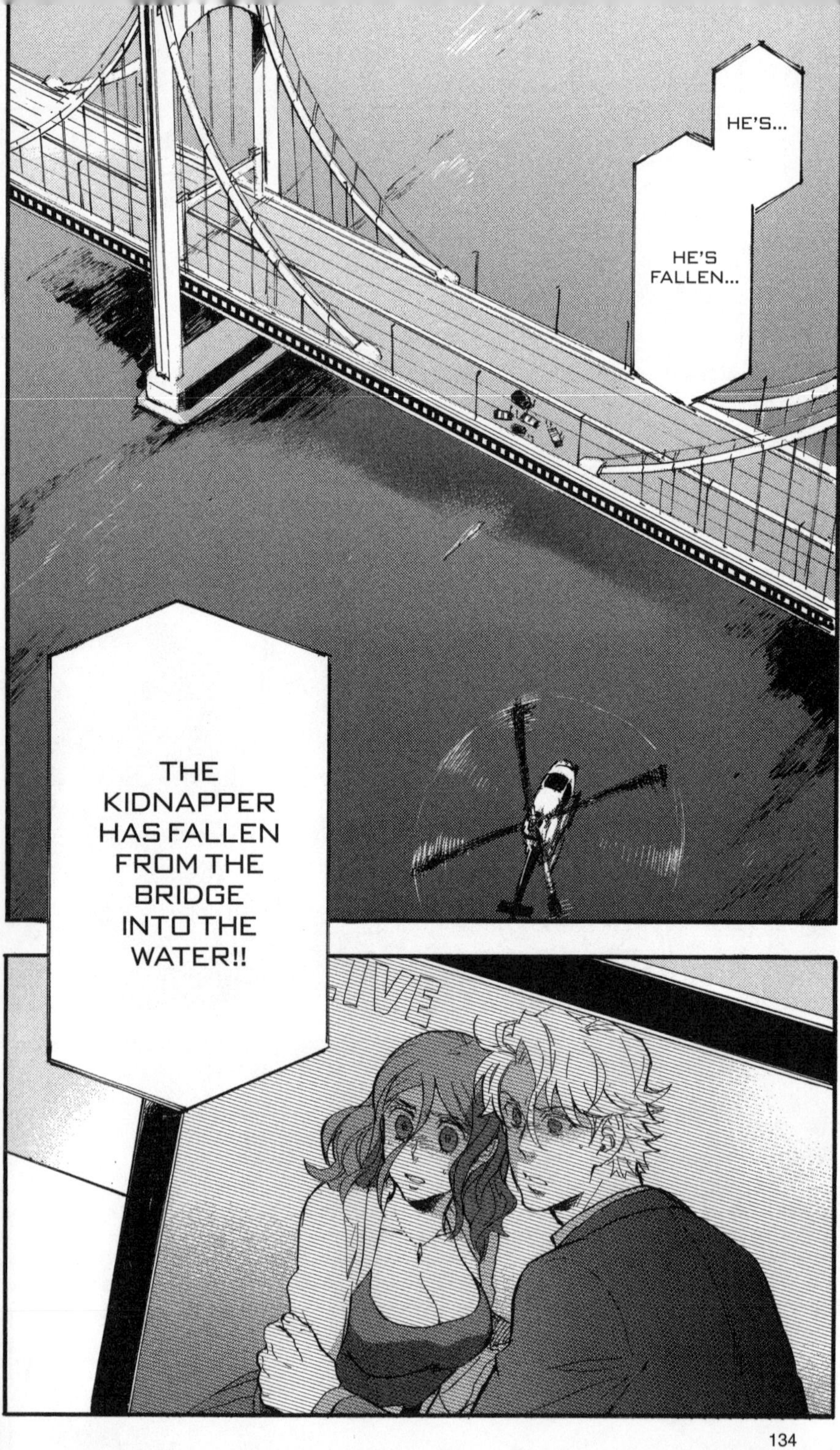
HE'S...
HE'S FALLEN...
THE KIDNAPPER HAS FALLEN FROM THE BRIDGE INTO THE WATER!!
LIVE

# CHAPTER sixty-five

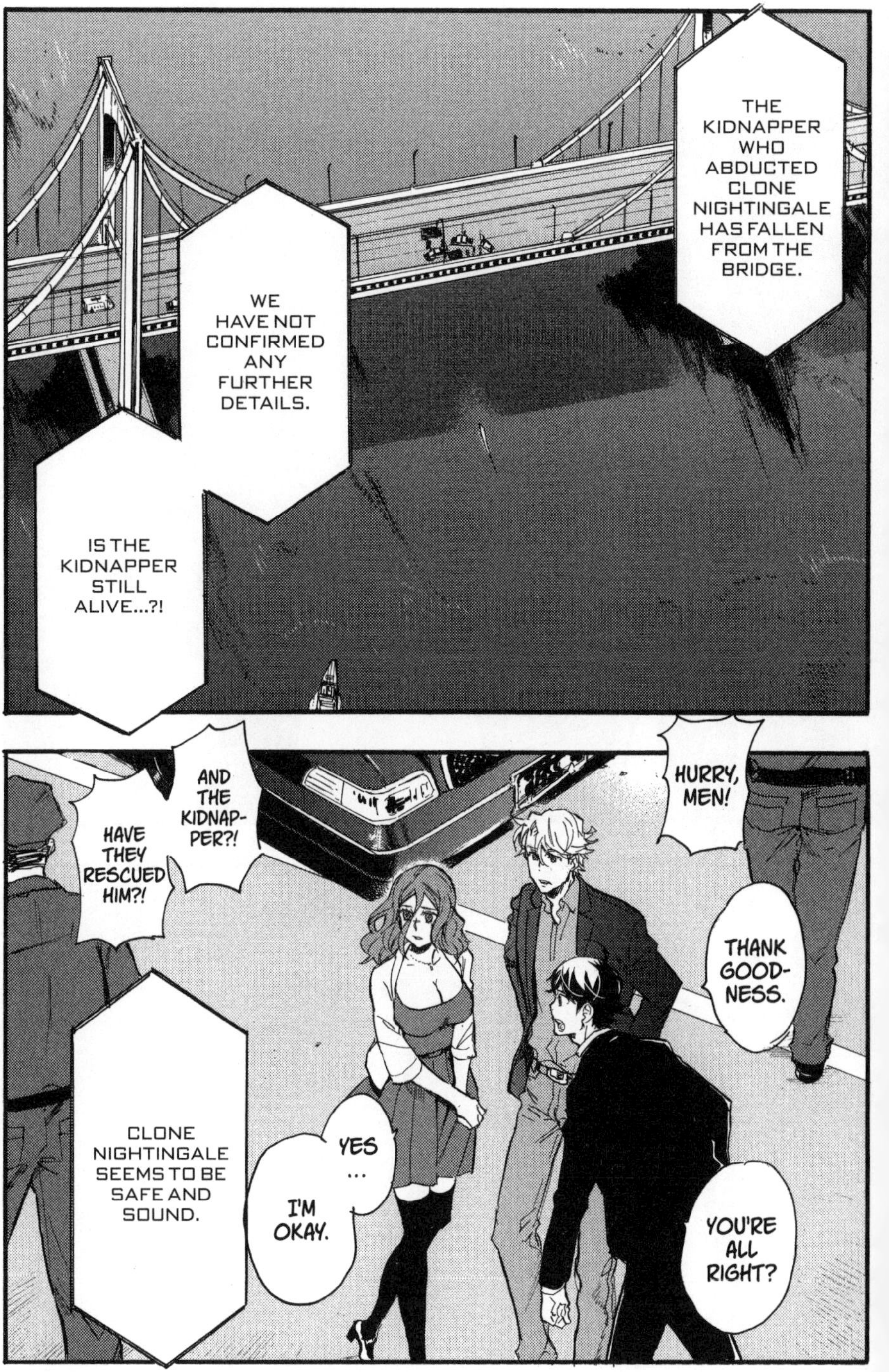
THE KIDNAPPER WHO ABDUCTED CLONE NIGHTINGALE HAS FALLEN FROM THE BRIDGE.
WE HAVE NOT CONFIRMED ANY FURTHER DETAILS.
IS THE KIDNAPPER STILL ALIVE...?!
HURRY, MEN!
AND THE KIDNAP-PER?!
HAVE THEY RESCUED HIM?!
THANK GOOD-NESS.
YOU'RE ALL RIGHT?
YES... I'M OKAY.
CLONE NIGHTINGALE SEEMS TO BE SAFE AND SOUND.

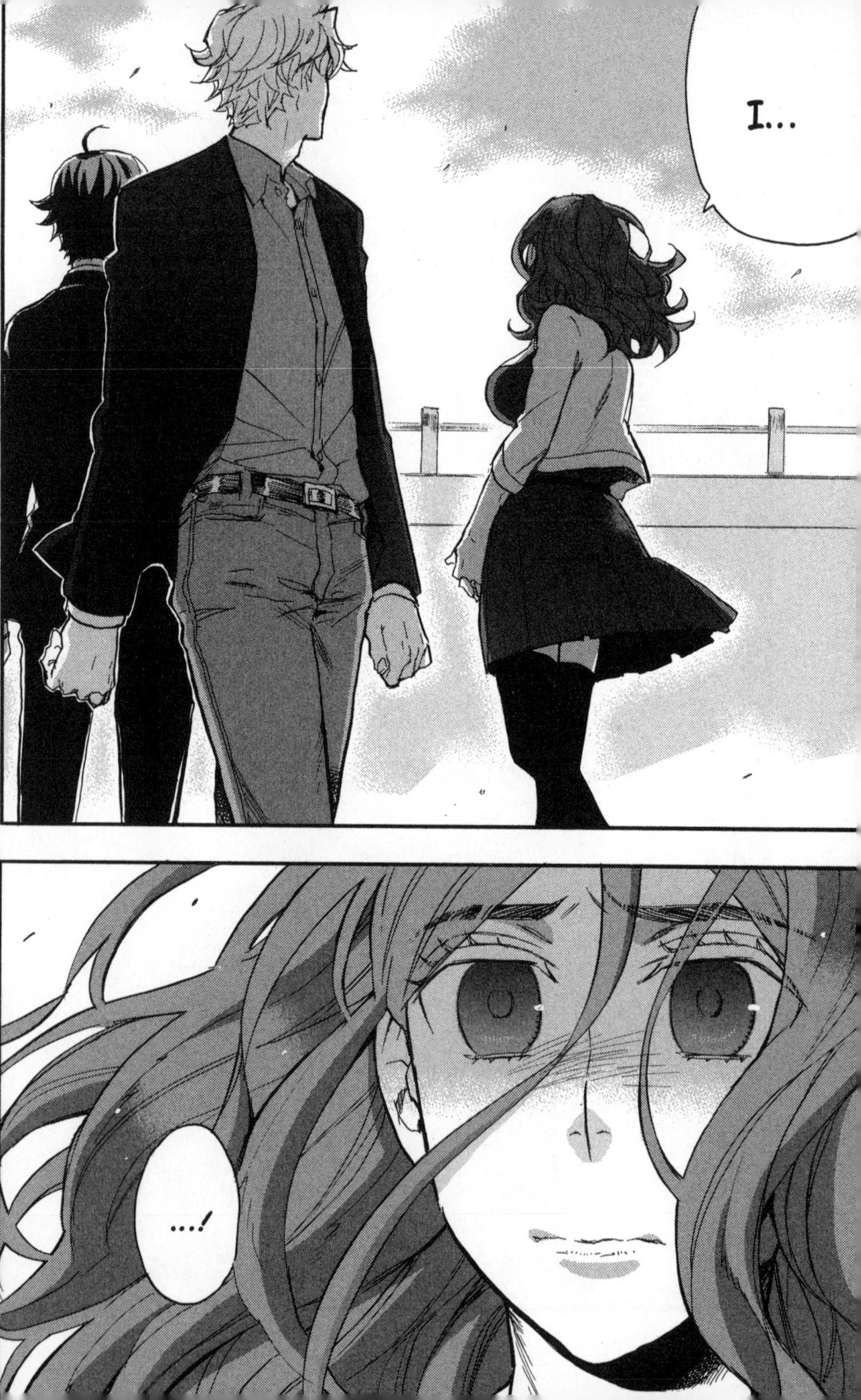
I...
...!

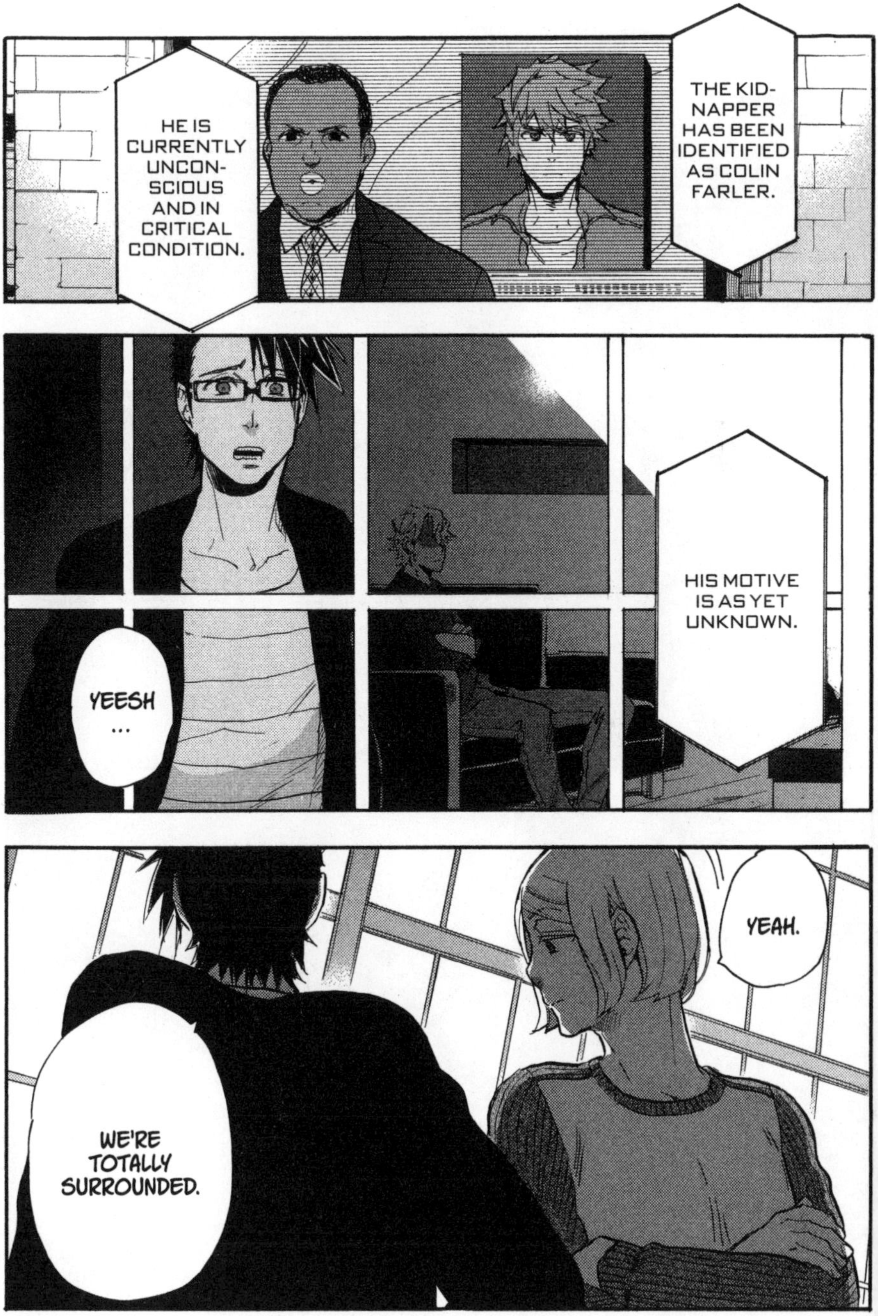
THE KID-NAPPER HAS BEEN IDENTIFIED AS COLIN FARLER.
HE IS CURRENTLY UNCON-SCIOUS AND IN CRITICAL CONDITION.
HIS MOTIVE IS AS YET UNKNOWN.
YEESH ...
YEAH.
WE'RE TOTALLY SURROUNDED.

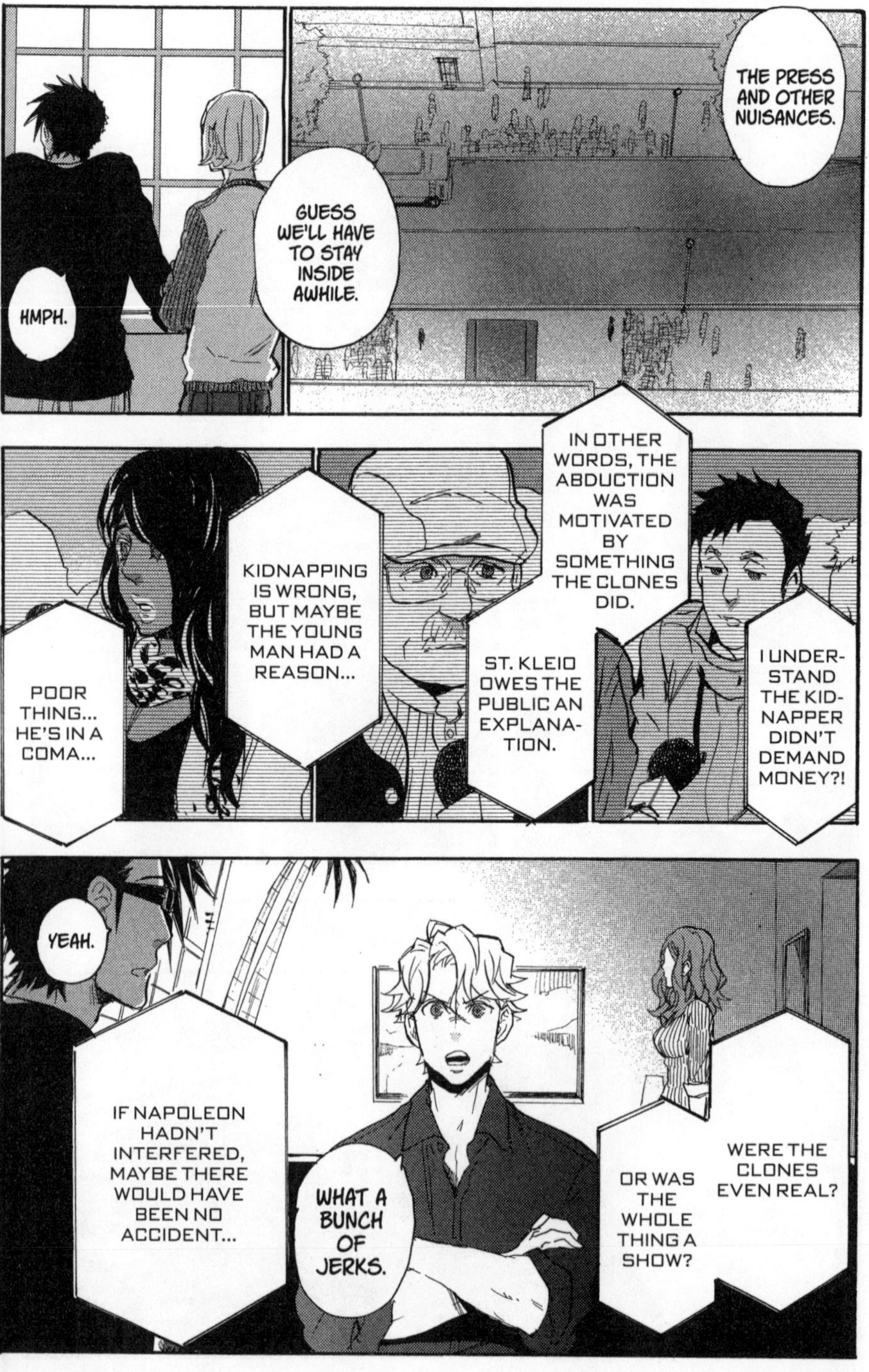
THE PRESS AND OTHER NUISANCES.
GUESS WE'LL HAVE TO STAY INSIDE AWHILE.
HMPH.
I UNDER-STAND THE KID-NAPPER DIDN'T DEMAND MONEY?!
IN OTHER WORDS, THE ABDUCTION WAS MOTIVATED BY SOMETHING THE CLONES DID.
ST. KLEIO OWES THE PUBLIC AN EXPLANA-TION.
KIDNAPPING IS WRONG, BUT MAYBE THE YOUNG MAN HAD A REASON...
POOR THING... HE'S IN A COMA...
WERE THE CLONES EVEN REAL?
OR WAS THE WHOLE THING A SHOW?
WHAT A BUNCH OF JERKS.
IF NAPOLEON HADN'T INTERFERED, MAYBE THERE WOULD HAVE BEEN NO ACCIDENT...
YEAH.

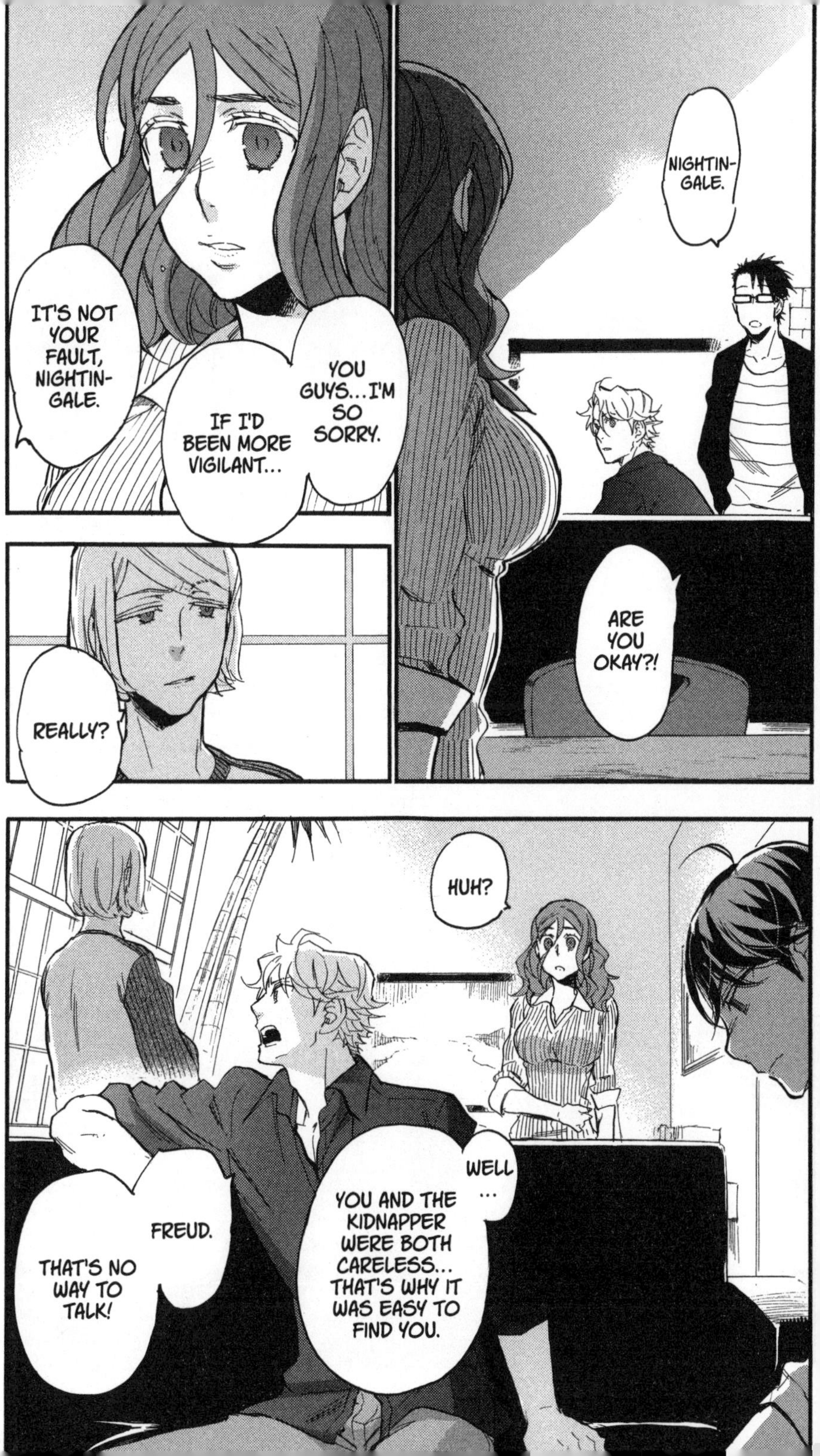
NIGHTIN-GALE.
ARE YOU OKAY?!
YOU GUYS...I'M SO SORRY.
IF I'D BEEN MORE VIGILANT...
IT'S NOT YOUR FAULT, NIGHTIN-GALE.
REALLY?
HUH?
WELL...
YOU AND THE KIDNAPPER WERE BOTH CARELESS... THAT'S WHY IT WAS EASY TO FIND YOU.
FREUD.
THAT'S NO WAY TO TALK!

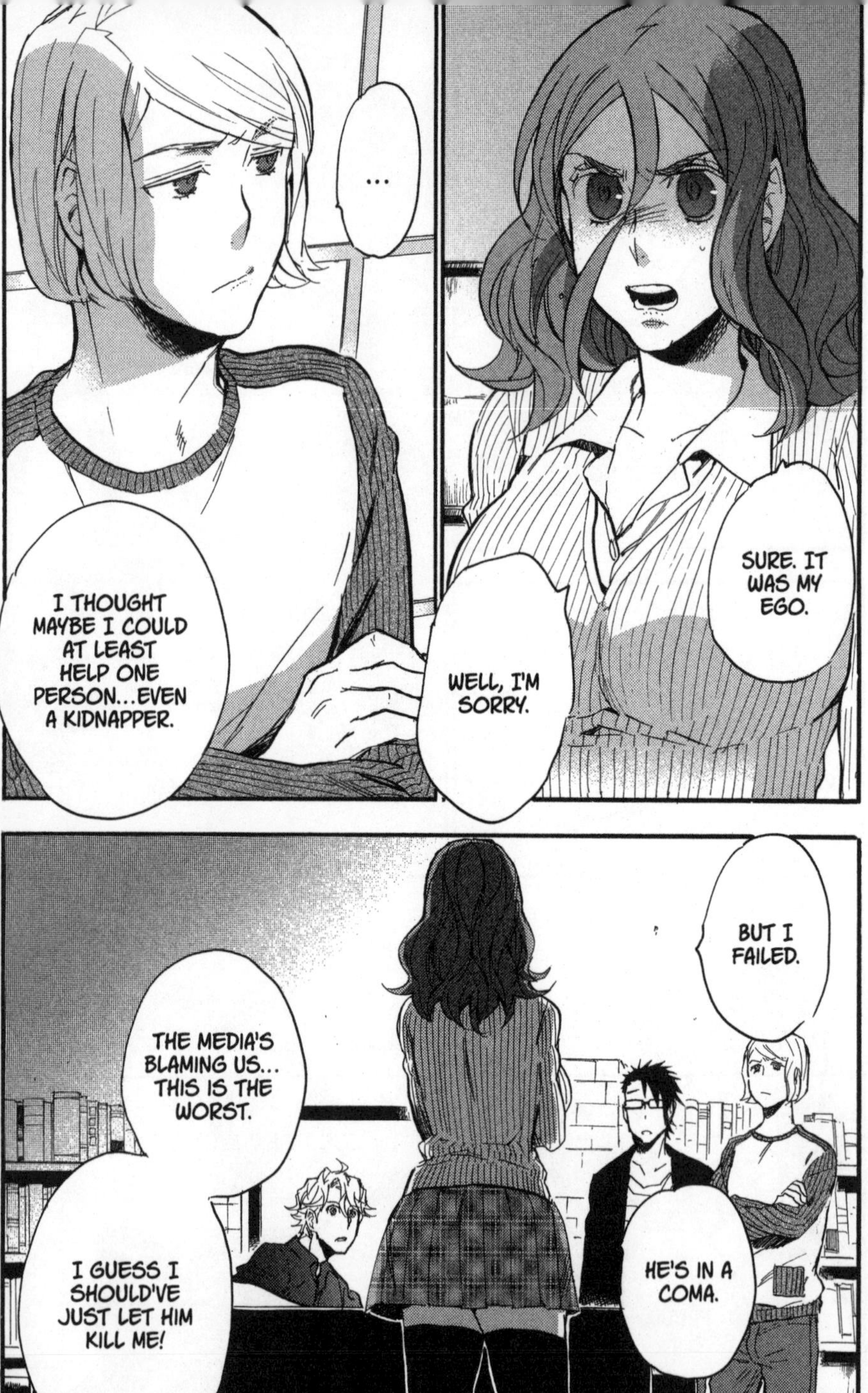
SURE. IT WAS MY EGO.
WELL, I'M SORRY.
...
I THOUGHT MAYBE I COULD AT LEAST HELP ONE PERSON...EVEN A KIDNAPPER.
BUT I FAILED.
THE MEDIA'S BLAMING US... THIS IS THE WORST.
HE'S IN A COMA.
I GUESS I SHOULD'VE JUST LET HIM KILL ME!

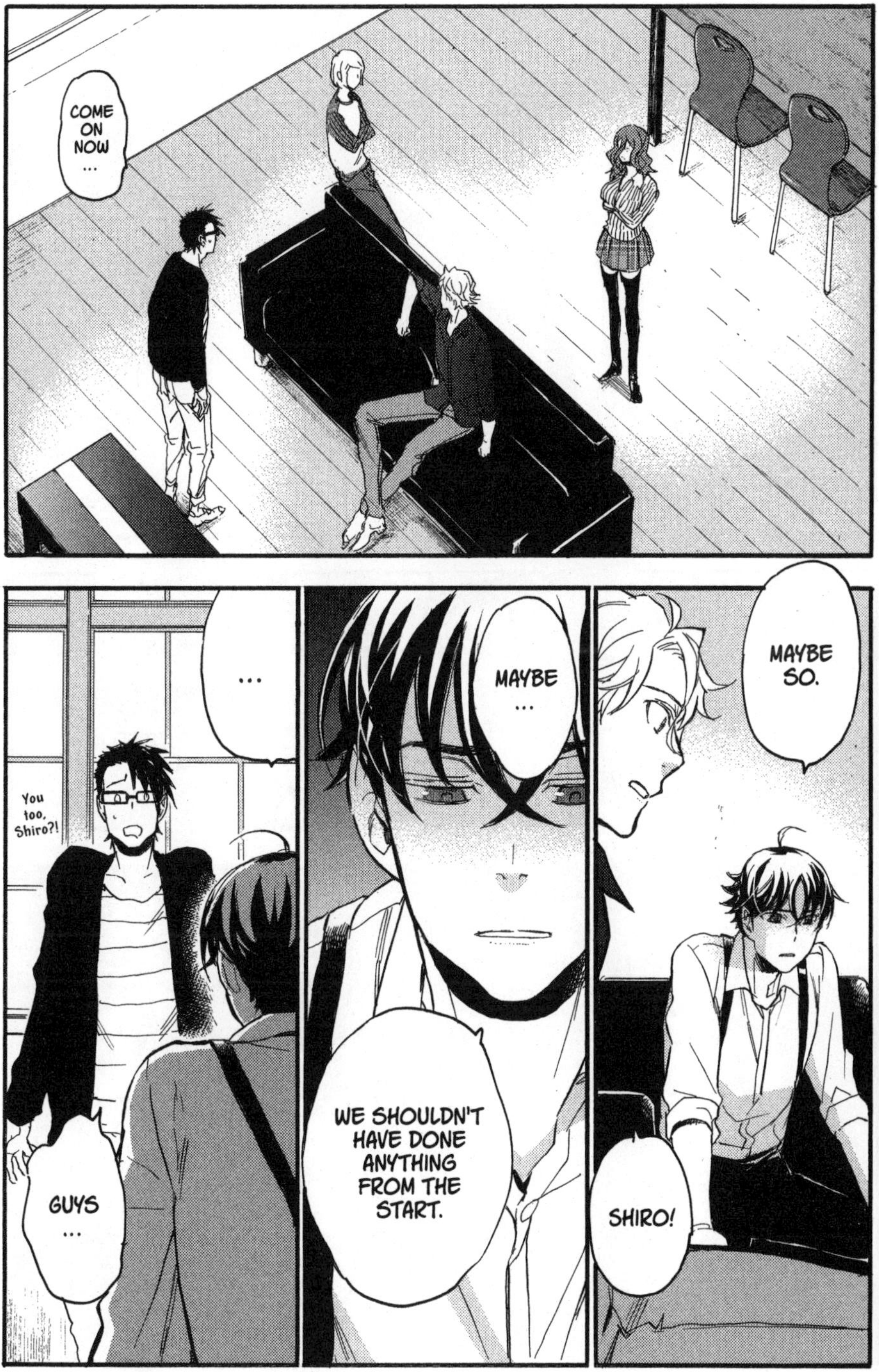
COME ON NOW ...
MAYBE SO.
SHIRO!
MAYBE ...
WE SHOULDN'T HAVE DONE ANYTHING FROM THE START.
...
You too, Shiro?!
GUYS ...

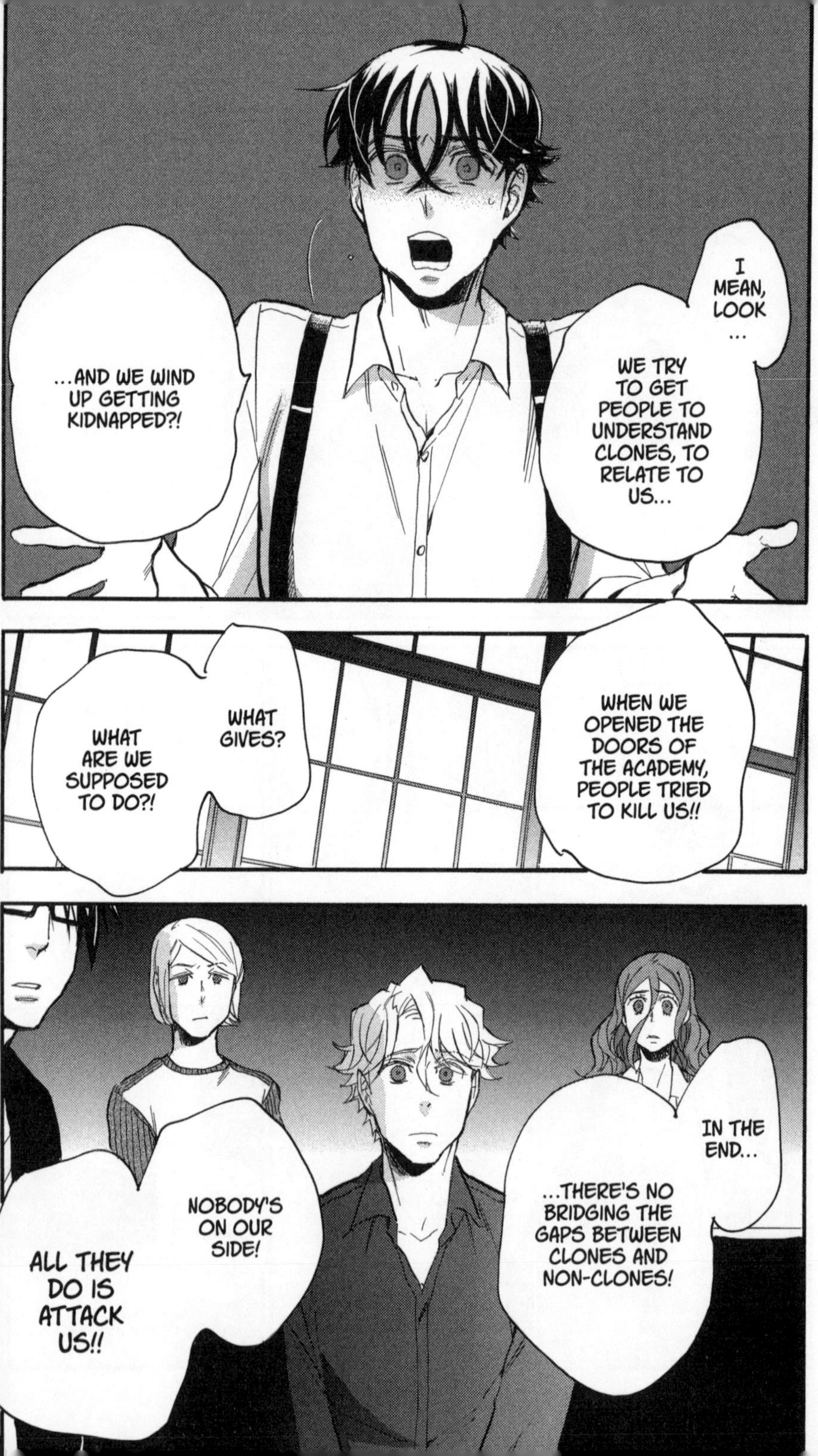
I MEAN, LOOK...
WE TRY TO GET PEOPLE TO UNDERSTAND CLONES, TO RELATE TO US...
...AND WE WIND UP GETTING KIDNAPPED?!
WHEN WE OPENED THE DOORS OF THE ACADEMY, PEOPLE TRIED TO KILL US!!
WHAT GIVES?
WHAT ARE WE SUPPOSED TO DO?!
IN THE END...
...THERE'S NO BRIDGING THE GAPS BETWEEN CLONES AND NON-CLONES!
NOBODY'S ON OUR SIDE!
ALL THEY DO IS ATTACK US!!

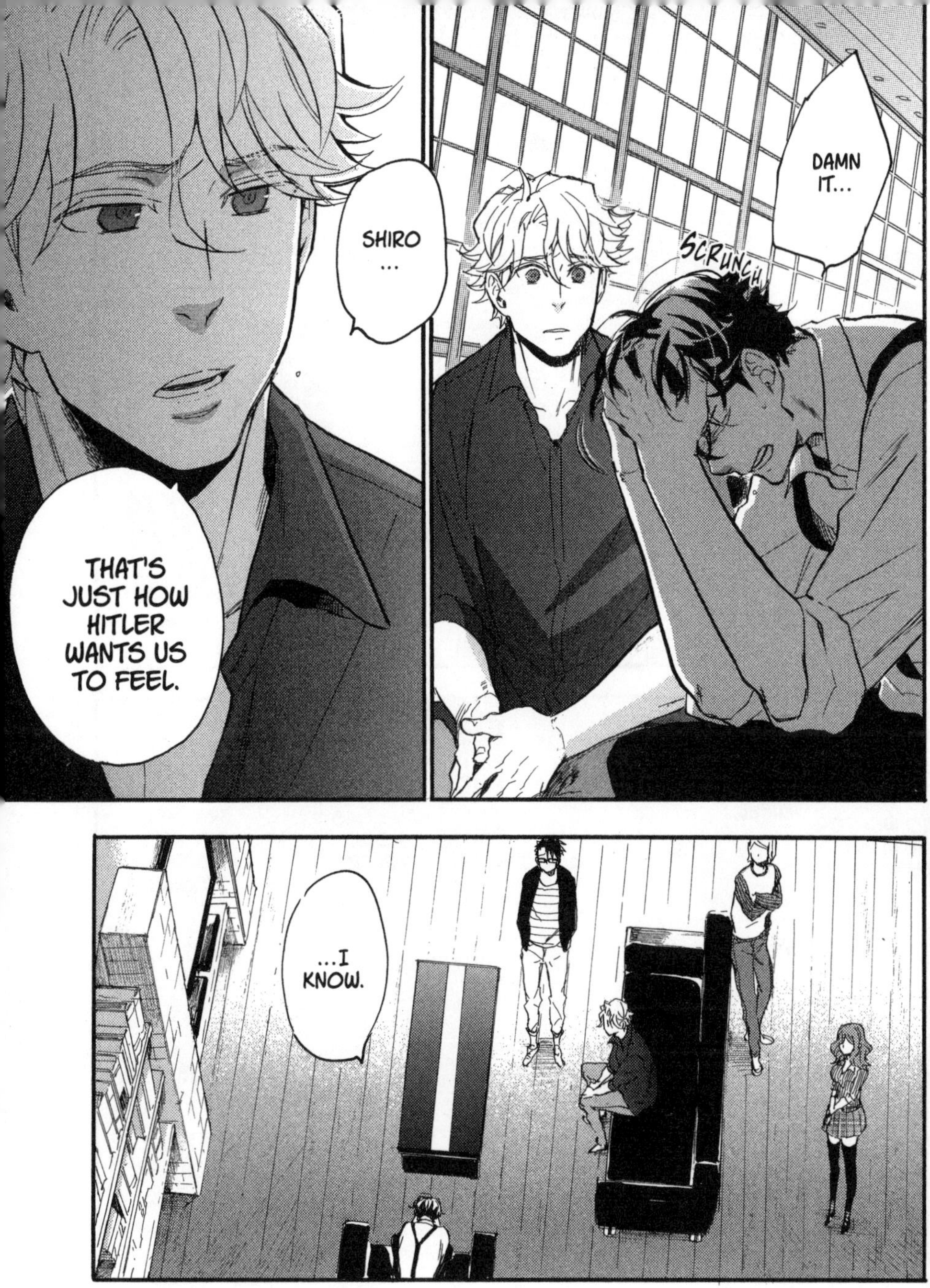
DAMN IT...
SCRUNCH
SHIRO ...
THAT'S JUST HOW HITLER WANTS US TO FEEL.
...I KNOW.

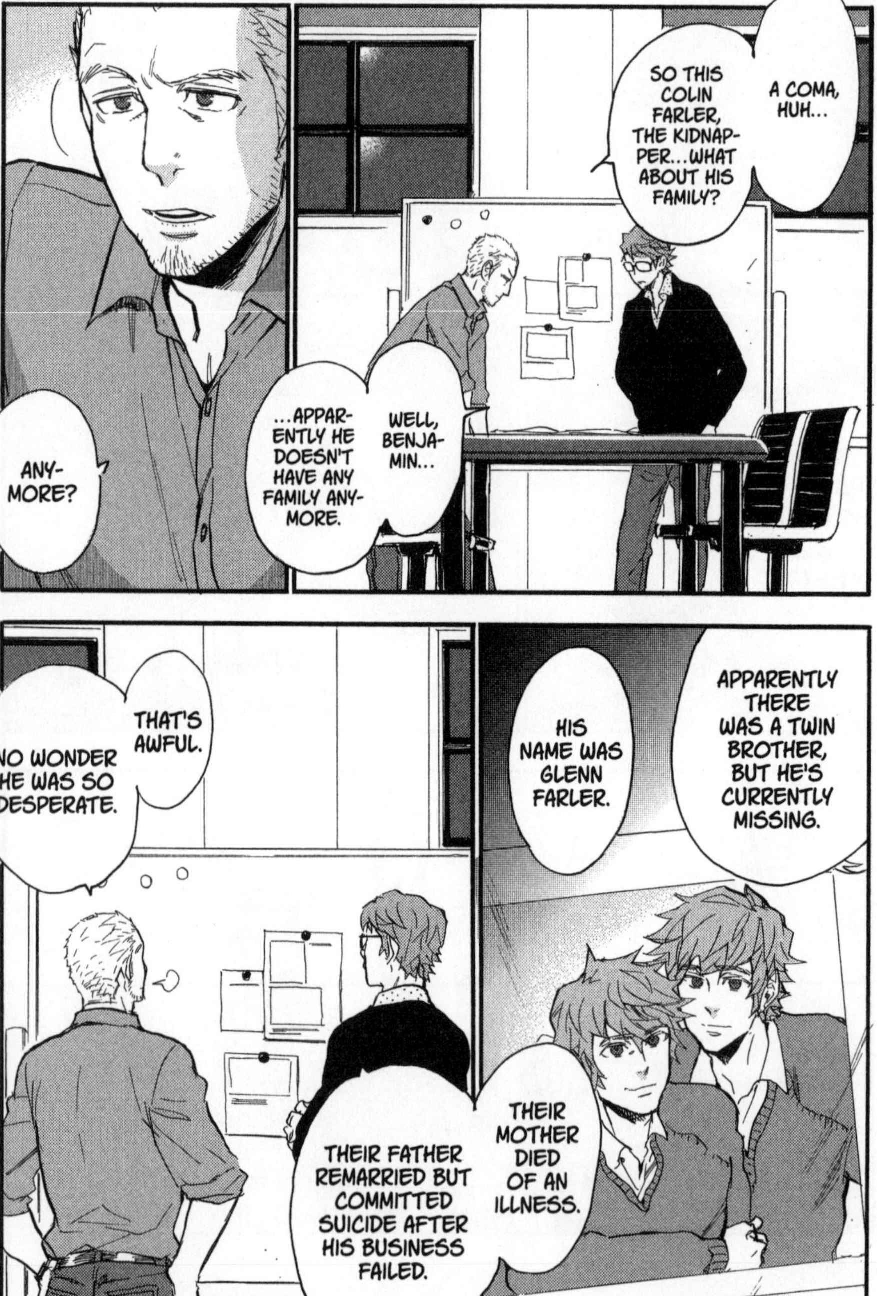
A COMA, HUH...
SO THIS COLIN FARLER, THE KIDNAPPER...WHAT ABOUT HIS FAMILY?
WELL, BENJAMIN...
...APPARENTLY HE DOESN'T HAVE ANY FAMILY ANYMORE.
ANYMORE?
APPARENTLY THERE WAS A TWIN BROTHER, BUT HE'S CURRENTLY MISSING.
HIS NAME WAS GLENN FARLER.
THEIR MOTHER DIED OF AN ILLNESS.
THEIR FATHER REMARRIED BUT COMMITTED SUICIDE AFTER HIS BUSINESS FAILED.
THAT'S AWFUL.
NO WONDER HE WAS SO DESPERATE.

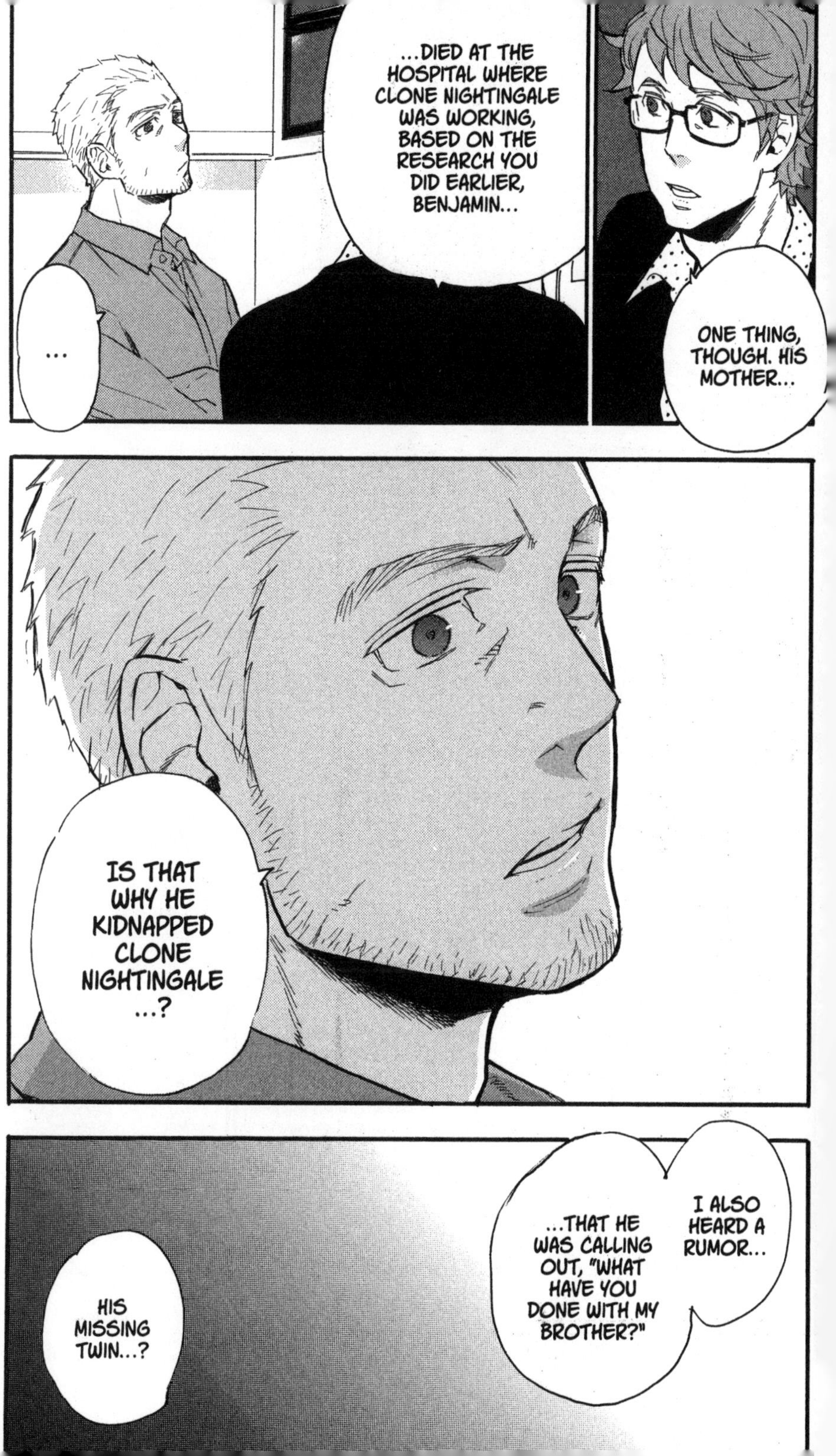
ONE THING, THOUGH. HIS MOTHER...
...DIED AT THE HOSPITAL WHERE CLONE NIGHTINGALE WAS WORKING, BASED ON THE RESEARCH YOU DID EARLIER, BENJAMIN...
...
IS THAT WHY HE KIDNAPPED CLONE NIGHTINGALE ...?
I ALSO HEARD A RUMOR...
...THAT HE WAS CALLING OUT, "WHAT HAVE YOU DONE WITH MY BROTHER?"
HIS MISSING TWIN...?

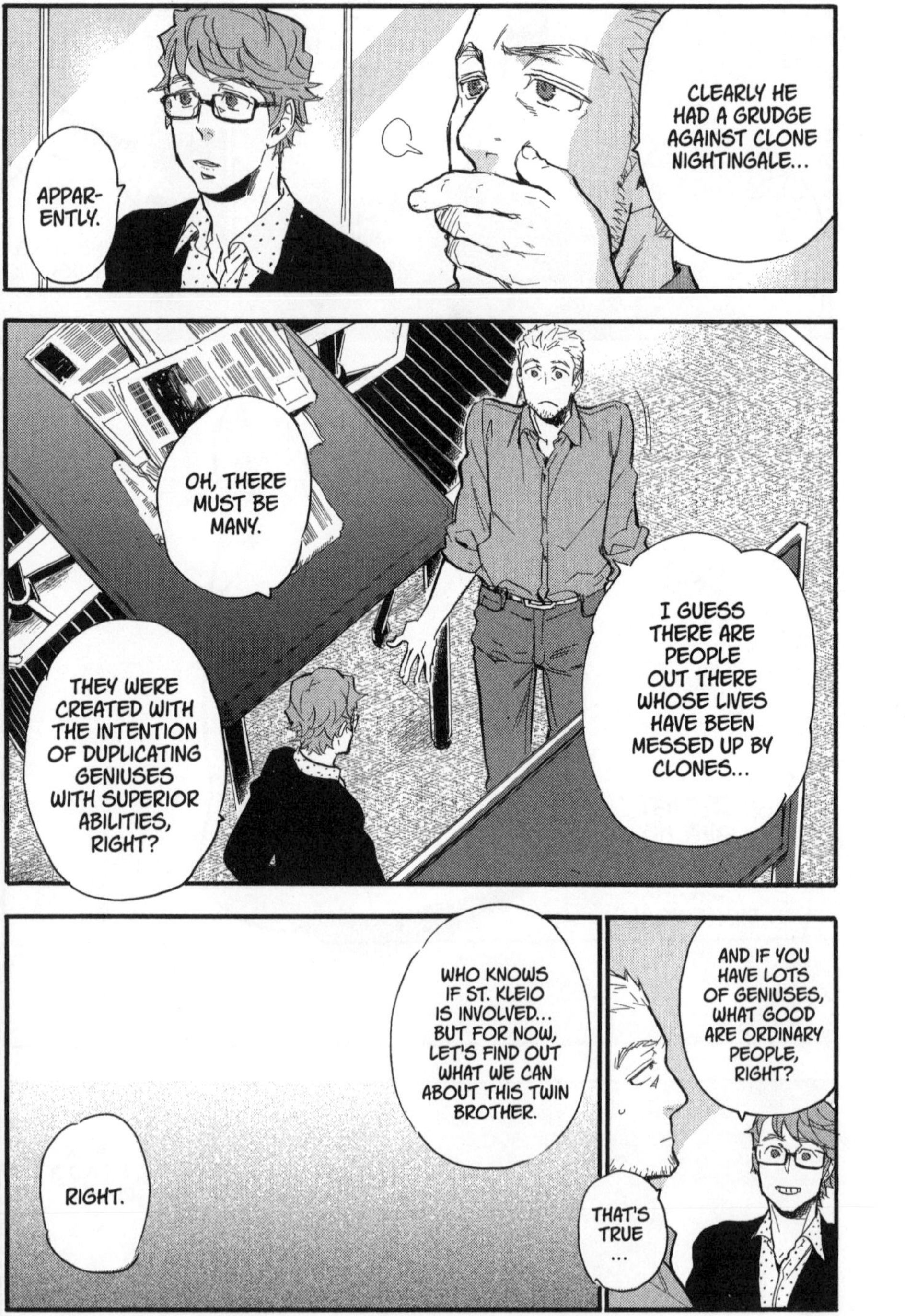
CLEARLY HE HAD A GRUDGE AGAINST CLONE NIGHTINGALE...
APPAR-ENTLY.
I GUESS THERE ARE PEOPLE OUT THERE WHOSE LIVES HAVE BEEN MESSED UP BY CLONES...
OH, THERE MUST BE MANY.
THEY WERE CREATED WITH THE INTENTION OF DUPLICATING GENIUSES WITH SUPERIOR ABILITIES, RIGHT?
AND IF YOU HAVE LOTS OF GENIUSES, WHAT GOOD ARE ORDINARY PEOPLE, RIGHT?
THAT'S TRUE ...
WHO KNOWS IF ST. KLEIO IS INVOLVED... BUT FOR NOW, LET'S FIND OUT WHAT WE CAN ABOUT THIS TWIN BROTHER.
RIGHT.

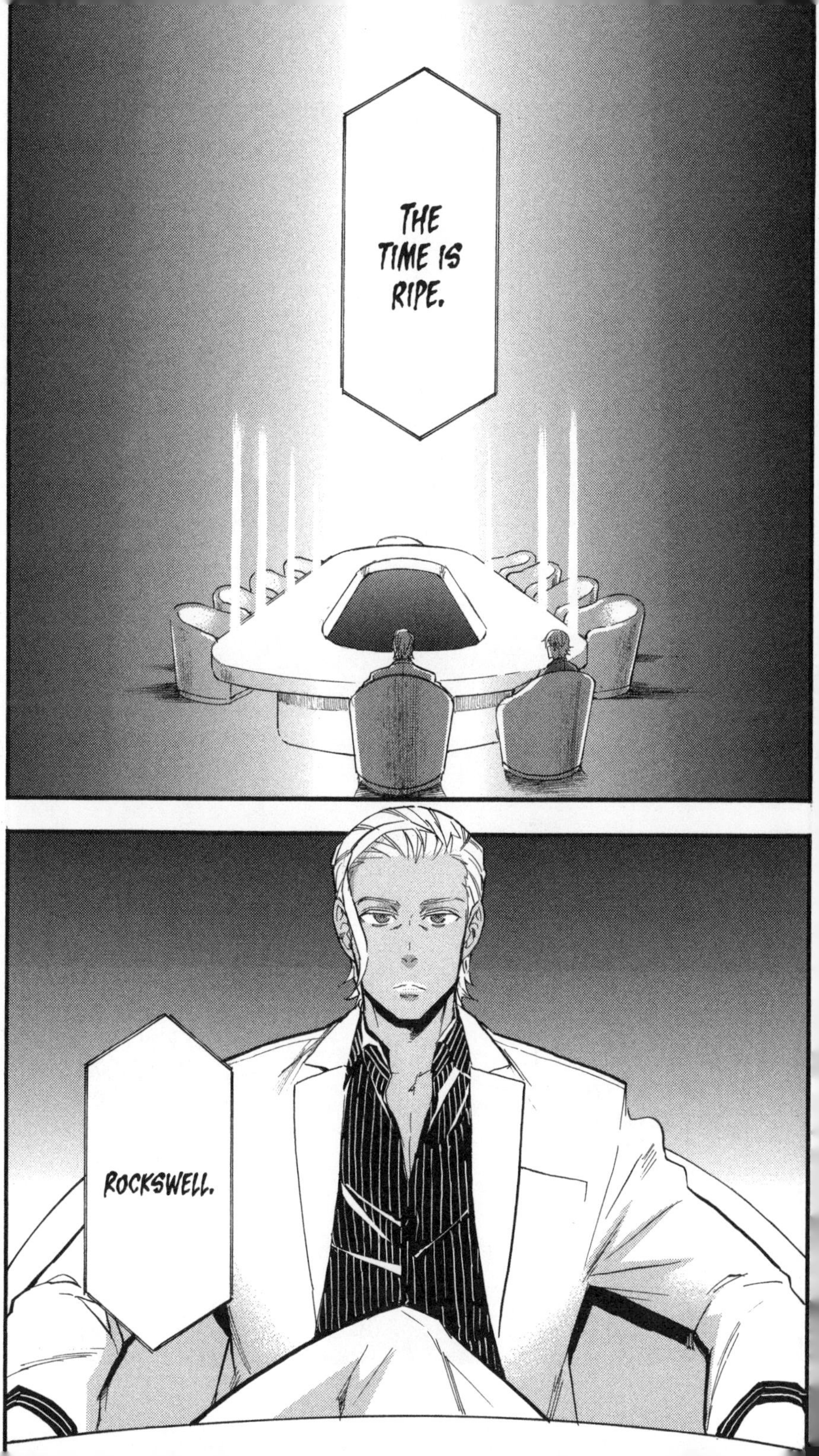
THE TIME IS RIPE.
ROCKSWELL.

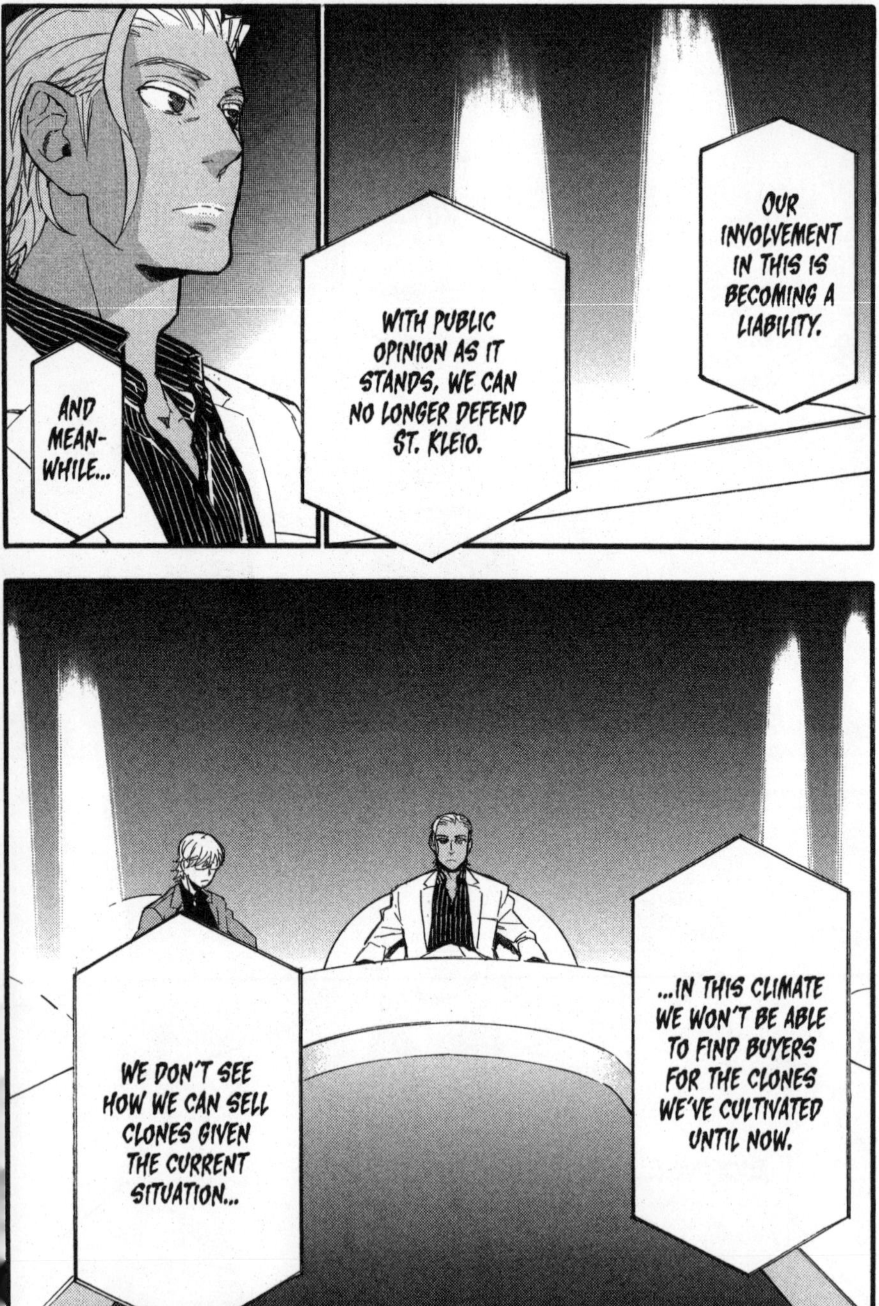
OUR INVOLVEMENT IN THIS IS BECOMING A LIABILITY.
WITH PUBLIC OPINION AS IT STANDS, WE CAN NO LONGER DEFEND ST. KLEIO.
AND MEAN-WHILE...
...IN THIS CLIMATE WE WON'T BE ABLE TO FIND BUYERS FOR THE CLONES WE'VE CULTIVATED UNTIL NOW.
WE DON'T SEE HOW WE CAN SELL CLONES GIVEN THE CURRENT SITUATION...

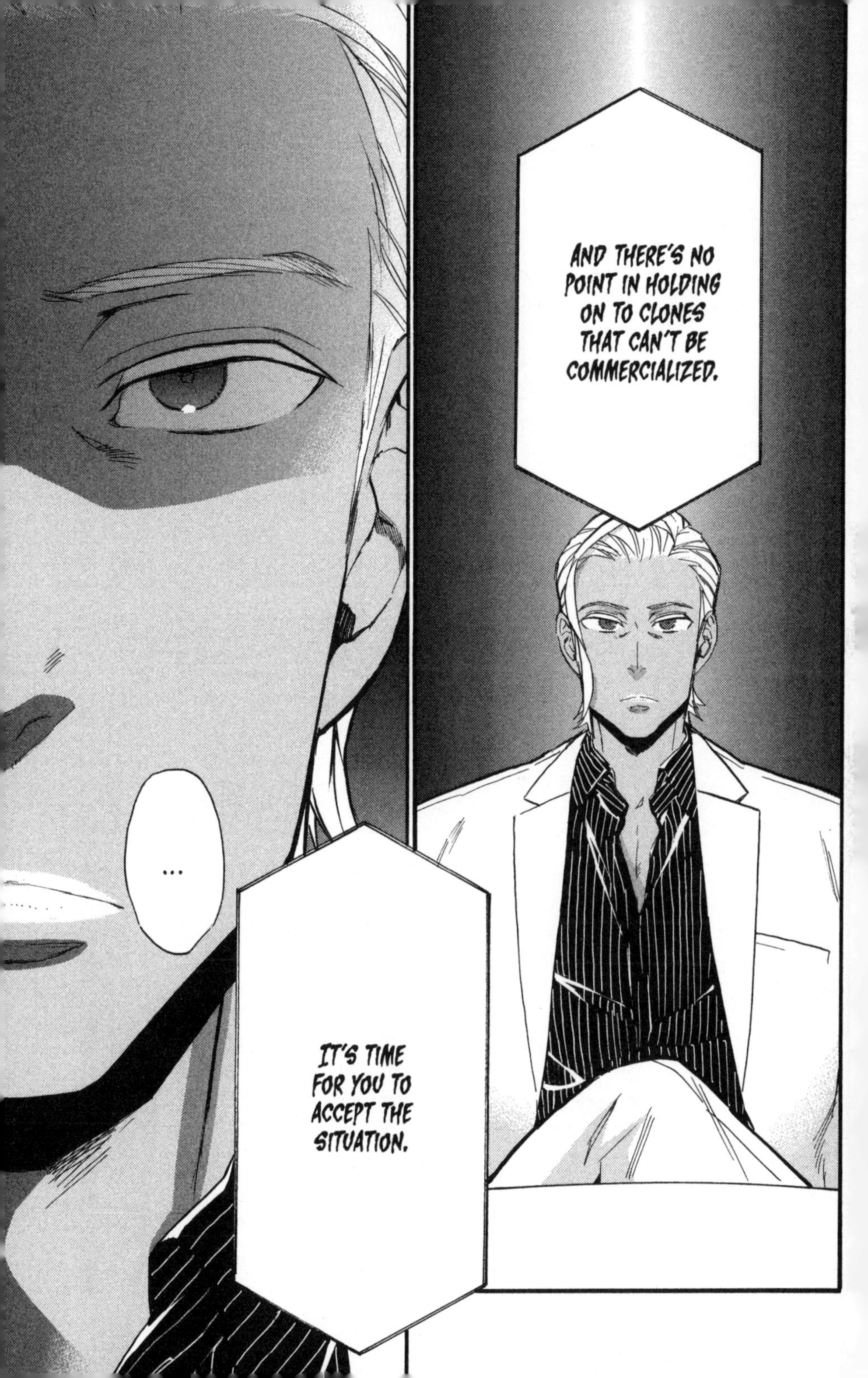
AND THERE'S NO POINT IN HOLDING ON TO CLONES THAT CAN'T BE COMMERCIALIZED.
...
IT'S TIME FOR YOU TO ACCEPT THE SITUATION.

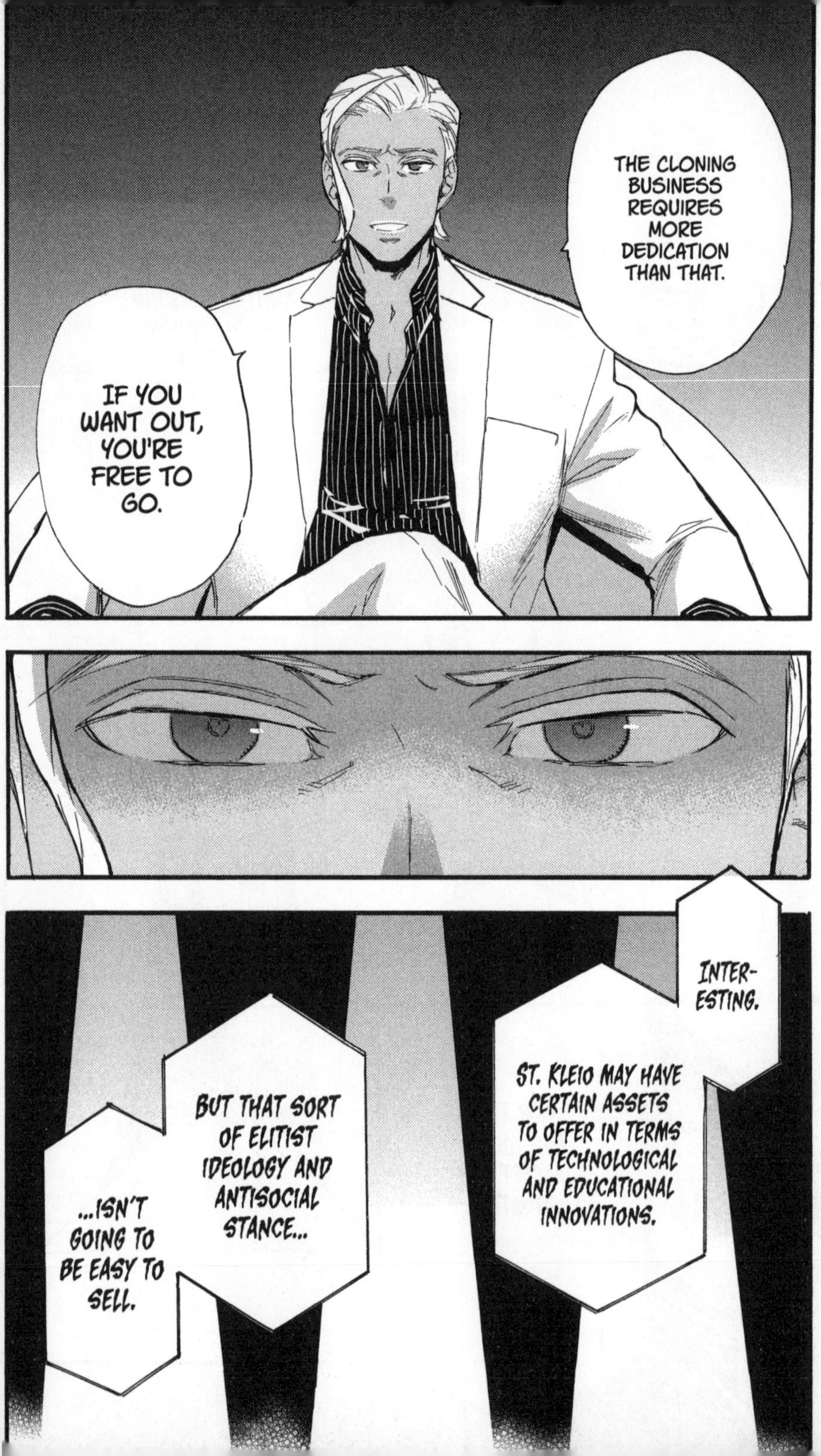
THE CLONING BUSINESS REQUIRES MORE DEDICATION THAN THAT.
IF YOU WANT OUT, YOU'RE FREE TO GO.
INTER-ESTING.
ST. KLEIO MAY HAVE CERTAIN ASSETS TO OFFER IN TERMS OF TECHNOLOGICAL AND EDUCATIONAL INNOVATIONS.
BUT THAT SORT OF ELITIST IDEOLOGY AND ANTISOCIAL STANCE...
...ISN'T GOING TO BE EASY TO SELL.

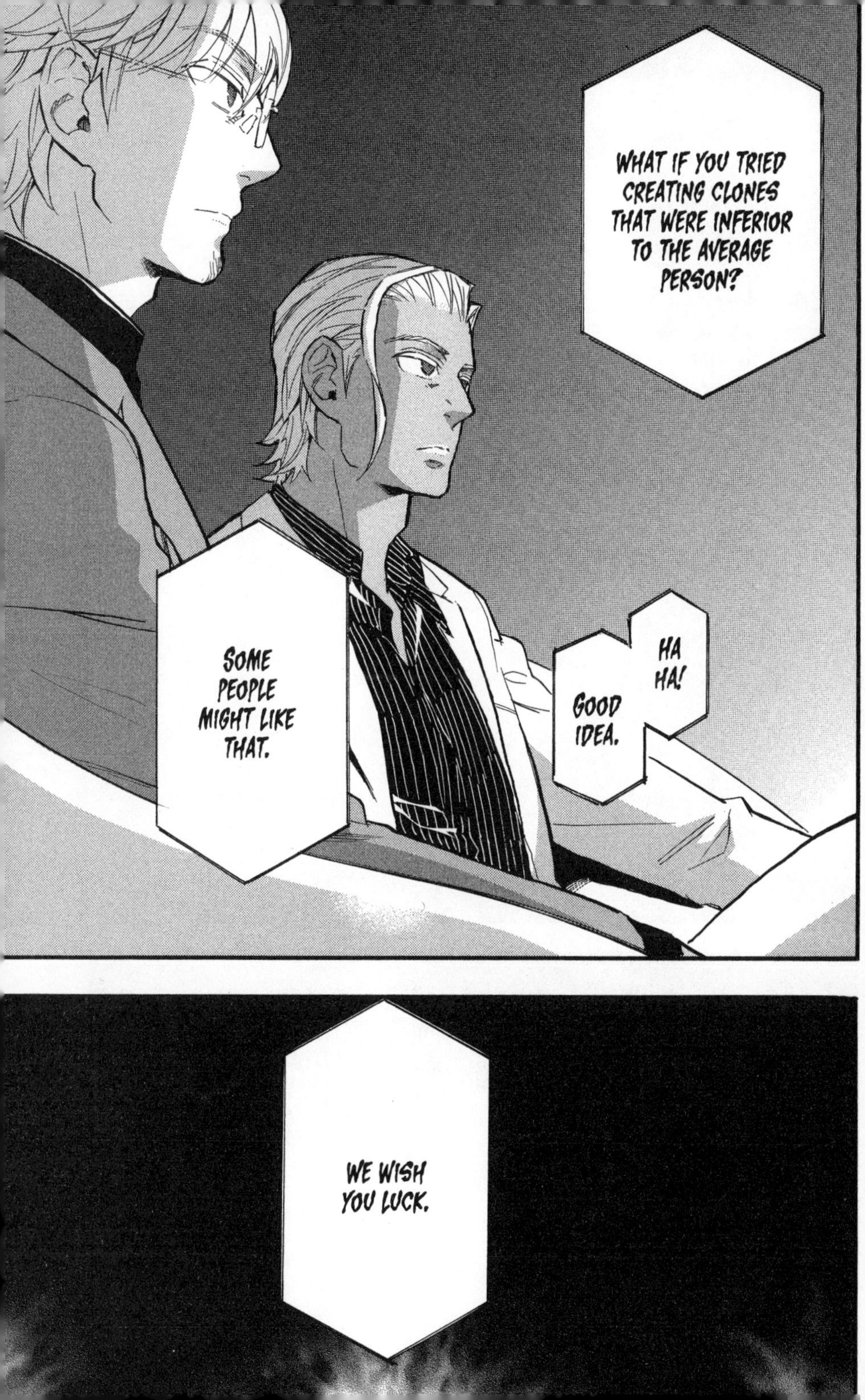
WHAT IF YOU TRIED CREATING CLONES THAT WERE INFERIOR TO THE AVERAGE PERSON?
HA HA! GOOD IDEA.
SOME PEOPLE MIGHT LIKE THAT.
WE WISH YOU LUCK.

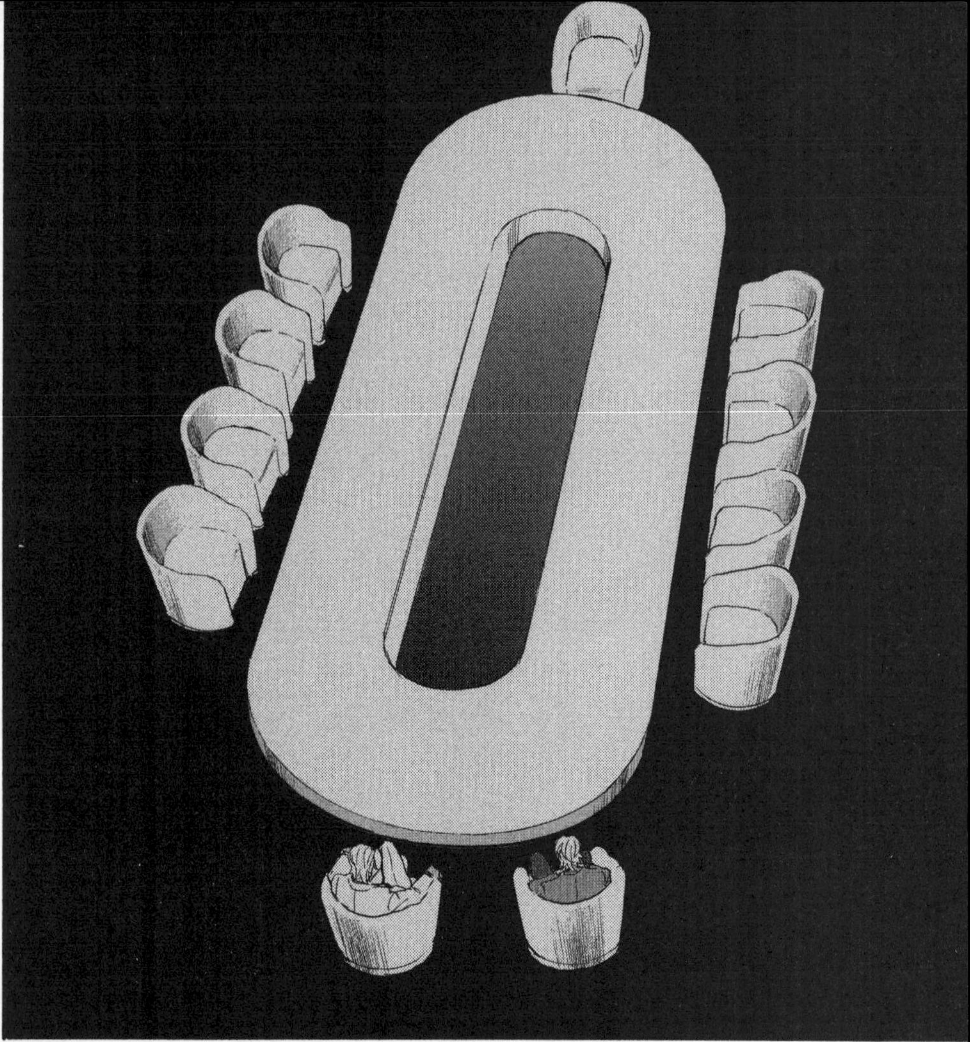

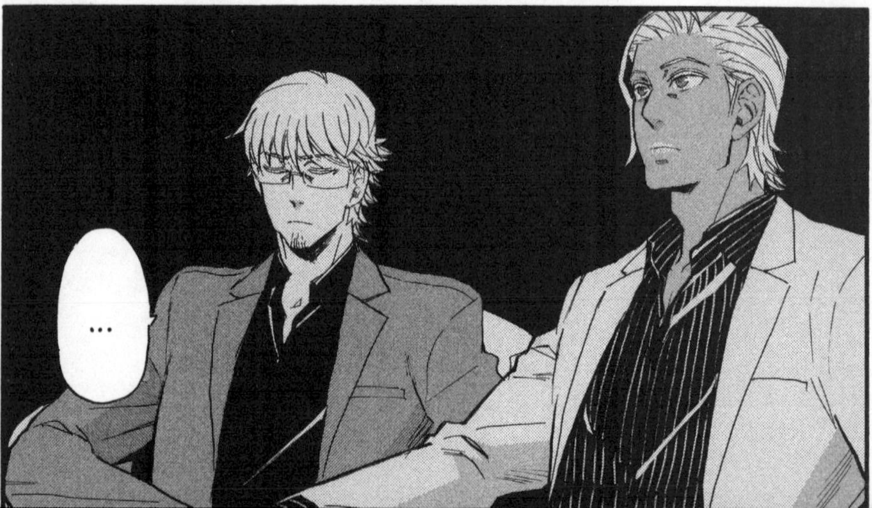
...

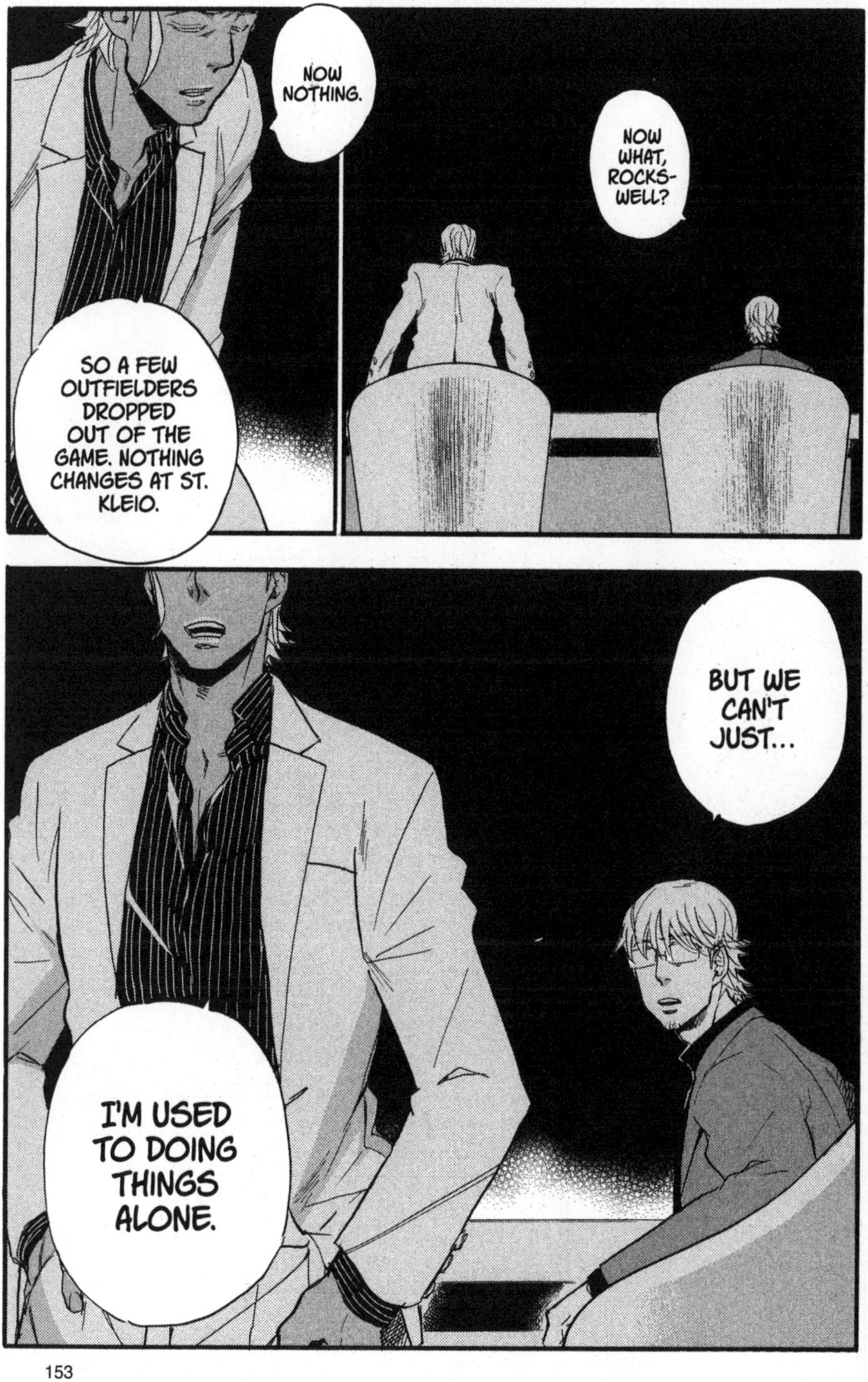
NOW WHAT, ROCKS-WELL?
NOW NOTHING.
SO A FEW OUTFIELDERS DROPPED OUT OF THE GAME. NOTHING CHANGES AT ST. KLEIO.
BUT WE CAN'T JUST...
I'M USED TO DOING THINGS ALONE.

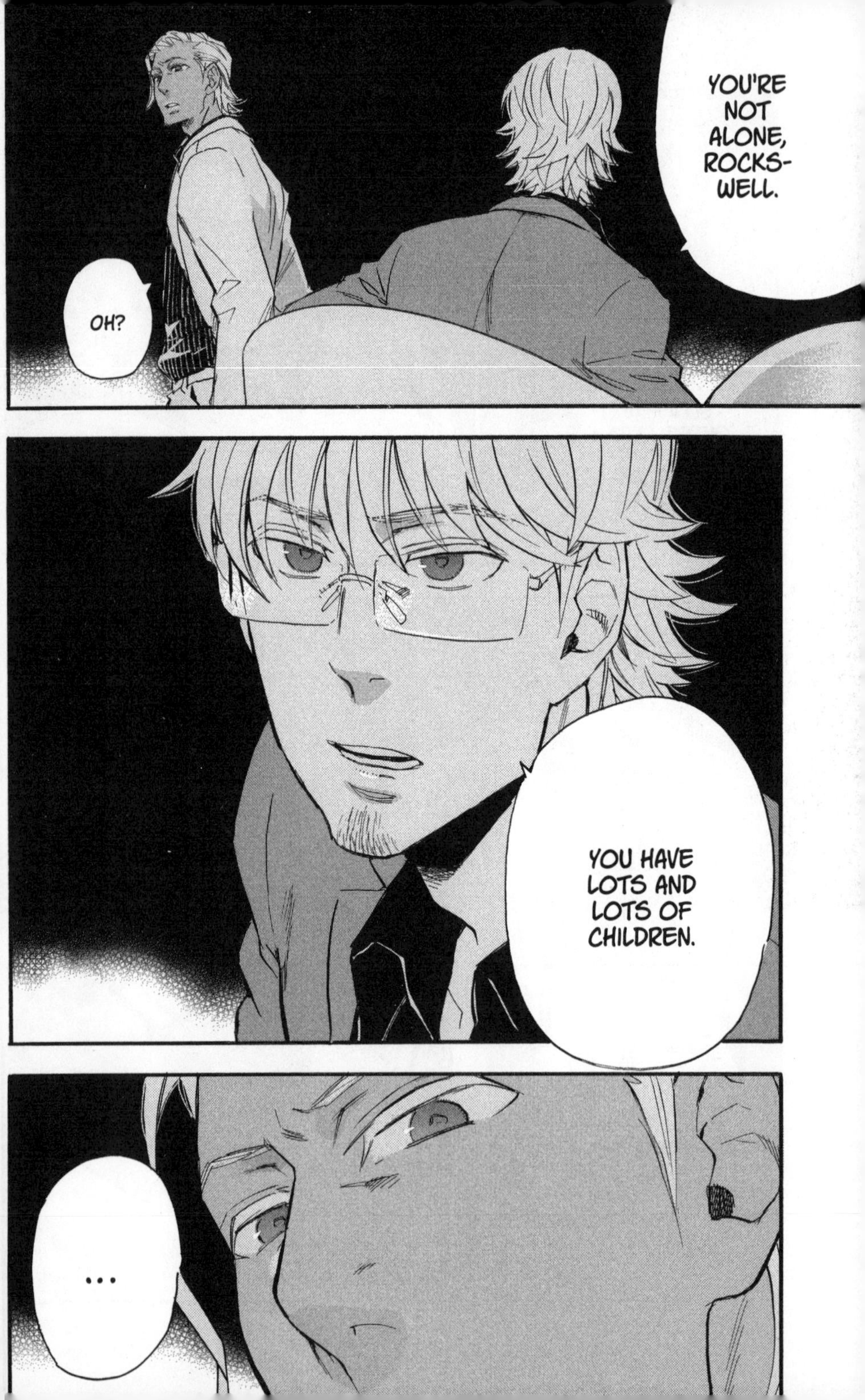
YOU'RE NOT ALONE, ROCKS-WELL.
OH?
YOU HAVE LOTS AND LOTS OF CHILDREN.
...

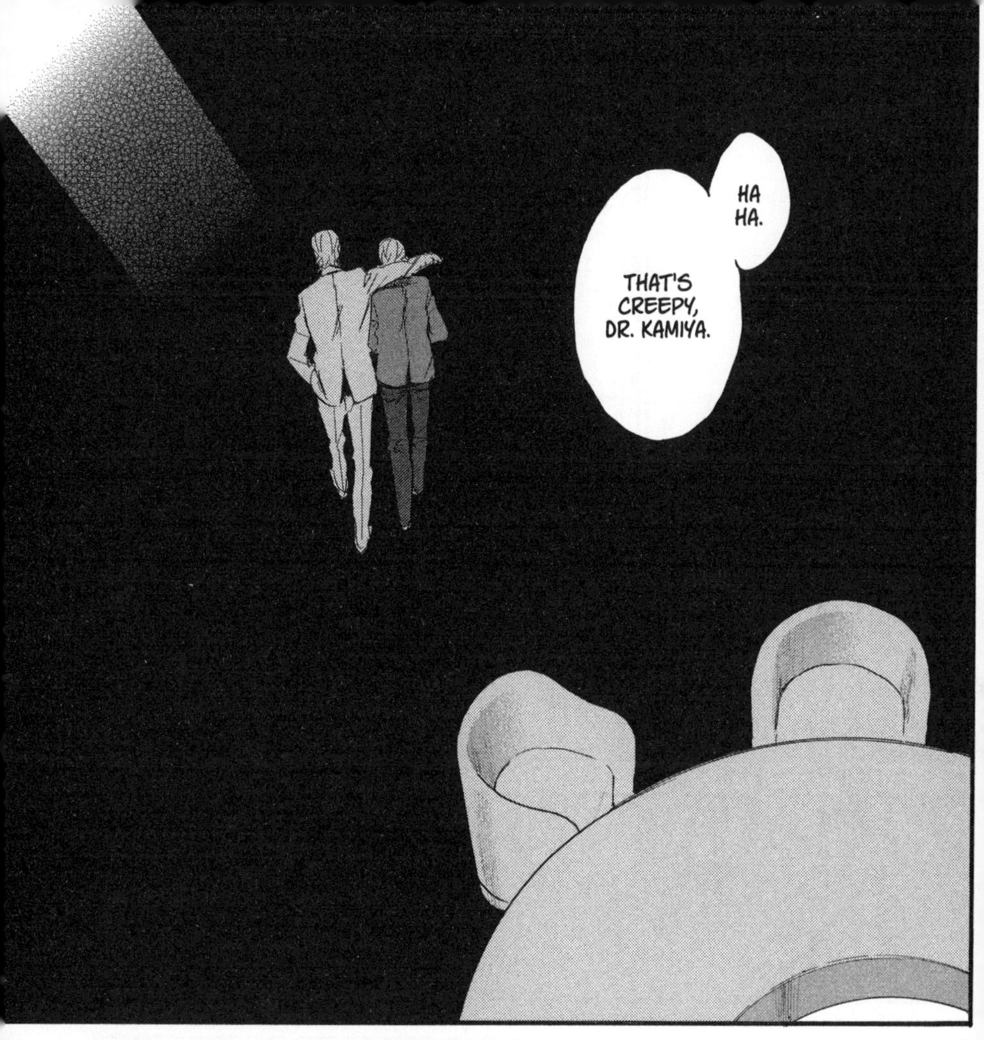
HA HA.
THAT'S CREEPY, DR. KAMIYA.

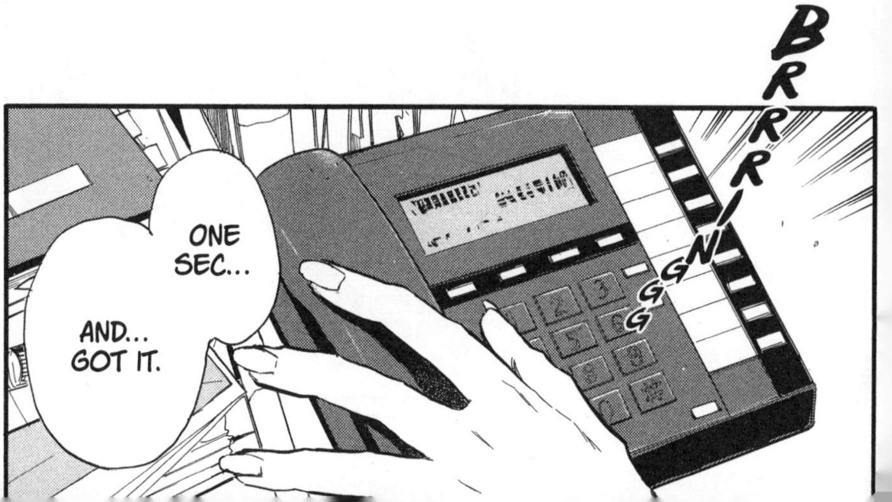
BRRRINGGG
ONE SEC...
AND... GOT IT.

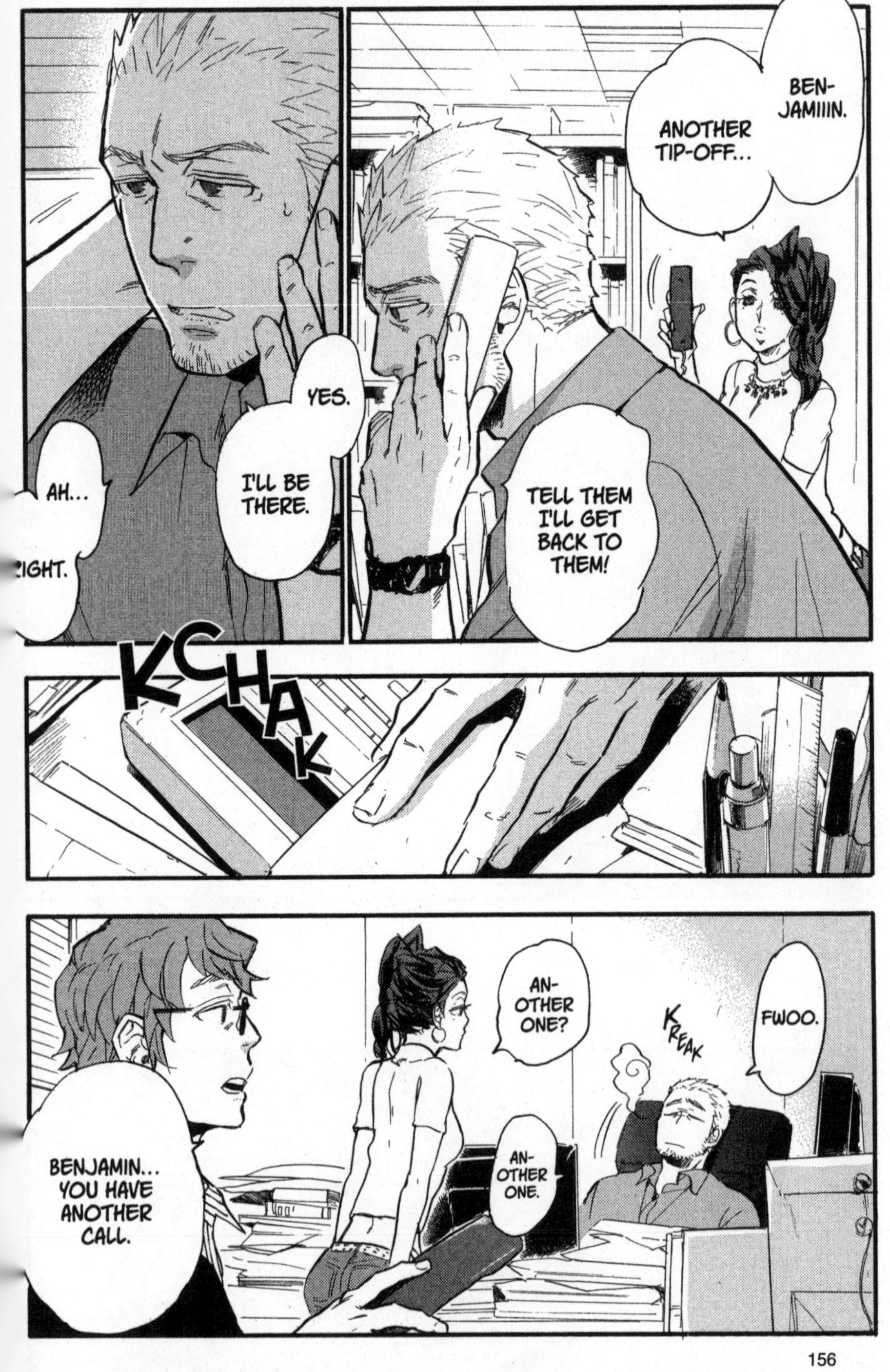
BEN-JAMIIIN.
ANOTHER TIP-OFF...
TELL THEM I'LL GET BACK TO THEM!
YES.
I'LL BE THERE.
AH...
RIGHT.
KCHAK
FWOO.
KREAK
AN-OTHER ONE?
AN-OTHER ONE.
BENJAMIN... YOU HAVE ANOTHER CALL.

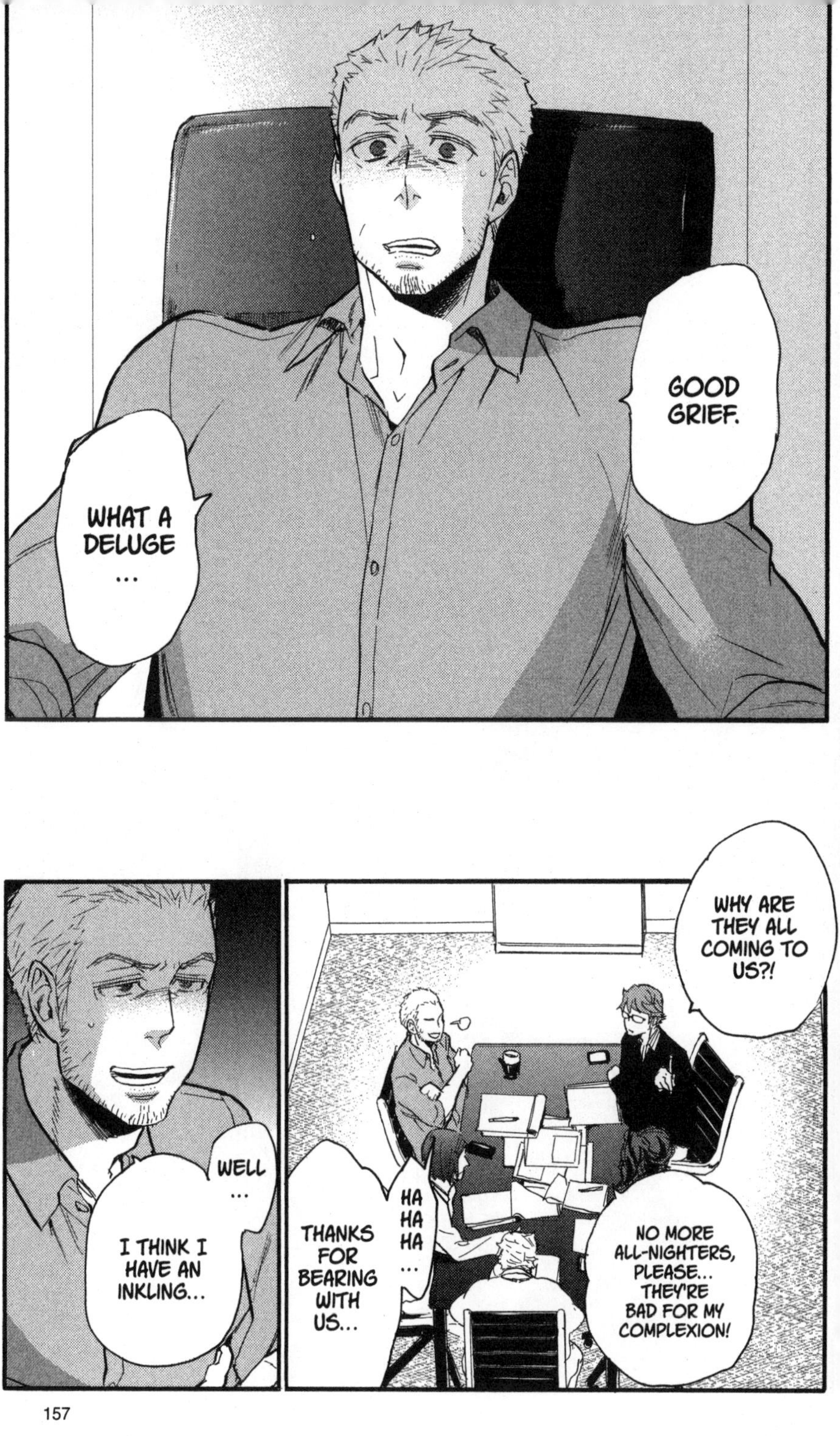
GOOD GRIEF.
WHAT A DELUGE ...
WHY ARE THEY ALL COMING TO US?!
NO MORE ALL-NIGHTERS, PLEASE... THEY'RE BAD FOR MY COMPLEXION!
HA HA HA ...
THANKS FOR BEARING WITH US...
WELL ...
I THINK I HAVE AN INKLING...

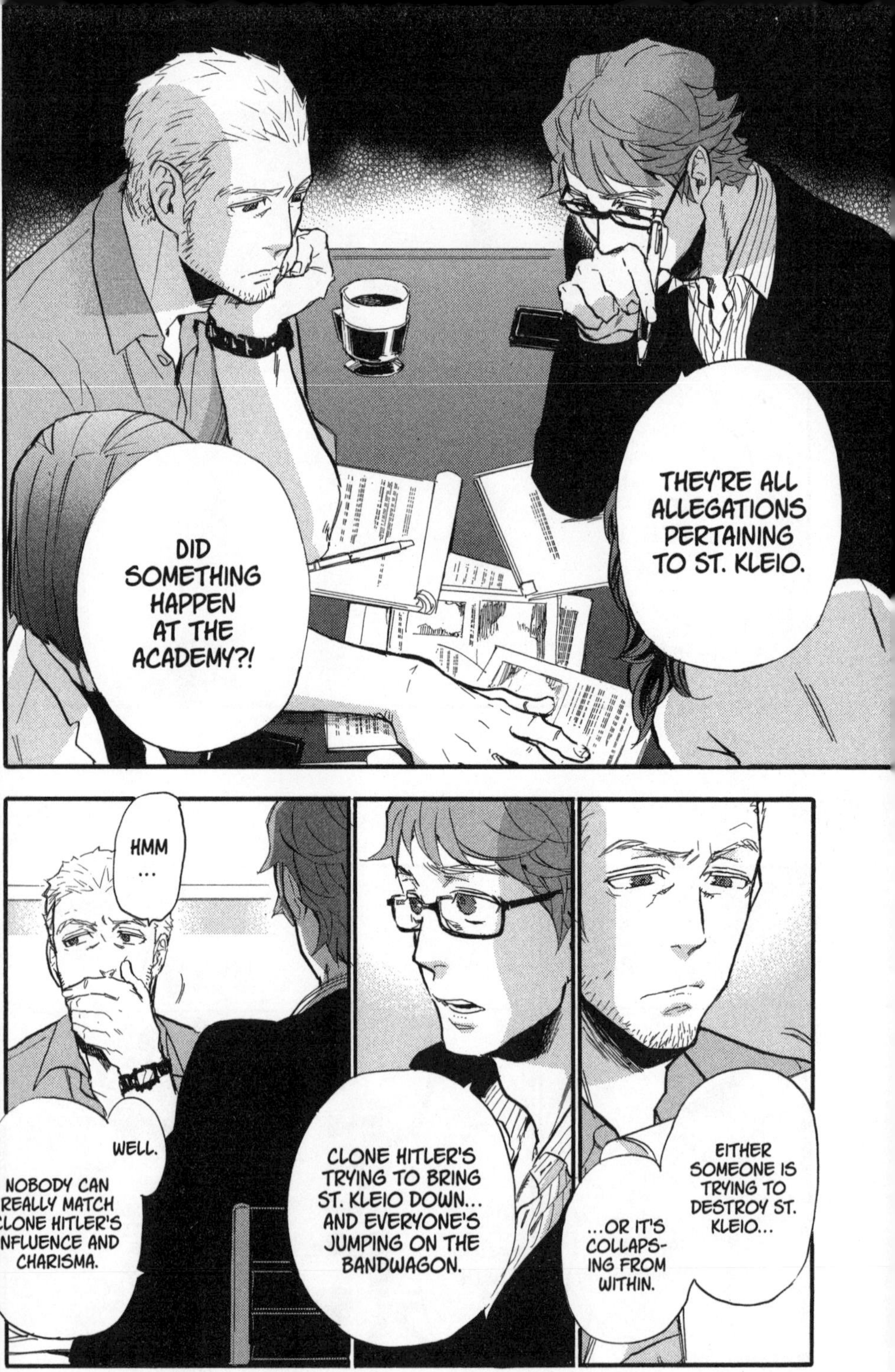
THEY'RE ALL ALLEGATIONS PERTAINING TO ST. KLEIO.
DID SOMETHING HAPPEN AT THE ACADEMY?!
EITHER SOMEONE IS TRYING TO DESTROY ST. KLEIO...
...OR IT'S COLLAPS-ING FROM WITHIN.
CLONE HITLER'S TRYING TO BRING ST. KLEIO DOWN... AND EVERYONE'S JUMPING ON THE BANDWAGON.
HMM ...
WELL.
NOBODY CAN REALLY MATCH CLONE HITLER'S INFLUENCE AND CHARISMA.

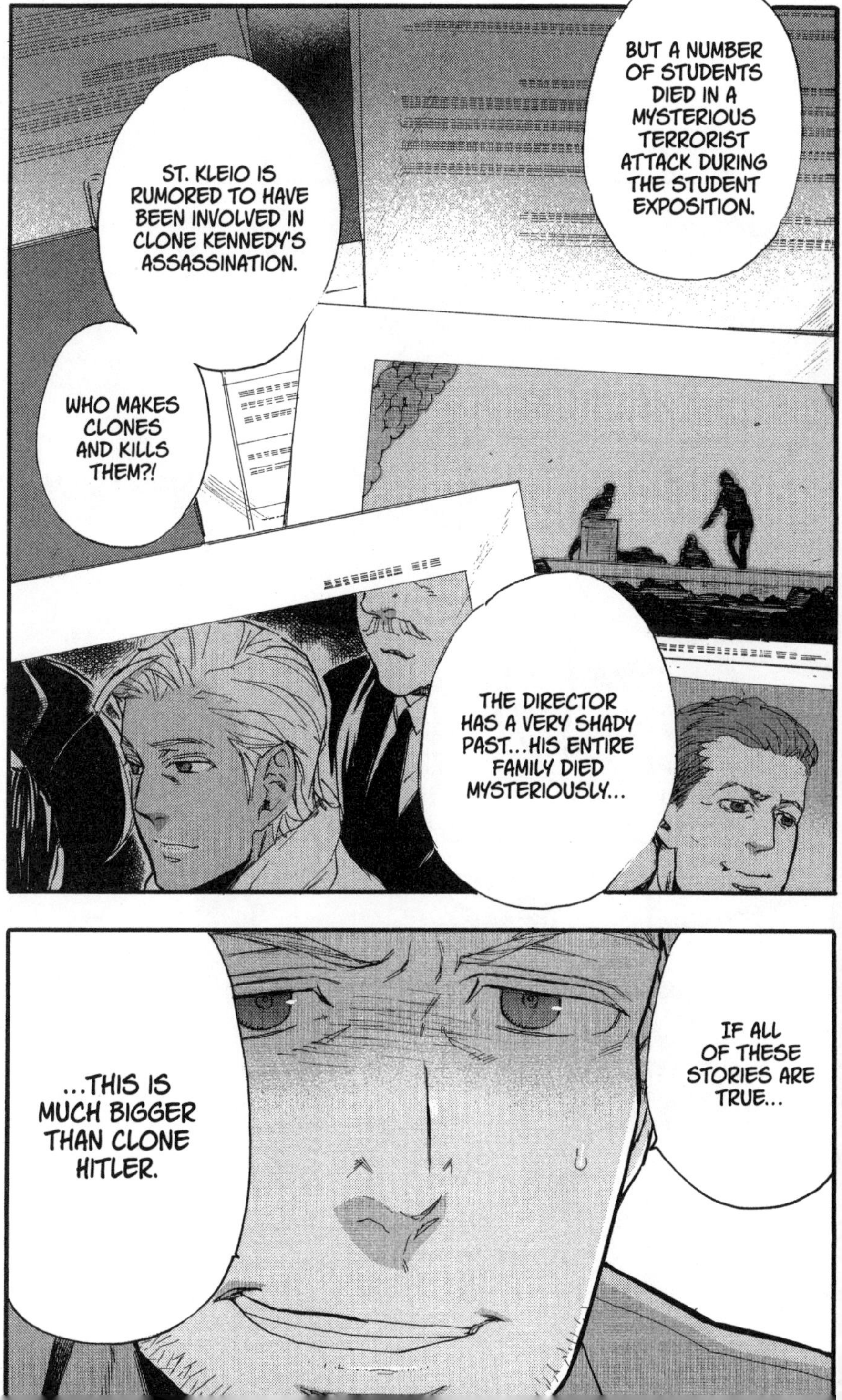
BUT A NUMBER OF STUDENTS DIED IN A MYSTERIOUS TERRORIST ATTACK DURING THE STUDENT EXPOSITION.
ST. KLEIO IS RUMORED TO HAVE BEEN INVOLVED IN CLONE KENNEDY'S ASSASSINATION.
WHO MAKES CLONES AND KILLS THEM?!
THE DIRECTOR HAS A VERY SHADY PAST...HIS ENTIRE FAMILY DIED MYSTERIOUSLY...
IF ALL OF THESE STORIES ARE TRUE...
...THIS IS MUCH BIGGER THAN CLONE HITLER.

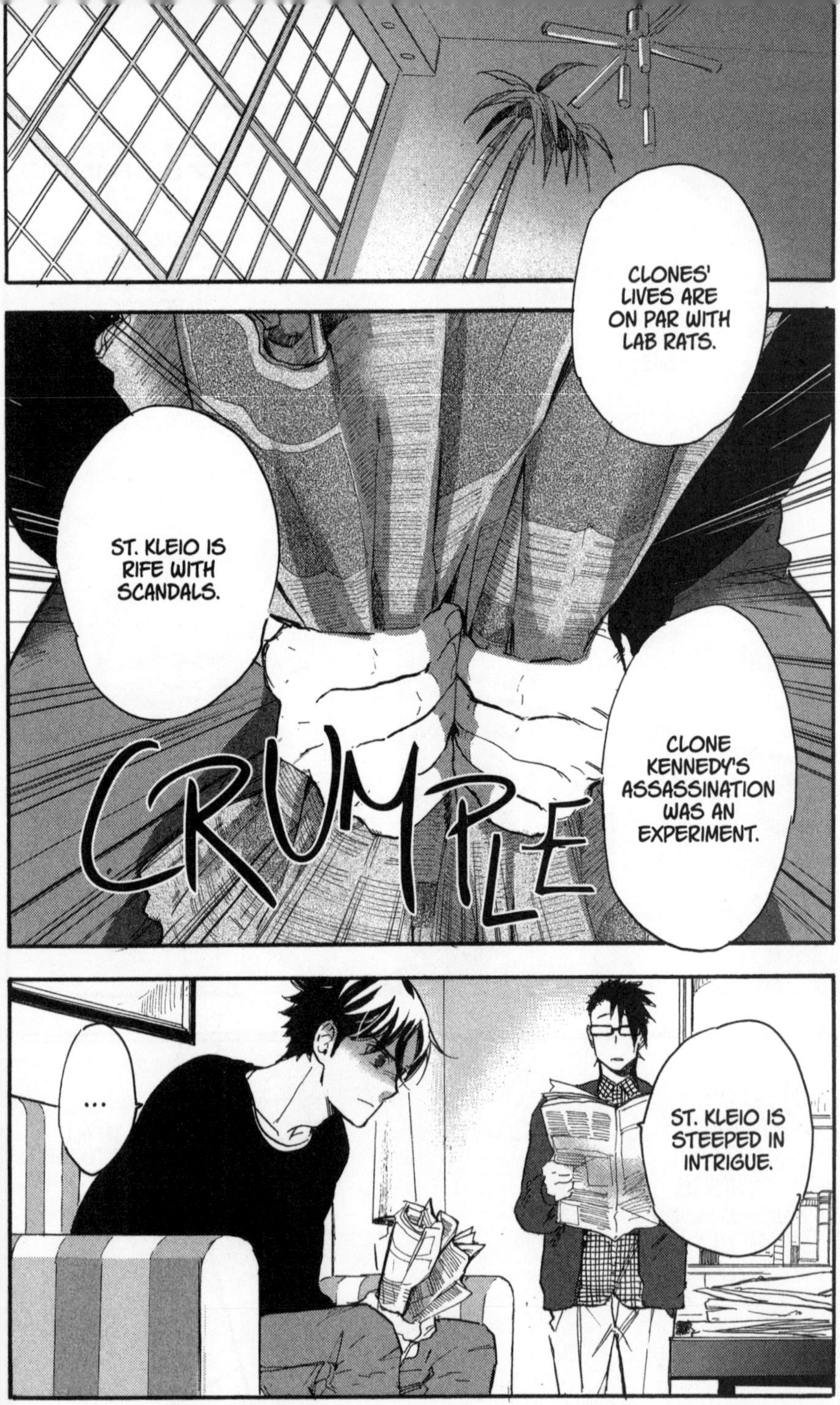
CLONES' LIVES ARE ON PAR WITH LAB RATS.
ST. KLEIO IS RIFE WITH SCANDALS.
CLONE KENNEDY'S ASSASSINATION WAS AN EXPERIMENT.
CRUMPLE
ST. KLEIO IS STEEPED IN INTRIGUE.
...

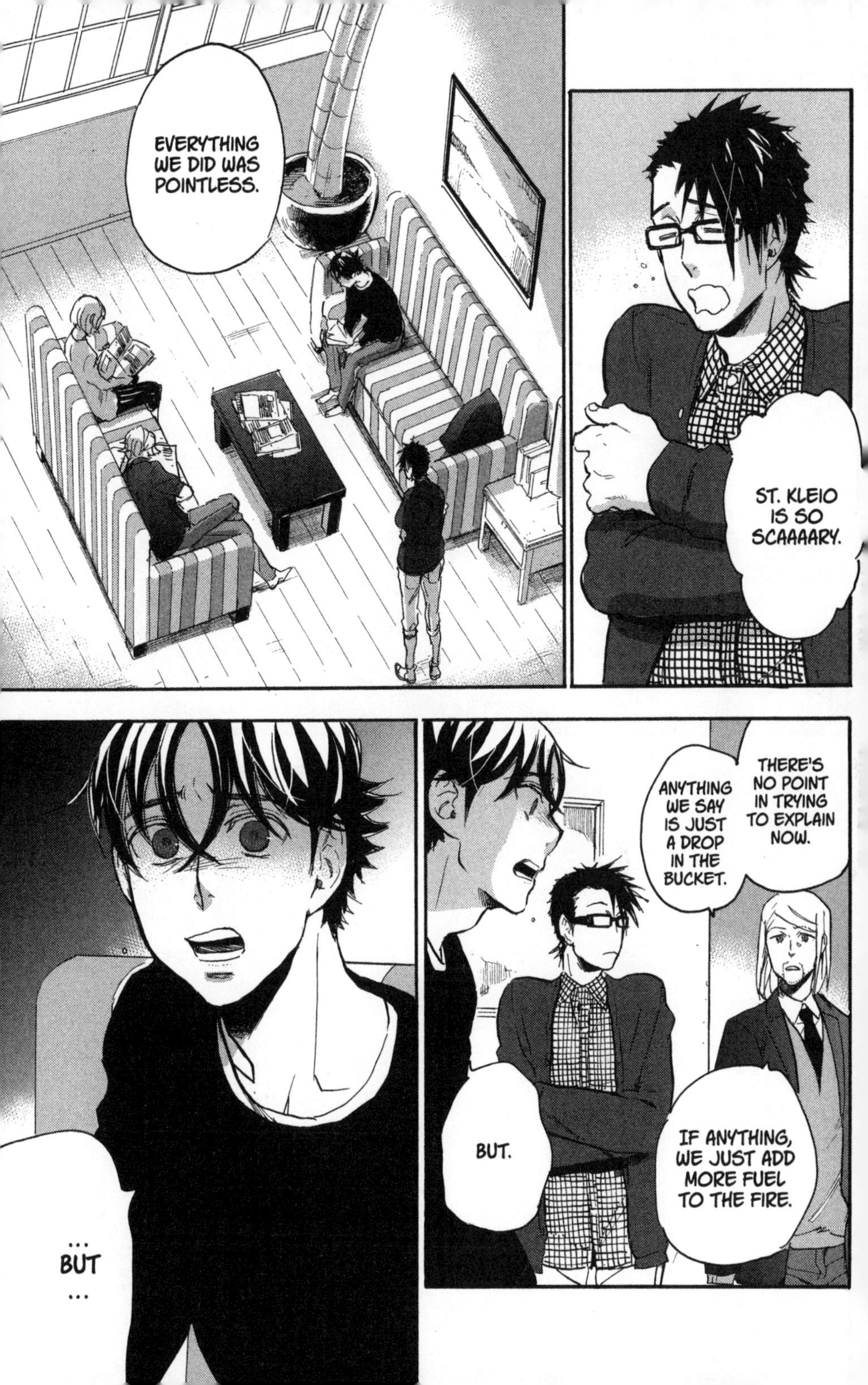
ST. KLEIO IS SO SCAAAARY.
EVERYTHING WE DID WAS POINTLESS.
THERE'S NO POINT IN TRYING TO EXPLAIN NOW.
ANYTHING WE SAY IS JUST A DROP IN THE BUCKET.
IF ANYTHING, WE JUST ADD MORE FUEL TO THE FIRE.
BUT.
... BUT ...

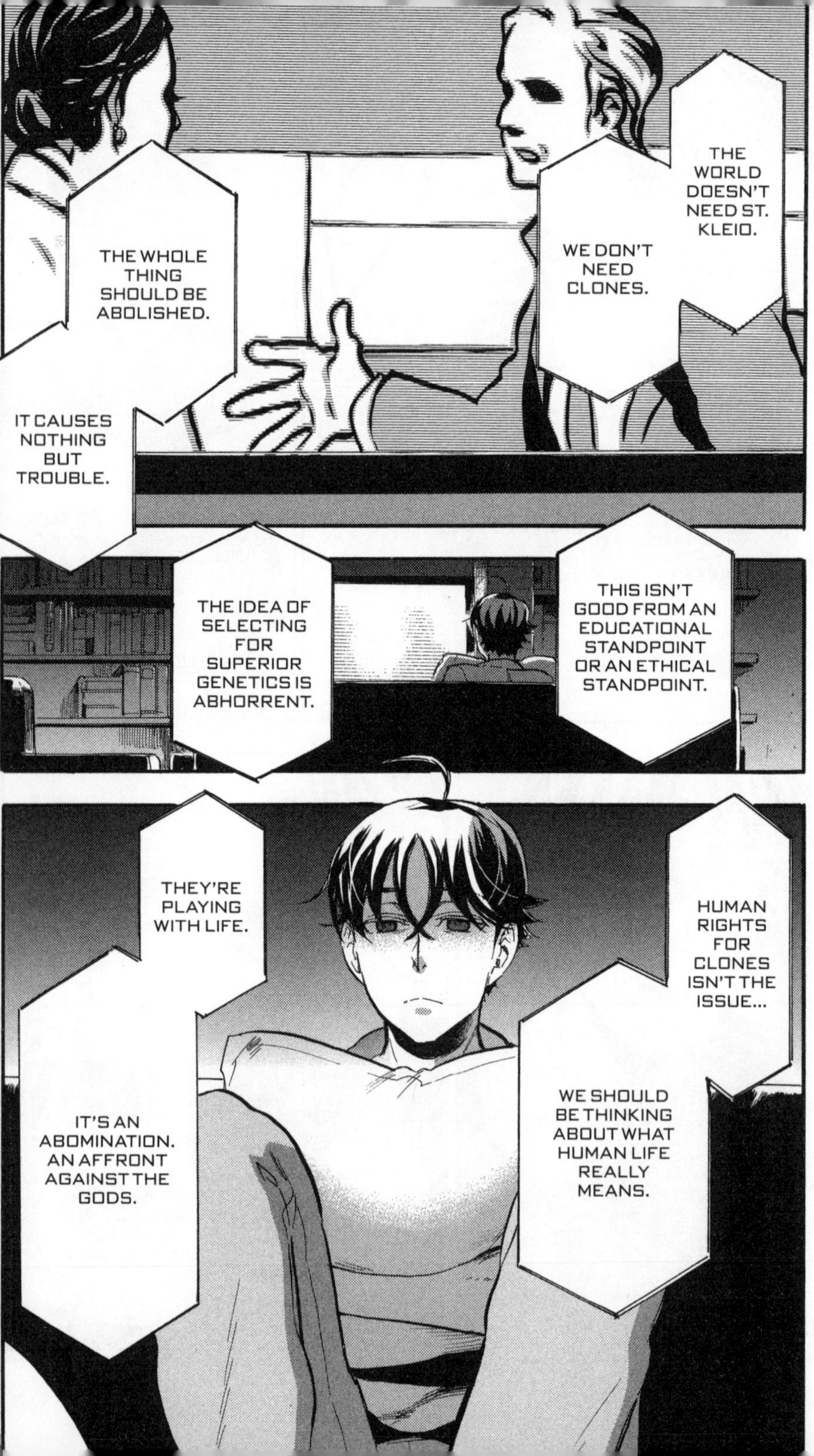
THE WORLD DOESN'T NEED ST. KLEIO.
WE DON'T NEED CLONES.
THE WHOLE THING SHOULD BE ABOLISHED.
IT CAUSES NOTHING BUT TROUBLE.
THIS ISN'T GOOD FROM AN EDUCATIONAL STANDPOINT OR AN ETHICAL STANDPOINT.
THE IDEA OF SELECTING FOR SUPERIOR GENETICS IS ABHORRENT.
HUMAN RIGHTS FOR CLONES ISN'T THE ISSUE...
THEY'RE PLAYING WITH LIFE.
WE SHOULD BE THINKING ABOUT WHAT HUMAN LIFE REALLY MEANS.
IT'S AN ABOMINATION. AN AFFRONT AGAINST THE GODS.

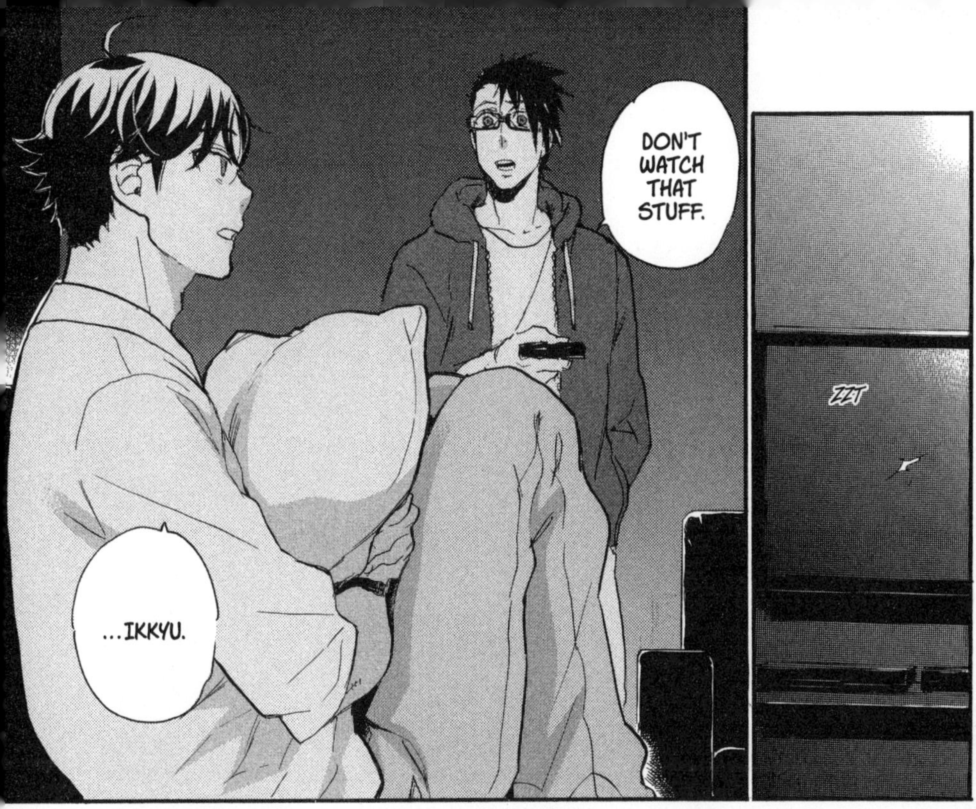
DON'T WATCH THAT STUFF.
ZZT
...IKKYU.
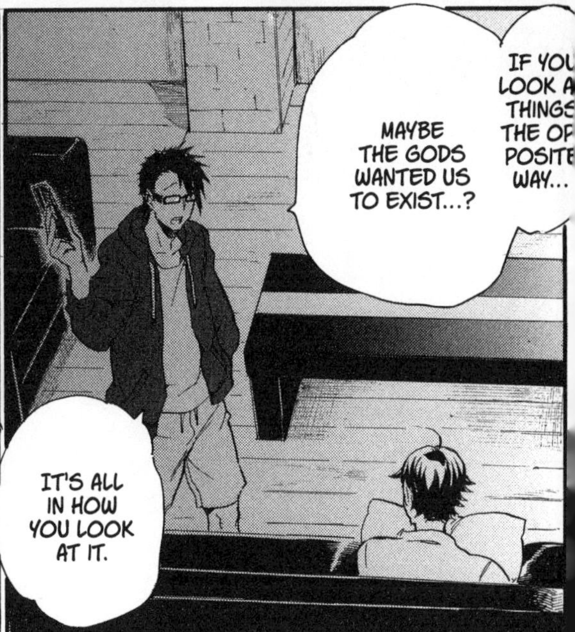
IF YOU LOOK A THINGS THE OP POSITE WAY...
MAYBE THE GODS WANTED US TO EXIST...?
IT'S ALL IN HOW YOU LOOK AT IT.
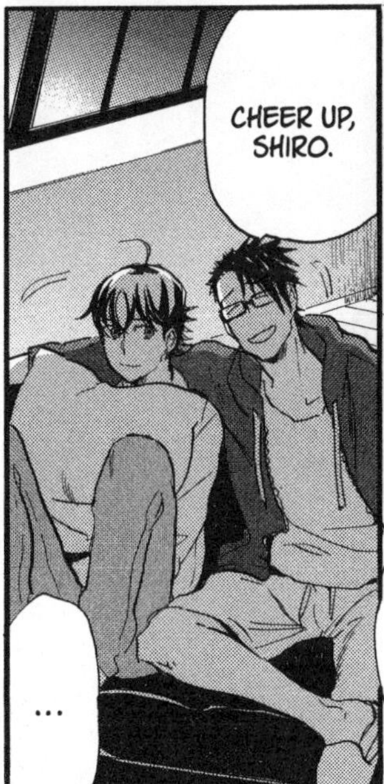
CHEER UP, SHIRO.
...

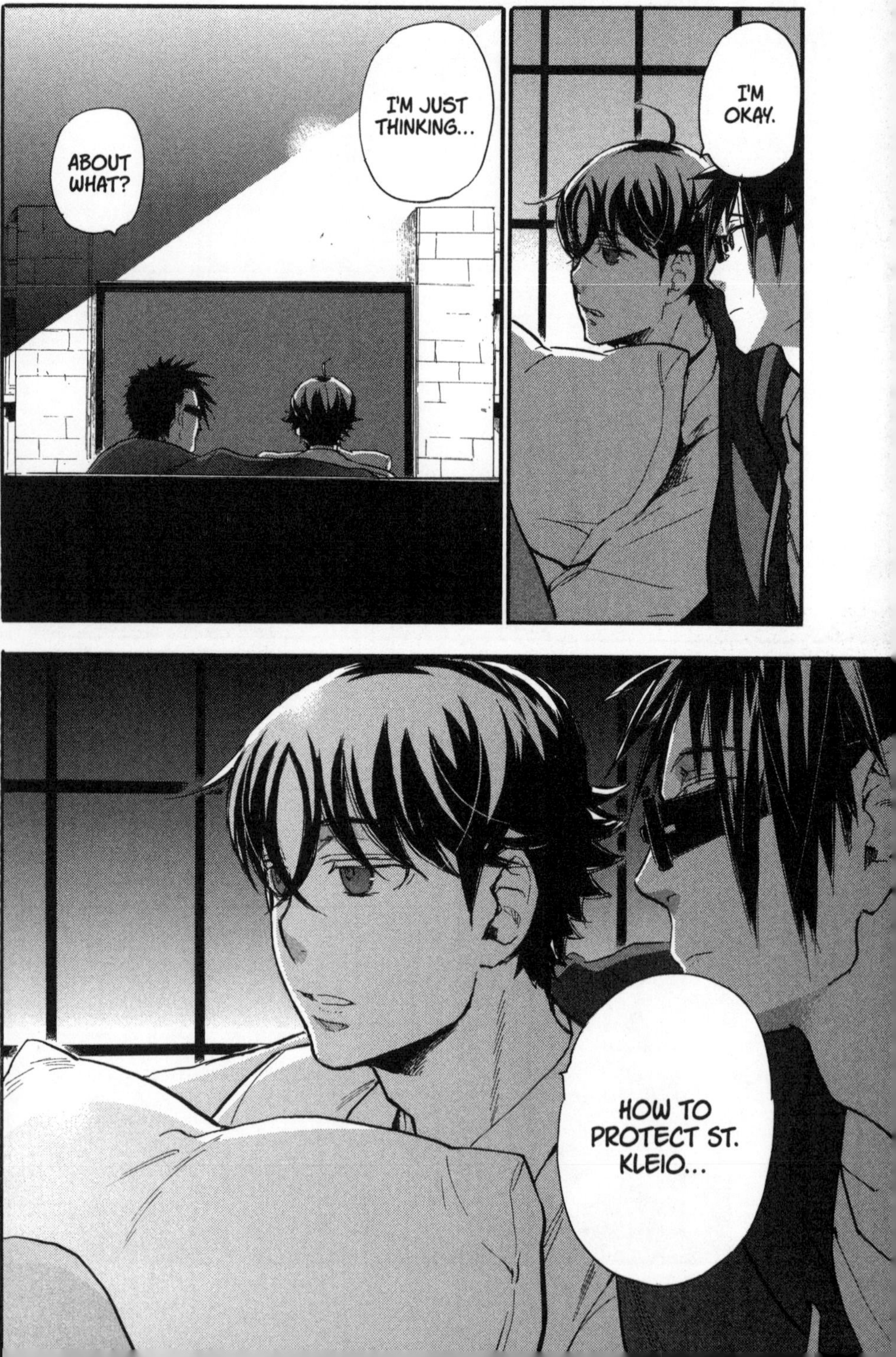
I'M OKAY.
I'M JUST THINKING...
ABOUT WHAT?
HOW TO PROTECT ST. KLEIO...

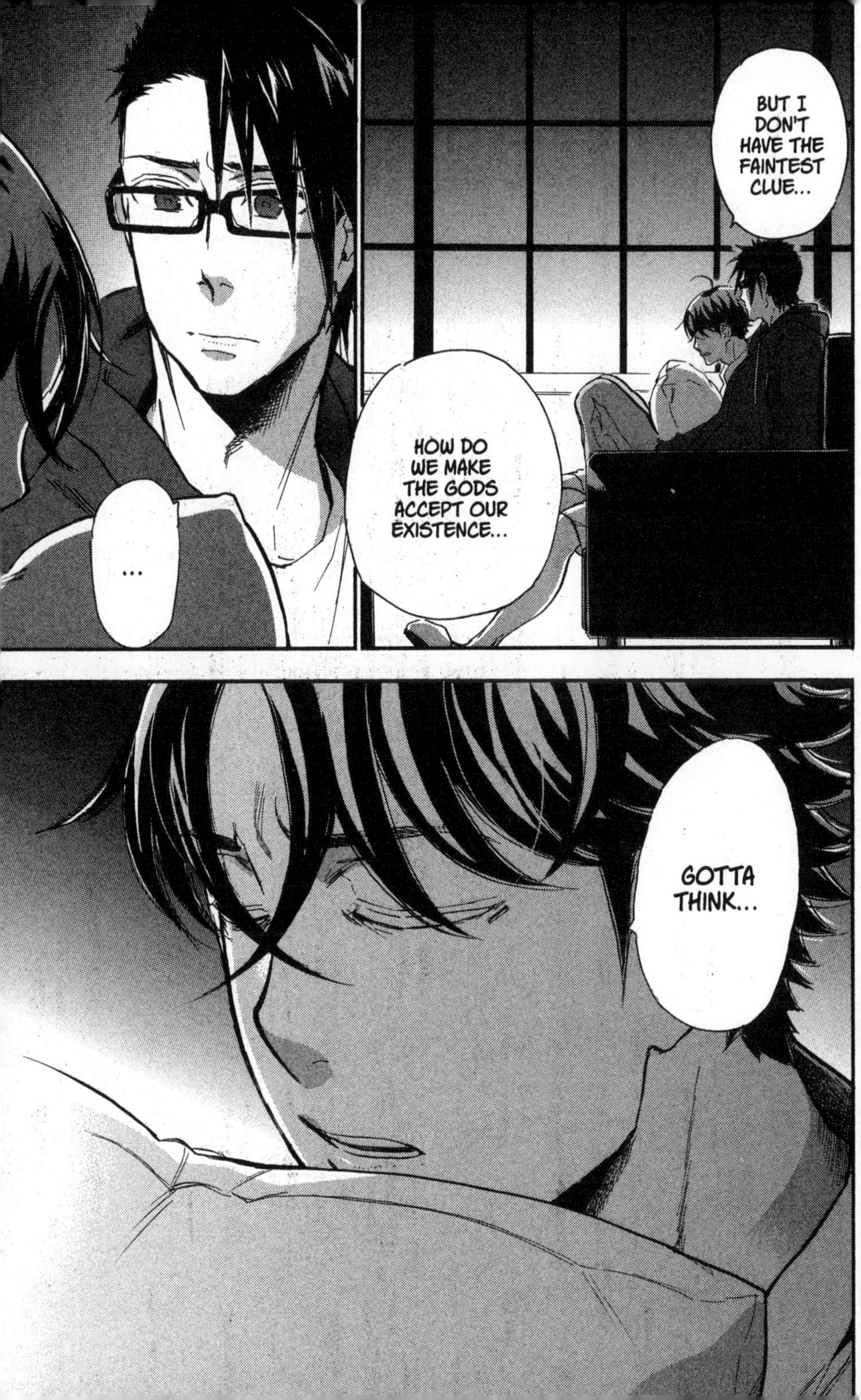
BUT I DON'T HAVE THE FAINTEST CLUE...
HOW DO WE MAKE THE GODS ACCEPT OUR EXISTENCE...
...
GOTTA THINK...

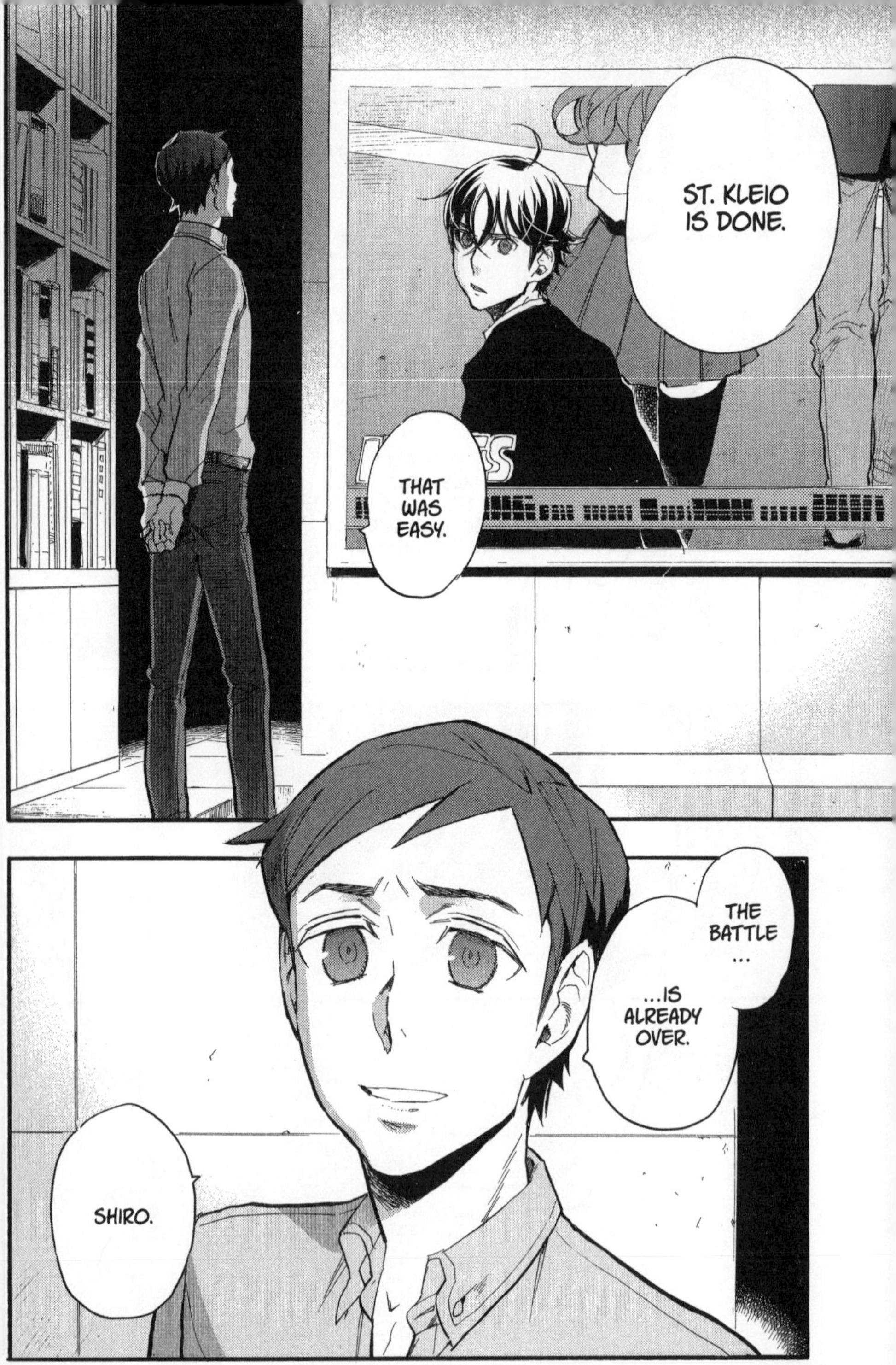
ST. KLEIO IS DONE.
THAT WAS EASY.
THE BATTLE ...
...IS ALREADY OVER.
SHIRO.

# CHAPTER sixty-six

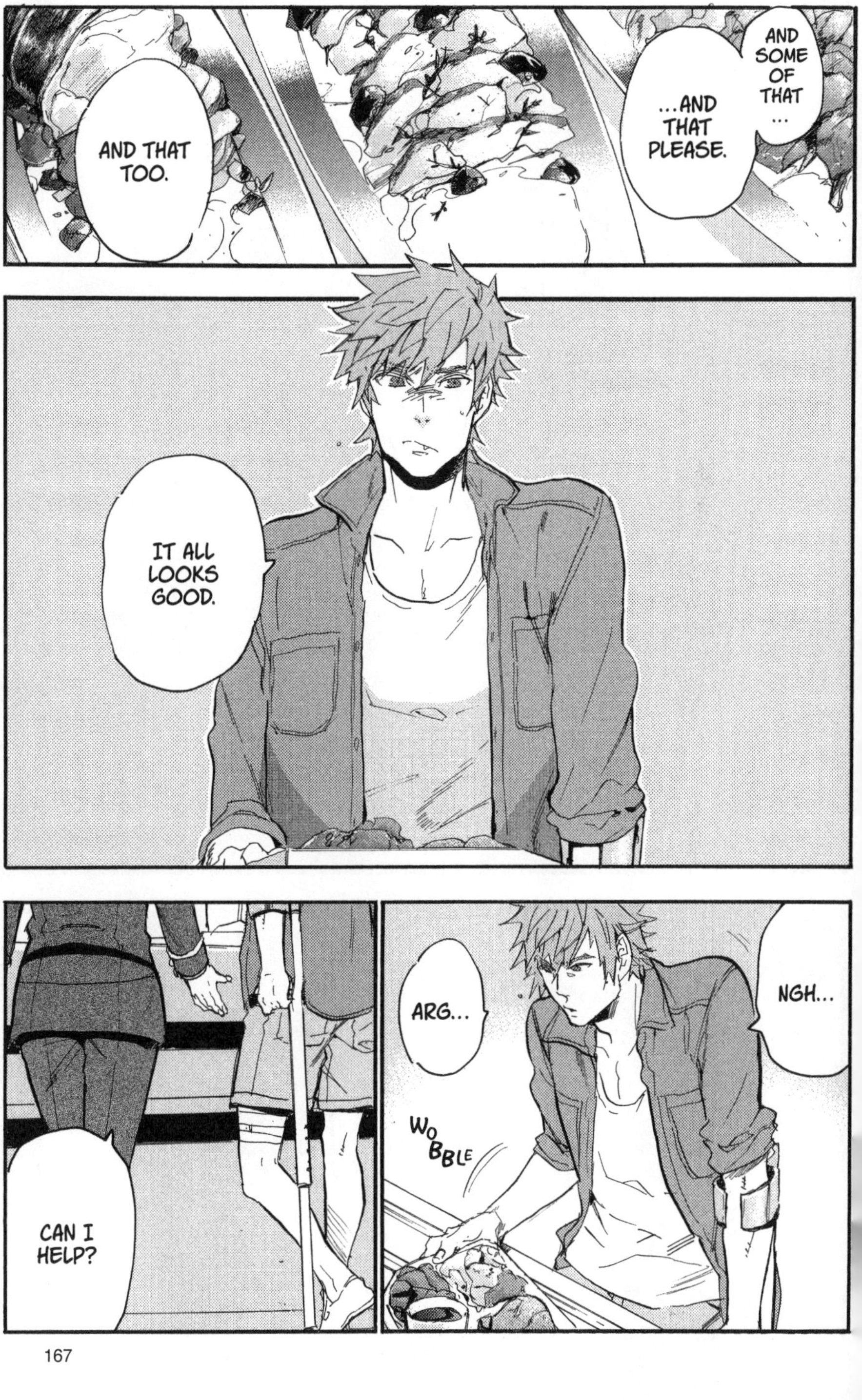
AND SOME OF THAT...
...AND THAT PLEASE.
AND THAT TOO.
IT ALL LOOKS GOOD.
NGH...
ARG...
WOBBLE
CAN I HELP?

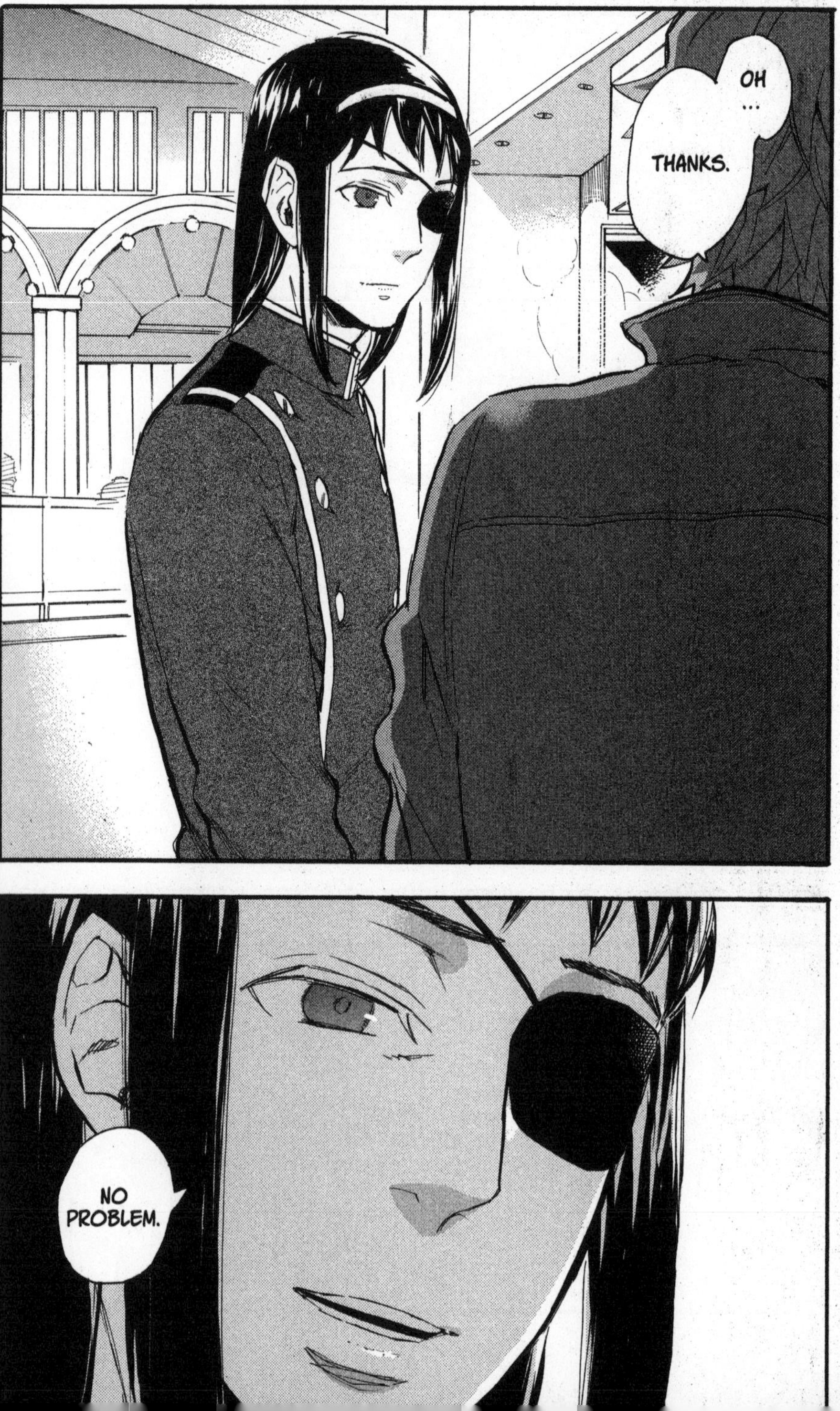
OH ...
THANKS.
NO PROBLEM.

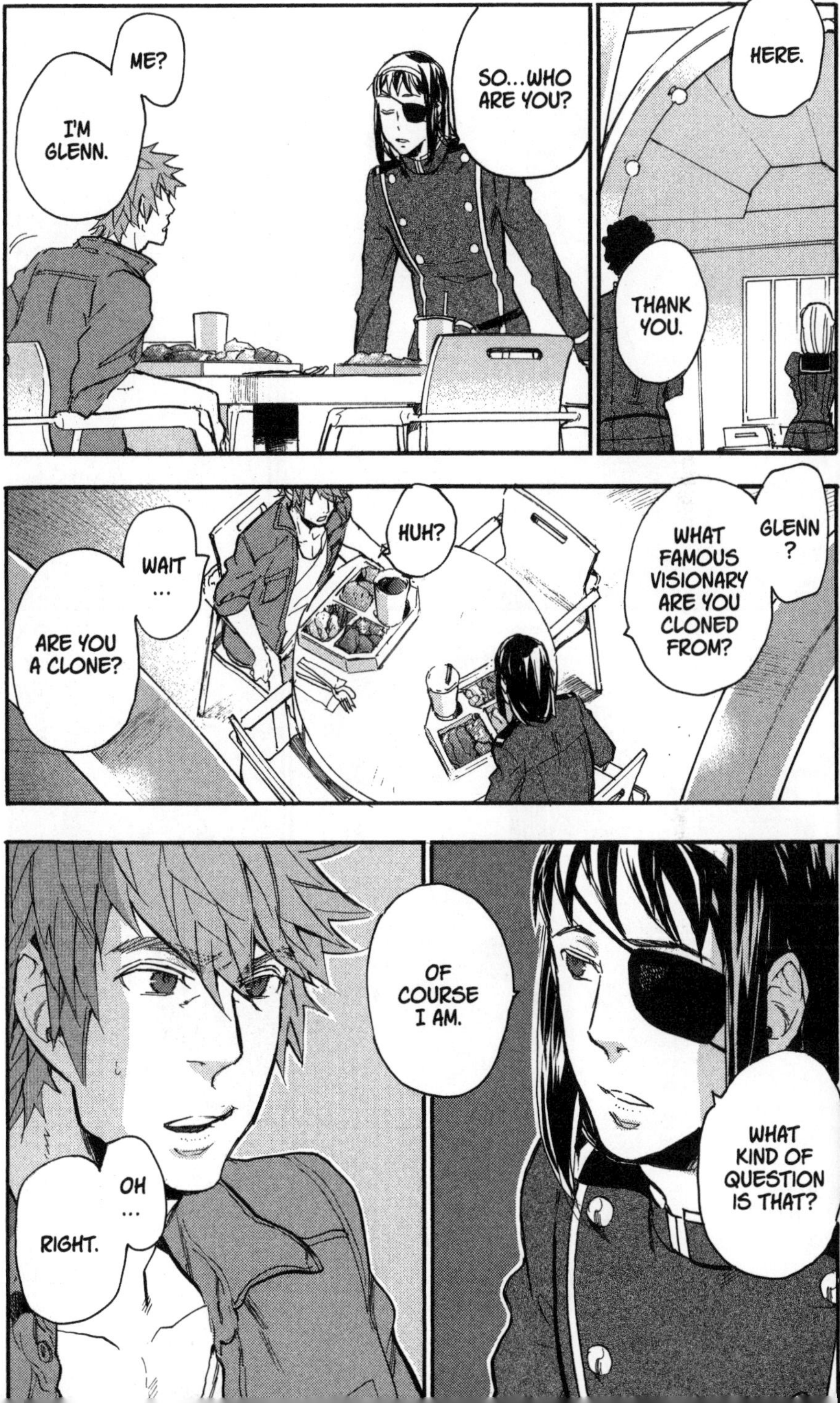
HERE.
THANK YOU.
SO...WHO ARE YOU?
ME?
I'M GLENN.
GLENN?
WHAT FAMOUS VISIONARY ARE YOU CLONED FROM?
HUH?
WAIT...
ARE YOU A CLONE?
OF COURSE I AM.
WHAT KIND OF QUESTION IS THAT?
OH...
RIGHT.

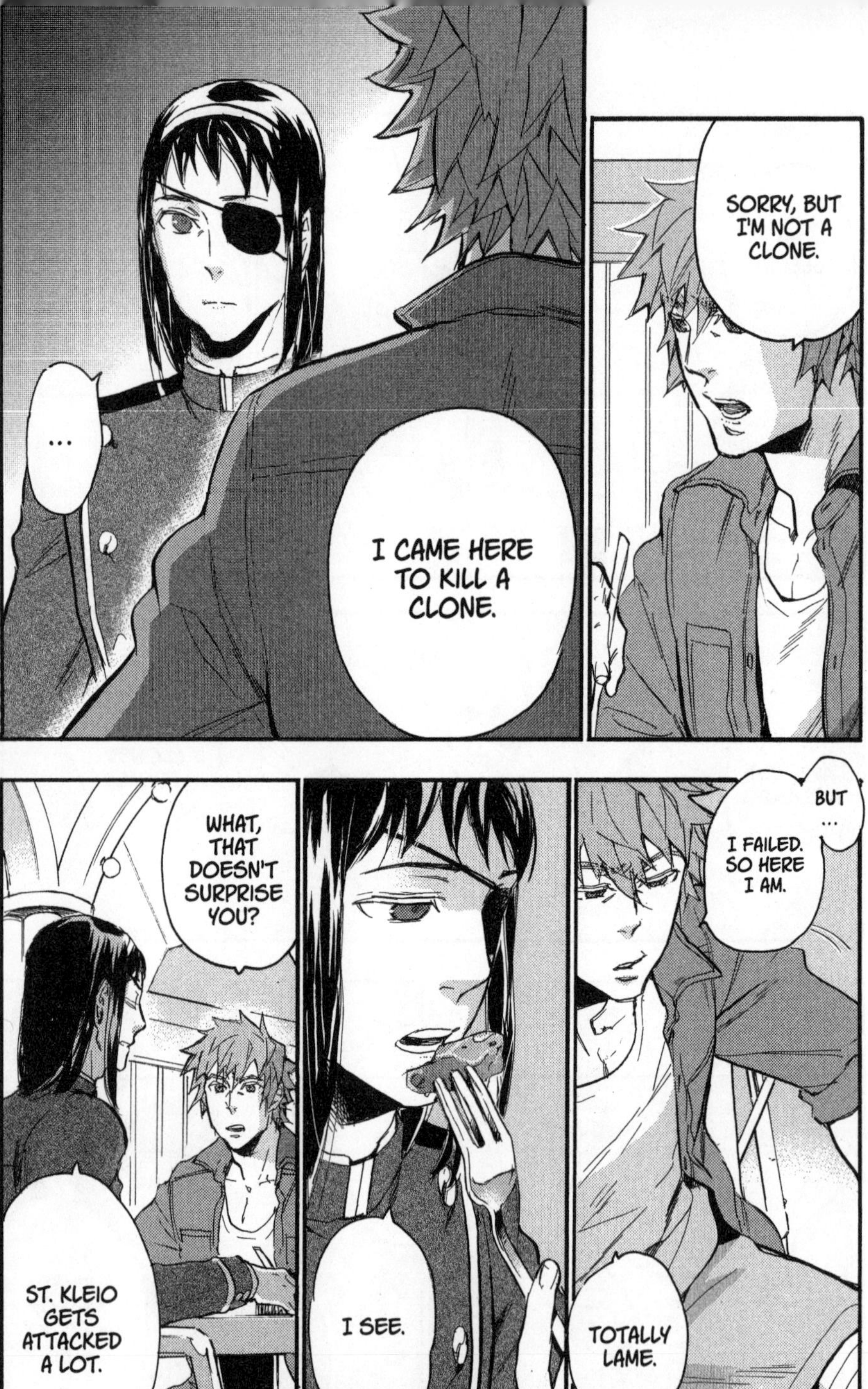
SORRY, BUT I'M NOT A CLONE.
I CAME HERE TO KILL A CLONE.
...
BUT ...
I FAILED. SO HERE I AM.
TOTALLY LAME.
I SEE.
WHAT, THAT DOESN'T SURPRISE YOU?
ST. KLEIO GETS ATTACKED A LOT.

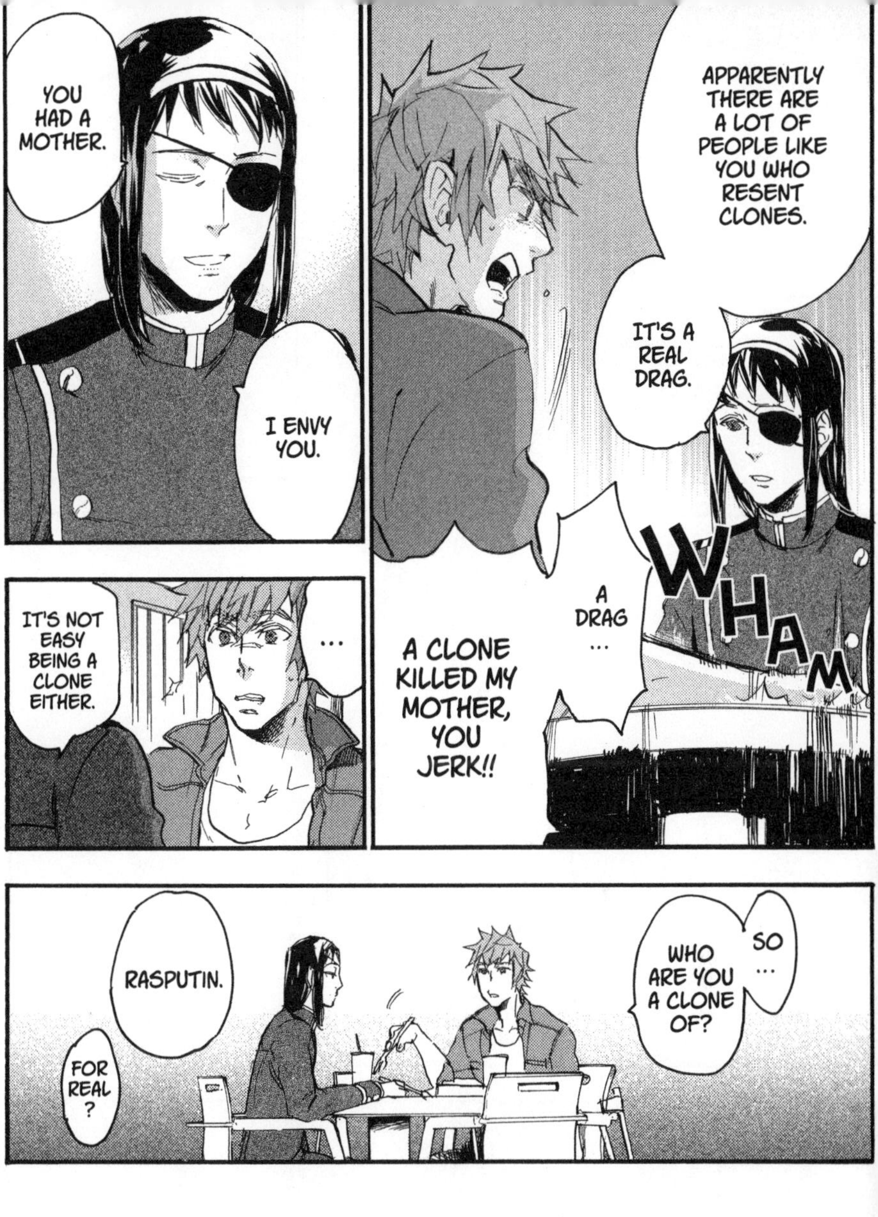
APPARENTLY THERE ARE A LOT OF PEOPLE LIKE YOU WHO RESENT CLONES.
IT'S A REAL DRAG.
WHAM
A DRAG ...
A CLONE KILLED MY MOTHER, YOU JERK!!
YOU HAD A MOTHER.
I ENVY YOU.
...
IT'S NOT EASY BEING A CLONE EITHER.
SO ...
WHO ARE YOU A CLONE OF?
RASPUTIN.
FOR REAL ?

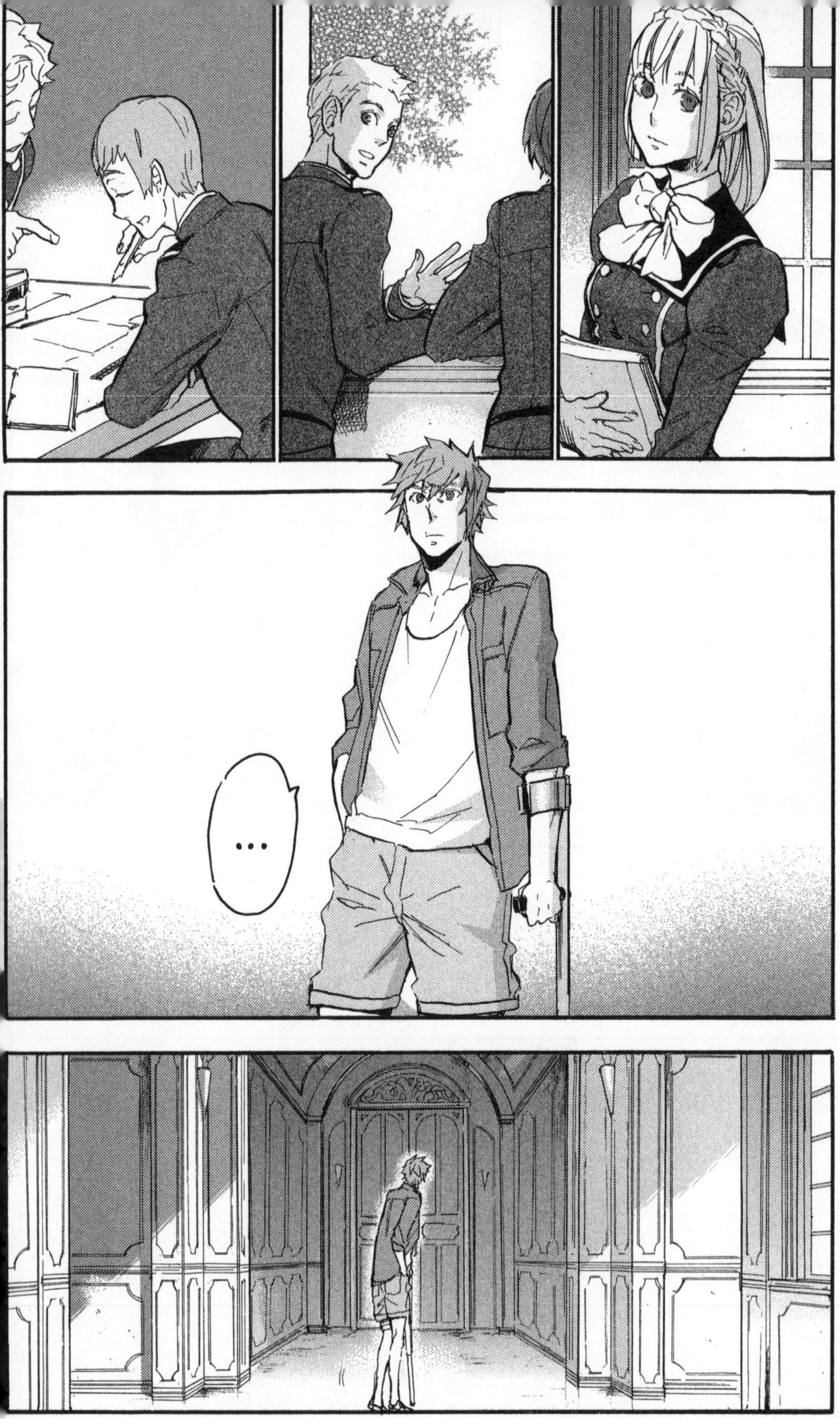
...

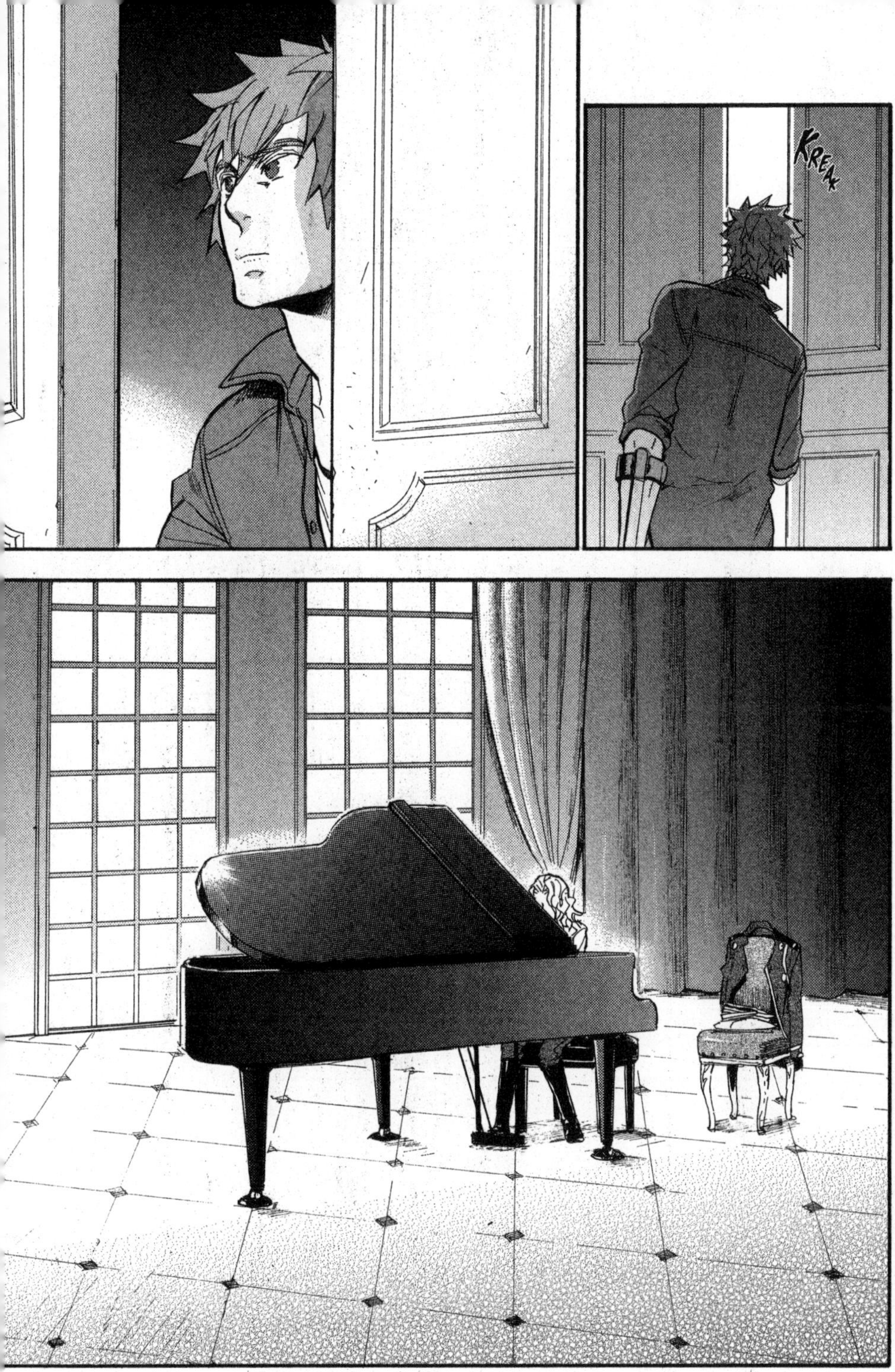
KREAK

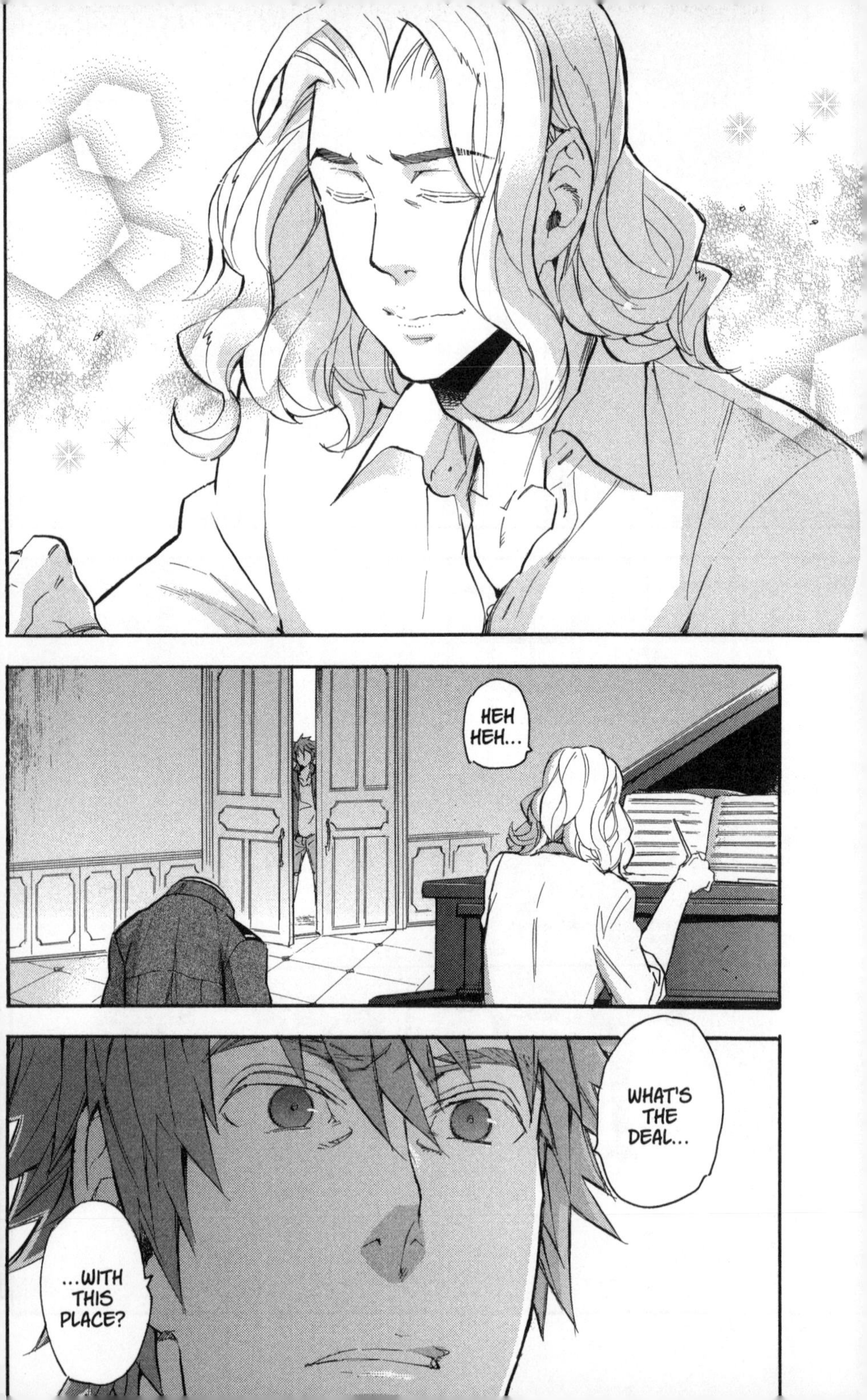
HEH HEH...
WHAT'S THE DEAL...
...WITH THIS PLACE?

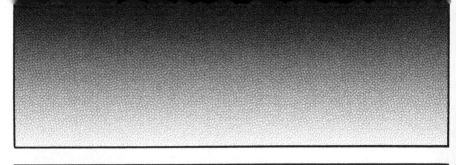

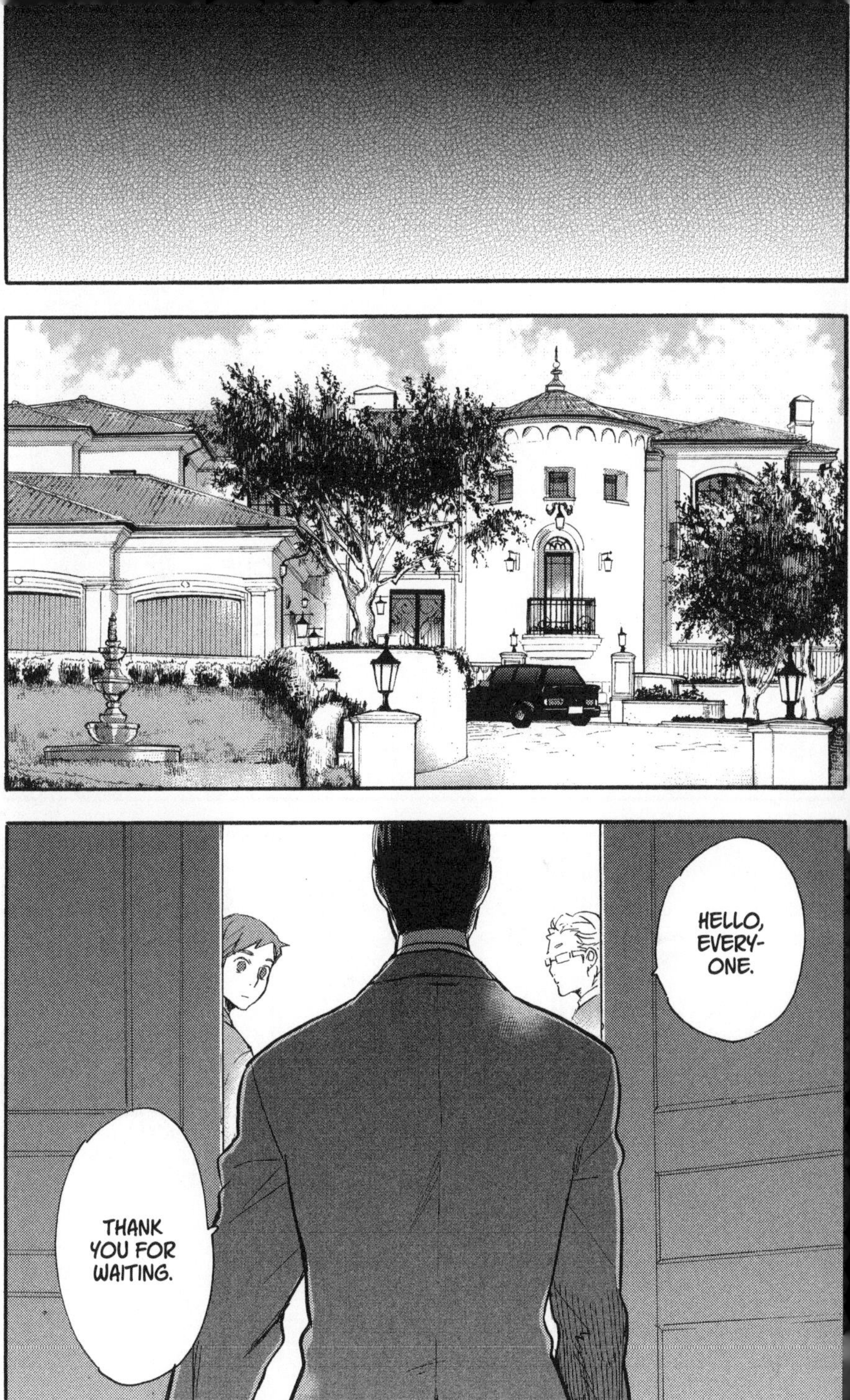
HELLO, EVERY-ONE.
THANK YOU FOR WAITING.

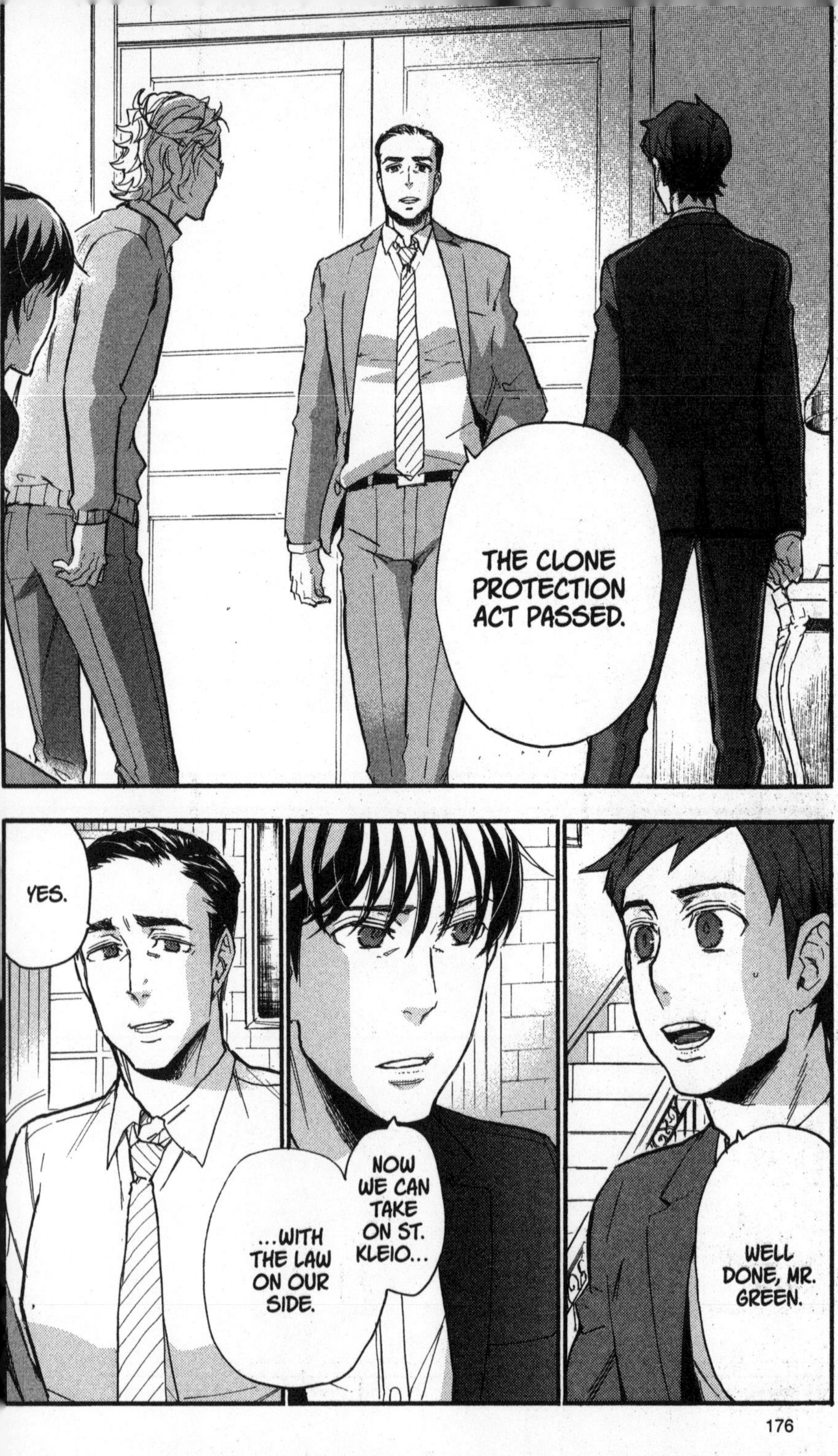
THE CLONE PROTECTION ACT PASSED.
WELL DONE, MR. GREEN.
NOW WE CAN TAKE ON ST. KLEIO...
...WITH THE LAW ON OUR SIDE.
YES.

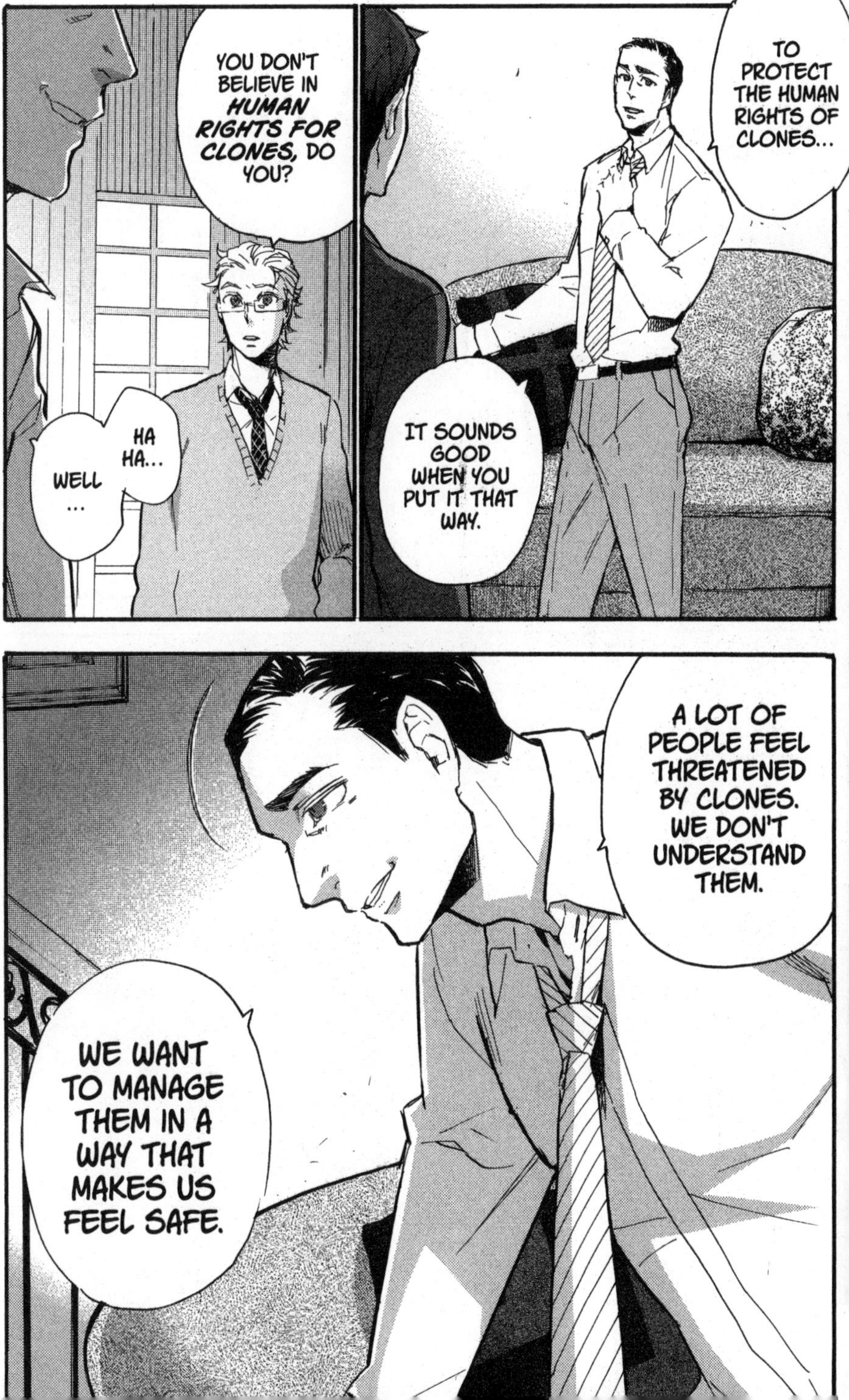
TO PROTECT THE HUMAN RIGHTS OF CLONES...
IT SOUNDS GOOD WHEN YOU PUT IT THAT WAY.
YOU DON'T BELIEVE IN *HUMAN RIGHTS FOR CLONES*, DO YOU?
HA HA...
WELL...
A LOT OF PEOPLE FEEL THREATENED BY CLONES. WE DON'T UNDERSTAND THEM.
WE WANT TO MANAGE THEM IN A WAY THAT MAKES US FEEL SAFE.

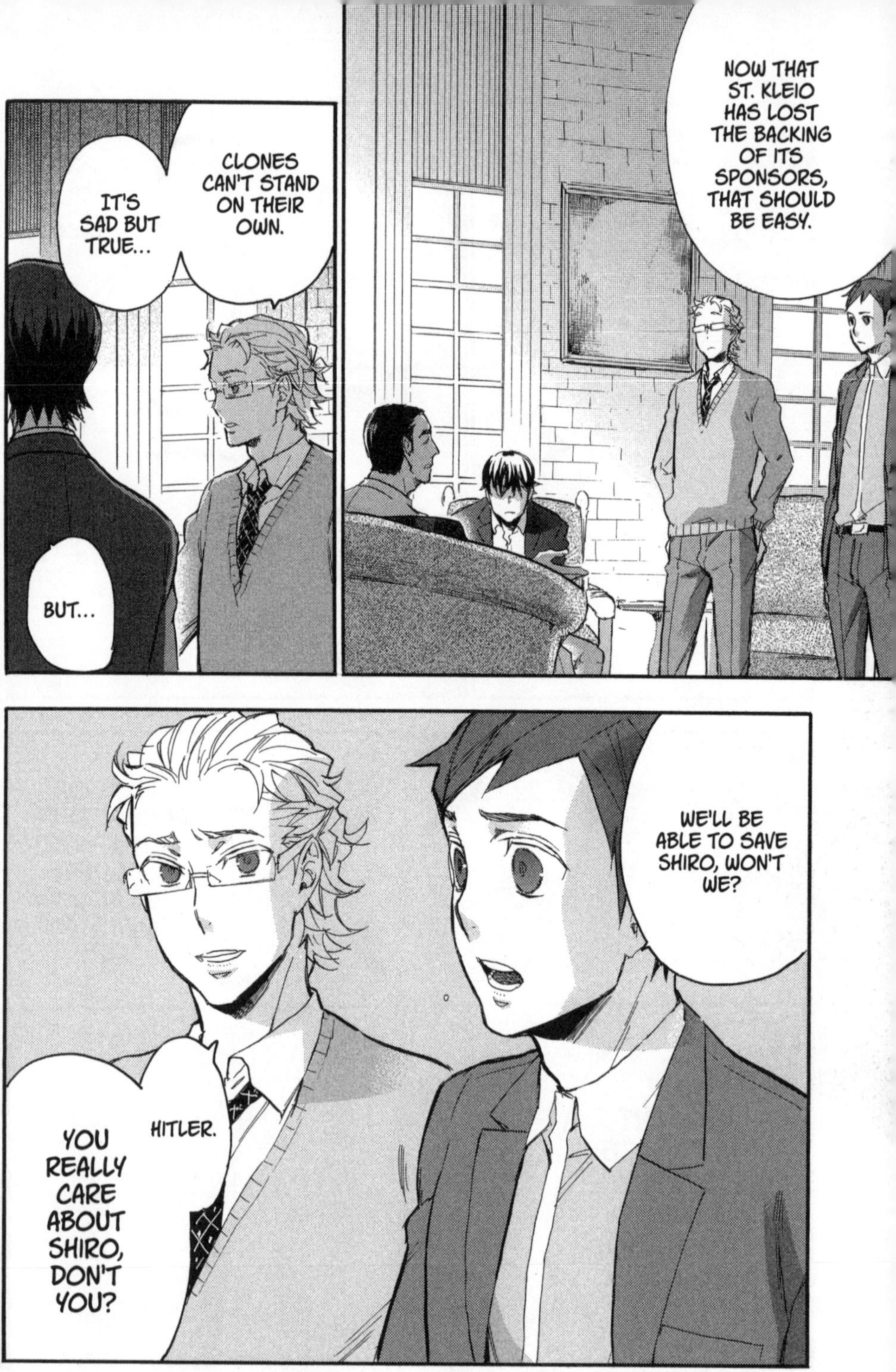
NOW THAT ST. KLEIO HAS LOST THE BACKING OF ITS SPONSORS, THAT SHOULD BE EASY.
CLONES CAN'T STAND ON THEIR OWN.
IT'S SAD BUT TRUE...
BUT...
WE'LL BE ABLE TO SAVE SHIRO, WON'T WE?
HITLER.
YOU REALLY CARE ABOUT SHIRO, DON'T YOU?

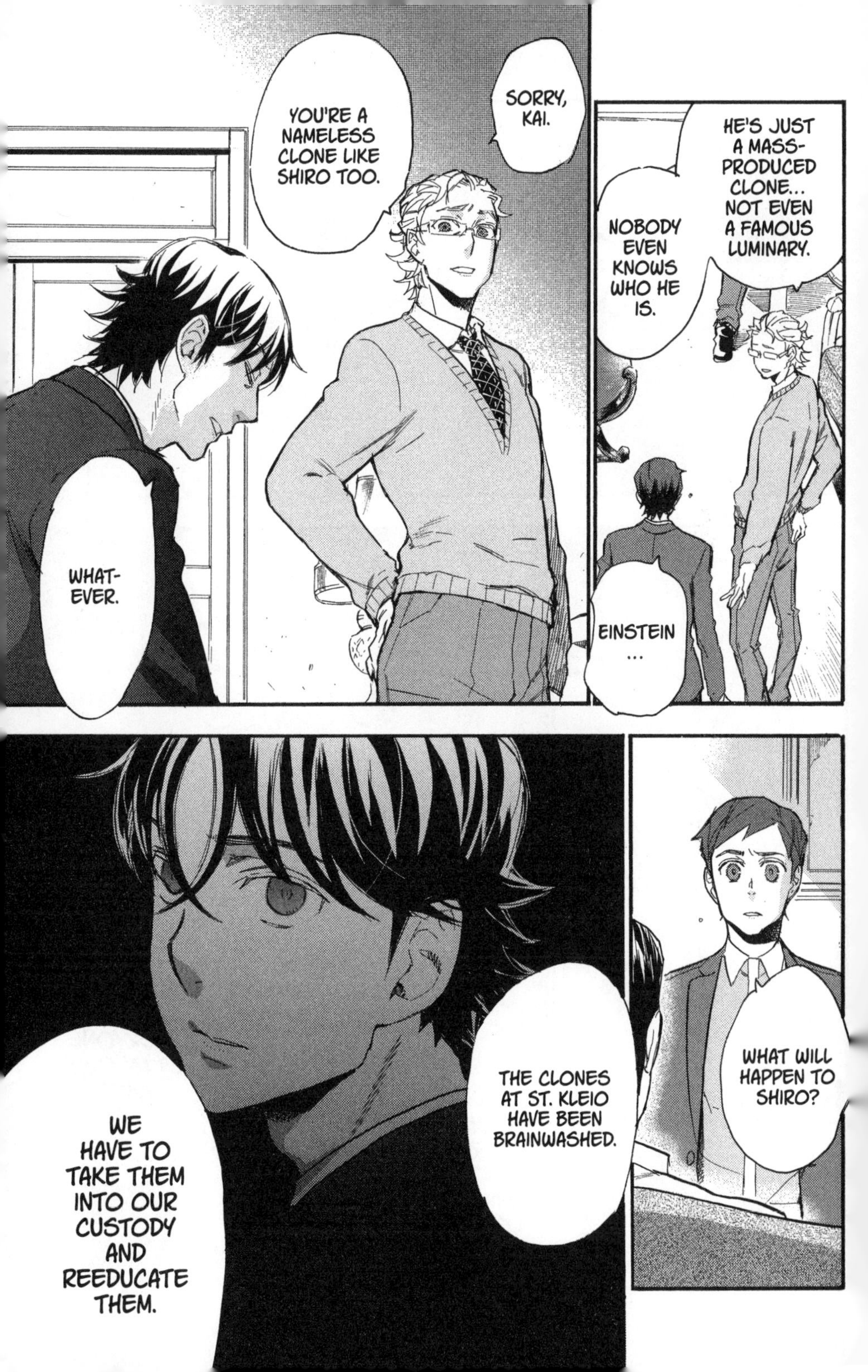
HE'S JUST A MASS-PRODUCED CLONE... NOT EVEN A FAMOUS LUMINARY.
NOBODY EVEN KNOWS WHO HE IS.
EINSTEIN...
SORRY, KAI.
YOU'RE A NAMELESS CLONE LIKE SHIRO TOO.
WHAT-EVER.
WHAT WILL HAPPEN TO SHIRO?
THE CLONES AT ST. KLEIO HAVE BEEN BRAINWASHED.
WE HAVE TO TAKE THEM INTO OUR CUSTODY AND REEDUCATE THEM.

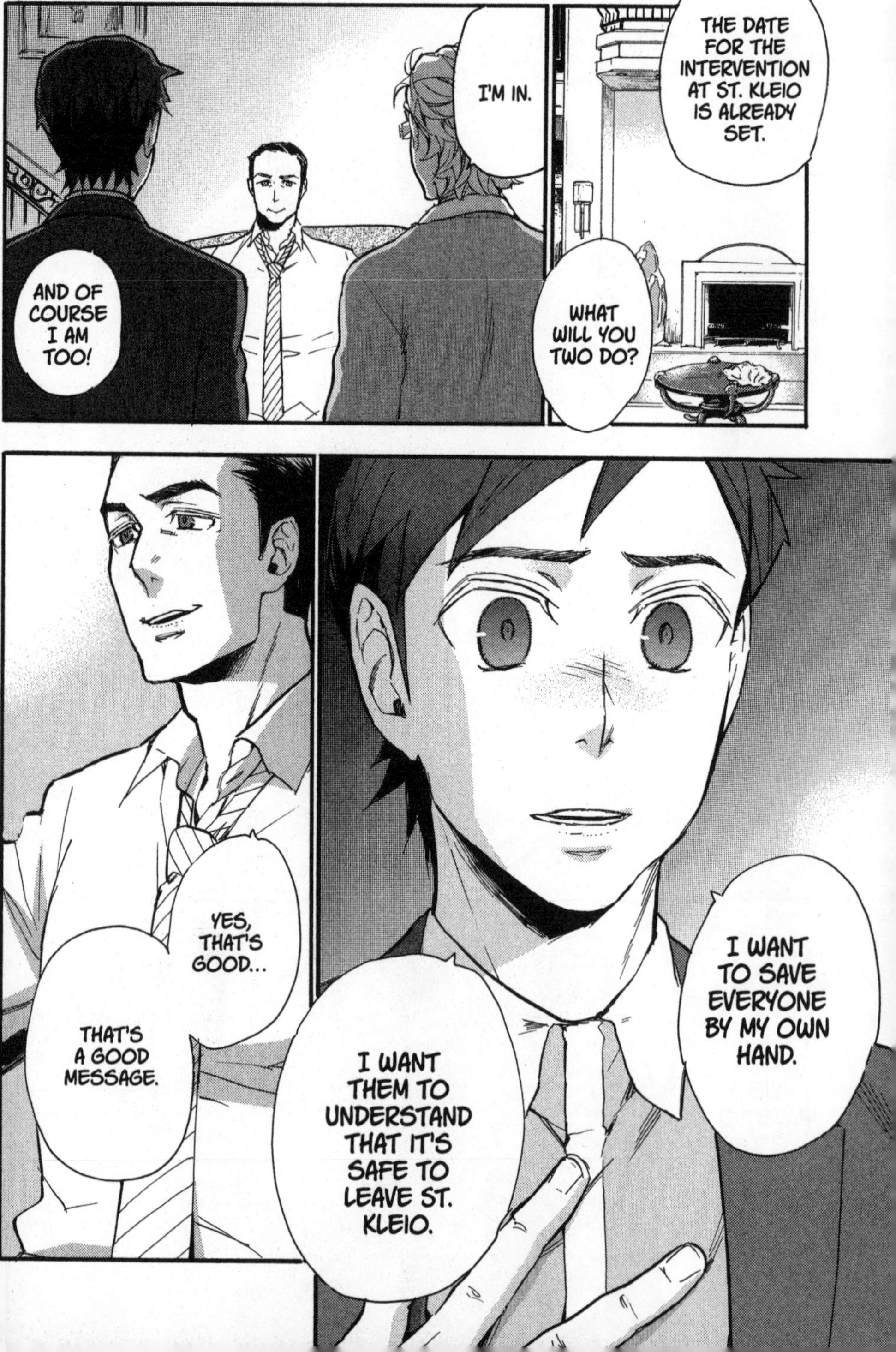
THE DATE FOR THE INTERVENTION AT ST. KLEIO IS ALREADY SET.
WHAT WILL YOU TWO DO?
I'M IN.
AND OF COURSE I AM TOO!
I WANT TO SAVE EVERYONE BY MY OWN HAND.
I WANT THEM TO UNDERSTAND THAT IT'S SAFE TO LEAVE ST. KLEIO.
YES, THAT'S GOOD...
THAT'S A GOOD MESSAGE.

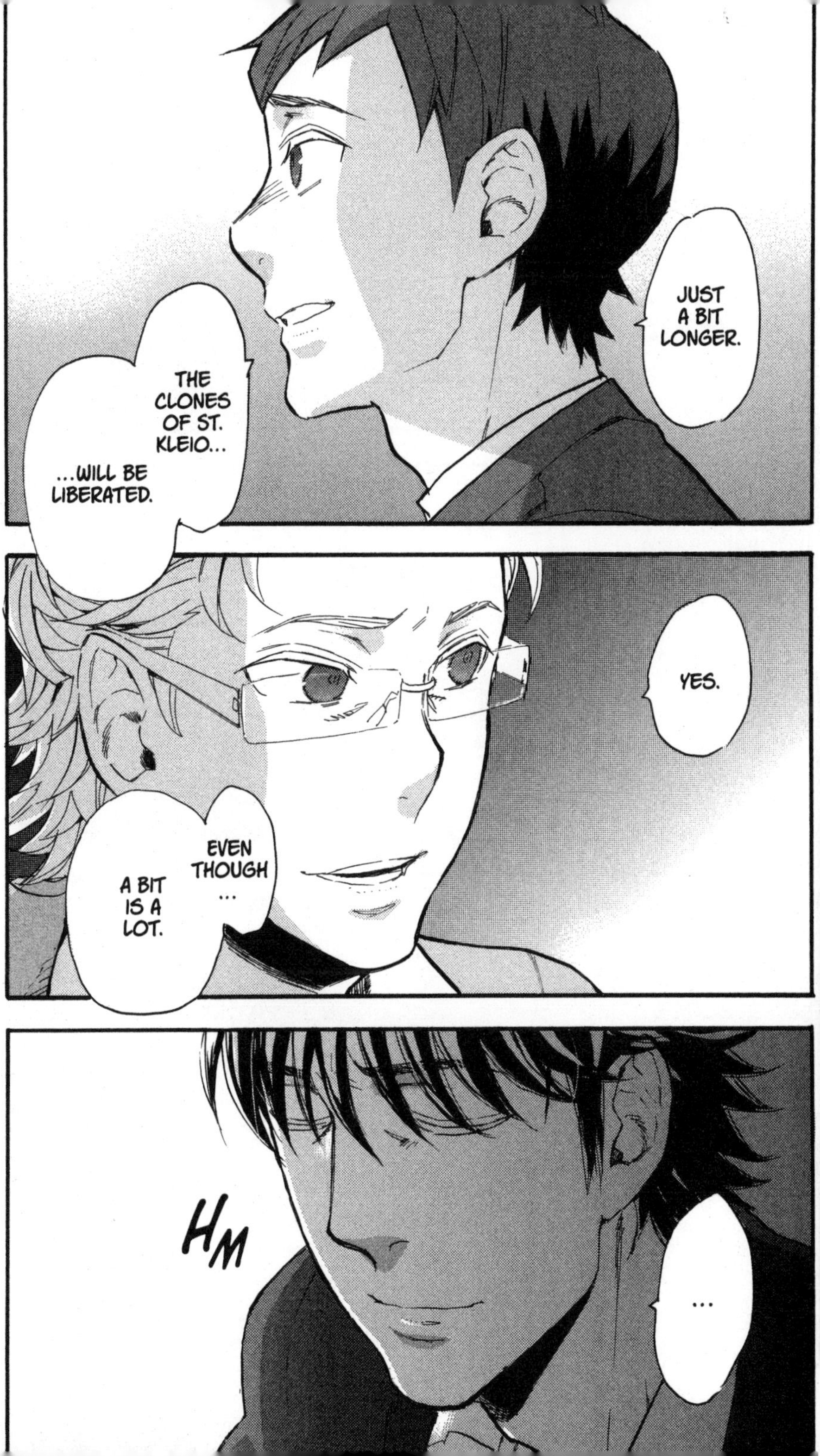
JUST A BIT LONGER.
THE CLONES OF ST. KLEIO...
...WILL BE LIBERATED.
YES.
EVEN THOUGH...
A BIT IS A LOT.
...
HM

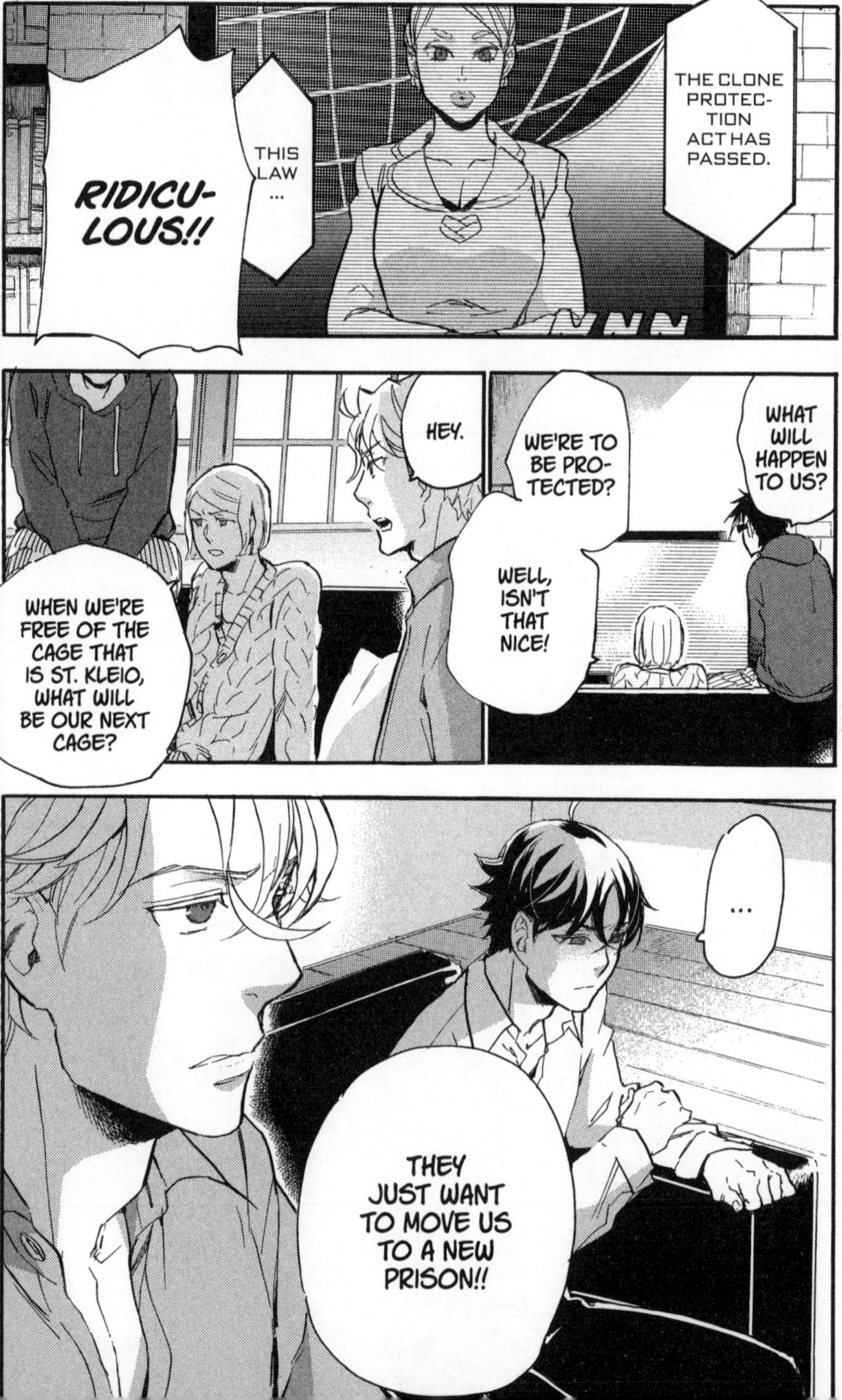
THE CLONE PROTECTION ACT HAS PASSED.
THIS LAW ...
RIDICULOUS!!
NNN
WHAT WILL HAPPEN TO US?
WE'RE TO BE PROTECTED?
HEY.
WELL, ISN'T THAT NICE!
WHEN WE'RE FREE OF THE CAGE THAT IS ST. KLEIO, WHAT WILL BE OUR NEXT CAGE?
...
THEY JUST WANT TO MOVE US TO A NEW PRISON!!

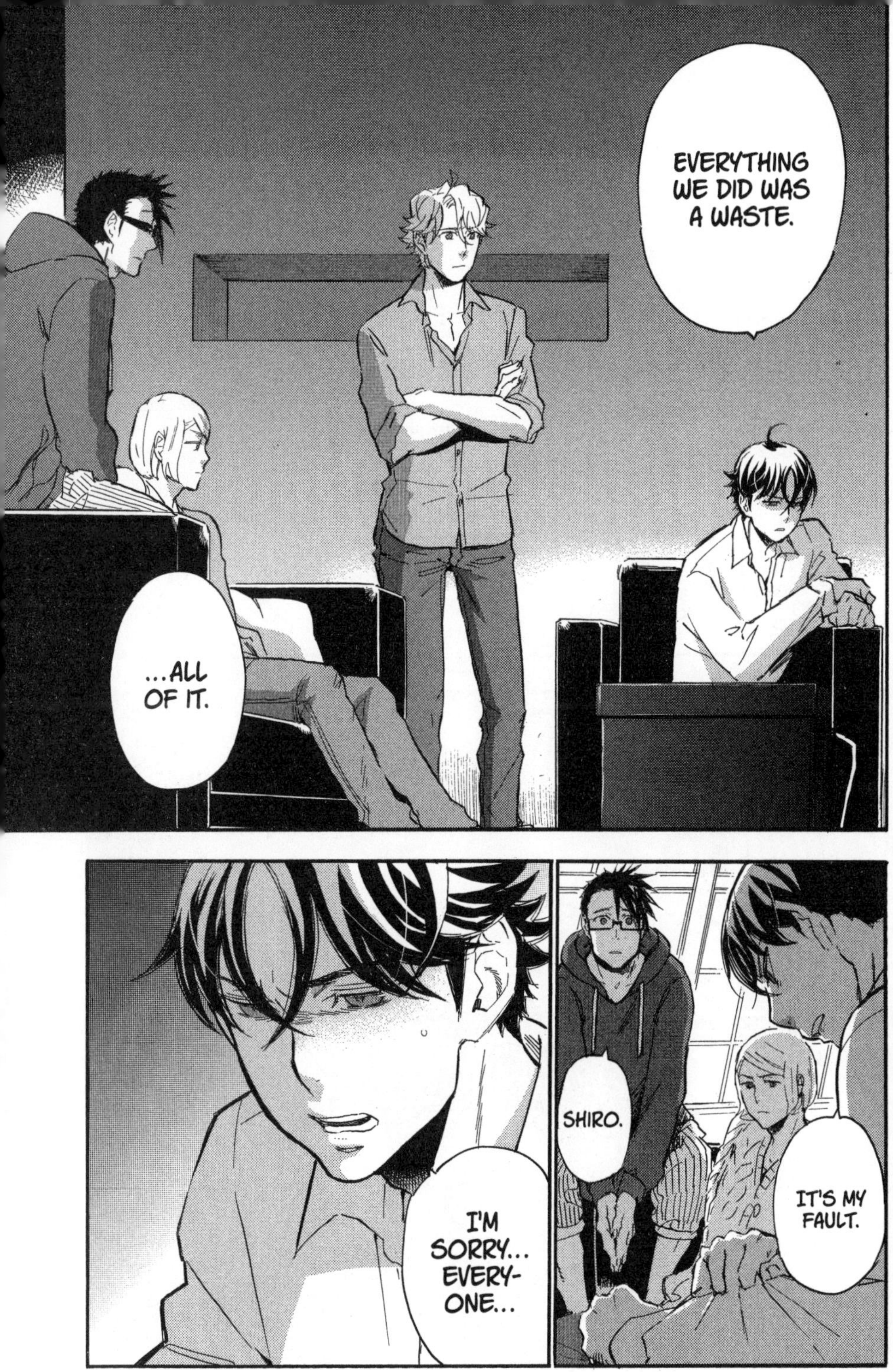
EVERYTHING WE DID WAS A WASTE.
...ALL OF IT.
IT'S MY FAULT.
SHIRO.
I'M SORRY... EVERY-ONE...

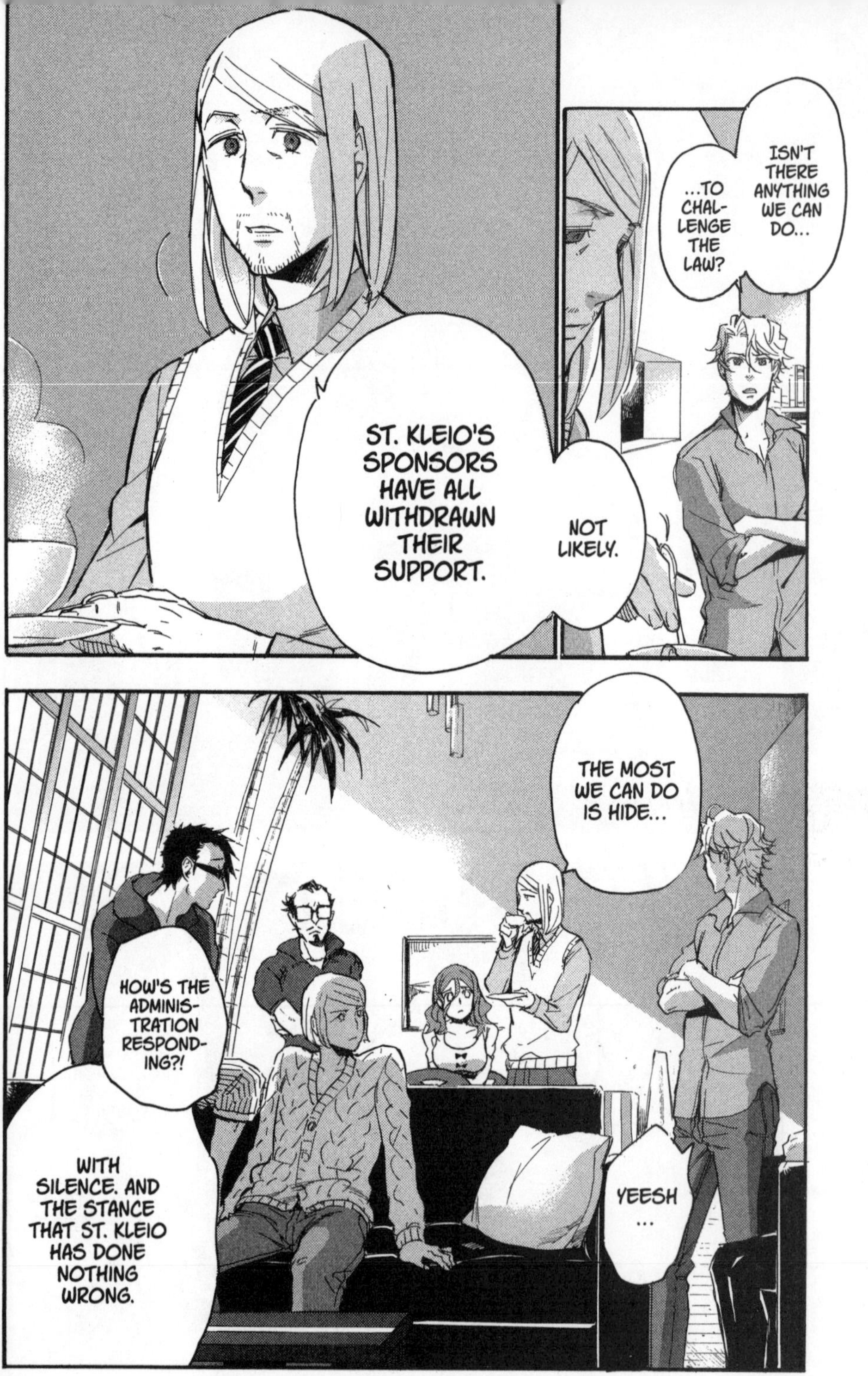

ISN'T THERE ANYTHING WE CAN DO...
...TO CHALLENGE THE LAW?
NOT LIKELY.
ST. KLEIO'S SPONSORS HAVE ALL WITHDRAWN THEIR SUPPORT.
THE MOST WE CAN DO IS HIDE...
YEESH ...
HOW'S THE ADMINISTRATION RESPONDING?!
WITH SILENCE. AND THE STANCE THAT ST. KLEIO HAS DONE NOTHING WRONG.

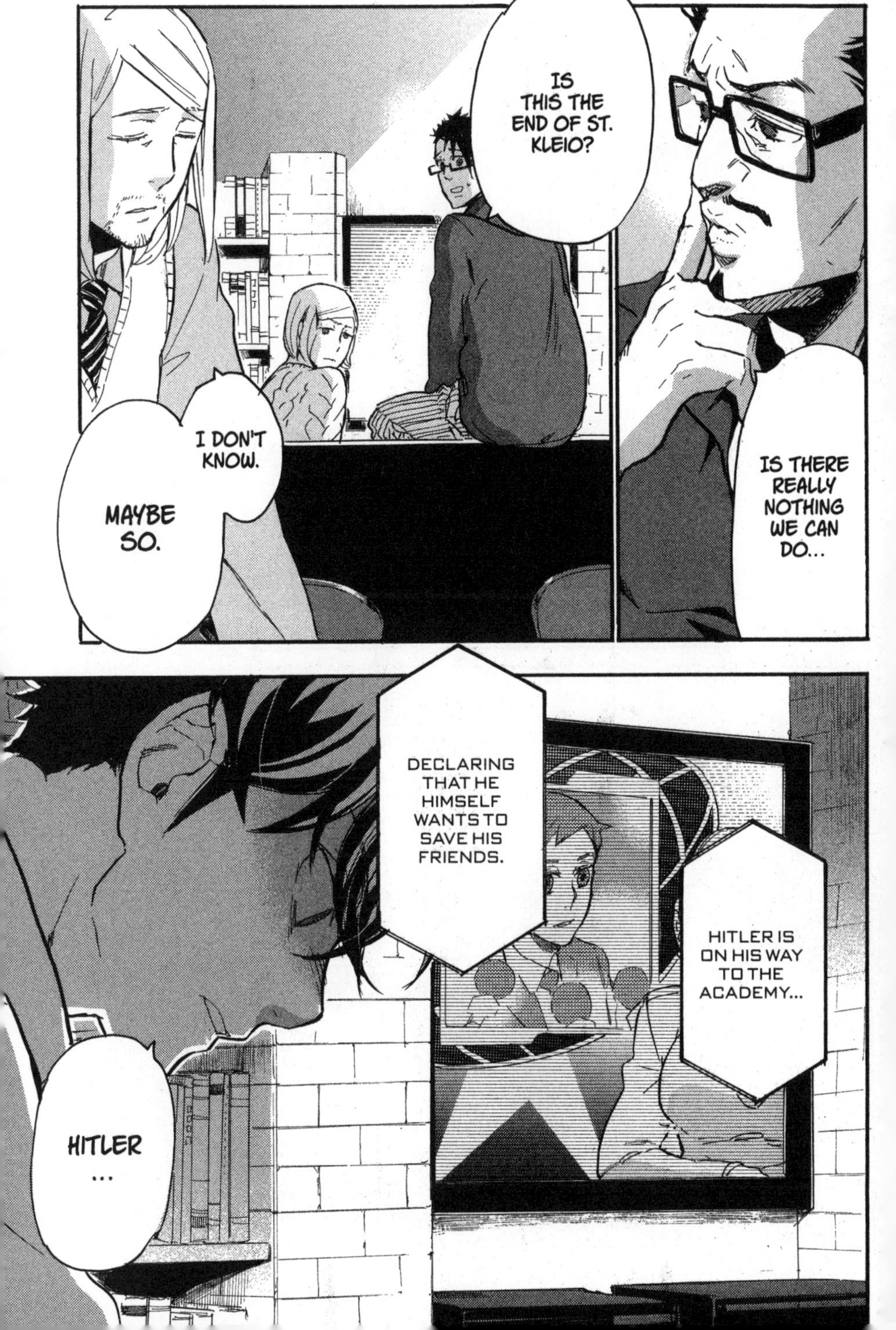
IS THERE REALLY NOTHING WE CAN DO...
IS THIS THE END OF ST. KLEIO?
I DON'T KNOW.
MAYBE SO.
HITLER IS ON HIS WAY TO THE ACADEMY...
DECLARING THAT HE HIMSELF WANTS TO SAVE HIS FRIENDS.
HITLER...

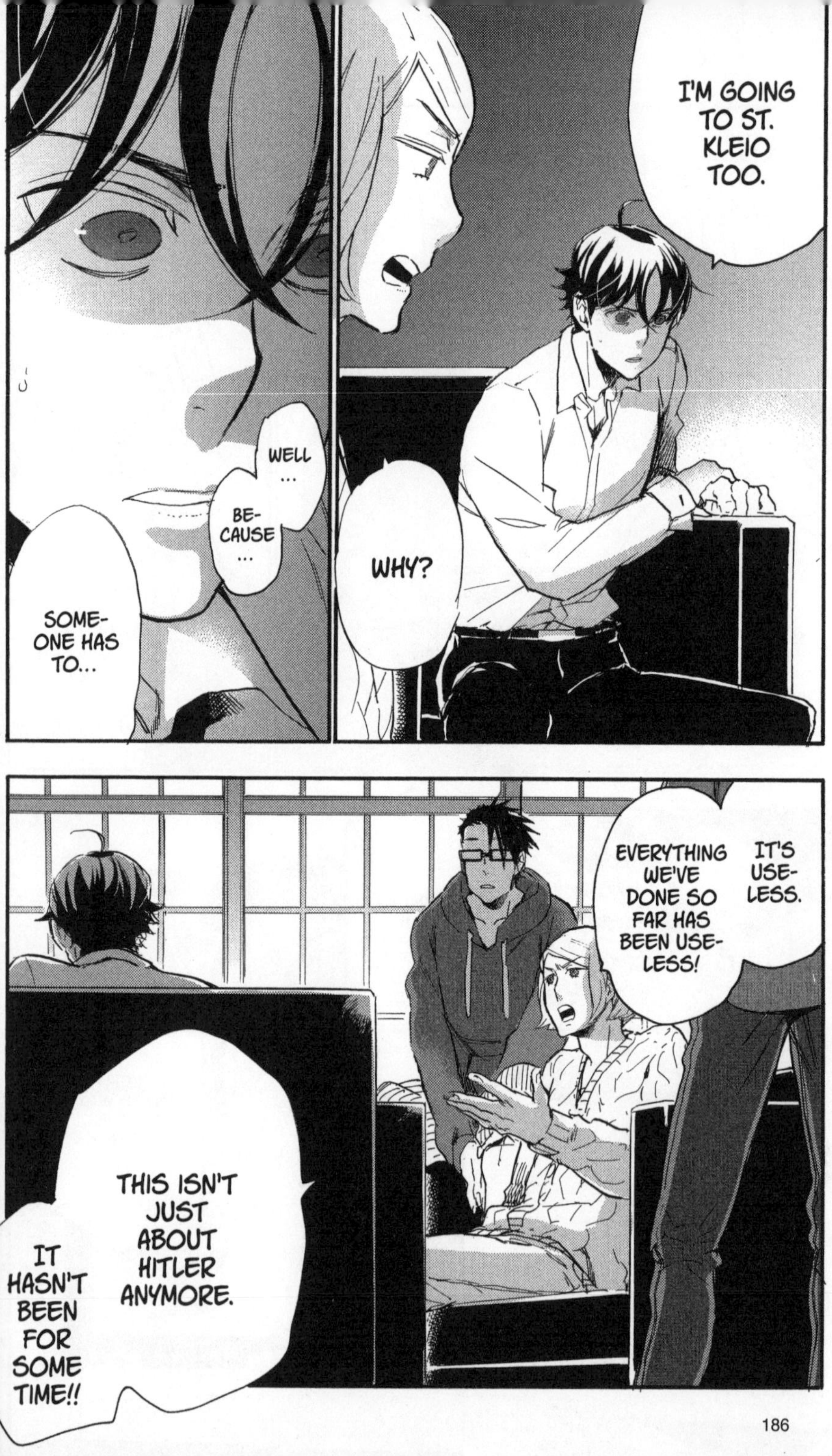
I'M GOING TO ST. KLEIO TOO.
WHY?
WELL ... BE-CAUSE ...
SOME-ONE HAS TO...
IT'S USE-LESS.
EVERYTHING WE'VE DONE SO FAR HAS BEEN USE-LESS!
THIS ISN'T JUST ABOUT HITLER ANYMORE.
IT HASN'T BEEN FOR SOME TIME!!

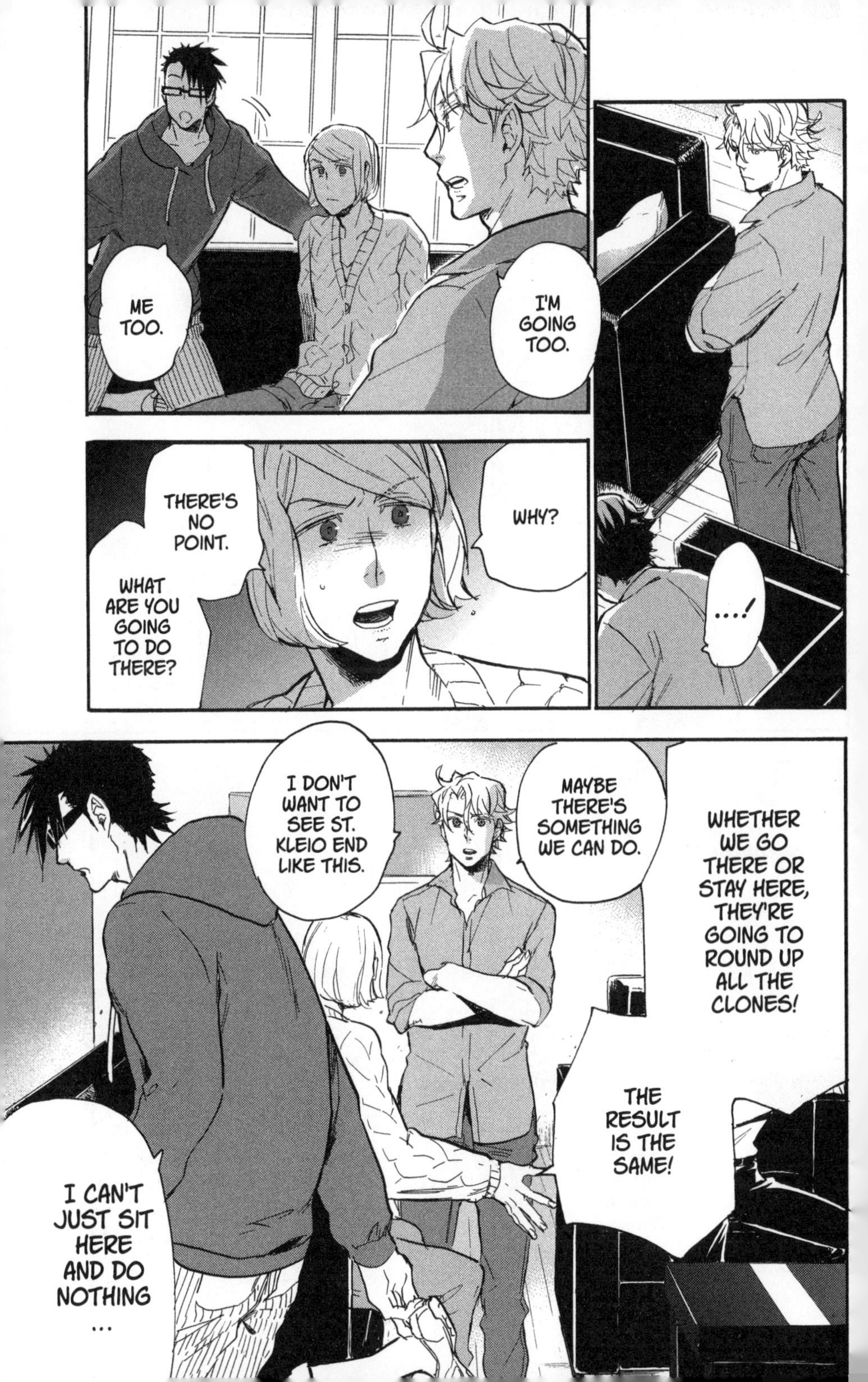
...!
I'M GOING TOO.
ME TOO.
WHY?
THERE'S NO POINT.
WHAT ARE YOU GOING TO DO THERE?
WHETHER WE GO THERE OR STAY HERE, THEY'RE GOING TO ROUND UP ALL THE CLONES!
THE RESULT IS THE SAME!
MAYBE THERE'S SOMETHING WE CAN DO.
I DON'T WANT TO SEE ST. KLEIO END LIKE THIS.
I CAN'T JUST SIT HERE AND DO NOTHING...

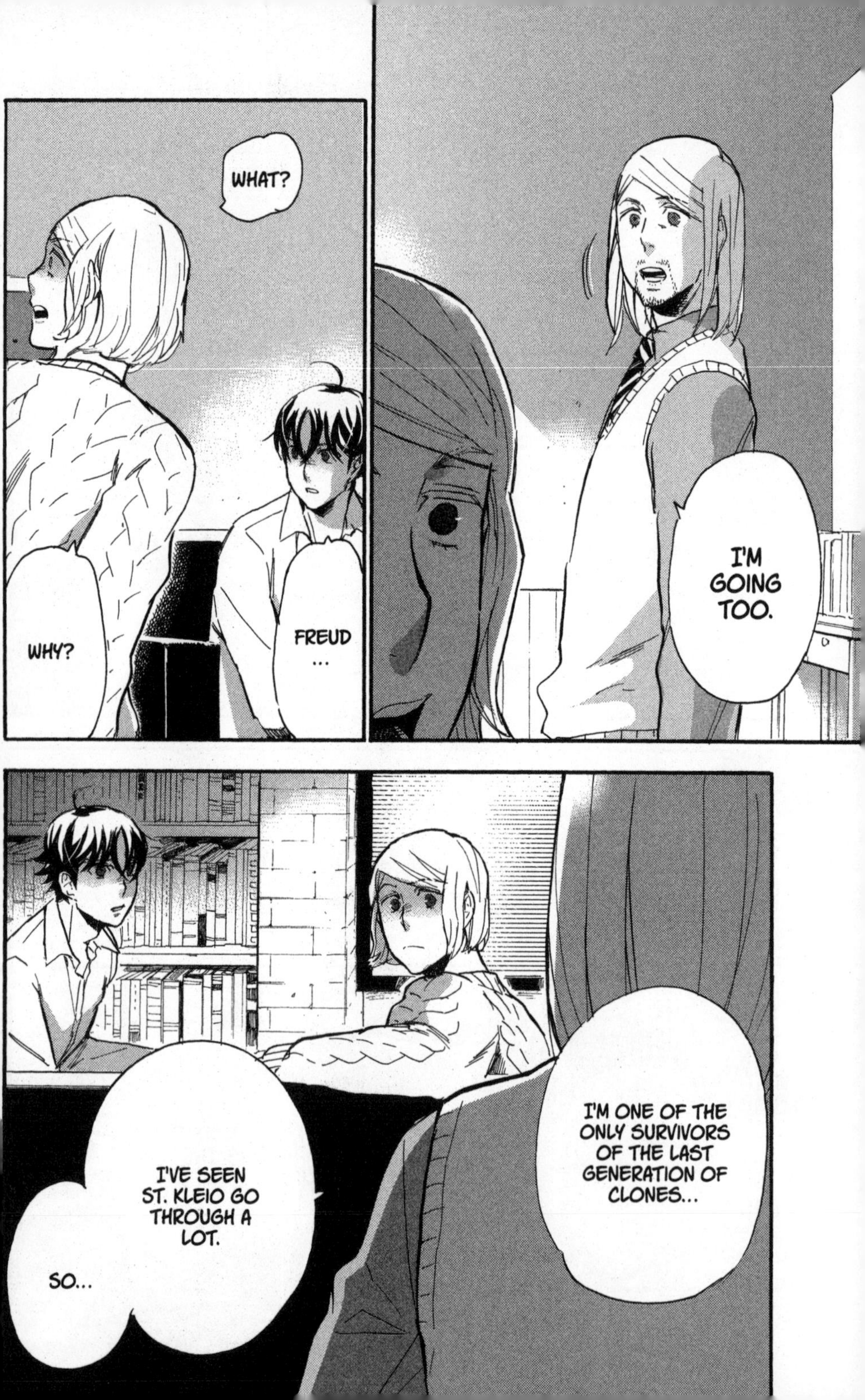
I'M GOING TOO.
WHAT?
FREUD ...
WHY?
I'M ONE OF THE ONLY SURVIVORS OF THE LAST GENERATION OF CLONES...
I'VE SEEN ST. KLEIO GO THROUGH A LOT.
SO...

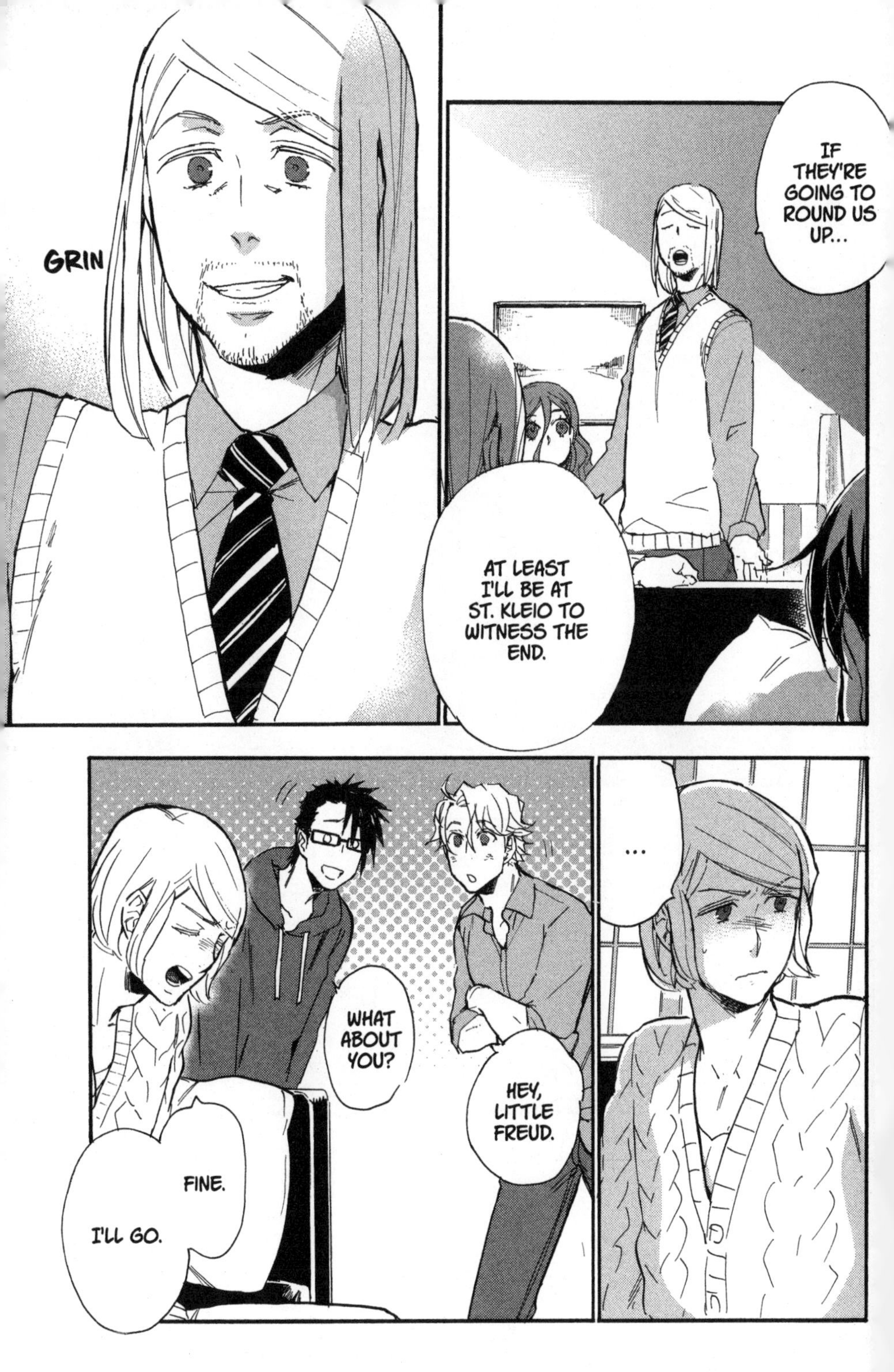
IF THEY'RE GOING TO ROUND US UP...
AT LEAST I'LL BE AT ST. KLEIO TO WITNESS THE END.
GRIN
...
HEY, LITTLE FREUD.
WHAT ABOUT YOU?
FINE.
I'LL GO.

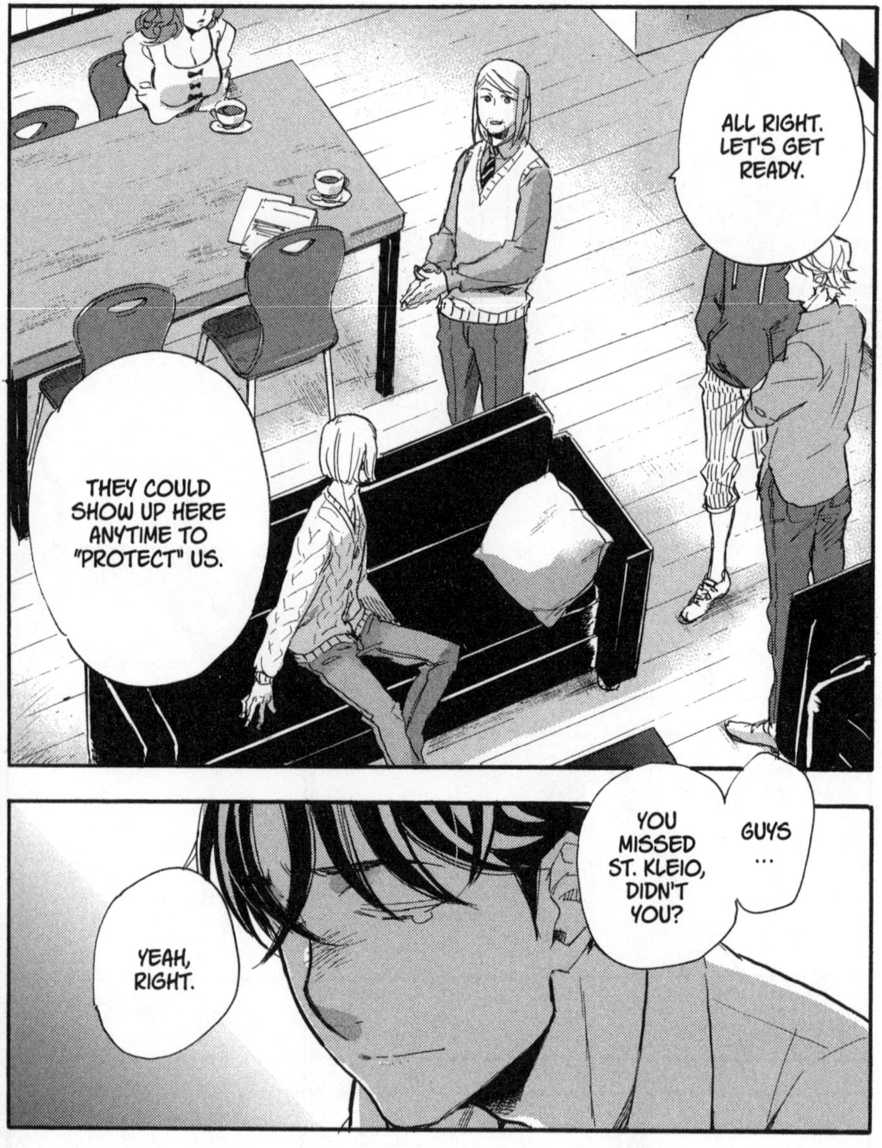
ALL RIGHT. LET'S GET READY.
THEY COULD SHOW UP HERE ANYTIME TO "PROTECT" US.
GUYS ...
YOU MISSED ST. KLEIO, DIDN'T YOU?
YEAH, RIGHT.

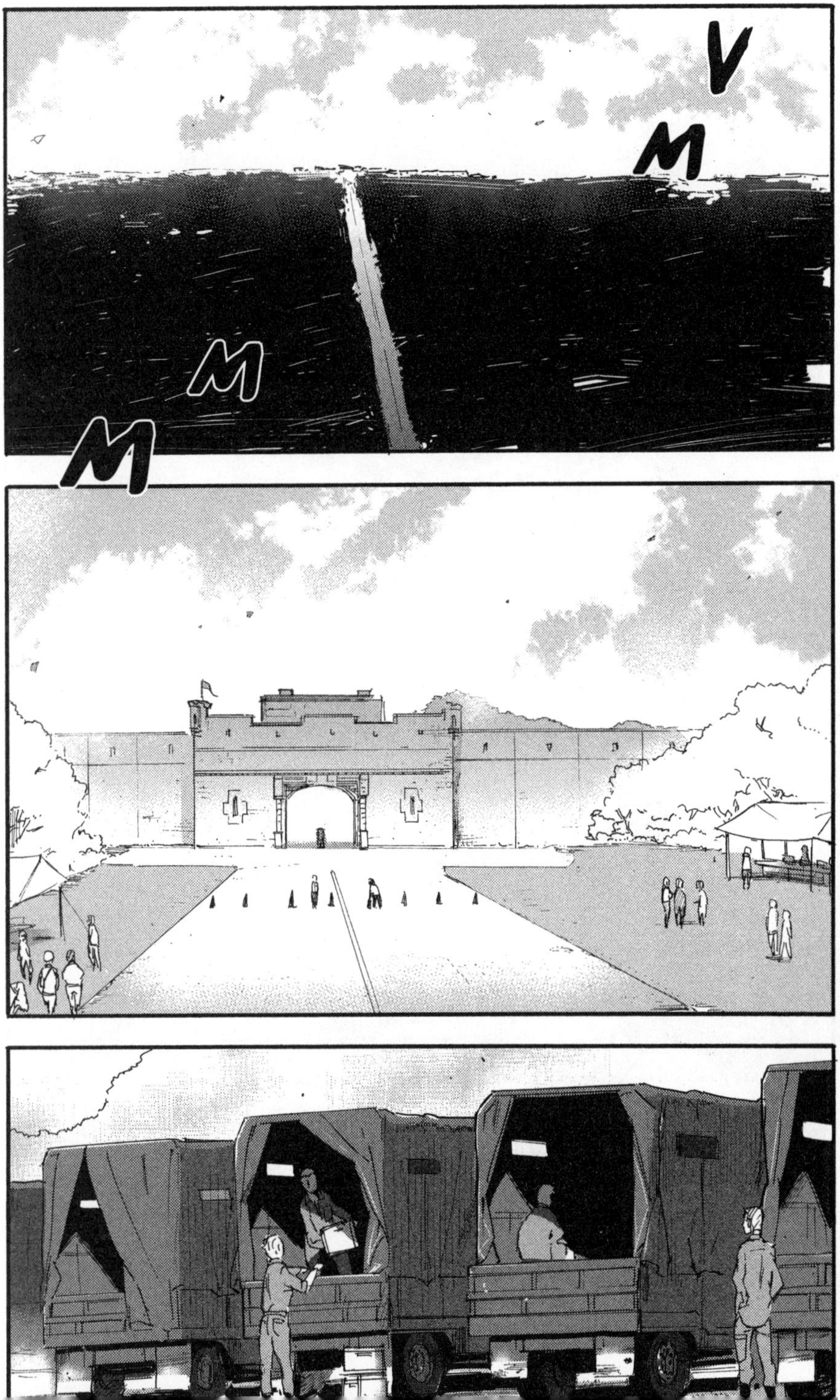
V
M
M
M

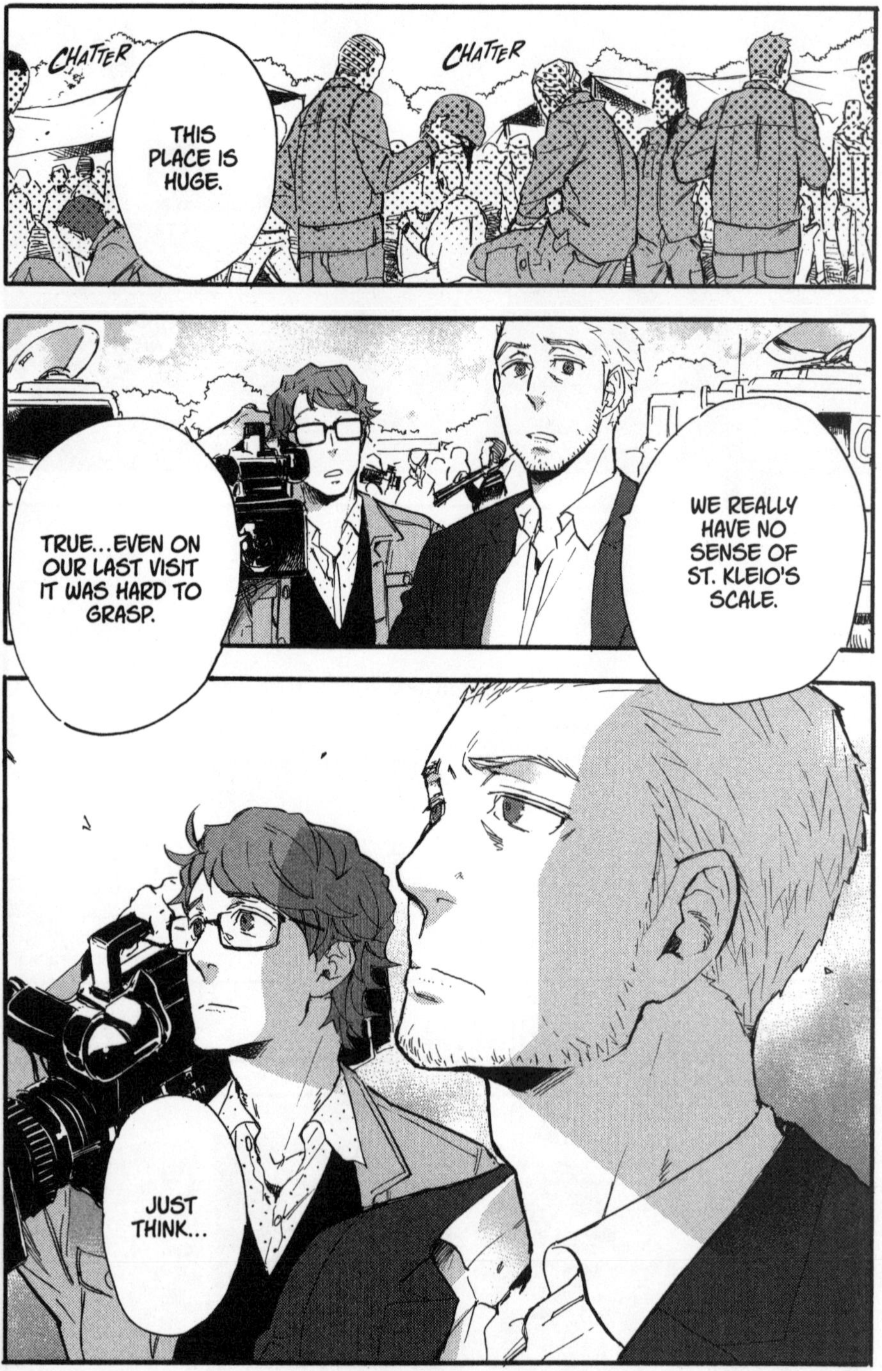
CHATTER
CHATTER
THIS PLACE IS HUGE.
WE REALLY HAVE NO SENSE OF ST. KLEIO'S SCALE.
TRUE...EVEN ON OUR LAST VISIT IT WAS HARD TO GRASP.
JUST THINK...

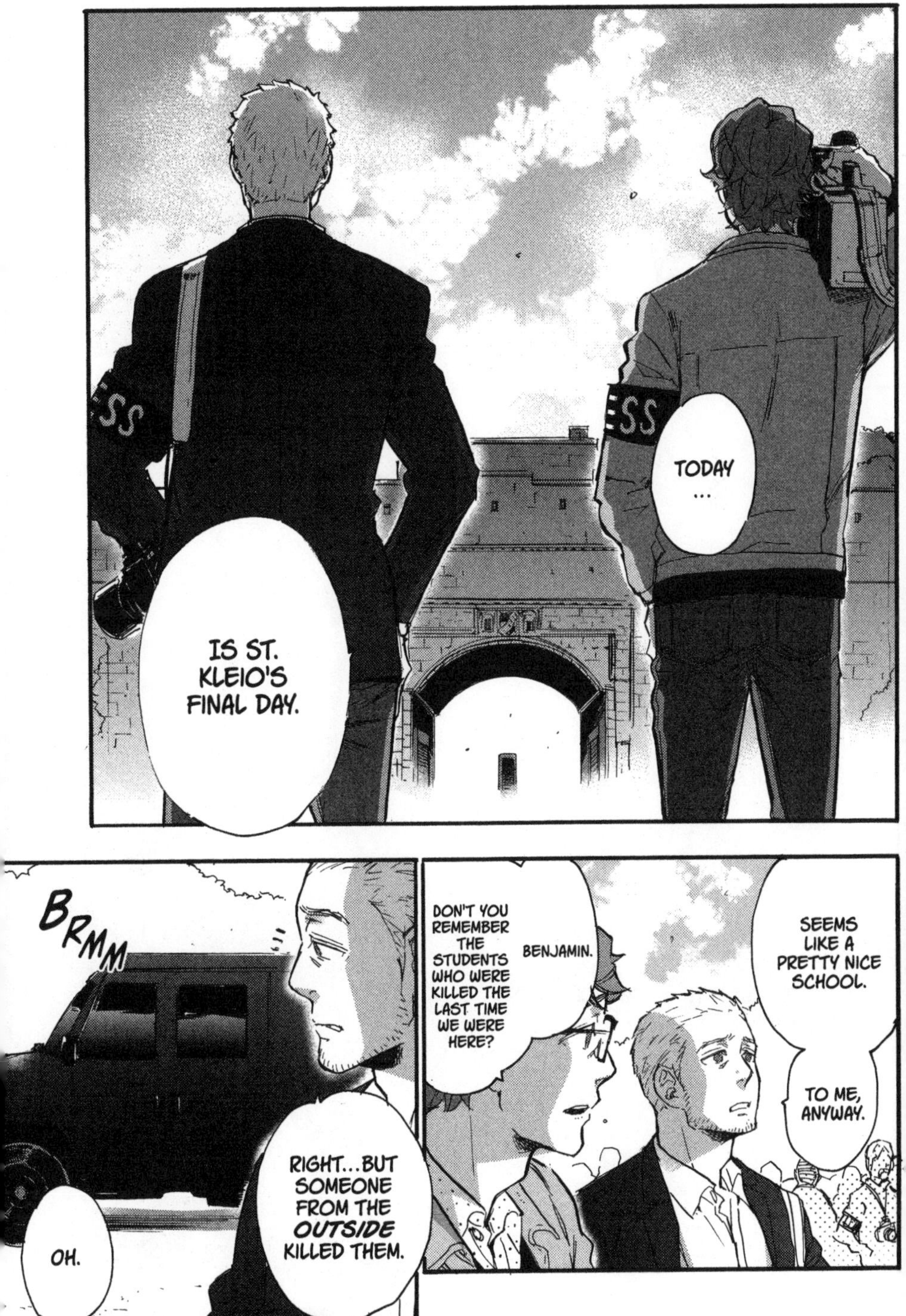
TODAY ...
IS ST. KLEIO'S FINAL DAY.
SEEMS LIKE A PRETTY NICE SCHOOL.
TO ME, ANYWAY.
BENJAMIN.
DON'T YOU REMEMBER THE STUDENTS WHO WERE KILLED THE LAST TIME WE WERE HERE?
RIGHT...BUT SOMEONE FROM THE OUTSIDE KILLED THEM.
BRMM
OH.

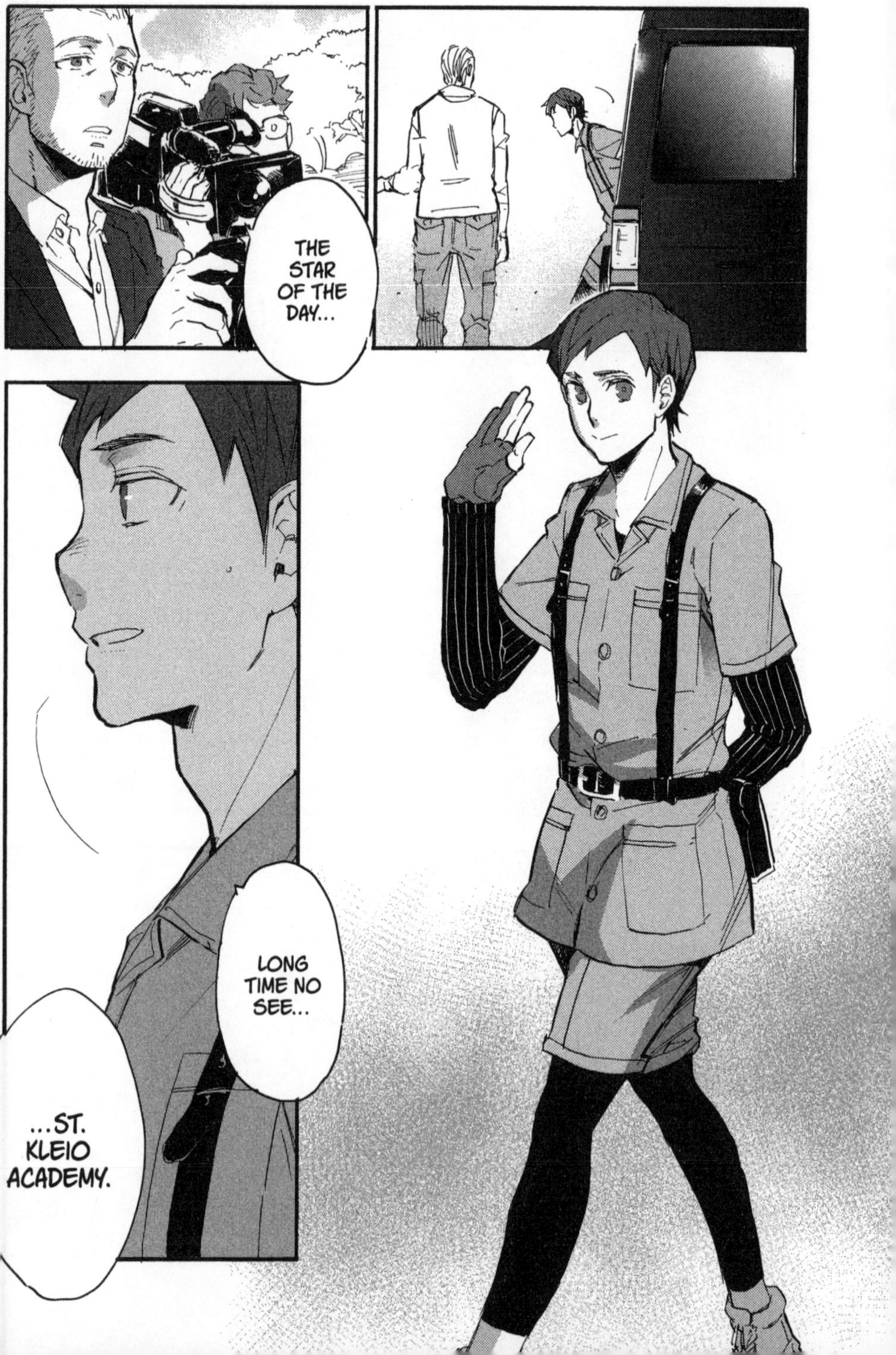
THE STAR OF THE DAY...
LONG TIME NO SEE...
...ST. KLEIO ACADEMY.

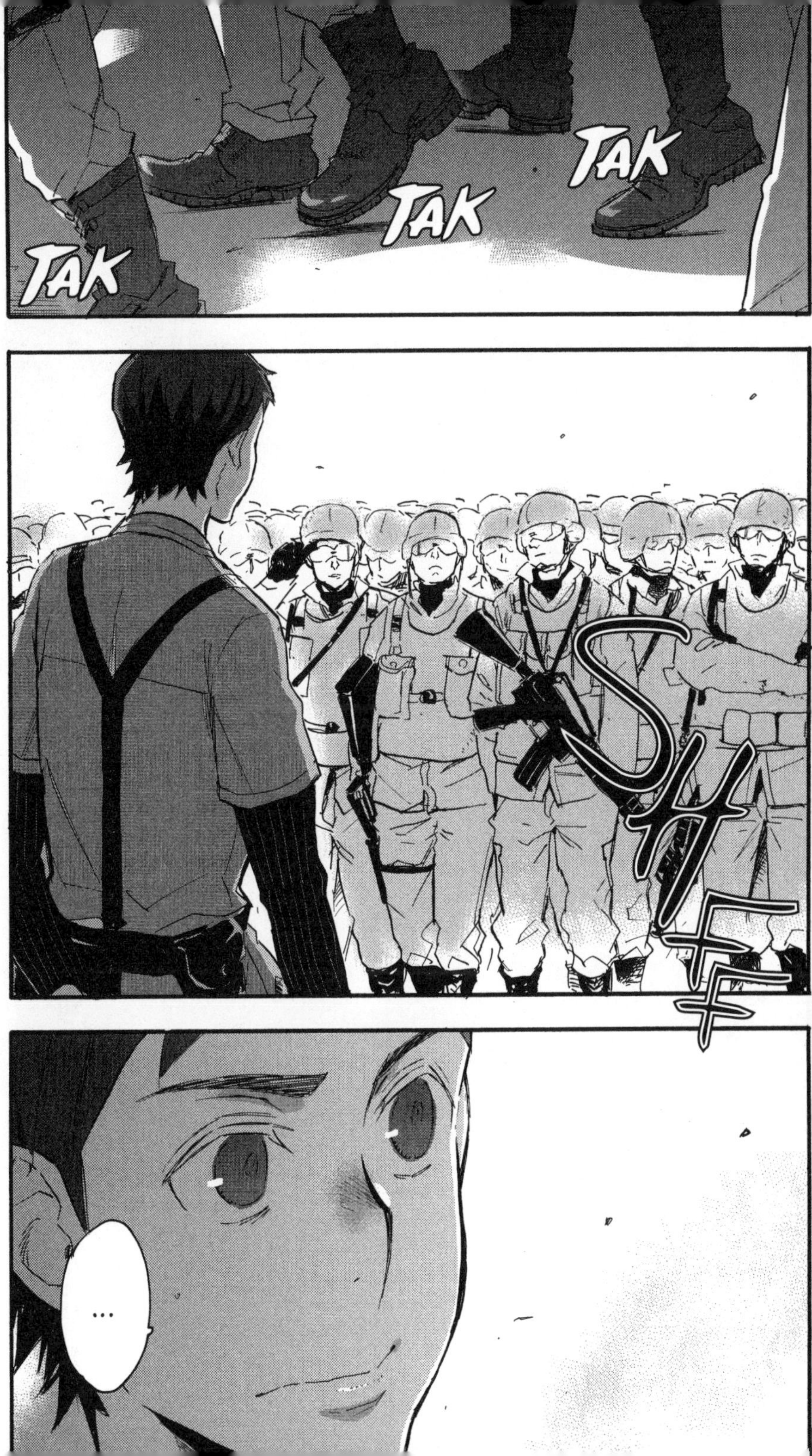
TAK
TAK
TAK
SHFF
...

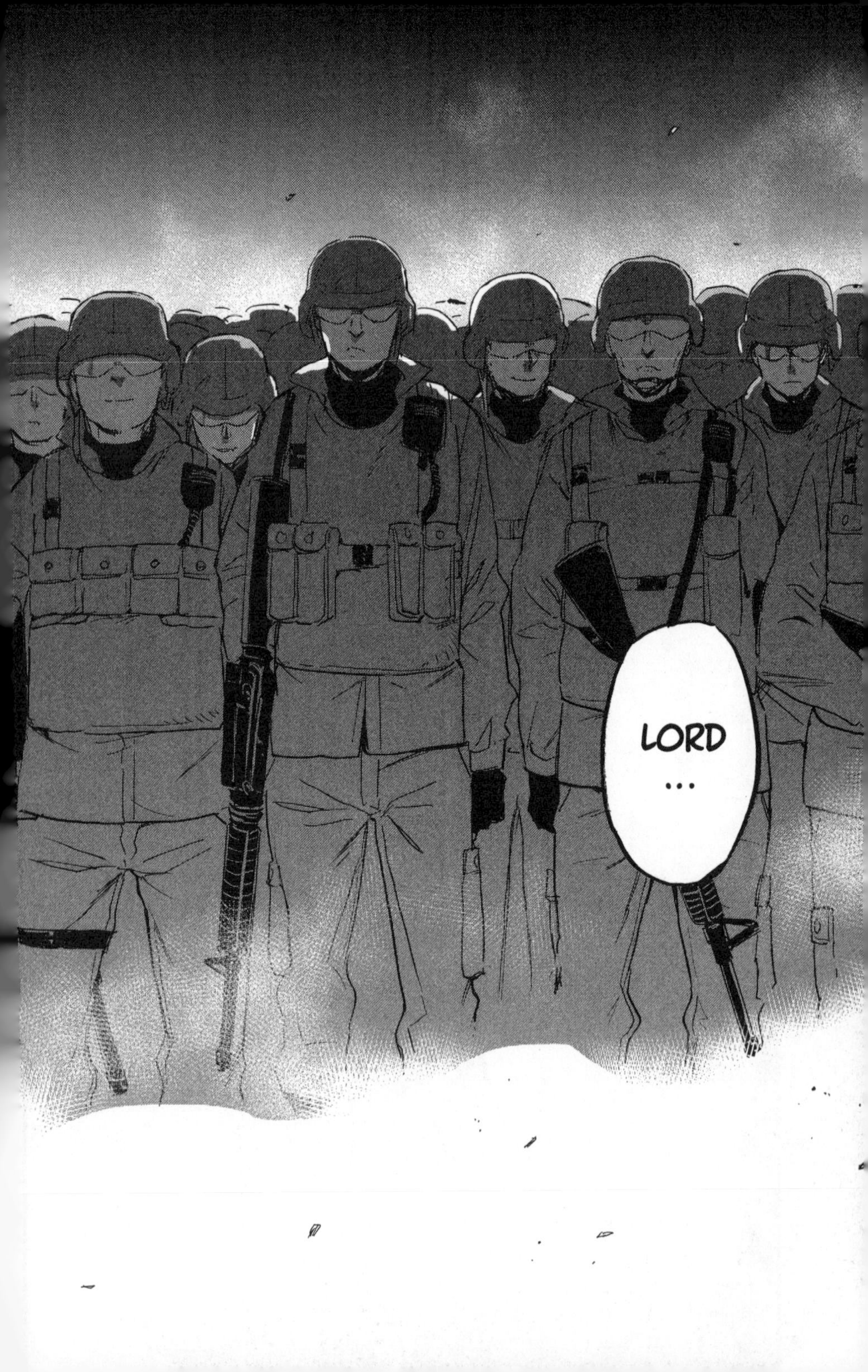
LORD
...

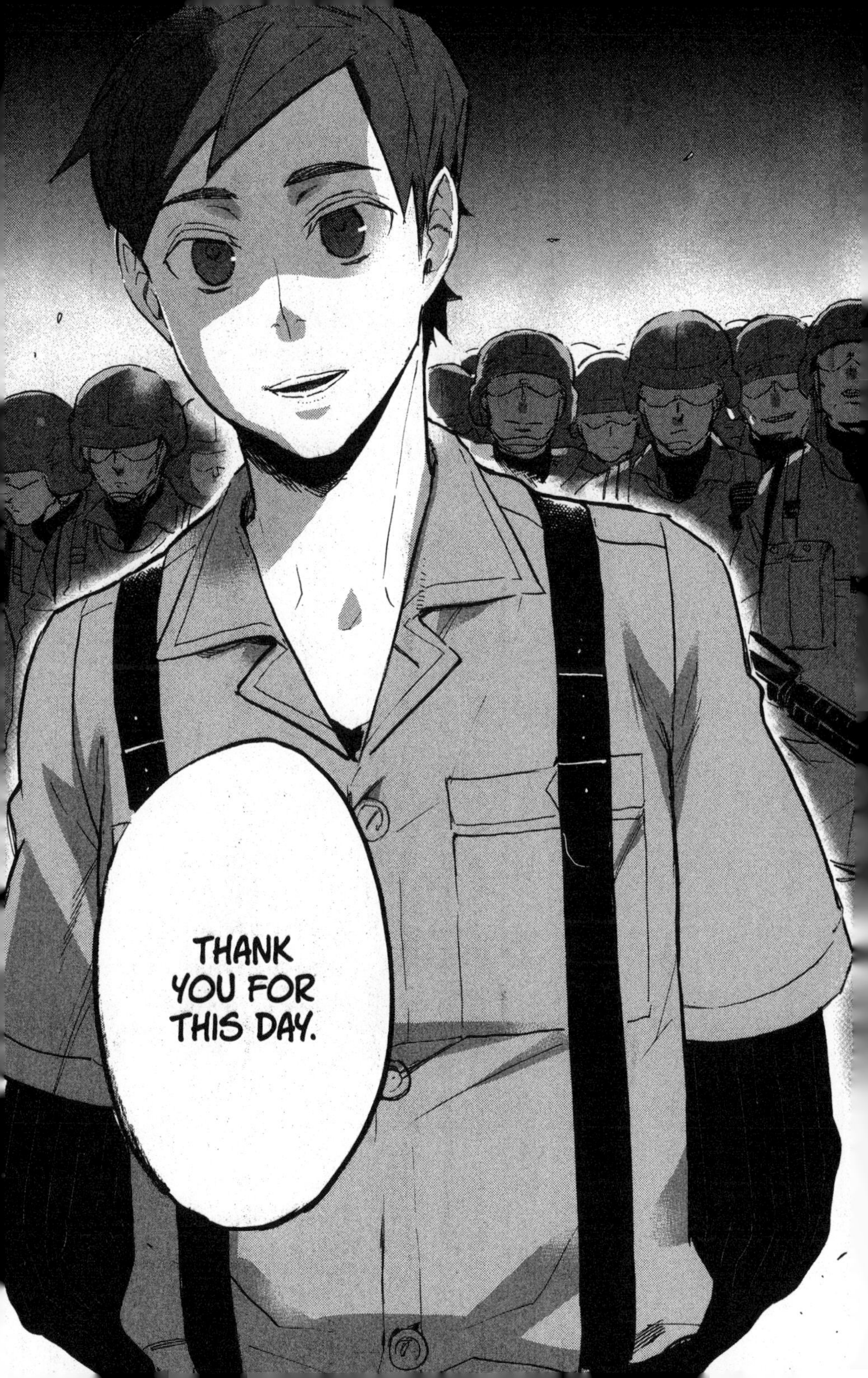
THANK YOU FOR THIS DAY.

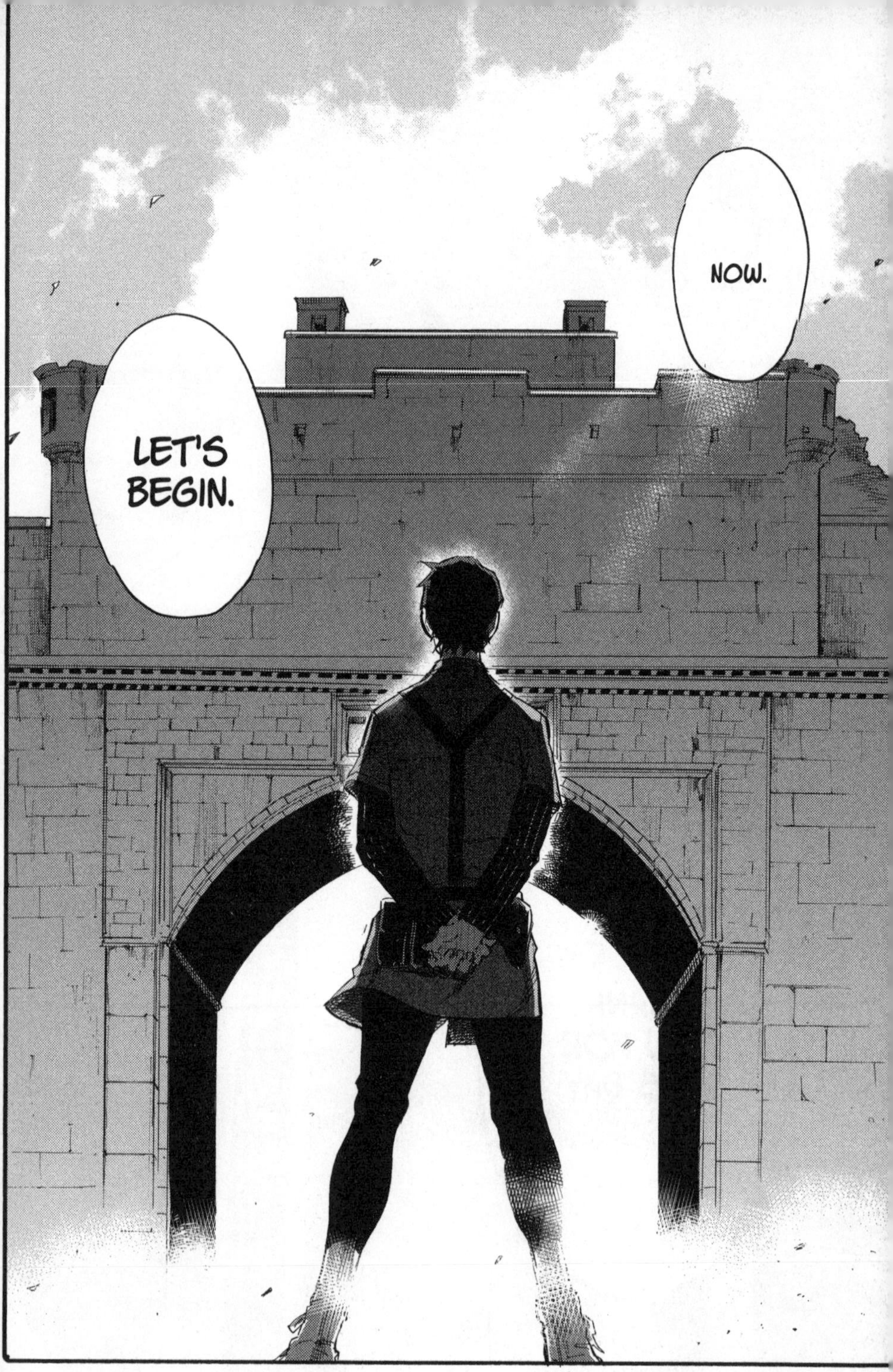
NOW.
LET'S BEGIN.

afterschool charisma

VOLUME ELEVEN

end

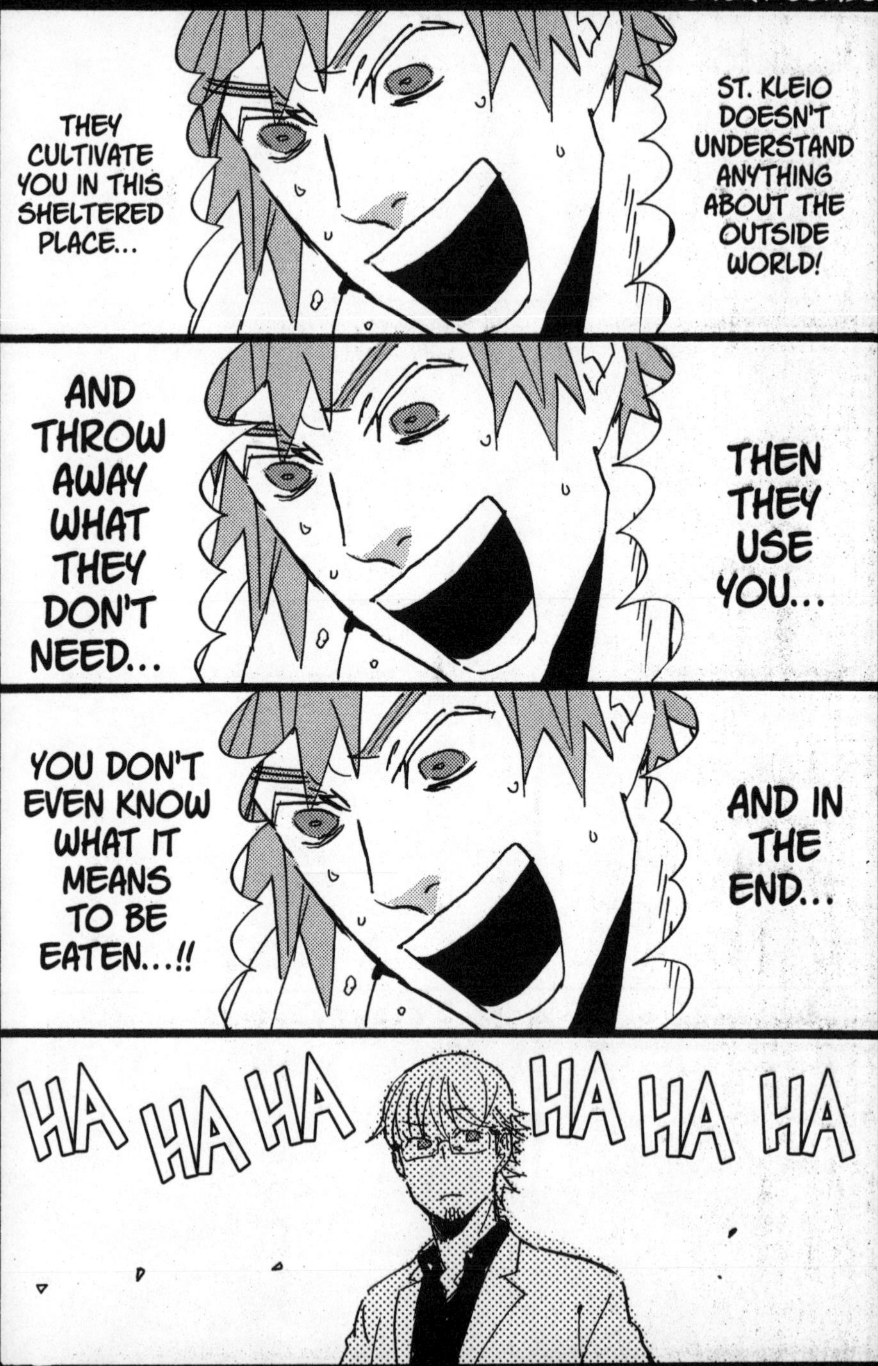
ST. KLEIO DOESN'T UNDERSTAND ANYTHING ABOUT THE OUTSIDE WORLD!
THEY CULTIVATE YOU IN THIS SHELTERED PLACE...
THEN THEY USE YOU...
AND THROW AWAY WHAT THEY DON'T NEED...
AND IN THE END...
YOU DON'T EVEN KNOW WHAT IT MEANS TO BE EATEN...!!
HA HA HA
HA HA HA

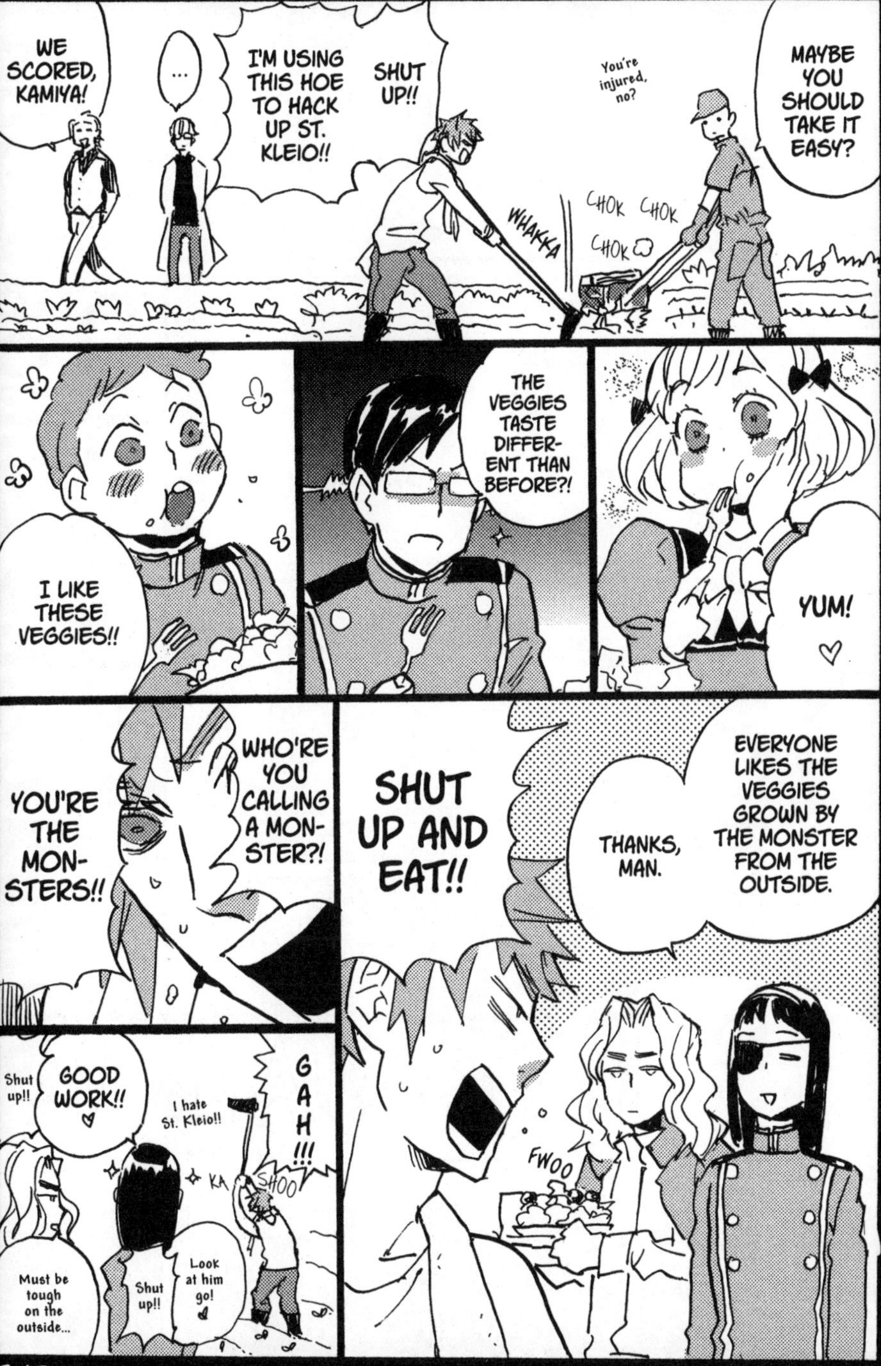
MAYBE YOU SHOULD TAKE IT EASY?
You're injured, no?
CHOK CHOK
CHOK
WHAKKA
SHUT UP!!
I'M USING THIS HOE TO HACK UP ST. KLEIO!!
...
WE SCORED, KAMIYA!
YUM! ♡
THE VEGGIES TASTE DIFFER-ENT THAN BEFORE?!
I LIKE THESE VEGGIES!!
EVERYONE LIKES THE VEGGIES GROWN BY THE MONSTER FROM THE OUTSIDE.
THANKS, MAN.
SHUT UP AND EAT!!
FWOO
WHO'RE YOU CALLING A MON-STER?!
YOU'RE THE MON-STERS!!
GAH!!!
KA
SHOO
I hate St. Kleio!!
GOOD WORK!! ♡
Shut up!!
Look at him go!
Shut up!!
Must be tough on the outside...

END

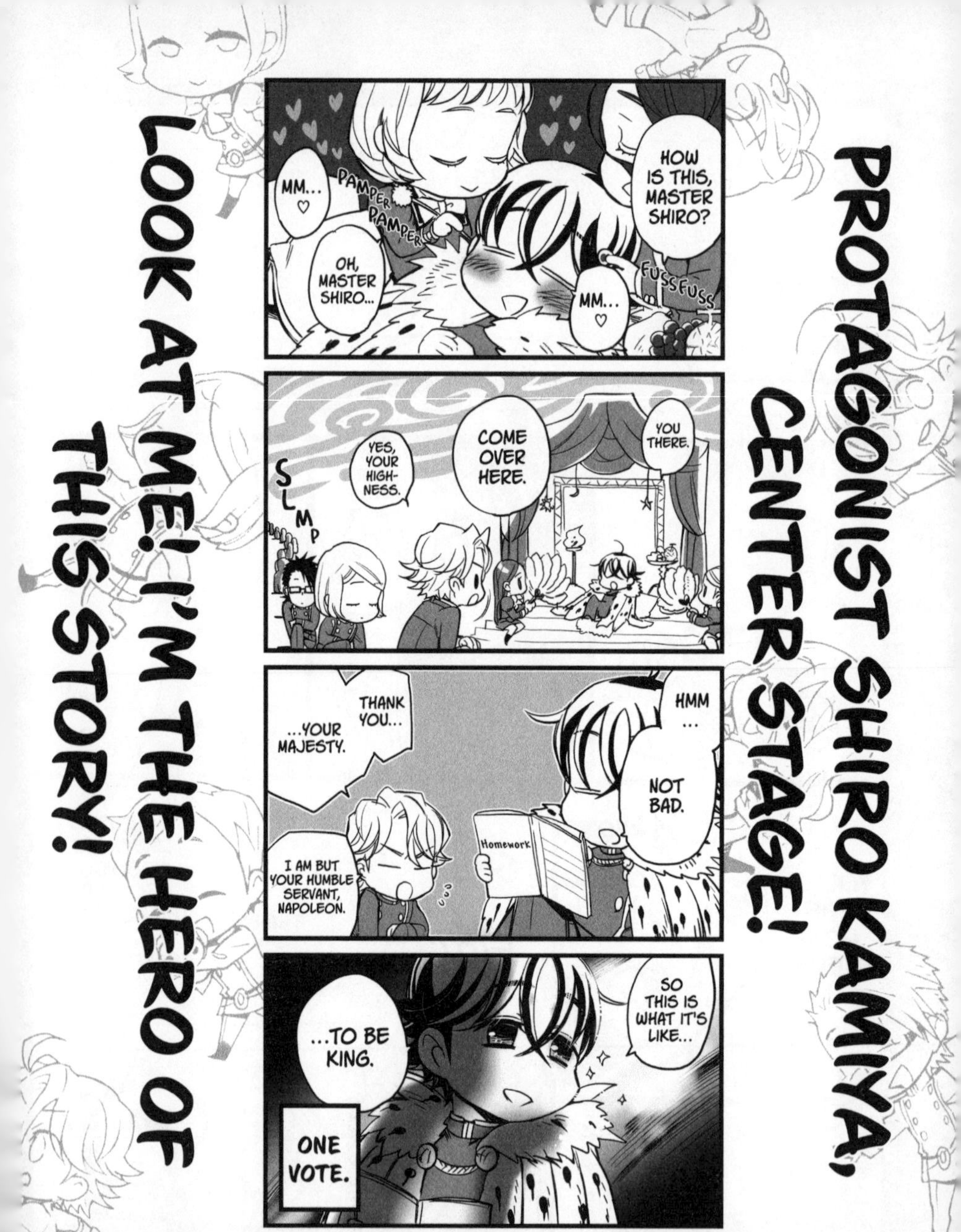
PROTAGONIST SHIRO KAMIYA, CENTER STAGE!
HOW IS THIS, MASTER SHIRO?
FUSSFUSS
MM... ♡
MM... ♡
PAMPER PAMPER
OH, MASTER SHIRO...
YOU THERE.
COME OVER HERE.
YES, YOUR HIGHNESS.
SLMP
HMM...
NOT BAD.
THANK YOU...
...YOUR MAJESTY.
Homework
I AM BUT YOUR HUMBLE SERVANT, NAPOLEON.
SO THIS IS WHAT IT'S LIKE...
...TO BE KING.
ONE VOTE.
LOOK AT ME! I'M THE HERO OF THIS STORY!

A SPECIAL FOUR-PANEL COMEDY FOR THOSE OF YOU WHO CAN'T HANDLE THE MAIN STORY BECAUSE IT'S TOO SERIOUS!

SHIRO...WHO...?

...SORRY, WE LIED!

# AFTERSCHOOL CHARISMA
## VOLUME 11
### VIZ SIGNATURE EDITION

### STORY & ART BY **KUMIKO SUEKANE**

HOKAGO NO CHARISMA Vol. 11
by Kumiko SUEKANE
© 2009 Kumiko SUEKANE
All rights reserved.
Original Japanese edition published by SHOGAKUKAN.
English translation rights in the United States of America and Canada
arranged with SHOGAKUKAN.

Original Japanese cover design by Mitsuru KOBAYASHI (GENI A LÒIDE)

TRANSLATION –○– CAMELLIA NIEH
TOUCH UP ART & LETTERING –○– ERIKA TERRIQUEZ
DESIGN –○– FAWN LAU
EDITOR –○– MEGAN BATES

Printed in the U.S.A.

Published by VIZ Media, LLC
P.O. Box 77010
San Francisco, CA 94107

10 9 8 7 6 5 4 3 2 1

First printing, December 2015

www.viz.com

**VIZ SIGNATURE**
WWW.SIGIKKI.COM

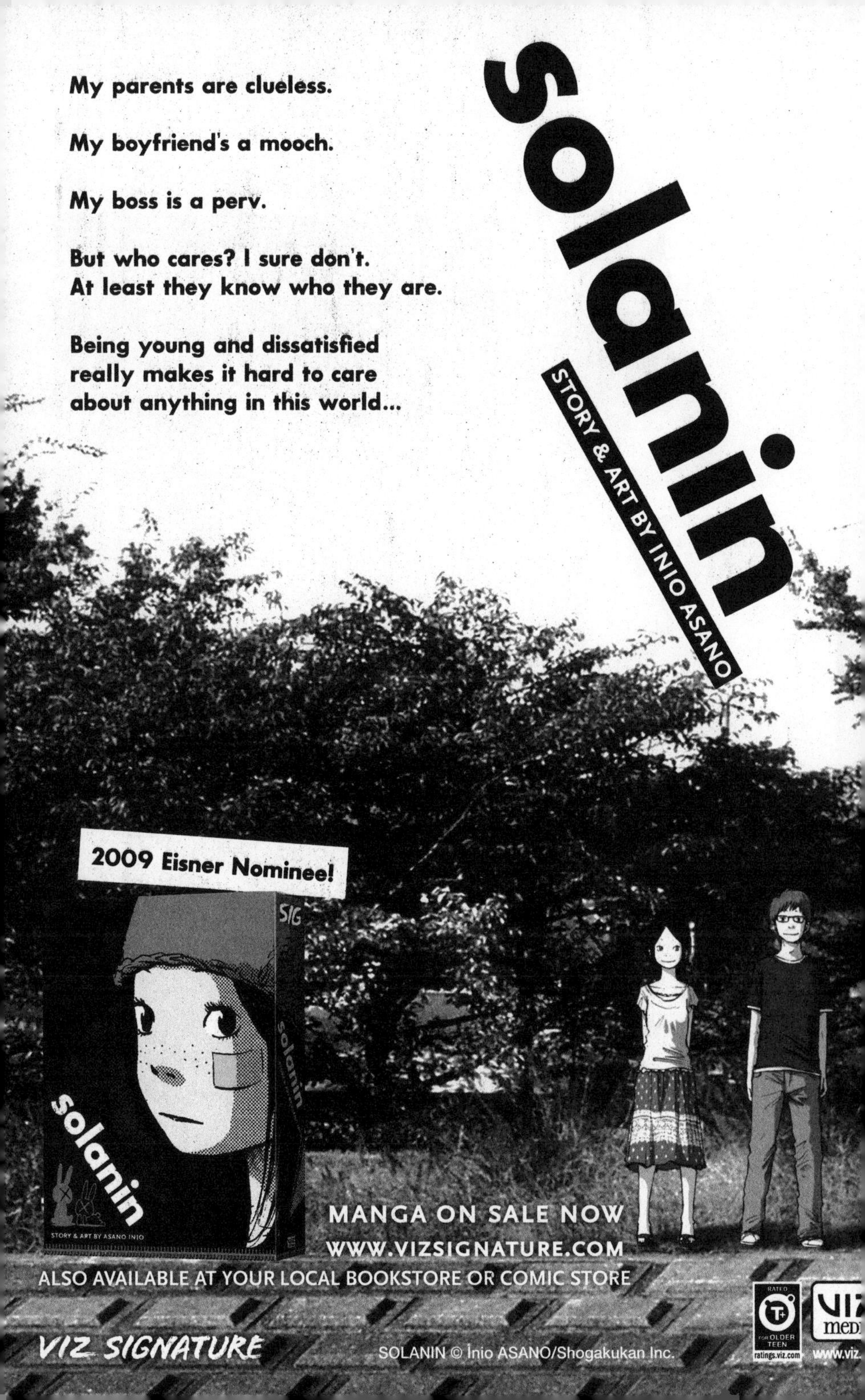
My parents are clueless.
My boyfriend's a mooch.
My boss is a perv.
But who cares? I sure don't.
At least they know who they are.
Being young and dissatisfied
really makes it hard to care
about anything in this world...
solanin
STORY & ART BY INIO ASANO
2009 Eisner Nominee!
SIG
solanin
solanin
STORY & ART BY ASANO INIO
MANGA ON SALE NOW
WWW.VIZSIGNATURE.COM
ALSO AVAILABLE AT YOUR LOCAL BOOKSTORE OR COMIC STORE
VIZ SIGNATURE
SOLANIN © Inio ASANO/Shogakukan Inc.
RATED
T+
FOR OLDER TEEN
ratings.viz.com

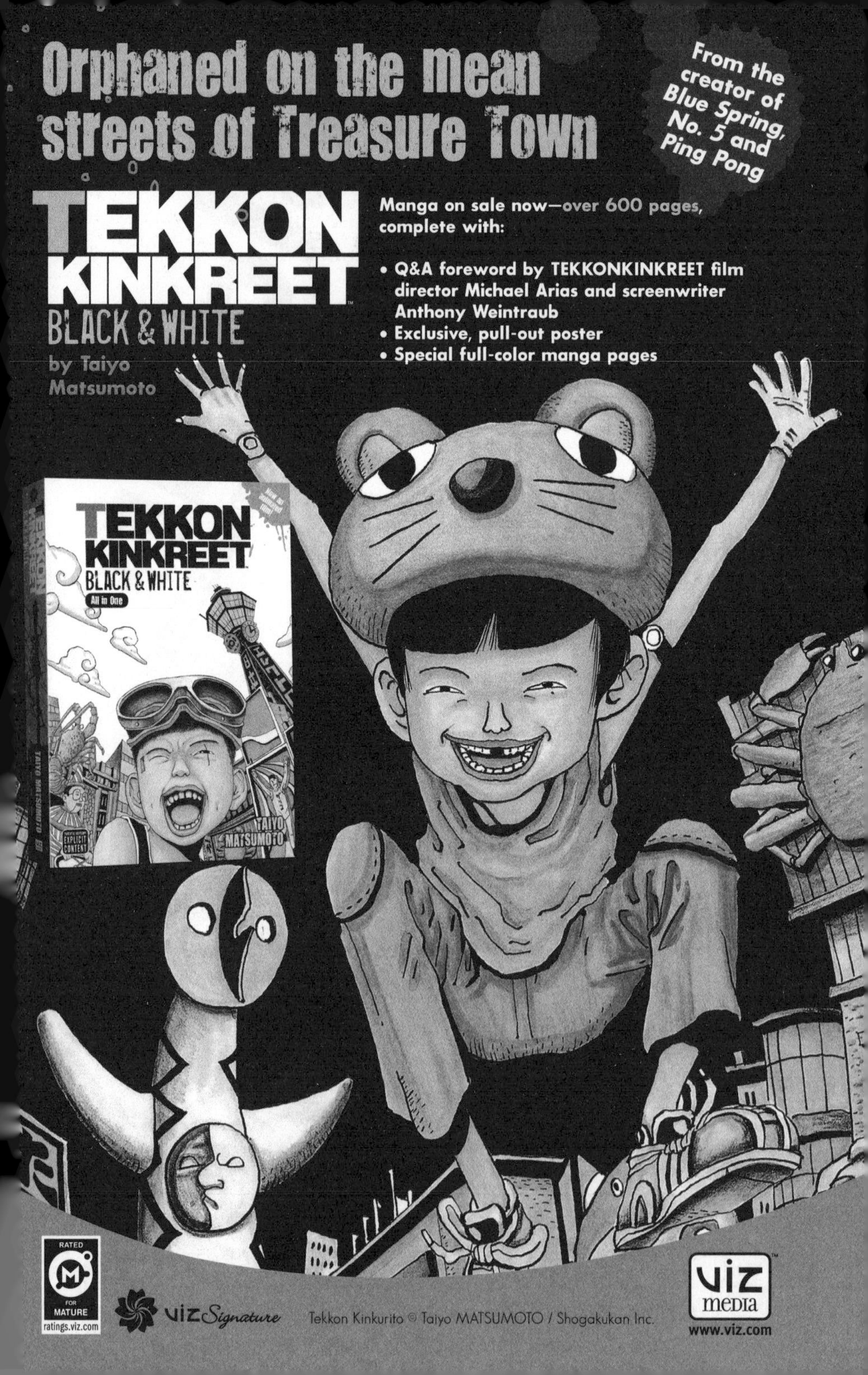

Orphaned on the mean streets of Treasure Town
From the creator of Blue Spring, No. 5 and Ping Pong
TEKKON KINKREET BLACK & WHITE
by Taiyo Matsumoto
Manga on sale now—over 600 pages, complete with:
• Q&A foreword by TEKKONKINKREET film director Michael Arias and screenwriter Anthony Weintraub
• Exclusive, pull-out poster
• Special full-color manga pages
TEKKON KINKREET BLACK & WHITE
All in One
TAIYO MATSUMOTO
EXPLICIT CONTENT
RATED M FOR MATURE
ratings.viz.com
VIZ Signature
Tekkon Kinkurito © Taiyo MATSUMOTO / Shogakukan Inc.
VIZ media
www.viz.com

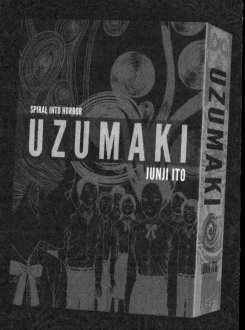

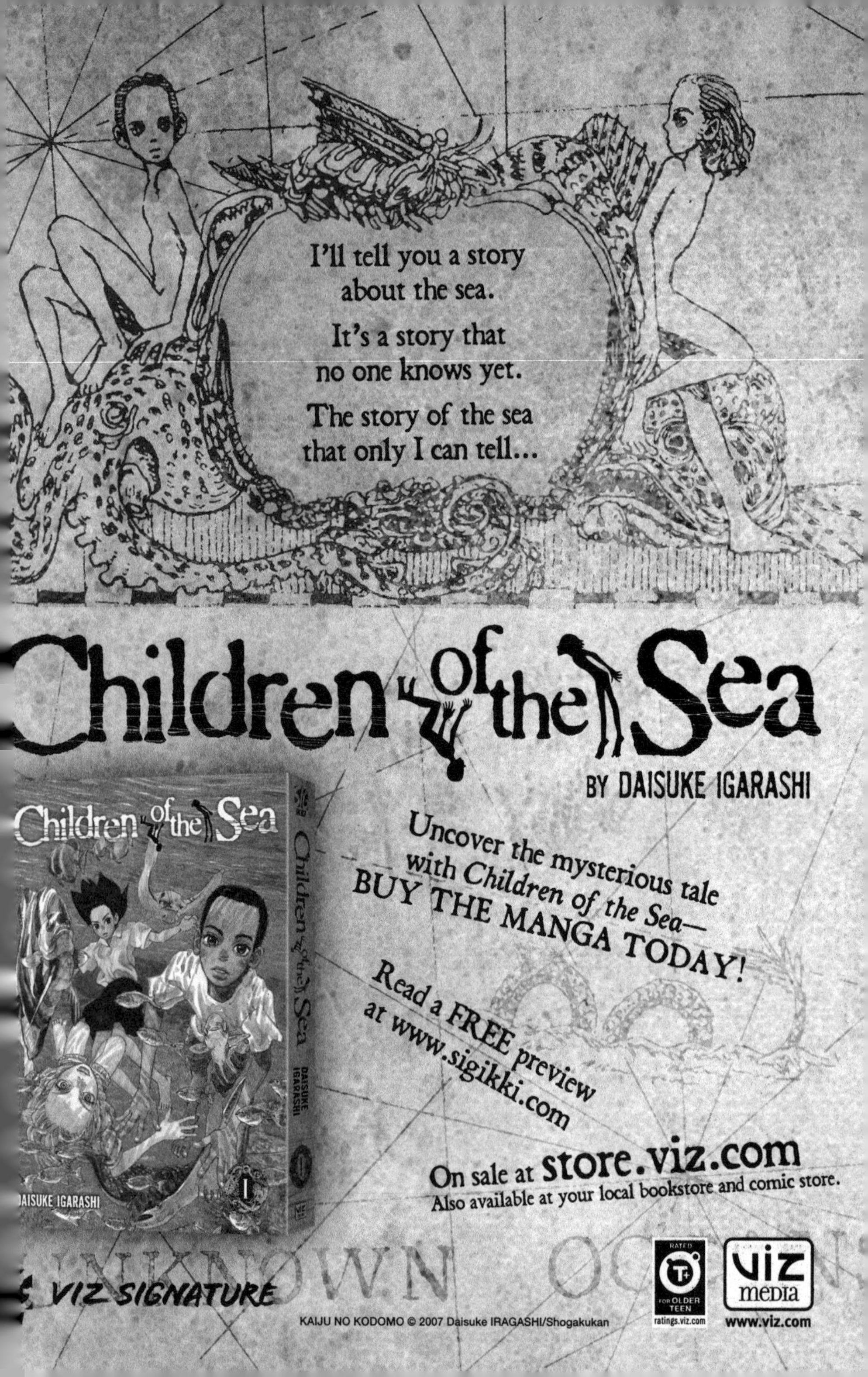
I'll tell you a story
about the sea.
It's a story that
no one knows yet.
The story of the sea
that only I can tell...
Children of the Sea
BY DAISUKE IGARASHI
Children of the Sea
DAISUKE IGARASHI
DAISUKE IGARASHI
1
Uncover the mysterious tale
with *Children of the Sea*—
BUY THE MANGA TODAY!
Read a FREE preview
at www.sigikki.com
On sale at store.viz.com
Also available at your local bookstore and comic store.
UNKNOWN OCEANS
VIZ SIGNATURE
KAIJU NO KODOMO © 2007 Daisuke IRAGASHI/Shogakukan
RATED T+ FOR OLDER TEEN
ratings.viz.com
VIZ media
www.viz.com